'one saved always saved'
cf fallen from grace
p 91f

BLACK'S NEW TESTAMENT COMMENTARIES

GENERAL EDITOR: HENRY CHADWICK, D.D.

THE FIRST EPISTLE TO THE CORINTHIANS

BLACK'S NEW TESTAMENT COMMENTARIES

THE GOSPEL ACCORDING TO ST. MATTHEW
Floyd V. Filson

THE GOSPEL ACCORDING TO ST. MARK
Sherman E. Johnson

THE GOSPEL ACCORDING TO ST. LUKE
A. R. C. Leaney

THE GOSPEL ACCORDING TO ST. JOHN
J. N. Sanders and B. A. Mastin

THE ACTS OF THE APOSTLES
C. S. C. Williams

THE EPISTLE TO THE ROMANS
C. K. Barrett

THE FIRST EPISTLE TO THE CORINTHIANS
C. K. Barrett

THE SECOND EPISTLE TO THE CORINTHIANS
C. K. Barrett

THE EPISTLE TO THE PHILIPPIANS
F. W. Beare

THE FIRST AND SECOND EPISTLES TO THE THESSALONIANS
Ernest Best

THE PASTORAL EPISTLES
Timothy I & II, and Titus
J. N. D. Kelly

THE EPISTLE TO THE HEBREWS
H. W. Montefiore

THE EPISTLES OF PETER AND OF JUDE
J. N. D. Kelly

THE JOHANNINE EPISTLES
J. L. Houlden

THE REVELATION OF ST. JOHN THE DIVINE
G. B. Caird

COMPANION VOL. I
THE BIRTH OF THE NEW TESTAMENT
C. F. D. Moule

A COMMENTARY ON
THE FIRST EPISTLE TO THE CORINTHIANS

C. K. BARRETT, D.D., F.B.A.
PROFESSOR OF DIVINITY, UNIVERSITY OF DURHAM

SECOND EDITION

ADAM & CHARLES BLACK
LONDON

FIRST PUBLISHED 1968
SECOND EDITION 1971
REPRINTED 1973, 1976, 1978, 1979
A. AND C. BLACK (PUBLISHERS) LIMITED
35 BEDFORD ROW, LONDON WC1

ISBN 0 7136 1253 3

PRINTED AND BOUND IN GREAT BRITAIN BY
BILLING & SONS LTD, GUILDFORD, LONDON AND WORCESTER

PREFACE

A good deal of what I wrote in the Preface to my Commentary (in this series) on the Epistle to the Romans applies to this commentary too. Again the translation is intended to aid the notes by expressing as accurately as possible, in as plain English as possible, what Paul said. There is in the new book more Greek than in the old, because (to put the matter in a nutshell) there is no 'Sanday and Headlam' for 1 Corinthians, and the student, being less well served, needs more help; but again it will be easily possible for those who know no Greek to skip every word of it.

The commentator's debt to his predecessors is not so overwhelming as in Romans, but there are useful books, from which I have learnt much. Most of these appear in the list of abbreviations, but I am surprised, on looking through my manuscript, to see that I have not actually referred to, though I have been helped by, the commentaries by G. G. Findlay and F. W. Grosheide. Other books that might have been quoted more fully are W. Schmithals, *Die Gnosis in Korinth* (1956), and U. Wilckens, *Weisheit und Torheit* (1959); but I have referred to these in 'Christianity at Corinth'. I have found it more useful to quote K. Barth's *Church Dogmatics* (which contains many expository discussions of 1 Corinthians) than his book on 1 Corinthians (*The Resurrection of the Dead*; E.T., 1933).

I am indebted to the General Editor, Professor Henry Chadwick, for pressing me to undertake the Corinthian Epistles, and for his patience in waiting for the treatment of 1 Corinthians which now appears. He will probably have to exercise even more patience over 2 Corinthians—surely the most difficult book in the New Testament. I hope, however, to be able without undue delay to offer as complete an account of Paul's dealings with the most troublesome of his churches as the nature of the sources, and my own ability, permit. I believe that the church in our generation needs to rediscover the apostolic Gospel; and for this it needs the Epistle to the Romans. It needs also to rediscover the relation between this Gospel and its order, discipline, worship, and ethics; and for this it needs the First Epistle to the Corinthians. If it makes these discoveries, it may well find itself broken; and this may turn out to be the meaning of the Second Epistle to the Corinthians.

C. K. BARRETT

Durham
April 1967

CONTENTS

Preface	v
Abbreviations	ix
Introduction	1
Analysis of the Epistle	28
Translation and Commentary	30
Index of Names and Subjects	401
Index of Greek Words and Phrases	409

ABBREVIATIONS

Adam	C. K. Barrett, *From First Adam to Last*, 1962.
Allo	E. B. Allo, *Saint Paul : Première Épître aux Corinthiens* (*Études Bibliques*), 1956.
Bachmann	P. Bachmann, *Der erste Brief des Paulus an die Korinther*, fourth edition, with supplements by E. Stauffer, 1936.
Background	C. K. Barrett (ed.), *The New Testament Background : Selected Documents*, 1956.
Barth, *C.D.*	K. Barth, *Church Dogmatics*, 1936–1962.
Bauer[1]	W. Bauer, *Griechisch-Deutsches Wörterbuch zu den Schriften des Neuen Testaments und der übrigen urchristlichen Literatur*, 1952.
B.D.[2]	F. Blass, *Grammatik des neutestamentlichen Griechisch*, revised by A. Debrunner, 1949.
Betz	H. D. Betz, *Lukian von Samosata* (*Texte und Untersuchungen*, 76), 1961.
Bultmann, *Theology*	R. Bultmann, *Theologie des Neuen Testaments*, 1948–1953. E.T.: *Theology of the New Testament*, 1965.
Calvin	J. Calvin, *The First Epistle of Paul the Apostle to the Corinthians* (tr. J. W. Fraser), 1960.
'Cephas and Corinth'	C. K. Barrett, 'Cephas and Corinth', in *Abraham unser Vater, Festschrift für Otto Michel* (ed. O. Betz, M. Hengel, P. Schmidt), 1963, pp. 1-12.
'Christianity at Corinth'	C. K. Barrett, 'Christianity at Corinth', in *Bulletin of the John Rylands Library* 46 (1964), pp. 269-97.
Daube	D. Daube, *The New Testament and Rabbinic Judaism*, 1956.
W. D. Davies	W. D. Davies, *Paul and Rabbinic Judaism*, 1948.
E.T.	English translation.

[1] See also the English edition by W. F. Arndt and F. W. Gingrich (1957).

[2] The same paragraph references apply to the English edition by R. W. Funk (1961).

EVV	English Versions.
Harris	W. B. Harris, *The First Epistle of St Paul to the Corinthians*, 1958.
Heim	K. Heim, *Die Gemeinde des Auferstandenen*, ed. F. Melzer, 1949.
Héring	J. Héring, *La Première Épître de saint Paul aux Corinthiens* (*Commentaire du Nouveau Testament* VII), 1949. E.T.: *The First Epistle of Saint Paul to the Corinthians*, 1962.
Hurd	J. C. Hurd, *The Origin of 1 Corinthians*, 1965.
J.T.S.	*The Journal of Theological Studies.*
Knox, *Gentiles*	W. L. Knox, *St Paul and the Church of the Gentiles*, 1939.
Kümmel	See Lietzmann.
Lietzmann	H. Lietzmann, *An die Korinther I, II* (*Handbuch zum Neuen Testament* 9), fifth edition with supplements by W. G. Kümmel, 1969.
Lightfoot	J. B. Lightfoot, *Notes on Epistles of St Paul*, 1895.
Lipsius-Bonnet	R. A. Lipsius and M. Bonnet, *Acta Apostolorum Apocrypha*, 1959.
L.S.	H. G. Liddell and R. Scott, *A Greek-English Lexicon*, new edition by H. S. Jones and R. McKenzie, n.d.
M. i	J. H. Moulton, *A Grammar of New Testament Greek*, Volume I, Prolegomena, 1908.
M. ii	The Same: Volume II, Accidence and Word-Formation, by J. H. Moulton and W. F. Howard, 1929.
M. iii	The Same: Volume III, Syntax, by N. Turner, 1963.
T. W. Manson, *Studies*	T. W. Manson, *Studies in the Gospels and Epistles*, ed. by M. Black, 1962.
M.M.	J. H. Moulton and G. Milligan, *The Vocabulary of the Greek Testament*, 1914–1929.
Moffatt	J. Moffatt, *The First Epistle of Paul to the Corinthians*, 1938.
Moule	C. F. D. Moule, *An Idiom Book of New Testament Greek*, 1953.
N.T.S.	*New Testament Studies.*
Robertson	A. T. Robertson, *A Grammar of the Greek New Testament in the Light of Historical Research*, 1919.

ABBREVIATIONS

Robertson-Plummer	A. Robertson and A. Plummer, *A Critical and Exegetical Commentary on the First Epistle of St Paul to the Corinthians* (*International Critical Commentary*), 1914.
Romans	C. K. Barrett, *A Commentary on the Epistle to the Romans* (Black's New Testament Commentaries), 1962.
RV	Revised Version.
S.B.	H. L. Strack and P. Billerbeck, *Kommentar zum Neuen Testament aus Talmud und Midrasch*, 1922–1961.
Schlatter	A. Schlatter, *Paulus der Bote Jesu*, 1962.
Schoeps, *Paulus*	H. J. Schoeps, *Paulus*, 1959. E.T.: *Paul*, 1961.
Schweitzer, *Mysticism*	A. Schweitzer, *The Mysticism of Paul the Apostle* (tr. W. Montgomery), 1931.
Schweizer	E. Schweizer, *Church Order in the New Testament* (*Studies in Biblical Theology* 32), 1961.
Sevenster, *Seneca*	J. N. Sevenster, *Paul and Seneca* (*Novum Testamentum* Supplement IV), 1961.
Stauffer	See Bachmann.
Studia Paulina	*Studia Paulina in honorem J. de Zwaan* (ed. J. N. Sevenster and W. C. van Unnik), 1953.
'Things Sacrificed to Idols'	C. K. Barrett, 'Things Sacrificed to Idols', in *N.T.S.* xi (1965), pp. 138-53.
T.W.N.T.	*Theologisches Wörterbuch zum Neuen Testament*, ed. by G. Kittel and G. Friedrich, 1933– . See also the English translation.
Weiss	J. Weiss, *Der erste Korintherbrief* (*Kritisch-exegetischer Kommentar über das Neue Testament*—Meyer), 1910.
Wendland	H. D. Wendland, *Die Briefe an die Korinther* (*Das Neue Testament Deutsch* 7), 1946.
Whiteley	D. E. H. Whiteley, *The Theology of St Paul*, 1964.
Z.N.T.W.	*Zeitschrift für die neutestamentliche Wissenschaft und die Kunde der älteren Kirche.*
Zuntz	G. Zuntz, *The Text of the Epistles*, 1953.

Note: The usual sigla are employed for New Testament manuscripts and versions. They are explained in all good editions of the Greek New Testament.

INTRODUCTION

I. Corinth

Corinth was situated at the south-western extremity of the isthmus that connects the mainland of Greece with the Peloponnese. It was part of a complex that included, one and a half miles to the north, Lechaeum on the Gulf of Corinth, and, seven and a quarter miles to the east, Cenchreae on the Saronic Gulf (Rom. xvi. 1). The region was not fertile, but its economic advantages were great. It controlled the land route between north and south, and also acted as a land link, indispensable until the cutting of the Corinth Canal (begun but given up by Nero, and only completed in 1893), in the sea route between east and west. From time to time this control of the portage of ships had military significance;[1] it must constantly have been important in commerce, and as early as Homer the phrase 'wealthy Corinth' occurs (*Iliad*, ii.570; cf. xiii.664). The plain in which Corinth is situated is dominated by the hill which served as acropolis to the city, Acrocorinth, rising to 1857 feet. Economic and military advantages combined in favour of Corinth,[2] and it is not surprising that it reached a position of eminence in the ancient world; it is perhaps more surprising that it never achieved preeminence.

In 146 B.C. a sharp line is drawn through the history of Corinth, when Rome brought the Achaean League to an end. After the decisive engagement at Leucopetra, on the Isthmus, the consul Lucius Mummius was able to occupy Corinth

[1] See e.g. Thucydides viii. 7: The Spartans sent off three full citizens (*Spartiatae*) to Corinth in order that when they had brought the boats over the Isthmus as quickly as possible from the other sea to that by Athens they might order them all to sail to Chios.

[2] See e.g. Plutarch, *Aratus* XVI, XVII (1034): . . . Acrocorinth, a very high mountain, rising up out of the midst of Greece [that is, between the Peloponnese and the Epirus], when garrisoned, stands in the way and cuts off all the land within the Isthmus from commerce and passage and military campaigning, and prevents traffic both by land and by sea, and makes him who rules and holds the place with a garrison master. . . . The place has always been fought for by all, by kings and rulers. . . .

without a blow. The citizens were killed, or sold into slavery; the city itself was levelled with the ground, and rebuilding was forbidden. The territory became public land of Rome, except part that was given to the neighbouring state of Sicyon, on the understanding that henceforward Sicyon, in place of Corinth, would maintain the Isthmian Games. After 100 years of desolation Corinth was refounded by Julius Caesar as a Roman colony.

New Corinth naturally possessed the topographical characteristics of the old city; otherwise it bore little relation to its predecessor. Today, the traveller can see little of the Greek city but half a dozen columns of the temple of Apollo; the Roman foundation is much better represented. But this was already substantially true in the time of Pausanias,[1] whose account contrasts the old with the new. For example, '... yearly sacrifices were instituted in their honour, and a figure of Terror (δεῖμα) erected. The latter still remains to our day ... But since the destruction of Corinth by the Romans and the disappearance of the ancient Corinthians the sacrifices are no longer performed by the colonists, nor do the children cut their hair or wear black clothes' (Pausanias, II. iii. 7). The new settlers, to whom the traditions of Corinth meant little, were drawn from various parts of the Empire; many would be discharged soldiers. No doubt there were Greeks among them, but it is impossible to think of the Corinth of Paul's day as in any way distinctively Greek. That there were Jews in Corinth is shown by an inscription[2] consisting of the broken words '[Syn]agogue of the Hebr[ews]' (... ΓΩΓΗ ΕΒΡ ...), and probably part of the lintel of the door of the synagogue. The date of this inscription cannot be narrowly determined, but it gives sufficient confirmation to Acts xviii. 4 (he discoursed in the synagogue every Sabbath). New Corinth was thus a cosmopolitan city. The immoral reputation of old Corinth (words derived from the name Corinth seem to have been used in the Old Comedy with the meanings *to practise fornication*, *whoremonger*, and the like) may not be simply carried across a century; it cannot however

[1] G. Roux, *Pausanias en Corinthe* (1958), p. 29, gives 155±—170± as the date of Pausanias's second book, in which he describes Corinth.

[2] See *Background*, p. 50.

be said that the new foundation went out of its way to redeem the past. In Paul's day, Corinth was probably little better and little worse than any other great sea port and commercial centre of the age.

It was probably not a lurid reputation that put Paul in terror when he first visited Corinth (1 Cor. ii. 3), but the sense of his vocation and responsibility. He had nothing to preach but Christ crucified (ii. 2), and he had resolved to make use of no human arts in setting forth this theme (i. 17; ii. 1). Notwithstanding this (or perhaps, as Paul himself would have said, because of this), his preaching effected the conversion of many in Corinth, of whom the first (at least, the first in Achaea, probably the first in Corinth since we know of no Achaean town evangelized before Corinth) were the household of Stephanas (xvi. 15). Paul had laid the only conceivable foundation for a Christian church—Jesus Christ himself (iii. 10 f.); others were to build upon this foundation, and the superstructure turned out to be less satisfactory than the base on which it rested. The church of God in Corinth was by no means free from blemishes and wrinkles. This may have been due in part to the number and variety of the builders. Apollos undoubtedly worked in Corinth (iii. 6). It is probable but not quite certain that Peter did so also.[1] As a result of this, and no doubt because of their own imperfectly Christianized contentiousness too, the church membership, though not completely split into factions, tended to break down into groups, each appealing to the name of a Christian leader (i. 11 f.). The disunity of the church manifested itself on these lines perhaps but on others also at the Lord's Supper, where rich and poor were marked out in different groups (xi. 18-22). Other blemishes appeared on the surface of Corinthian church life. There were public litigation among the members (vi. 1-8), a notorious case of immorality (v. 1-5), disputes over the legitimacy of eating food that had been sacrificed to idols (viii. 1-13; x. 14–xi. 1), and disagreements about the propriety of marriage (vii. 1-40), and the admissibility of sexual relations outside marriage (vi. 12-20). The Christian doctrine of resurrection appeared to have been denied (xv. 12), and Paul's own apostleship questioned (iv. 3, 15; ix. 1 f.).

[1] See ix. 5; also 'Cephas and Corinth'.

Meanwhile Paul had left Corinth, but had not been without contact with the church there. He had been informed of the existence of parties in the church by members of Chloe's household (i. 11). We know nothing, and can conjecture little, about these persons. It is probable that they did not make their journey at the instance of the church in order to convey information to Paul, but acted as messengers incidentally when on other business. Stephanas, Fortunatus, and Achaicus, however, seem to have acted as representatives of the church (xvi. 17 f.). It does not appear that they conveyed a gift (contrast Phil. iv. 18); this would surely have been mentioned more specifically. They may have carried the letter referred to in 1 Cor. vii. 1 (see the notes); if they did not carry it we do not know who did. Paul for his part had written a letter to Corinth (v. 9); it had been misunderstood, and he uses the present letter to correct the false impression that had been given. This 'Previous Letter', as it is often called, may have been entirely lost. Some have found part of it in 2 Cor. vi. 14–vii. 1; this opinion will be discussed in the commentary on 2 Corinthians. For the view that some part or parts of the Previous Letter are to be found in 1 Corinthians see below, pp. 12-17.

The history of Paul's dealings with Corinth (and it is little enough of their history that we know) has been sketched so far, as is right, on the basis of Paul's own certainly genuine writings alone.[1] The story as told in Acts is, however, consistent with it. According to Acts, Paul reached Corinth after his visit to Athens (Acts xviii. 1). He encountered Aquila and Priscilla (xviii. 2f.; cf. 1 Cor. xvi. 19, where the lady's name is Prisca), and made use of the synagogue, with greater freedom when Silas and Timothy joined him (Acts xviii. 4f.). Difficulties with the Jews led to a mission directed more specifically to Gentiles (especially perhaps God-fearers, who stood between the synagogue and the Gentile world—cf. xviii. 7, which shows Paul at work in the house of Titius Justus, a God-fearer), but the synagogue-ruler Crispus (cf. 1 Cor. i. 14) was converted (Acts xviii. 6 ff.). With divine encouragement, Paul continued his ministry for eighteen months.

At this point (xviii. 12-17), Acts narrates the appearance of

[1] See Hurd, pp. 41 f.

Paul before Gallio,[1] who was proconsul in charge of Achaea probably from summer A.D. 51. It is reasonable to infer (though the dates may be a year or so out) that Paul reached Corinth in about March 50, and stayed there till about September 51.

In due course Paul left Corinth for Syria (xviii. 18), touched at Ephesus, with a promise to return (xviii. 19 ff.), and brought his so-called second journey to a close (xviii. 22 f.). Here Acts mentions Apollos, his instruction by Priscilla and Aquila, and his journey to Achaea, which almost certainly included a visit to Corinth. In chapter xix Paul is back in Ephesus, and his ministry there occupies Acts xix. 1–xx. 1, and lasted two years and three months (xix. 8, 10; xx. 31, *three years*, is not inconsistent with this). In the course of it Paul is said to have sent Timothy and Erastus into Macedonia (xix. 22), while himself making plans for such a journey (xix. 21). These journeys may reasonably correspond with those mentioned in 1 Cor. xvi. 5, 10; if so, and as far as the chronology of Acts may be trusted, we have a fairly precise means of dating our epistle. Allowing for some time in Antioch, and for the journey through the 'upper region' (Acts xix. 1), Paul will have reached Ephesus again in the late summer of 52; the Pentecost he was anxious to spend in Jerusalem (xx. 16) will have been that of 55; the Pentecost of 1 Cor. xvi. 8 that of 53, or more probably 54. The most probable date for 1 Corinthians is therefore in the early months of 54, or possibly towards the end of 53.

The epistle was not a successful document. Affairs in Corinth, and relations between the Corinthian church and the apostle, deteriorated. It seems that Paul paid a visit to Corinth, which ended in something near disaster, certainly in deep sorrow for him (2 Cor. ii. 1; xii. 14, 21; xiii. 2). He wrote a severe letter, which cost him many tears (2 Cor. ii. 4; vii. 8). He sent Titus to Corinth, and was overjoyed to hear good news from him (2 Cor. vii. 6 f.). But seeds of bitterness had been sown; Paul was abused by those who should have defended him (2 Cor. xii. 11), and his place was usurped by rivals who, though outwardly more impressive, lacked the inward authorization, and the conformity with the passion of Christ, that

[1] The dates of Gallio's proconsulship are given by an inscription found at Delphi; see *Background*, pp. 48 f., and *Romans*, pp. 4 f.

marked Paul's apostolic work (2 Cor. xii. 12 f.). These events can be pieced together and told in detail only on the basis of detailed study of 2 Corinthians, and will accordingly be fully discussed in the Introduction to the Commentary on that epistle. Here we may note only that at the close of the first century the Corinthian church appears, if we may trust Clement of Rome, in the old light. Worthy presbyters had been deposed, and the church was splitting into factions (1 Clement xliv; xlvi; xlvii).

Two special attempts to reconstruct the history of the Corinthian church in greater detail call for attention. The first is that of J. C. Hurd.[1] In his acute and penetrating study Dr Hurd, using 1 Corinthians as his source, explores the content of Paul's original preaching in Corinth, of his 'Previous Letter', and of the Corinthian reply. In a word, his conclusion is that the Corinthians had remained a good deal closer to the original preaching than Paul himself had done. During his ministry in Corinth, Paul (according to Dr Hurd) had maintained that 'it was best for a man not to touch a woman' (1 Cor. vii. 1). He himself was unmarried and believed that others should be like himself. He approved and encouraged 'spiritual marriages'. In regard to food sacrificed to idols, he had taught that 'all things were lawful' (x. 23), and that idols had no real existence (viii. 4). 'We all have knowledge', he had said (viii. 1), and behaved as one outside the law (ix. 21). In worship, he had himself freely spoken with tongues (xiv. 18), and had permitted women to go without veils (this follows from the fact that behind xi. 2 there appears to be a Corinthian claim to be following Paul's own instructions). As far as the future was concerned, 'he had assured the Corinthians of the imminence of the Parousia, but had said nothing of any need for a change of bodies or for resurrection to enter the Kingdom. There was no reason to talk of resurrection, since the time before the end was so short that there was no expectation of death; nor was there any reason to discuss a change of bodies, since this subject . . . was dependent upon Paul's later explanation of the resurrection of those believers who had died' (p. 285). Baptism and in particular the Lord's Supper 'held death in check and guaranteed that all who believed would remain alive to the end' (p. 287).

[1] See Abbreviations, p. x.

Paul's enthusiastic preaching of a law-free Gospel included these points.

The Previous Letter marked a change. It was written in order to commend and enforce the provisions of the Apostolic Decree (see Acts xv. 20, 29; xxi. 25), which touched on two main points, immorality and idolatry ((a) idol meat, (b) pollutions of idols). The Previous Letter, as reconstructed by Dr Hurd, deals with precisely these points. It commended marriage, as a remedy against fornication, and required separation from immoral men; and it condemned idolatrous practices, forbidding outright the use of food sacrificed to idols, urging caution in the use of tongues, and requiring women to be veiled. In addition, the Previous Letter explained that deceased Christians would be raised up, so as to receive their share in the kingdom of God, and mentioned the collection for the poor. When the Corinthians received this letter they were naturally puzzled, and wrote to Paul, putting to him a number of questions. What do you really mean? Are we to marry, or not? Are we to eat food sacrificed to idols, or not? Must the women wear veils, or not? Do you expect us to believe that corpses will get up out of their graves? How is it that some have died, even though they have been baptized and taken the bread and wine of the Lord's Supper?

In answer to these queries Paul wrote 1 Corinthians, a balanced statement, avoiding the extremes both of his early enthusiasm, and of the excessive caution of the Previous Letter. It is good, Dr Hurd thinks, to have the mature thought of the canonical letter, but he is evidently not without regret that the 'younger, more vigorous Paul, fired with enthusiasm in his new faith, less cautious in his theological statements than he later became, little conscious of the weaknesses of human nature' (p. 287) is lost to us.

There are many fine insights in Dr Hurd's book, and it has been fully referred to here in the hope that students of 1 Corinthians will pursue Dr Hurd's argument for themselves and follow him as far as they can. Such studies must throw light on the meaning of 1 Corinthians. Two points however are bound to cast some doubt on the reconstruction as at present proposed. (1) Only a very short time is available for Paul's thought to move (as is suggested) from thesis through antithesis to synthesis. It was shown above to be probable that Paul left Corinth in about September 51, and wrote 1 Corinthians in the early months of 54, or possibly even of 53. That is, within an interval of about twenty-seven months (or possibly even of fifteen), Paul preached his original Gospel in Corinth, exercised a *volte face* to the reactionary views of the Previous Letter, and finally established the stable position of 1 Corinthians. This is not impossible; it cannot be said to be probable. (2) Neither in 1 Corinthians nor elsewhere does Paul mention the Apostolic Decree. His silence may be due to embarrassment; it is more probably due either to ignorance or to the fact that he did not recognize the Decree as having any authority, at least over his churches. Our knowledge of the origin, scope, purpose, and authority of this Decree is in fact so small that to build upon it means almost inevitably to erect one hypothesis upon another. It seems to me very improbable that one of Paul's motives in writing the Previous Letter was to commend the Decree to Corinth.

Taken as a whole, 1 Corinthians scarcely gives the impression that Paul was playing for safety in the interests of 'theological and institutional readjustment and redefinition' (p. 288). There is little institutionalism in 1 Corinthians, and there is a great deal of fresh, creative, and exciting theological thinking.

H. W. Montefiore, in his commentary on the Epistle to the Hebrews,[1] has made the suggestion that Hebrews was written by Paul's colleague Apollos, after he had returned to Ephesus from the visit to Corinth recorded in Acts xix. 1 and had heard of difficulties in the Corinthian church. Unable, or unwilling (cf. 1 Cor. xvi. 12), to visit Corinth, he wrote his epistle instead. The epistle, though well-intentioned and in itself admirable, had some unfortunate results, which are reflected in 1 Corinthians, which Paul wrote not long afterwards in order to deal with a situation which was partly the same as that which Apollos had been dealing with, but had also in part come into being through Apollos's intervention. Bishop Montefiore is able to find a number of passages in 1 Corinthians (especially in 1 Cor. i-iv) which reflect the circumstances brought into being by Hebrews.

[1] Black's New Testament Commentaries (1964).

Apollos's letter led to the formation of an Apollos-party; it is this (Bishop Montefiore thinks) that Paul has chiefly in mind in his discussion of the parties. 'Cephas enters the argument (1 Cor. i. 12, iii. 22) but the real question of the moment concerns only Paul and Apollos (1 Cor. iii. 5, iv. 6)' (p. 22). Paul was in a difficult position. He 'had apparently the highest opinion of Apollos, who seems later to have been his friend and companion (Titus iii. 13). He did not write a word against him, yet it would seem that he alluded to the Epistle that Apollos had written, and to the wrong use that was being made of this letter by the mutinous Corinthians' (pp. 22 f.). Bishop Montefiore brings out the following points of contact.

Hebrews	*1 Corinthians*
ii. 3 (note the use of βεβαιοῦν)[1]	i. 6, 8
Hebrews is a notably eloquent work	ii. 1, 4
v. 14; vi. 1 had led the Corinthians to think that they were mature (τέλειοι), which Paul doubts	ii. 2, 6
iv. 12, 13; v. 13 ff.	ii. 10-16; cf. iv. 5. Paul insists that Christian discrimination is a gift of the Spirit
v. 12	iii. 2
vi. 7 f.	iii. 6, 8, 9
vi. 1, 3	iii. 10, 11
vi. 8	iii. 13-15: Paul 'seems to have softened the rigorism of Apollos' (p. 25)
The Corinthians had inferred from Apollos's letter that the only true temple was in heaven. Why then need they live holy lives on earth?	iii. 16 f.; cf. 2 Cor. vi. 16

[1] The difference here hardly seems to justify the description of the author of Hebrews as 'semi-Pelagian' and of Paul as 'semi-Augustinian'.

Hebrews—contd.	*1 Corinthians*—contd.
iii. 2-6 Hebrews is expressed in terms of Old Testament interpretation	iv. 1 f., 4 iv. 6. Paul recalls the Corinthians 'to the scriptural limits of Apollos's teaching' (p. 26), or perhaps warns them that Apollos's exegesis goes far enough
iii. 1, 12; vi. 1; cf. xiii. 7. Apollos calls his readers his brothers	iv. 14, 16. Paul can call the Corinthians his children
x. 25, 26, 27. Apollos reproves his readers for absenting themselves from Christian worship, which would include the eucharist; this is unforgivable	xi. 20, 25, 27, 29, 30, 32. In the next stage of development the Corinthians attended and abused the eucharist. Again Paul is less rigorous, and sees the result as chastening rather than condemnation

If Bishop Montefiore's hypothesis is correct it adds a great deal to our understanding of the historical background out of which 1 Corinthians arose. It should however be viewed with caution, and no use will be made of it in this commentary. Whether Apollos wrote Hebrews is a question not to be discussed here.[1] It may be that he did; but, even so, if the view of 1 Corinthians i-iv, and especially of iii, that I have taken is correct, it was not Apollos but Cephas whom Paul saw as a possible source of peril to his work. Apollos was always his friend and colleague, as Bishop Montefiore rightly sees, and Paul mentions him rather than any other rival because, precisely for this reason, it was easier to do so.

Most of Bishop Montefiore's parallels are too slight and fanciful to carry conviction. It is sad that we do not know more of the historical circumstances that lay behind the writing of 1 Corinthians, but we must probably be content to reconcile

[1] The suggestion, as Montefiore points out, is not new; it was made by Luther. There is a good deal to be said for it, though not enough to remove it from the realm of conjecture.

ourselves to ignorance; and we may perhaps allow ourselves to render Paul's own advice in 1 Cor. iv. 6 as: It is better not to read too much between the lines.

II. The Epistle

The account that has been given of Paul's dealings with the Corinthian church assumes both the authenticity and the integrity of 1 Corinthians. The former calls for no defence. No serious scholar questions it. To manufacture a document which in every other line reflects the concerns of the fifties of the first century, and the personal characteristics of Paul, is a task that would have proved far beyond the powers of any Christian at the end of the century. Moreover, Clement of Rome, writing to the Corinthians in about A.D. 95,[1] not merely quotes but refers specifically to the epistle (1 Clement xlvii. 1-3):

> Take up the epistle of the blessed apostle Paul. What did he write to you first of all, in the beginning of the Gospel? Of a truth, he charged you spiritually concerning himself and Cephas and Apollos, because even then you had formed parties.

On the next page, in chapter xlix, we find Clement composing a hymn to love, which is evidently based upon, though it is but a pale shadow of, 1 Cor. xiii. There are other quotations and allusions.

Ignatius of Antioch (*c.* A.D. 112) also echoes the language of 1 Corinthians. See for example Ignatius, *Ephesians* xvi. 1 (Those who corrupt houses shall not inherit the kingdom of God); xviii. 1 (Where is the wise man? Where is the disputant?); *Trallians* xii. 3; *Romans* iv. 3 (Not as Peter and Paul do I charge you; they were apostles . . . they were free); v. 1; ix. 2 (I am the last of them, and one hurried into the world before his time (ἔκτρωμα)); *Philadelphians* iii. 3. Further than this there is no need to go. The evidence for the use of 1 Corinthians is older, clearer, and more widespread than that for any other book of

[1] This is the usually accepted date of 1 Clement; see however E. T. Merrill, *Essays in Early Christian History* (1924), pp. 235-41, who suggests a date in the neighbourhood of A.D. 140. This would diminish, but not seriously, the evidential value of the epistle.

the New Testament. No doubt Christians of the post-apostolic age found it of great practical use.

The integrity of 1 Corinthians is another matter. Paul wrote the document; but did he write it all at once? Does it embody parts of more than one letter? Discussion of these questions must begin from the observation that Paul's dealings with Corinth were more complicated than appears on the surface of the New Testament. It is certain (a) that he visited Corinth on an occasion not recorded in Acts—2 Cor. ii. 1; xii. 14, 21; xiii. 1 f. imply a 'sorrowful visit', which would make the forthcoming visit (cf. Acts xx. 2) not his second but his third; and (b) that he wrote at least four letters to Corinth (1 Cor. v. 9; 2 Cor. ii. 3-9; vii. 8). It may be that of these four letters two only have been preserved (1 and 2 Corinthians), the other two having been completely lost; it is however worthwhile to explore the hypothesis that in the two canonical letters parts of more than two of the original documents have been combined. Very many students see in 2 Corinthians a composite letter; this matter will be pursued in the commentary on 2 Corinthians. Relatively few have adopted a similar hypothesis for 1 Corinthians.

A simple form of analysis is suggested by J. Héring,[1] who notes three points in the epistle as marks of composition. These are (a) the contradiction between iv. 19 (where Paul says he will soon come to Corinth), and xvi. 5-9 (where he explains that his coming will be delayed); (b) the contradiction between x. 1-22 (which takes a rigorist attitude over pagan sacrificial food), and viii. 1-13 and x. 23–xi. 1 (where the matter is treated simply as a question of charity to the weak); (c) the abrupt renewal of the discussion of Paul's apostleship in chapter ix, when it seemed to have been completed in chapter iv. On the basis of these observations, Dr Héring constructs two letters, which, he claims, are coherent:

A: i. 1–viii. 13; x. 23–xi. 1; xvi. 1-4, 10-14.

B: ix. 1–x. 22; xi. 2–xv. 58 (though chapter xiii stands apart); xvi. 5-9, 15-24.

The order of events is as follows:

(a) Paul received information from Chloe's people.

[1] See Abbreviations, p. x.

(b) The same people, or perhaps Sosthenes, handed him a letter from Corinth, containing questions about marriage and food sacrificed to idols.

(c) Paul wrote A, announcing the arrival of Timothy, who was perhaps already on the way, and promising his own speedy arrival. Chloe's people may have conveyed this letter.

(d) Stephanas, who had taken Paul's side in Corinth, arrived at Ephesus with alarming news: the Corinthians doubted Paul's apostleship, doubted the resurrection, and were generally out of hand.

(e) Paul wrote B, sending it by Stephanas, who, he hoped, might still arrive before Timothy. He himself was staying in Ephesus.

An editor attached B to A, perhaps because the beginning of B had become illegible; he removed x. 23–xi. 1 from its original setting and joined it to x. 1-22, because it dealt with the same subject; and he put personal notes together to form chapter xvi.

An example of a more elaborate kind of partition theory is provided by J. Weiss.[1] The part of the theory that relates to 1 Corinthians may be given most simply in Weiss's own words in *The History of Primitive Christianity* (1937), i. 356 f.

> (1) Paul's first letter (A) containing a vigorous attack on participation in idolatry, fornication, the unveiling of women, improper conduct at the common meal; written at Ephesus not long before his departure (1 Cor. xvi. 8 f.). It consists of 1 Cor. x. 1-23; vi. 12-20; xi. 2-34; xvi. 7(?), 8 f.; perhaps xvi. 20 f.; 2 Cor. vi. 14–vii. 1. In this letter Paul announces a visit.
>
> (2) Letter from the church to Paul (1 Cor. vii. 1), possibly brought by Stephanas, Fortunatus, and Achaicus; it reaches the Apostle possibly while he was still in Ephesus, possibly only after he had gone to some other place in the province.
>
> (3) Paul in danger of his life at Ephesus; he leaves the city, stays in the province. He sends on Timothy and Erastus to Macedonia (Acts xix. 22) and to Corinth (1 Cor. iv. 17; xvi. 10 f.), the latter probably with a letter containing his

[1] In his commentary (see Abbreviations, p. xi), and in *The History of Primitive Christianity* (E.T., 1937).

answer to the questions of the Corinthians and comprising 1 Corinthians chapters vii; viii; ix; x. 24–xi. 1; xii; xiii; xiv; xv; xvi. 1-6, perhaps also verses 7 and 15-19. (This is letter B1). He again announces his coming (xvi. 1 ff.).

(4) Paul receives a report from Macedonia about the readiness of the churches there to have a share in the collection, perhaps through Gaius and Aristarchus (Acts xix. 29); he sends Titus and two brethren through Macedonia to Corinth to wind up the matter of the collection (2 Cor. viii). About this time, or soon after,

(5) The household of Chloe arrive with reports of the party disputes.

(6) Paul writes, in considerable agitation, a letter B2, comprising 1 Cor. i. 1-9; i. 10–vi. 11; xvi. 10-14 and perhaps also verses 22 ff. This he sends to Corinth either along with B1 or, if this had already been despatched, by itself. He once more announces his coming and that very soon.[1]

The student should piece together the documents as Dr Héring and Weiss (who are good representatives of the method employed) reconstruct them, and read them through. He will find that in the historical contexts that these scholars provide for them they make quite good sense. The fact that each reconstruction makes good sense is an argument against both, for they cannot both be right, and the sense that one makes, and quite possibly the sense that both make, must be due to the scholar making the reconstruction.

It is often advanced as an argument against partition theories that there is no textual evidence in their support. This argument has no weight. The evidence of the MSS. can tell us nothing about the state of the Pauline (or, for that matter, of any other) literature before its publication. That what we call 1 Corinthians was published in the form in which we now know it is certain; but this does not prove that the form we know was not put together out of a number of pieces.

The essential question that must be asked and answered is whether 1 Corinthians makes sense in its present form, or is so

[1] Weiss's reconstruction of the Corinthian story continues, but the rest concerns only 2 Corinthians.

manifestly inconsistent with itself that its illogical movement and internal contradictions can be remedied only by separating the discordant parts into different letters written on different occasions.[1] This is primarily a question for exegesis, and an Introduction must refer the reader forward to the main body of the commentary, where such matters are discussed as from time to time they arise. It must also be remembered that far more difficult problems arise in 2 Corinthians than in 1 Corinthians, and I hope to return to the whole question of partition and integrity in the Introduction to the Commentary on the second epistle. At present I record the view that no partition theory in regard to 1 Corinthians seems more probable than that Paul simply wrote the letter through, beginning with chapter i and finishing with chapter xvi, and summarize some of the weightiest arguments in favour of it.

(1) 1 Corinthians is a long letter. When it was written Paul was energetically engaged in vigorous evangelistic and pastoral activity, and may at the same time have been earning his living by working at a trade. How much leisure he had for writing we do not know; probably not much. This means that the writing of the letter will have been spread over some time; it may well have been laid aside from time to time, and taken up again after an interval. A letter written in such circumstances may be expected to show occasional inconsistencies, and passages in which the same topic is looked at from different points of view. Fresh news may reach the writer; plans may change with changing needs and opportunities.

(2) There is no serious difficulty in regard to Paul's plans for his own movements. Apart from the lapse of time which may have intervened between the writing of chapter iv and chapter xvi, the two chapters are conceived in different terms. In chapter iv Paul is giving a lively warning to men who are behaving as if they were never likely to see their apostle again. 'Don't make any mistake! I shall be back in Corinth again, and before some of you think. Then we shall know not only what these people can say but what they can do.' In chapter xvi,

[1] Where theological consistency is concerned, it is not easy to see that much is gained by separating the supposedly contradictory elements by an interval of a few months.

Paul is soberly writing out his plans. 'I shall come—and indeed reasonably soon—to Corinth, but I am committed in Ephesus till Pentecost.'

(3) Timothy causes a little more trouble: iv. 17 says that he has already been sent; xvi. 10 says not 'When he comes' but 'If he comes'—there is some doubt whether he will arrive. See the commentary on these passages. The most probable solution is that Timothy (alone or with Erastus) had been sent into Macedonia, with some discretion in regard to the question whether he should continue his journey as far as Achaea.

(4) The crux of the matter lies in chapter ix. The following questions are raised. Why is the theme of apostleship reopened? How can chapter ix be connected with chapter viii? Why is the discussion of food sacrificed to idols, begun in chapter viii, dropped, and then resumed (with apparently somewhat different treatment) in chapter x? One answer suffices for all these questions, but it needs the support of detailed exegesis, which is given in the commentary. In the question of food sacrificed to idols, Paul is dealing with a very complex problem. It is complicated in two ways. (a) It is necessary to distinguish between the mere consumption of food, and the consumption of food in a particular context which gives to the act of eating the significance of idolatry. (b) It is necessary to bear in mind both Christian freedom, and the obligation of Christian love, which may on occasion limit freedom. These points explain apparent inconsistencies in Paul's treatment of sacrificial food; they also account for chapter ix. Paul has appealed to the Corinthians for voluntary limitation of their freedom and surrender of their rights. He immediately adds that he is not asking them for what he himself will not give. He has voluntarily surrendered his own apostolic rights. At this point he could have stopped and picked up the main thread once more, but characteristically he pauses to ask, Why? The answer is that he has limited his enjoyment of his undoubted rights in the interests of the Gospel (ix. 12, 15, 18, 22 f.). This leads him to consider the nature of the Gospel, and thus to the dangerous folly of those who dare to think that they are automatically preserved from sin and judgement by the sacraments. Now he takes up again the main theme of sacrificial food in the light of the new insights afforded by his digressions.

The integrity of 1 Corinthians is a question on which differences of opinion will no doubt continue to exist. The suggested reconstructions, of which two examples have been given here, are by no means impossible, though their variety indicates the large subjective element that enters into them, and the more elaborate they become the harder it is to understand the editorial process by which the epistle was given its present form. As long, however, as it seems that the epistle as it stands makes reasonably good sense, historically and theologically, the balance of probability will remain with the view that we have it substantially as it left the author's hands.

III. The Contribution of 1 Corinthians

(a) To the Development of Theology

1 Corinthians is anything but a work of systematic theology. It is a practical letter addressed to a single, though complex, situation, aimed at telling its readers not so much what they ought to think as what they ought to do—or ought not to do. The practical advice, however, is consciously grounded in theological principles which can usually be detected; and, more important, the problems with which Paul deals seem to have reacted upon his theological views, or at least to have had a catalytic effect in pushing forward developments that might otherwise have taken place more slowly. The theology that underlies the counsel contained in 1 Corinthians is best studied as it emerges in the course of the epistle, and must therefore be sought in the body of the commentary. In the following pages no attempt is made to give a full account of 'Pauline theology', or even of the theology of 1 Corinthians; their aim is rather to pick out some of the points at which circumstances in Corinth obliged Paul to develop his theological thought.

(1) *Christology*. There was no evident Christological error at Corinth to compel Paul to develop positive Christological views; two points however led him to think on Christological lines.

The first is concerned with *wisdom* (σοφία). It will be shown below in the commentary[1] that the word wisdom is used in 1 Corinthians in at least four ways. There were some in Corinth

[1] See also 'Christianity at Corinth', pp. 275-86.

to whom wisdom was primarily a manner of preaching, involving the use of logical and rhetorical devices which were designed to convince the hearer, whose conviction (if it were achieved) would thus rest upon the devices employed. The argument was carried over to him on the strength of the case which the speaker could make for it. It was necessary for Paul to point out that this was not how he understood Christian preaching, which for him was a placarding of that supremely unconvincing folly, Christ crucified, a placarding which derived its effectiveness not from the human wisdom with which it was conducted but from its own subject-matter—Christ himself, and the power of the self-evidencing Spirit of God which accompanied it. Christ himself was the true wisdom. But, in addition, wisdom (sometimes perhaps *knowledge*—γνῶσις) was being represented as the stuff of salvation itself. It was not only a method of commending a way of salvation, it was itself the way of salvation, the way, that is, by which men might find their entry into glory in the heavenly world. Again, Paul had to set over against this false wisdom the true wisdom—Christ himself. He was indeed a hidden wisdom, since by no human standards would anyone suspect that the crucified Jesus was the power and wisdom of God, nor did acceptance of him open the way to immediate bliss, but to a life of disciplined obedience. Yet, in the Corinthian context, if Paul's understanding of Christianity was to be maintained, the equation must be made: Christ is the Wisdom of God.

This equation did not immediately lead Paul to a developed wisdom Christology, such as begins to appear in Colossians and Hebrews, but the roots of this kind of Christology are to be found in 1 Corinthians, not only in the discussion of Wisdom in chapters i and ii, but also, and especially, in viii. 6, where Christ (through whom are all things, including ourselves) takes on the characteristics of the personified Wisdom of, for example, the Wisdom of Solomon. It is not necessary here to expound this thought; it is sufficient to note that it arises and develops in the Corinthian situation.

A second Christological development occurs in Paul's discussion of the doctrine of the resurrection, a discussion necessitated by Corinthian error in the matter (xv. 12). It was not Paul's belief that men were immortal, or that they would be raised up, in their own right. As men they were under sentence of death—a sentence which had been justly pronounced on Adam (Gen. ii. 17; iii. 19), and inherited by all his descendants. That mankind now had a new hope of a new future was due simply to the fact that the crucified Jesus had been raised from the dead, and raised as the first fruits of all those who had fallen asleep. He thus stood to the new humanity in the same relation as Adam to the old. He was in fact the last Adam, the heavenly man corresponding to the 'man of dust' of the creation narratives in Genesis. In what sense did Christ correspond to Adam? Paul appears to allude to the vision of Dan. vii. 13, where a human figure appears with the clouds of heaven, and thus begins to draw upon two realms of thought: that proper to Jewish Son-of-man apocalyptic, and that of the wide-spread speculations about a primal or archetypal man. It is not possible to say on the basis of 1 Corinthians[1] how much Paul thought it right to borrow, and what he made of his borrowings, but it is possible to see how the necessity of arguing with the Corinthians (together, no doubt, with other causes) led him to important Christological development.

(2) *Anthropology*. 1 Cor. vi. 12 f. reflects a characteristic, and superficially convincing, Corinthian argument. It was deduced from Paul's preaching of a Gospel that meant freedom from legalism that all things were lawful, and this conclusion was supported by an argument based on an analogy of human functions. Man is no longer bound by food laws; foods were made for the belly and the belly for foods, and it does not matter what foods are used, since they and the belly alike have only a transient existence and cannot affect man's eternal destiny. By similar reasoning (it was urged) man's sexual life may be freed from restriction. Neither male nor female sexual organs will survive death, so that while life lasts each may be freely and promiscuously used to gratify the appetite of the other. It is clear that Paul could not assent to this argument without abandoning Christian morality altogether; but where was the difference between sexual and other appetite to be found?

Paul is faced with a related problem when he discusses the

[1] See in addition Rom. v. 12-21; Phil. ii. 6-11; also *Adam* (Index, s.v. Adam).

resurrection of the dead. He contends for a continuity[1] between the body of the present life and the body of the life to come. But is this credible? What kind of continuity does he mean?

How Paul deals with these questions should appear in the course of the commentary. The only observation to be made here is that these problems led Paul to think about the relation between flesh (σάρξ) and body (σῶμα), to develop his conception of the two kinds of body, natural and spiritual (σῶμα ψυχικόν and σῶμα πνευματικόν), and to consider the bearing of deeds done in the body upon the essential life and identity of man. These distinctions and relationships are handled more firmly in 2 Corinthians, and especially in Romans; it seems however that they were forced upon the apostle's attention when he wrote 1 Corinthians.

(3) *Judaism and Other Religions.* Paul's Christian faith grew up in tension with the Jewish religion, which he had abandoned in order to become a Christian. There can be no doubt that he was aware of the pressure of the old religion throughout his Christian life, and there were times and places in which it was brought more forcefully to his attention than in Corinth, at least in the period up to the writing of 1 Corinthians. There was however some Judaizing pressure,[2] in the context of which Paul worked out his view of the complete irrelevance of current Judaism which he states in vii. 19. It is, again, probably not a coincidence that it is in 1 Corinthians that Paul states the principle of ix. 20 ff. With complete elasticity of practice[3] he regulates his behaviour in terms of his environment, with the single-minded intention of winning converts to the faith. There has probably been no other period, and no other person, in whom this alternating attitude, now observant, now neglectful, of the Torah, could have been for a moment practical; what is significant is Paul's grasp of the principle that all things must be done 'in the interests of the Gospel' (διὰ τὸ εὐαγγέλιον).

In Corinth, Paul was obliged to confront not only Judaism but also a variety of other religions, well provided with gods and lords (viii. 5) who were worshipped in temples and by the

[1] For the nature of this continuity see the commentary on chapter xv; also M. E. Dahl, *The Resurrection of the Body* (*Studies in Biblical Theology* No. 36; 1962).

[2] See T. W. Manson, *Studies*, pp. 191-207, 216.

[3] Cf. H. Chadwick, 'All things to All Men', in *N.T.S.* i. 261-75.

sacrifice of various kinds of food. I have argued above (p. 16; see also the commentary) that the various passages in 1 Corinthians in which Paul deals with the question of food sacrificed to idols are not inconsistent with one another; it is however true that in them we can see Paul feeling his way towards a clear statement of Christian principle and policy in this matter. Further, he allows a limited degree of analogy between the pagan feasts which he deplores as instituting communion with demons, and the Christian feast. The Christian feast too is a communion, though with a different Lord. Possibly he means to imply also that, in its own unique way, the Christian feast is a sacrificial meal, as were those of the heathen temples. Though not the occasion of a sacrifice it was held in consequence and celebration of a sacrifice (cf. v. 7). The setting of the Christian supper sent him back to Israel in the wilderness, with its baptism into Moses, and its spiritual drink and food; it also obliged him to think out, in the light of pagan parallels, the mode in which it afforded communion with Christ crucified. Paul's preaching and arguing were nothing if not Christian, but he conducted them (as one may see from this epistle) in sensitive awareness of his environment.

(4) *Apostleship and the Pattern of Christian Life.* It is not until 2 Corinthians that this theme will be heard with full clarity, but it is already sounded in the first epistle. How may an apostle be known? The Corinthian answer appears to have been: by eloquent speech; by an impressive theology of a gnostic kind; by authoritarian behaviour. By none of these criteria did Paul qualify. He refused the media of argument and rhetoric, accepted the hardships of a pioneer, and behaved towards his converts with the gentleness of a father rather than the outward authority of a master. It would probably be true to say that Paul knew instinctively that his was the right method, but Corinth made him face and answer the question, What is an apostle and how may he be recognized? It was this that drove him back upon his commission from the risen Christ, and the fact that, as Christians, the Corinthians were his own begetting. He had laid the foundation of their society. These were observable facts, and they did give Paul a real authority, but in the end it was the Lord only who would vindicate the apostle and his work; to

outward appearance an apostle might provide but a derisory spectacle. Not even his own clear conscience was a relevant factor.

In all this, Paul and his fellow-apostles did not stand apart from the church as a whole, but manifested, as a particularly clear example, the pattern of Christian life. Corinth also forced upon Paul the necessity of formulating a hierarchy of values. There is good reason to think that of all the gifts of the Spirit the one most highly prized in Corinth was that of speaking with tongues. It was one that Paul himself possessed; if Dr Hurd[1] is right, he had taught the Corinthians to practise and esteem it. This may or may not be correct; if it is, reflection on the Corinthian situation had led Paul to revise his judgement, and to see the real stuff of Christian living not in superficially impressive gifts, but in love. It would be foolish to suggest that this truth struck Paul for the first time when he wrote 1 Corinthians; indeed, there is some reason to think that the material contained in 1 Cor. xiii may have been in existence before Paul used it in this letter. But Corinth gave him occasion for thought, and the opportunity of setting out in complete clarity his understanding of Christian priorities.

(b) To our Knowledge of the Primitive Church

1 and 2 Corinthians together constitute perhaps the most valuable of all the documents available to the historian of the apostolic age. Material most suitable to a discussion of 2 Corinthians is deferred to a later volume; here some of the most important conclusions that may be derived from 1 Corinthians are summarized. More details are to be found in the commentary.

(1) *Chronology*. This subject has already been discussed, when the question of the date and background of the epistle was considered (pp. 3 ff.). Unless we are prepared to make conjectures which (though some of them are probable) are not capable of proof, 1 Corinthians supplies only a bare outline of the events

[1] Op. cit. p. 281. Hurd of course does not suggest that Paul ever taught the Corinthians that speaking with tongues was the most important spiritual gift.

that led up to its composition—the founding visit, the Previous Letter, a letter from Corinth, and visits from Chloe's people, and Stephanas, Fortunatus, and Achaicus. We may reasonably, though not certainly, add the visit to Corinth of Cephas[1] as well as that of Apollos. In addition, two further points may be made.

1 Corinthians gives us some information about Paul's ministry in Ephesus. In xv. 30 ff. Paul says: Why do we too go in danger every hour? If it was on purely human terms I fought with wild beasts at Ephesus, what good does that do me? It does not seem probable (see the commentary) that this refers to a literal encounter with wild beasts in the arena; it nevertheless bears witness to an experience of great danger and hardship, and probably of fierce resistance to Paul's preaching. It thus adds vivid colour to the 'many adversaries' of xvi. 9.

1 Corinthians contains the earliest extant reference (except perhaps the general statement of Gal. ii. 10) to Paul's collection for the poor saints. An account of this activity of Paul's[2] belongs to the commentary on 2 Corinthians; but it should be noted that it had already begun, and that arrangements had been made in the churches of Galatia (xvi. 1).

(2) *The structure of the church*. The social make-up of the church in Corinth is described without flattery in i. 26. It did not contain many who, by human standards, were wise, powerful, or well-born. It contained slaves (vii. 21), but was not entirely servile in status (vii. 23).

The several members (and they would hardly have been Corinthian if they had not shown a good measure of individualism) were united in a fellowship so close that it could be compared to a body (x. 17; xii. 12-27), every part of which was bound up with and reacted upon every other. As the image of the body suggests, however, the group was an organism rather than an organization; at least, practically no trace of organization is revealed to us in the letter. In particular there seems to have been little or no formal leadership. The church's meeting for

[1] See 'Cephas and Corinth'.

[2] See D. Georgi, *Die Geschichte der Kollekte des Paulus für Jerusalem* (*Theologische Forschung: Wissenschaftliche Beiträge zur kirchlich-evangelischen Lehre* 38), 1965; also K. F. Nickle, *The Collection* (*Studies in Biblical Theology* No. 48), 1966.

the Lord's Supper is described without any reference to a president; indeed, xi. 33 may imply that there was no such person. There was no treasurer to whom subscriptions could be paid (xvi. 2). It may have been to some extent a natural human desire that led to the formation of the groups that attached themselves to the names of Paul, Apollos, Cephas, and Christ. If this was so, Paul made no attempt to remedy the situation by asserting his own authority and claim to the allegiance of the whole church. He was no more than a steward (iv. 1), and, though conscientious (iv. 4), not a very impressive one (iv. 9-13). He was, however, the evangelist to whom the Corinthians owed their Christian existence, and as such could speak of himself as their father (iv. 14 f.); as a father he could when necessary use a stick (iv. 21).

The beginnings of organization show themselves in the emergence of the household of Stephanas, and others who do Christian work, and cooperate in the running and discipline of the community (xvi. 15 f.); also in the wide range of spiritual gifts bestowed on the church. See the commentary on xii. 28. Beside the apostles stand prophets and teachers. It is not easy on the basis of 1 Corinthians alone to describe the functions and assess the position of the second and third groups. Prophecy was evidently a local gift in the sense that, like speaking with tongues, it was exercised by members of the local church. Prophets may however to some extent have travelled from church to church, doing some at least of the work of apostles. Teachers probably were local, but we must admit that we do not know, and cannot from 1 Corinthians deduce, what they taught, or how, and to whom, they taught it. Among the other gifts seem to be those of rendering practical service, and taking a lead, or giving advice. These hardly call for comment here.

The Corinthian church in the fifties (and this will doubtless apply to many contemporary societies) had no clearly marked form or structure. It was intensely alive; many spiritual gifts were exercised within it; many persons made their contributions, some large, some small, some quiet and solid, some showy and ephemeral. Paul appears to have made no conscious effort to give the church a permanent shape, but it is possible to see (with the aid of other New Testament books) how Christian life tended to create its own forms on the lines of the ministry of the word, loving service, and community discipline.[1]

(3) *Institutions of the Church.* It is not to be expected that a body thus provided with no more than a loose and gradually developing structure should have evolved a set of rigid institutions; the noun itself is perhaps an unhappy one, but even in Corinth things did to some extent happen in recurring patterns, and no society can exist long without adopting some more or less stable practices.

Probably all Christians were baptized on admission to the church, though Paul was not in a position to give first hand testimony to this, since he had not himself baptized many of his converts, and had indeed only a somewhat hazy idea whom he had baptized (i. 14-17). The argument of x. 1-13 suggests that some Christians overvalued (or it might be better to say, misinterpreted) their baptism, regarding it as a prophylactic which it was never intended to be, and xv. 29, at least on some interpretations, implies in Corinth a similar magical view of the efficacy of the rite.

Those who were members of the church met from time to time in assembly. At these meetings, prophecy and speaking with tongues were practised, and each member had some sort of contribution to make to the proceedings: a word of knowledge or of wisdom, a piece of teaching or revelation, given as prophecy or in a tongue (xii. 8; xiv. 26). Paul's instructions suggest that the meetings were sometimes tumultuous, even chaotic; they were certainly not dull. They were not confined to members of the church; unbelieving outsiders might find their way in (xiv. 23). The extent to which women were permitted to take part is hard to assess because it is difficult to reconcile xi. 5 and xiv. 34; see the notes on these passages. If Paul was (as he may have been) uneasy about their public appearances, this may well have been because, as is hardly surprising, the Corinthians found it difficult to regulate relations between the sexes; on the one hand, chapter v bears witness to a case of immorality shocking by even heathen standards, and, on the other, chapter vii reveals an ascetic view of sex—even if vii.

[1] See 'The Ministry in the New Testament', in *The Doctrine of the Church*, edited by Dow Kirkpatrick (1964), pp. 39-63.

25-38 does not reflect an early form of the custom, known at later points in church history, of spiritual marriages.

Sometimes when the church assembled it was to eat a common meal. The commentary (see the notes on x. 16-21; xi. 17-34) inevitably lays some stress upon the special Corinthian aberrations which Paul was obliged by circumstances to censure; here it will be more important to see what may be regarded as the norm behind the aberrations. Thus from the fact that Paul complains that while one member of the church goes hungry another gets drunk, we may deduce that the meal was a real meal (and not merely a symbolic one), and that it involved ideally a pooling of resources by rich and poor members. It included a recital of the events of the Lord's death, and thus looked backward, as well as forward to the Lord's return; whether the recital included the 'Words of Institution' we cannot be sure. It is usually assumed that this was so because Paul quotes them (xi. 24 ff.), but though he uses the words of Jesus to bring the Corinthian church to a right understanding of what they are about it cannot necessarily be inferred from this that the words were used at every assembly.

For further details, and some attempt to bring out the meaning of the Christian actions described and alluded to, reference must be made to the commentary. There is scarcely a paragraph in the epistle that does not bear historical witness to what was happening at Corinth, and theological witness to the positive and creative criticism of this that Paul believed was applied by the Gospel. It is this fact that gives 1 Corinthians its unique importance within the New Testament. It is not the fullest and clearest statement of Paul's Gospel; for this we must turn to Romans. Nor is it the letter that shows Paul's own heart most clearly, for in this respect it is surpassed by 2 Corinthians, and perhaps by other epistles too. But it has the great value of showing theology at work, theology being used as it was intended to be used, in the criticism and establishing of persons, institutions, practices, and ideas. 'As Biblical theology, theology is the question as to the foundation, as practical theology it is the question as to the aim, as dogmatic theology it is the question as to the content, of the language peculiar to the Church.'[1] As

[1] K. Barth, *C.D.* I. i. 3.

students of the New Testament we cannot distinguish biblical, practical, and dogmatic theology, but in 1 Corinthians we see the primary theological conviction of the apostle interrogating a particular church in all these ways; and not only the substance of the conviction but the manner of the interrogation are given us for our learning.

ANALYSIS OF THE EPISTLE

A. INTRODUCTION i. 1-9

1. i. 1-3: Address
2. i. 4-9: Thanksgiving

B. NEWS FROM CORINTH i. 10–vi. 20

(a) Wisdom and Division at Corinth i. 10–iv. 21

3. i. 10-17: The Corinthian groups
4. i. 18-31: The word of the cross
5. ii. 1-5: Simple testimony
6. ii. 6-16: Wisdom, false and true
7. iii. 1-4: Even true wisdom unsuitable for babes
8. iii. 5-17: Paul and Apollos
9. iii. 18-23: Paul, Apollos, Cephas, and Christ
10. iv. 1-5: Servants of Christ, and their work
11. iv. 6-13: The Corinthians and their apostles
12. iv. 14-21: The Corinthians and their apostle; Paul's plans

(b) Fornication v. 1-13

13. v. 1-13: Fornication inside and outside the church

(c) Litigation vi. 1-11

14. vi. 1-11: There should be no litigation—or grounds for it

(d) The Root of the Trouble vi. 12-20

15. vi. 12-20: The root of the trouble

C. A LETTER FROM CORINTH vii. 1–xvi. 4

(a) Marriage and Related Questions vii. 1–40

16. vii. 1-7: Behaviour within marriage
17. vii. 8-24: Christian and mixed marriages, slavery and freedom
18. vii. 25-40: Virgins

(b) FOOD SACRIFICED TO IDOLS viii. 1 – xi. 1

19. viii. 1-13: Source of the trouble—exaltation of knowledge over love
20. ix. 1-27: Even an apostle will renounce his rights for the sake of the Gospel
21. x. 1-13: Even baptized communicants are not secure
22. x. 14-22: Christianity inconsistent with idolatry
23. x. 23 – xi. 1: Nature, extent, and limitations of Christian freedom

(c) THE CHRISTIAN ASSEMBLY xi. 2-34

24. xi. 2-16: Men and women
25. xi. 17-34: The Supper

(d) SPIRITUAL GIFTS xii. 1 – xiv. 40

26. xii. 1-3: The fundamental test: (a) Jesus is Lord
27. xii. 4-31: Diversity of gifts in one body
28. xiii. 1-13: The fundamental test: (b) Love
29. xiv. 1-40: The tests applied to tongues and prophecy

(e) THE RESURRECTION xv. 1-58

30. xv. 1-11: The common Gospel
31. xv. 12-22: Implications of the Gospel
32. xv. 23-28: Christian Apocalypse (a)
33. xv. 29-34: *Ad hominem* arguments for and about resurrection
34. xv. 35-49: The old manhood and the new
35. xv. 50-58: Christian Apocalypse (b)

(f) THE COLLECTION xvi. 1-4

36. xvi. 1-4: Instructions and plans for the collection

D. CONCLUSION xvi. 5-24

37. xvi. 5-12: Wider setting of Paul's plans
38. xvi. 13-24: Last words to the church, and greetings

TRANSLATION AND COMMENTARY

A. INTRODUCTION

1. i. 1-3. ADDRESS

(1) Paul, called to be an apostle of Christ Jesus through God's will, together with Sosthenes his brother Christian, (2) to the church of God that is in Corinth, made up of men who are sanctified in Christ Jesus,[1] by divine call saints, together with all who, in every meeting-place, call on the name of our Lord Jesus Christ—their Lord and ours. (3) I wish you grace and peace from God our Father and the Lord Jesus Christ.

As in every epistle, Paul uses the conventional Greek letter-formula, A to B, greeting. As in every epistle, so here, the formula undergoes Christian expansion, in the definition of the sender and the recipients, and in the greeting. The expansion in this letter is not so extensive as that in Romans (i. 1-7), but it raises difficult problems of text, grammar, and interpretation.

Paul describes himself as **called to be an apostle.** It is probable that the word *called* (κλητός) should stand in the text, though A D omit it, and the longer text (with κλητός) might as well be an assimilation to Rom. i. 1 as the shorter text (without κλητός) to 2 Cor. i. 1. It is in favour of the text with *called* that it raises a problem (which a copyist might well have thought to remove by dropping the word) over the connection of **through God's will.** Does this refer to the calling, or to the apostleship? 2 Cor. i. 1 points decisively to the latter, though Gal. i. 15 favours the former. Not merely the actual call, on the Damascus road (Acts xxvi. 16 ff.) or in Jerusalem (xxii. 21), but

[1] *Made up of . . . Jesus* is placed immediately after *church of God* by P[46] B D* G it.

the whole of Paul's apostolic activity is determined by God's will. The proclamation of the good news is itself part of the good news, and Paul's ministry within the church is part of the constitutive divine act by which the church is created. Hence Paul's delicately balanced authority, which will be called in question, and much misunderstood, in the course of the epistles (e.g. 1 Cor. iv; ix. 1-23; 2 Cor. iv. 1-15; x-xiii). Hence also the lack of authority of those who, however impressive in their gifts, conduct, and human relations, have not been appointed by God's will, by which alone men are appointed to valid service (cf. e.g. 2 Cor. x. 12-18; xi. 12-23).

Paul does not stand alone. **Sosthenes** is not, apparently, an apostle, but he is a **brother Christian**; literally, *the brother*. The term is a common one among Christians (e.g. Matt. xxiii. 8). It is true that it represents the correct relationship between Christians who in Christ Jesus are all sons of the one Father, and must therefore recognize that among them the ordinary distinctions of sex, race, and class have ceased to exist (Gal. iii. 28; Col. iii. 11), but true also that the word has a history of use in Judaism (e.g. 2 Macc. i. 1; Josephus, *War* ii. 122, of the Essenes), and in pagan social and religious life also (see Bauer and L.S. s.v.). The Gospel supplied a new basis in reality, and generated warmth of feeling, but it did not create a wholly new vocabulary. According to Acts xviii. 17, a Sosthenes who was a ruler of the Corinthian synagogue was brought before Gallio's judgement seat and beaten. It is not said in Acts that this Sosthenes became a Christian. According to the Western text of Acts xviii. 17 he was beaten by all *the Greeks*—presumably as a Jew; but probably *the Greeks* should be omitted, and the implication may be that Greeks and Jews joined in beating Sosthenes, the former because he was a Jew, the latter possibly because he had become a Christian, or at least had failed to secure a conviction against Paul. We cannot be certain that the Sosthenes who joined Paul in writing to Corinth had earlier been a leading Corinthian Jew, but it is at least possible, and perhaps more than possible. There is no doubt that Paul is the senior partner; or that Sosthenes genuinely is a partner.

Paul and Sosthenes write **to the church of God that is in** 2

Corinth. The word *church* (ἐκκλησία) occurs twenty-two times in 1 Corinthians, and further discussion of its meaning will be found below (e.g. pp. 260 f., 287-96). The church in Corinth evidently consists of a group of persons who will assemble to read (or hear) Paul's letter, but it is what it is not because it bears some particular human structure, but because it is **made up of men who are sanctified in Christ Jesus.** It is God's act in sanctifying them (that is, in separating them for himself) and not any act of their own that makes these men into the church. Paul uses the same word, as here, for a local assembly of Christians, and for the whole company of Christian believers (xv. 9; perhaps xii. 28; cf. the use of the plural or its equivalent: iv. 17; vii. 17; xi. 16; xiv. 33). This is an important fact, which should be brought out in translation by using the same English word for both purposes. That which exists in Corinth is, so far as Corinth is concerned, the church of God, wanting in nothing save numbers. It cannot afford to neglect other similar manifestations of the whole church (thus Paul will urge the Corinthians to join in charitable service to the Palestinian Christians —xvi. 1-4), and must take note of universal Christian beliefs and practices (iv. 17; vii. 17; xi. 16; xiv. 33-6), but it is the church, and not simply a fraction of it.

The words *made up . . . Christ Jesus* have a variable place in the MSS. and may not be part of the original text; see Zuntz, pp. 91 f. If they are omitted there is no loss, since their sense is repeated in the next words, **by divine call saints** (literally, *called*, *holy*). The Corinthian Christians, concerning whose morals we shall hear a number of complaints in the following pages, are *saints* (that is, holy persons) in the sense that they are God's people, as was Israel in former times; cf. e.g. Exod. xix. 6. They exist no longer to serve their own purposes but God's; hence, if they take their holiness seriously, the most important of moral consequences will flow from it. But it is not in itself a moral condition. See below, pp. 60 f., 141 ff. Here, as in verse 1, *called* (κλητός), a verbal adjective, comes near to being a substantive. Paul is a called person, who is an apostle; the Corinthians are called persons, who are holy (Moule, pp. 95 f.). The fact of the calling is as significant as that of the holiness (with which it is closely bound up); and the members of the Corinthian church, equally with the apostle, have their place, though a different place, in the purpose of God.

The next words, **together with all who . . . call on the name of our Lord Jesus Christ . . .,** could be connected with Paul and Sosthenes (verse 1), with the Corinthian recipients of the letter (verse 2a), or with the idea expressed in *by divine call saints*—the Corinthians share this calling with all their fellow-believers. Each possibility has its own difficulties. It is hard to see in what sense the whole company of Christians can join Paul and Sosthenes in addressing the church at Corinth; they simply are not doing so. This possibility can surely be excluded. Again, though there is a sense in which Paul by addressing one local church is addressing the whole church (see above), the letter is so personal that Paul can hardly have thought that all Christians would read it. It may be that this clause was added when the Pauline letters were collected, published, and recognized as canonical scriptures applying to the whole church (so e.g. Weiss). There is no textual evidence for this, but in the nature of things such evidence could not be expected; see Introduction, p. 14. As far as sense is concerned, the third possibility is best: Christians in Corinth are called to holiness, and in this they share a common vocation with all Christians. But this interpretation is the most difficult grammatically; see Lightfoot ad loc. Probably it is best to take the second interpretation, and to suppose that Paul is thinking not of the letter as a whole but of the Christian greeting he is about to express. If he wishes grace and peace for the church at Corinth, so he does for believers elsewhere.

To call upon the name of Christ is to put one's trust in him, and to address him in prayer and worship; cf. Romans x. 13 (quoting Joel iii. 5 (EVV, ii. 32); Weiss perhaps makes too much of the distinction between Romans, where he takes the main point to be conversion, and 1 Corinthians, where he thinks the emphasis is on liturgical invocation). This invocation of Christ is made **in every meeting-place.** The noun (τόπος) means as a rule simply *place*; but there is evidence (see T. W. Manson, *Studies*, pp. 208 f.) that it was used by Jews to refer to their own meeting-places (synagogues), and though *in every place* would make good sense here the sentence is more pointed if the technical meaning is applied. The word could refer to Jewish meeting-places, and indicate Jewish Christians who maintained a Christian witness within the framework of the synagogue; more probably (since Paul appears to be thinking of all Christians rather than of Jewish Christians only) the reference is to Christian meeting-places, for which the Jewish word had been borrowed. Naturally we are not at this date to think of buildings specially erected for the purpose; cf. xvi. 19, *the church that meets in their house*. It is possible that in some areas the majority of a Jewish community was converted, and that the synagogue was then taken over for Christian use; there is no ground for thinking that this happened in Corinth.

In the translation the last words of verse 2 are given as **their Lord and ours.** No noun is expressed in the Greek (*theirs and ours*), and the pronouns could refer to *meeting-place*: all who call upon the name of our Lord Jesus Christ in every meeting-place, their meeting-place and ours. This makes sense but is very trite: it is more probable that Paul is making the point that all Christians share a common holiness because they share a common Lord. Ulrich Wickert (*Z.N.T.W.* 50 (1959), pp. 73-82) adds the observation that Paul, having in mind the exhortation to unity that he is shortly to deliver (see i. 10), is concerned here to bring out his own solidarity with the Corinthians (who would be included in *ours*). 'I write to you in fellowship with all who call on the name of our Lord (and thus in fellowship with you too, you factious—cf. 1 Cor. xi. 16—Corinthians); for I am one with them, as indeed we are all one, wherever we are willing to turn to the Lord' (p. 80).

A non-Christian Greek would send his correspondent greeting (*χαίρειν*); a Jew would wish him peace. Paul prays for his
3 readers **grace** (*χάρις*) **and peace** (for the combination cf.
Apoc. Baruch lxxviii. 2; 2 Macc. i. 1), and sees both as coming **from God our Father and the Lord Jesus Christ.** Grace and peace do not play in 1 and 2 Corinthians the great theological role that they have in Romans; Paul is here less concerned to state theological principle than to emphasize its practical consequences. But the theological principle is always there; for grace, see especially 2 Cor. viii. 9, and the context; for peace, 1 Cor. vii. 15. Grace is the antecedent being and act of God

which are the ground of all Christian existence (cf. 1 Cor. xv. 10); peace is the outcome of God's redemptive act, the total state of well-being to which men are admitted (cf. Rom. v. 1). When one Christian wishes grace and peace to another he prays that he may apprehend more fully the grace of God in which he already stands, and the peace he already enjoys.

Each comes from God the Father and the Lord Jesus Christ; the Father is the source, Christ the means or agent; cf. viii. 6. Paul provides no ready-made doctrine of God or of Christ. What he believed about each must appear from his statements of what each has done; see the notes on i. 30; viii. 6; and, for Jesus as Lord, especially xii. 3 and the comment.

2. i. 4-9. THANKSGIVING

(4) I am constantly giving thanks to God for you, because of the grace of God that was given you in Christ Jesus. (5) For in every respect, in speech and knowledge of every kind, you were made rich in him, (6) as the preached testimony to Christ was confirmed in your own experience, (7) so that you come short in no gift of grace as you await the revelation of our Lord Jesus Christ. (8) He will keep you firm to the end,[1] so that you are irreproachable on the day of our Lord Jesus Christ. (9) God, through whom you were called into fellowship with his Son Jesus Christ our Lord, is faithful.

Paul again follows convention in continuing with a thanksgiving; naturally, his thanksgiving rests upon Christian grounds, and reflects the Christian standing of his readers. That is, it rests upon (ἐπί with the accusative is used 'of the occasion or cause'—L.S.) **the grace of God that was given you in** 4
Christ Jesus. For *grace* see the note on i. 3; here however the word has a developed sense, as in a number of Pauline passages where the same expression (ἡ χάρις ἡ δοθεῖσα) is used (Rom. xii.

[1] Instead of *to the end* (ἕως τέλους), P^{46} has the interesting variant *perfect* (τελείους); this is probably already a corruption (cf. Zuntz, p. 20).

3, 6; xv. 15; 1 Cor. iii. 10; Gal. ii. 9). The antecedent and universal grace of God encounters particular Christians as a divine gift, constituting their Christian life, and enabling them to perform services they are called to render in the church and for the world. The gift is given *in Jesus Christ*. This prepositional phrase may be taken either with the verb: it is in the unspeakable gift (2 Cor. ix. 15) of Christ that all other specific gifts are given (cf. Rom. viii. 32); or with *you*: it is to you in Christ, that is, to you in your being as Christians that the gift has been given. The two interpretations are very closely related, but the next verse suggests that the emphasis is on the latter.

In the translation the next verse is taken as giving an elucida-
5 tion of *the grace given you:* **For** (ὅτι) . . . **you were made rich.** It is possible to take the Greek conjunction (ὅτι) as dependent on *I give thanks: I give thanks . . . that* (ὅτι) *you were made rich.* The latter construction would however more naturally contain an *and*: 'I give thanks because of . . ., *and* that . . .'. The result of the bestowal of God's grace is that in Christ Christians are made rich; thus that they are rich is a sign that grace has been given. The wealth of the Christian life is a thought not uncommon in these epistles (iv. 8; 2 Cor. vi. 10; viii. 2, 7, 9; ix. 11; elsewhere Paul speaks as a rule of God's or Christ's wealth: Rom. ii. 4; ix. 23; x. 12; xi. 33; Phil. iv. 19); it appears that the Corinthians had exaggerated the measure of wealth that they possessed, and had not understood the terms on which Christians hold their riches in Christ (2 Cor. iv. 7). For the present however Paul is not calling in question the riches of divine grace that had been received in Corinth and of which he had probably been informed either by letter (cf. vii. 1) or orally by messengers (xvi. 17). That the information came from Corinth is suggested by the kinds of wealth listed. They had been made rich **in every respect;** we are not told however that they were rich in faith, hope, or love (cf. xiii. 13, and see below, p. 40), but **in speech and knowledge of every kind.** It will become evident as we read the epistle that these were the kinds of Christian wealth that made the strongest appeal to the Corinthians. Paul never questions that they were genuine gifts (e.g. xii. 8, 10; xiv. 1 f.), but he knows a more excellent way

(xii. 31). *Speech* presumably includes the gift of speaking with tongues (see xii. 10, 28; xiv. 2, etc.), but *of every kind* (which in Greek is written twice, with *speech* as well as *knowledge*) means that prophecy (xiv. 1), and every kind of Christian discourse (xii. 8) is included (not every kind of rhetorical art, as Weiss points out). A good deal of attention is given in 1 and 2 Corinthians to the phenomena of Christian speech, and here we may be content to point forward to later and more detailed discussions, especially in the commentary on chapter xiv. The same is true of knowledge; the word (*γνῶσις*) occurs at viii. 1, 7, 10, 11; xii. 8; xiii. 2, 8; xiv. 6; 2 Cor. ii. 14; iv. 6; vi. 6; viii. 7; x. 5; xi. 6; cf. the related theme of wisdom (*σοφία*; see i. 17, where it occurs for the first time); and see 'Christianity at Corinth', pp. 275-86. Whatever shades of meaning may appear in particular contexts, knowledge certainly refers to intellectual apprehension and application of Christian truth. It is thus evidently a good thing, but it is inferior to love, and may lead to an exaggerated individualism which loses concern for the neighbour (viii. 11). In itself, the word (*γνῶσις*, *gnosis*) does not necessarily point to the religious phenomenon described (with bewildering variety of definition) as gnosticism. In Greek, as in English, it is most often used in a plain, non-technical sense; it seems clear however that behind the frequent use of the word (ten times in 1 Corinthians; six times in 2 Corinthians; five times in the other Pauline letters (including Colossians but not Ephesians); eight times in the rest of the New Testament) there lies a specific set of religious ideas, current at Corinth, and perhaps elsewhere. In the present passage there is no basis for further detail, and no further account of Corinthian *gnosis* can be given at this point; see the commentary on vi. 12 f.; viii. 1; x. 23.

The agency (**as,** *καθώς*, suggests that preaching and enrich- 6
ment were concurrent and proportionate) that led to this enrichment of the Corinthians in speech and knowledge was preaching. Paul's words are literally *the testimony of Christ* (cf. ii. 1). The genitive might be subjective (*the testimony borne by Christ*), and this would be in line with the fact that in true preaching Christ himself speaks (cf. Rom. x. 14, 17, and the note in *Romans*, pp. 204 f.); but the present context (cf. i. 23, We preach Christ crucified; and ii. 2) suggests that it is objective

(the testimony to Christ). This objectively true proclamation (for its content see the notes on the passages referred to above, and *passim*) **was confirmed in your own experience** (literally, *in you*). The Holy Spirit himself, the donor of all spiritual gifts, guaranteed (cf. 2 Cor. i. 21; also verse 8, where the same verb—βεβαιοῦν—is used) the validity of the proclamation. There is no other validation of preaching than the work of the Spirit: the preacher's wisdom, piety, or ecclesiastical authorization have no comparable significance; cf. ix. 1; 2 Cor. xii. 11 f. *As* (perhaps, *in proportion as*; see above), however, the truth of the preaching is thus confirmed by the faith which it evokes, the church is built up in spiritual gifts; conversely, the church is truly built up only as it conforms to the Gospel (Héring).

The result is stated by Paul, with perhaps some measure of friendly exaggeration, and an echo of Corinthian self-praise:
7 **you come short in no gift of grace** (not: you lack no gift of grace—see Lightfoot). This is a simpler and more natural, and for that reason preferable, way of taking Paul's words than to suppose that he means that as Christians, however unworthy, the Corinthians have potentially at their disposal all that God bestows on men (cf. Rom. viii. 32); and it may reasonably be said that the troubles in Corinth were due not to a deficiency of gifts but to lack of proportion and balance in estimating and using them. Grace (χάρις), as we have seen, means primarily God's love active in Christ, but secondarily the operation of this love in the existence of Christians (cf. verse 4); *gift of grace* (χάρισμα; see Schweizer, 7 i and note 377) is a more particular and concrete actualization of God's grace. All Corinthian Christians had such gifts (xii. 4-7); so indeed have Christians generally (Rom. xii. 6).

Gifts of grace are a valuable, and indeed indispensable, accompaniment of Christian life, which without them would fail to bear witness to its supernatural origin. They are not however the end of Christian life, in which men **await the revelation of our Lord Jesus Christ.** This *revelation* is the manifestation of Christ when he comes from heaven at the winding up of history, the moment in hope of which the whole creation, including Christians, groans and travails (Romans viii. 22 f.). More will be said later in the epistle (xi. 26; xv. 23, 47, 52; xvi. 22; cf.

iii. 13; iv. 3; v. 5; vii. 29) about this coming of Christ in glory; all that need be said at the moment is that we have here a second definition of Christian existence. Christians are what they are because through the Holy Spirit they have received gifts of grace, and they are what they are because, having been redeemed and called by the historic work of Christ they now look for his coming to comsummate his achievement. They live in remembrance of what he has done, and in expectation of what he will do (cf. xi. 26). It was a characteristic Corinthian error (cf. iv. 8; note the *already*) to concentrate on the present with its religious excitement, and to overlook the cost at which the present was purchased (e.g. vi. 20), and the fact that the present is still incomplete. Paul partly, but not wholly, demythologizes primitive Christian apocalyptic (see *Adam*, p. 90).

Thought of **the day of our Lord Jesus Christ** (that is, the 8
day of judgement; cf. iii. 13; iv. 3; and the Old Testament 'day of the Lord', Amos v. 18, etc.) should have the effect of deflating Corinthian pomposity (e.g. v. 2), but it should not awaken terror. It is true that the Christian no more than any other man can maintain a standard of moral conduct sufficient to satisfy the divine Judge (even when his conscience is clear—cf. iv. 4), but he does not have to make himself **irreproachable;** it is Christ himself (not God, for it is very difficult to look back to verse 4 for the antecedent of the relative ὅς), the Judge, who **will keep** him **firm** (βεβαιώσει; cf. verse 6) **to the end** (primarily a temporal end; but 'ἕως τέλους easily moves over from a temporal meaning to the meaning "completely" '—Schlatter). This does not mean that they are morally perfect, but that the righteousness of Christ himself is given to them so that they may be acquitted at the Great Assize (cf. Rom. viii. 33). In describing the Christian's calm and joyful expectation of the coming Judge Paul is stating the doctrine of justification by faith without the use of the technical terms he employs elsewhere. More important however than man's faith is God's faithfulness, on which all depends. The goal (of acceptance at the day of Christ) is sure, notwithstanding man's unfaithfulness and, in particular, many Corinthian moral failures, because **God, through whom** 9
you were called into fellowship with his Son Jesus Christ, is faithful. *Fellowship* (κοινωνία) means not only personal

association but suggests also sharing in or sharing with, and can mean community (so that here the sense would be that God has called you into the community—that is, the church—of Jesus Christ). Paul's usage is against the simple equation of this word with *church* (cf. e.g. x. 16; 2 Cor. xiii. 13; Phil. i. 5; ii. 1; iii. 10), but the translation given here would be strengthened if it were possible to bring out at the same time that Christians in fellowship with Christ share, not in his being (so Barth), but in his relation with the Father. As in the Pauline expression 'in Christ' (see verse 4, and *Romans*, p. 127), the thought is that Christians share in the position of the exalted, eschatological Lord. This fact links up with the thought of God's faithfulness, which is the one guarantee of Christian existence, both in the present and in the future. God's faithfulness is the permanent expression of his love; this is the ultimate ground of Paul's thanksgiving. That he says nothing of an answering trust, love, endurance, and faithfulness on the Corinthians' part (Bachmann) is partly, but only partly, due to circumstances in Corinth.

B. NEWS FROM CORINTH

(a) WISDOM AND DIVISION AT CORINTH

3. i. 10-17. THE CORINTHIAN GROUPS

(10) I beg you, brothers, for the sake of our Lord Jesus Christ, that you may all be agreed in what you say, and that there may be no divisions[1] among you; rather, that you may be restored to unity of mind and opinion. (11) I make this appeal, my brothers, because it has been made known to me about you by the members of Chloe's household that there are contentions among you. (12) What I mean is this: each one of you has his own watchword—'I belong to Paul', 'I belong to Apollos', 'I belong to Cephas', 'I belong to Christ'. (13) Has Christ been shared out? Was Paul crucified for you, or were you

[1] P[46] and a few other witnesses have the singular, σχίσμα.

baptized into Paul's name? (14) I am thankful[1] that I baptized none of you except Crispus and Gaius, (15) because this means that none of you can say that you were baptized[2] into my name. (16) I did baptize the household of Stephanas too; besides that I do not know whether I baptized anyone else. (17) I baptized no more than a few of you for Christ did not send me to baptize, but to preach the Gospel, and to do so without rhetorical skill, lest the cross of Christ should be emptied of its significance.

The introductory parts of the epistle are now completed. There is a measure of formality in them, but the second paragraph (the thanksgiving) has pointed forward to the first major theme, which is now begun. A church full of individualistically conceived and employed spiritual gifts, especially when these gifts are preeminently in the realms of speculation and eloquence, runs some risk of division. The risk was being realized in Corinth. How far the process had gone is not easy to determine. Evidently the church was sufficiently united for Paul to feel confident that all its members would read (or hear) his letter; they all came together (though with unhappy results; xi. 17) for the common meal. But their tendency to form cliques laid upon their pastor his first task.

I beg you, brothers; this address is no formality. The appeal 10
rests upon the fact that they are *brothers* to him and one another. See the note on i. 1. It is also made **for the sake** (literally, *through the name*; 'by all that he is and is to you'—Moffatt) **of our Lord Jesus Christ.** You should be rightly related to your fellow-Christian not simply because you are both members of the same organization but because he is your brother for whom Christ died (viii. 11). Paul's words may mean also that he addresses his readers with the authority of Jesus Christ; such authority as he has (and it is not unlimited; iv. 1; 2 Cor. i. 24) is for the purpose of building them up (as a community; 2 Cor. x. 8; xiii. 10). The appeal is **that you may all be agreed in what you say** (literally, *that you may all say the same thing*). The expression

[1] The majority of MSS. add, by assimilation to other passages, *to* (*my*) *God*.

[2] Many MSS., including the Western Text, have *I baptized*—an attractive reading but probably due to assimilation to verses 14 and 16.

need not mean anything more precise than peaceful co-existence (Weiss quotes an inscription from the grave of a husband and wife; see also Thucydides iv. 20; v. 31). But it is used here because the Corinthians were saying different things (i. 12). Paul seeks the abandonment of such party slogans, **and that there may be no divisions among you.** A division is a rending, a tearing apart (σχίσμα). Paul does not say that the community was already torn into pieces; he asks that this may not be allowed to happen, **rather, that you may be restored to unity of mind and opinion.** The nets of Mark i. 19 were being *restored* (καταρτίζειν), put back into their proper state; the word is used by Herodotus (v. 28) for composing civil discord. Disunity is fundamentally a matter of *mind* and *opinion*, that is, of doctrine, and it is here that restoration and reconciliation must take place; neither at this point nor later does Paul suggest that the church can be mended by ecclesiastical politics.

11 The words **I make this appeal** are not in the Greek, but some such supplement is required by the **because** (γάρ) with which the new verse begins. Only after pointing in the right direction, towards unity of mind and thought, does Paul mention the information that has reached him, that all is not well at Corinth. The information was not sent officially from the church, and we can only conjecture whether it arrived before or after the letter (vii. 1) and the visit of Stephanas, Fortunatus, and Achaicus (xvi. 17). It was brought **by the members of Chloe's household.** Who Chloe was we do not know. The name was a cult title of Demeter, but was probably not uncommon in popular use (witness the well known story of Daphnis and Chloe, and Horace's passing infatuation (*Odes* iii. 9)). We do not know that the Chloe to whom Paul refers was a Christian, but apparently some of her dependants (slaves or freedmen) were. We do not know whether they belonged to the Corinthian church. They had travelled between Corinth and Ephesus, but may have been based on either the one city or the other. We hear no more of these travellers, but they may usefully remind us of the relative mobility of society in general, and of Christians, in the first century. The report Paul receives from them is that **there are contentions** (ἔριδες, a Pauline word: iii. 3; 2 Cor. xii. 20; Rom. i. 29; xiii. 13; Gal. v. 20; Phil. i. 15;

elsewhere in the New Testament only 1 Tim. vi. 4; Titus iii. 9) **among you.** The word *divisions* is now dropped. Actual cleavage had not yet taken place, but there were disputes and feeling was rising. For a third word of dissidence (αἱρέσεις) see xi. 19. The nature of the disputes is brought out in the next verse.

What I mean is this: each one of you has his own 12
watchword. The translation avoids a minor difficulty. Paul does not really mean that 'each one of you saith' (RV) . . .; the sense is given in iii. 4. Four *watchwords* are given: **'I belong to Paul', 'I belong to Apollos', 'I belong to Cephas'** (note that Paul usually has the Aramaic Cephas (iii. 22; ix. 5; xv. 5; Gal. i. 18; ii. 9, 11, 14), seldom the Greek Peter (Gal. ii. 7, 8)), **'I belong to Christ'.** Christian leaders have, voluntarily or involuntarily, become the focal points of dissension. The various groups must be considered first, then the general state of the Corinthian church implied.

The existence of a 'Paul-group' itself implies opposition to Paul in Corinth. That some made a point of standing by the founder of the church shows that there were others who if they did not assail his position at least regarded him as *démodé*, and preferred new missionaries. Paul has no thanks for those who vocally took his part; this will be because they exaggerated and thus falsified his views, or because from the point of view of the unity of the church they were no better than the rest; or perhaps for both reasons. It is doubtful whether any further references to the Paul-group are to be found in the epistle; there is nothing to suggest that they were a serious problem.

Apollos (it would be precious to suggest another missionary of the same name), after instruction by Priscilla and Aquila (Acts xviii. 26), visited Corinth (Acts xviii. 27–xix. 1), and evidently attracted partisans. He was (according to Acts xviii. 24) an Alexandrian, and though there is no reason to think that every Alexandrian Jew was a Philo the same context in Acts tells us that Apollos was learned (or eloquent: λόγιος). Paul never suggests any difference between Apollos and himself but rather goes out of his way to represent Apollos as his colleague (iii. 6-9). It may be that Apollos introduced into Corinth the pursuit of wisdom (σοφία; see i. 17, and the references there), but even this, though potentially a source of trouble (see Introduction, pp. 17 f.), did not constitute a serious difference, for Paul himself acknowledges that *we speak wisdom among the mature* (ii. 6). It is easy to understand that, in a church where gifts of the tongue were rated high (i. 5; xii. 8, 28; xiv. 26), the appearance of a particularly eloquent preacher should awaken partisanship, and some contempt for the founder, who was despised as a speaker (2 Cor. x. 10), and himself acknowledged his failings in this respect (2 Cor. xi. 6).

It is probable but not certain that Peter visited Corinth (see 'Cephas and Corinth'). It is easier to understand the emergence of a Cephas-group if he did so, but not impossible if he did not, for (as will appear in the study of 2 Corinthians) representatives of the Jerusalem apostles, not necessarily authorized by them, made their presence felt in the gentile churches. Peter himself was the great missionary, itinerant head of Jewish Christianity, as James was its stationary head, resident in Jerusalem. That the Cephas-group represented Jewish Christianity in some form is almost certainly true, and T. W. Manson is probably right in seeing their influence in pressure for the observance of food laws and the judicial rights of the community, and in a questioning of Paul's apostolic status. See vi. 1-11; viii. 1-13; ix. 1-12; x. 14-23, with the notes, and 'Christianity at Corinth' pp. 273, 296. We are dealing here with fundamental problems that touch not only the structure of the Corinthian church but the history of primitive Christianity as a whole. These problems cannot be dealt with on the basis of a single passage; they will be referred to as they arise in the text, and a fuller treatment may be looked for in the commentary on 2 Corinthians.

I belong to Christ. These words stand in all MSS. of 1 Corinthians, and if *Christ* did not seem an odd fourth partner after *Paul*, *Apollos*, and *Cephas* their genuineness would probably not have been questioned. It is however true that when Clement of Rome (writing *c.* A.D. 95) refers to the divisions mentioned in 1 Corinthians he gives only the first three names (1 Clement xlvii.2), and it is therefore possible that his copy of the epistle (the earliest of which we have any knowledge) did not contain the fourth. Possible, but not more than possible; for it is at least equally likely that Clement's memory was affected by iii. 22, or that, knowing the words *I belong to Christ*, he took them as

Paul's correction of the Corinthian dissidents. If we assume (as I think we must) that they did not creep in from a pious copyist's marginal comment, we may suppose them to be such a comment on the part of Paul. 'Others may profess their allegiance to this or that apostle; my allegiance is to Christ alone.' This avoids the difficulties inherent in a 'Christ-group' (did not all Christians belong to Christ?), and also, according to some, improves the connection with the next verse. It fails however to give due weight to the parallel form in which the four protestations of loyalty are expressed (if Paul had been making an interjection he would probably not have used an identical form of words). The difficulties are less great than is sometimes thought, and the connection, though not perhaps strictly logical, is reasonably good, for Paul knows perfectly well that those whose rallying cries were *Paul*, *Apollos*, and *Cephas*, nevertheless all professed to belong to Christ. They meant: We support the Christ proclaimed by Paul, by Apollos, by Cephas, the Christ whom we know without the mediation of a preacher; and to this attitude the rhetorical question, Is Christ divided? is a suitable reply.

If then the text is to be accepted as it stands in the MSS., and Paul is referring to a fourth Christian group in Corinth, what were its characteristics? There is no further explicit reference to the group (cf. perhaps 2 Cor. x. 7), and we can do no more than guess at its tenets, but there is in 1 Corinthians a quantity of controversial material that might apply to it (an alternative but less probable guess would name the Apollos-group, supposing this to be related to speculative Alexandrian Judaism), and T. W. Manson's short summary is probably not far wrong (*Studies*, p. 207): 'I should be very much inclined to think that they were a group for whom Christ meant something like "God, freedom, and immortality", where "God" means a refined philosophical monotheism; "freedom" means emancipation from the puritanical rigours of Palestinian barbarian authorities into the wider air of self-realization; and immortality means the sound Greek doctrine as opposed to the crude Jewish notion of the resurrection.'

J. Munck (*Paulus und die Heilsgeschichte* (1954), especially pp. 128-31; E.T., 136-9) has rightly emphasized (and the point has been made above) that the existence of these groups does not mean that the Corinthian church was split into completely disunited fragments. It was nevertheless in a dangerous condition, not simply because of the lack of love (viii. 1; cf. Rom. xiv. 15) that was evinced, important though this failing was, but also because the Corinthians had lamentably failed to understand the position of their evangelists and the substance of the Gospel itself. They did not belong to their teachers; their teachers belonged to them (iii. 21 ff.), part of the total gift God had made them in Christ. And Christ, to whom indeed they all belonged, was not to be thought of as one alternative leader among many but as the only possible foundation of the whole church (iii. 11—see the note).

Paul brings home the meaning of what is happening in Corinth
13 by a series of rhetorical questions. **Has Christ been shared out?** Some take these words not as a question but as a statement: The church has been divided, in some sense (cf. xii. 12, and the note) the church is Christ, therefore Christ has been divided. This is however a less probable view than that which takes the clause as a question. It is true that this clause does not contain the interrogative particle expecting a negative answer (*μή*) with which the next clause is provided, but a reason can be given for this (see below); and the verb (*μερίζειν*) means not simply 'to divide' but 'to divide up and distribute' (cf. vii. 17; 2 Cor. x. 13; Rom. xii. 3). Paul is asking, Do you suppose that there are fragments of Christ that can be distributed among different groups? There is no particle (*μή*; an alternative explanation is that this word may have accidentally dropped out before the first two syllables of *μεμέρισται*) because, whereas no one could conceivably answer the next question otherwise than in the negative, the present question, though its true answer is No, might seem to receive the answer Yes from the Corinthian situation. This is the point Paul is making. There is only one undivided Christ, and if you have him, and belong to him, it is trivial whether you attach yourself to Paul, Apollos, or Cephas. Conversely, no devotion to one of these human teachers can make up for not having Christ. Truly, Christ is not divided, but the Corinthian church is behaving as if he were.

Was Paul crucified for you? There is no doubt about the

answer to this question. No one can usurp the unique, once-for-all position of the historic Saviour. Compare the fact that Christ is preached as Christ *crucified* (verse 23); and note Paul's delicacy in using here, and in the next question, his own name rather than those of his colleagues. **Or were you baptized into Paul's name?** Again, the answer is clear, though it may well be that the convert held in special regard the man who baptized him (but see the note on vi. 11). Baptism in the early church seems regularly to have been into or in the name of Christ (e.g. Acts ii. 38; viii. 16), or into Christ (e.g. Rom. vi. 3); baptism into the name of the Trinity (Matt. xxviii. 19) was a somewhat later, but not very late, development. The phrase indicates that it is under the authority of Christ that the baptism takes place, and also that the person baptized becomes the property of Christ, is entered, as it were, to his account. See further *Romans*, pp. 121-30; *Adam*, pp. 107 ff.; and pp. 220 f. below. Paul does not own even a group of Corinthian Christians, and he is no lord over their faith (2 Cor. i. 24). Christ does own them (iii. 23), and is their Lord (xii. 3).

Paul is glad that events have been such as to make these facts
unmistakably clear. **I am thankful that I baptized none of** 14
you except Crispus and Gaius. Notwithstanding the further exceptions about to be mentioned Paul baptized few of his converts; we may suppose that his practice was the same in other churches too; for the reason see verse 17. *Crispus* is probably the synagogue head mentioned as an early convert in Acts xviii. 8. *Gaius* cannot be the Gaius mentioned at Acts xix. 29, since he was a Macedonian, nor the Gaius of Acts xx. 4, since he came from Derbe (if we accept the Western Text the same Macedonian Gaius may be meant here as in xix. 29). He is probably however to be identified with the Gaius mentioned in Rom. xvi. 23 as host of Paul and of all the church (in Corinth, or Cenchreae). This suggests that he, like Crispus, may have been an early convert.

The next verse, if translated literally, would give Paul's purpose in baptizing only Crispus and Gaius: *I acted so in order that no one* (ἵνα μή τις) *might say....* But the true reason for Paul's action is given in verse 17, and the present verse expresses
result rather than purpose. **This means that none of you can** 15

say that you were baptized into my name. See above on verse 13. Even if Paul had baptized all his converts he would not have baptized them into his own name, but there would have been a greater possibility of misunderstanding, especially in such a heathen environment as Corinth, where we have good reason to believe (see the notes on x. 5; xv. 29) that it was easy for sub-Christian ideas of the sacraments to enter the church.

A memory returns, illustrating Paul's manner of dictating his
16 letters without revision (Lietzmann): **I did baptize the household of Stephanas too; besides that I do not know whether I baptized anyone else.** There were a few others—Paul is not sure how many—in addition to Crispus and Gaius. *Stephanas* was one of the Corinthians who had visited Paul (xvi. 17), and may have been present as Paul wrote. Did the *household* of Stephanas, who were baptized, include young children, and should this verse therefore be used as evidence for the practice of infant baptism in New Testament times? The meaning of the word *household* (here, οἶκος), though it has been debated at great length, cannot be fixed with complete precision, but it should be noted that at xvi. 15 *the household* (here οἰκία, but the words are synonymous) *of Stephanas* are said to *have set themselves for service to the saints*. This could hardly be said of children, and the presumption is that in using this word Paul is thinking of adults. Like Crispus and Gaius, Stephanas was an early convert (xvi. 15).

It is hard to avoid the conclusion that this verse reveals at least a relative disparagement of baptism (and not simply of the role in baptism of the baptizer—Kümmel). Paul assumes that all Christians are baptized (xii. 13) but cannot remember whom he has, and has not, baptized. Probably he had himself baptized his first converts, and left them to deal with the rest (cf. John iv. 1 f.; Acts x. 48), though it may possibly be implied by vi. 11 that most Christians baptized themselves. It was not a matter that needed close attention on Paul's part.

17 **I baptized no more than a few of you** (these words, not in the Greek, are implied by the *for* (γάρ) with which the verse begins) **for Christ did not send me to baptize but to preach the Gospel.** More important in Paul's view than baptism, and certainly his own vocation, was preaching. It is this he means

to stress; he is not excusing himself (Bachmann) for having baptized so few of his converts. There is no need to expound here what Paul means by preaching the Gospel because, from this cue, he proceeds through the rest of the chapter, and much more of the epistle, to explain it. It is the essence of his apostleship (*sent* is ἀπέστειλεν, a verb cognate with the noun ἀπόστολος, apostle). Preaching was the spearhead of the Christian mission; only when evangelistic preaching had done its work would men, already convinced, penitent, and believing, seek baptism. For Paul's *sending* see the note on i. 1; 1 and 2 Corinthians are full of material that shows how Paul understood his mission.

The present verse adds hints, which will be taken up in the ensuing paragraphs, about both the content of the Gospel Paul preaches, and the manner in which he preaches it—**without rhetorical skill** (literally, *not in wisdom of speech*), **lest the cross of Christ should be emptied of its significance,** should 'dwindle to nothing, vanish under the weight of rhetorical argument and dialectic subtlety' (Lightfoot). Paul represents himself as a preacher, not as an orator. Preaching is the proclamation of the cross; it is the cross that is the source of its power. The convincing power of the cross could not be fully manifest if preaching shared too evidently in the devices of human rhetoric; if men are persuaded by eloquence they are not persuaded by Christ crucified. Hence Paul rejects *wisdom* (σοφία) as a rhetorical device. We shall see (see the notes on i. 19-22, 24, 30; ii. 1, 4-7, 13; iii. 19; xii. 8, and 'Christianity at Corinth', pp. 275-86) that he uses the word wisdom in other senses, both good and bad; and indeed here *wisdom* as a formal characteristic of skilful speech is not far from describing also the content of a preaching in which the cross may come to look like a foolish error.

With this observation Paul is fully launched on his epistle. As in Romans (cf. i. 16 ff.), mention of the Gospel sets his thought and language in motion. The theme has been brought out in a context determined by the Corinthian divisions, and these are still in mind to the end of chapter iv; but the underlying subject matter, which determines the treatment of division, is the Gospel, and the calling, responsibility, and duty of those who preach and those who hear it.

4. i. 18-31. THE WORD OF THE CROSS

(18) For the message of the cross is foolishness to those who are on the way to destruction, but to us[1] who are on the way to salvation it is God's power. (19) For it is written

I will destroy the wisdom of the wise,

And I will set aside the intelligence of the intelligent.

(20) Where is the wise man? Where is the scholar? Where is the disputant of this age? Has not God made the world's wisdom folly? (21) For since, by God's wise plan, the world, exercising its own wisdom, did not know God, God chose to save those who had faith by the folly of the Christian preaching. (22) Since Jews ask for signs and Greeks seek wisdom, (23) but we preach Christ crucified, to Jews a scandal, to Gentiles folly, (24) but to those who are called, both Jews and Greeks, Christ, God's power and God's wisdom. (25) For this, God's foolishness, is wiser than men, and this, God's weakness, is stronger than men.

(26) You can see what I mean, brothers, by looking at your own calling as Christians; for there are among you not many who are wise by human standards, not many who are powerful, not many who are nobly born. (27) But God chose what the world counts foolish in order to put to shame the world's wise men. And God chose what the world counts weak in order to put to shame what it counts strong, (28) and what the world counts base, and despised, even the things that did not exist, God chose, that he might do away with what did exist, (29) in order that no one might glory in God's presence. (30) But you are related to God in Christ Jesus, who as God's gift became wisdom for us, and righteousness and sanctification and redemption too; (31) in order that the written word might be fulfilled, 'If anyone is to glory, let him glory in the Lord.'

[1] Zuntz (p. 137), with the Western Text, omits ἡμῖν, reading *to those who are on the way....*

Up to this point, in dealing with the Corinthian divisions, Paul has argued truly enough, but somewhat superficially, as follows: I baptized few of my converts; therefore you cannot say that you were baptized into my name; therefore you ought not to say, I belong to Paul; by analogy you ought not to say, I belong to Apollos, or I belong to Cephas; and no one group should be allowed to say, I belong to Christ. A deeper treatment of the subject follows. The party slogans all bear witness to an overvaluing of human wisdom, and a failure to understand, or rightly value, the Gospel, which Paul was sent (i. 17) to preach. He now begins to expound the true meaning of divine and human wisdom, and of the Gospel. This is his intention, and it operates primarily within a Christian framework of motivation and development. There is however much to be said for the suggestion that his exposition is reminiscent of Jewish sermons (of which one may be preserved in Baruch iii. 9–iv. 4) preached on Ab 9 on the Haphtorah for the day (Jer. viii. 13–ix. 24). On this view, Paul, using the substance of a sermon he might have preached in a synagogue, quotes his text in verse 31. See H. St John Thackeray, *The Septuagint and Jewish Worship* (1921), p. 97.

Paul has just mentioned the cross of Christ, and takes this up
in the new paragraph: **The message** (λόγος) **of the cross.** 18
The genitive is not subjective, but denotes the theme of the *message*, or discourse. That by this Paul means nothing other than the Gospel, the constitutive basis of Christianity, is clear from what follows. The Gospel is simply a placarding (cf. Gal. iii. 1) of Christ crucified; its effect is twofold. It **is foolishness to those who are on the way to destruction, but to us who are on the way to salvation it is God's power** (cf. 2 Cor. ii. 15 f.). Both groups are described by present participles, and although the former is from a compound verb with a 'perfectivizing' preposition (ἀπολλυμένοις; see M. i. 114 f.) neither process can be thought of as complete. It is nevertheless true, as Kümmel points out (comparing Phil. i. 28 and Rom. viii. 24), that both terms, and the distinction between the two groups, are eschatological. Destruction and salvation (cf. Rom. i. 16, 18) are consummated at the last day (cf. Rom. ix. 22; xiii. 11). *Those who are on the way to destruction* find the Gospel

foolishness, and therefore reject it. Do they perish because they reject, or do they reject because they are perishing? This kind of question is often raised at the beginning of Paul's arguments; it is better answered at the end, when Paul has looked at the problems of predestination from all angles. No doubt he was well aware of the practical rejection of the Gospel on the ground that it was absurd to find the truth about God in a scene of crucifixion: wisdom could do much better than this. It is at first surprising to find that the counterpart of *foolishness* is not 'true wisdom' or 'God's wisdom', but *God's power*. This however is where Paul's understanding of the Gospel begins; cf. Rom. i. 16. Moreover, though Paul will in ii. 5 allow that there is a Christian wisdom, the admission was an awkward one to make in Corinth. For the moment at least the word wisdom is in bad odour.

19 Paul has the Old Testament on his side. **It is written,**

I will destroy the wisdom of the wise,

And I will set aside the intelligence of the intelligent.

The quotation is from Isa. xxix. 14 and follows the LXX, except that for *I will set aside* the LXX has *I will hide*. Paul's variation may be due to Psalm xxxii. 10 (LXX: The Lord scatters the counsels of the Gentiles, he sets aside the reasonings of the peoples, he sets aside the counsels of rulers), but in any case he has made the quotation more suitable to the context in which he uses it; 'setting aside' could be regarded as a radical form of 'hiding'. It is evident that the *wisdom* spoken of here is a wisdom of this world (cf. verse 20), a wisdom that leaves God out of account and is man-centred (and hence is closely related to 'works'—Schlatter). This is the supposed wisdom of those who reject the Gospel as folly. The sense of the word *wisdom* (*σοφία*) is already changed from i. 17, for it is no longer a way of speaking but a way of thinking; the two are however alike, and closely related, in their essential man-centredness. The quotation supports Paul in what he has already said, but takes him a stage further; not only is the wisdom of this world mentioned in the Old Testament, the Old Testament predicts its overthrow. There is moreover further Old Testament material to the same effect.

20 **Where is the wise man? Where is the scholar? Where**

is the disputant of this age? Has not God made the world's wisdom folly? Paul's use of the Old Testament is here allusive rather than argumentative; cf. Isa. xix. 11 f.; xxxiii. 18; xliv. 25; Job. xii. 17. As the next verse will make clear, God has now acted so as to expose what the world considers wisdom as the folly that it truly is, and so to put to flight arrogant and self-assertive wise men, scholars, and disputants. *Of this age* (αἰών) and *of the world* (κόσμος) appear to be used synonymously. This corresponds to the double meaning (in late Hebrew) of *'olam*, and (more important) to the natural affinity between apocalyptic eschatology and philosophical idealism. This age, in contrast with the age to come, and this world, in contrast with the other world, are not two completely distinct dualisms. The new age and the new world, which are under God's immediate authority, will see the end of man-centred wisdom (cf. ii. 6 ff., and for the sense iii. 19).

God made the world's wisdom folly (that is, revealed it as folly; almost 'made a fool of it') by doing what it had failed to do, and by doing this in a way which the wise men of the world dismissed as foolish. **For since, by God's wise plan** (σοφία), **the** 21
world, exercising its own wisdom, did not know God, God chose to save those who had not wisdom but **faith** not by their own wisdom but **by the folly of the Christian preaching.** We have seen that the word *wisdom* (σοφία) is used in two bad senses; it is also used in two good senses. Here it refers to a scheme, or plan, prepared and enacted by God for the salvation of mankind. It is not a plan that men would ever have thought of because it operates through Christian preaching which, since it is focused upon the cross (verse 18), will inevitably be judged by worldly standards to be not wisdom but folly. This seems to be the sense of the verse, but some (see in addition to many of the commentaries G. Bornkamm, *Gesammelte Aufsätze* II (1959), pp. 120 f.) take the preposition *by* (*ἐν*, *in*) in a local sense, and understand the passage in terms of the wisdom of God manifest in his works; even in the midst of this revelation the world did not recognize God. See however Lightfoot, p. 161.

Paul appears to be contradicting the claim that the world, by the exercise of its wisdom, did know God; this means that by the world's wisdom Paul understands something akin to gnosticism, which offered a knowledge of God in which men might find salvation. This had failed to achieve what it professed and the failure was part of God's purpose. Expressed in mythological terms, this purpose is the whirling sword that kept the way into the Garden of Eden, and prevented access to the source of immediate knowledge and life (Gen. iii. 24). God is as truly manifest in his creation as any artist is manifest in his workmanship, but God is not apprehended in his creation because there is no manifestation of God that man's essentially self-regarding wisdom does not twist until it has made God in its own image (this is notoriously true of the gnostic God, who is the essence of self-love)—no manifestation, that is, except the manifestation in Christ crucified, which can be accepted as a revelation of God only by faith (cf. Rom. i. 19-24; *Romans*, pp. 35-8; *Adam*, pp. 17 ff.), which in the ignominous story of the dead Jew on the cross perceives and trusts the victorious love of God. Salvation (deliverance at the last day, anticipated in the present) is thus not by *gnosis* but by faith, not by wisdom but by the folly (as from the human standpoint it must appear) of the message Paul and his colleagues proclaim (κήρυγμα means not the act but the content of *preaching*).

22 **Since** (the word that introduced verse 21 is repeated, a little
loosely, to introduce a sharper restatement of the thought)
23 **Jews ask for signs and Greeks seek wisdom, but we**
(Christians) **preach** (proclaim as heralds; the cognate noun was
also used of the Cynic preacher—see Epictetus III. xxii. 69)
24 **Christ crucified, to Jews a scandal, to Gentiles folly, but**
to those who are called, both Jews and Greeks, Christ, God's power and God's wisdom. This is Paul's most brilliant epigrammatic description of the world in which the Gospel is preached, and of the Gospel itself. For the Jewish request for *signs* compare Mark viii. 11 (and parallels); also the Old Testament record of Israel's 'tempting the Lord' (e.g. Num. xiv. 11, 22). It implies a refusal to take God on trust; he must present his credentials in the form of visible and identifiable acts in which his claim upon men, and his ability to meet their need, are validated. The attitude in question, though often very religious in form, is fundamentally sceptical, and essentially egotistical. Notwithstanding the eminence of Greek philo-

sophical thought (which in fact is not particularly in mind here), *Greeks* does not mean Hellenes; this is shown by the synonymous use in the same sentence of *Gentiles*. The wisdom sought is that of gnosticism, religious thought without the practice of religion (in the cultic sense), a pretended revelation of God which was in truth a human speculative construction. In fact, in the Jewish demand for signs and the Greek quest for wisdom, we have the two expressions, religious and unreligious respectively, of man-in-the-world, man alienated from God and manifesting his rebellion in anthropocentric existence. Paul brackets Jews and Greeks together by a *both* ... *and* (καί ... καί —Zuntz, p. 200, omits the first καί with P46 F G Marcion) which can hardly be translated, but could be paraphrased, '*Both* Jews *and* Greeks are in error, Jews by asking for signs, Greeks by seeking wisdom'. It need not be said that, in the ancient world and at all times, these two expressions occur in an immense variety of mixed forms. There was for example Jewish gnosticism in Corinth. Religious egocentricity will inevitably find *Christ crucified* (the more so if Χριστός describes the office of Messiah, but probably, as usually in Paul, it is only a name), the theme of Christian preaching (cf. verse 18), *a scandal* (something that trips men up), for in the cross God does precisely the opposite of what he is expected to do; the intellectual egocentricity of wisdom-seeking Gentiles finds the same theme *folly*, because incarnation, crystallized in crucifixion, means not that man has speculated his way up to God but that God has come down to man where man is. If there are any who reach a different appraisal of the cross, they are not the exceptionally religious or the exceptionally learned, but those whom God has called (cf. i. 2). The precise force of the expression (αὐτοῖς δὲ τοῖς κλητοῖς) is not clear. Some have seen in the pronoun an 'appeal to personal experience' (Robertson-Plummer), but the pronoun draws attention to the persons rather than their inward feelings. It may be that Paul is referring back to the believers of verse 21, and redefines them. Viewed from one angle their characteristic is that they have faith: but a prior truth is that God has called them—the initiative is his. Whether his thought followed this line or not, it is certainly Paul's meaning that the acceptance of the Gospel, whether by Jews or

Greeks, is rooted ultimately in a divine, not a human, decision. He never works out fully the philosophical, or even the theological implications of this conviction, and has less to say on the subject in 1 and 2 Corinthians than in Romans; see especially Rom. ix-xi, and compare *Romans*, pp. 170 f., 186-91, 220 f., 227; *Adam*, p. 118. To the *called* (see i. 1 f.), Christ is *God's power and God's wisdom.* Compare i. 18, and the note. Here the language is fully balanced; corresponding to sign and scandal is God's power (cf. Rom. i. 16), to wisdom (as understood by the world) and folly, God's wisdom. Here wisdom is more than *wise plan.* As in i. 30 (cf. also viii. 6) wisdom is not merely the plan but the stuff of salvation. Paul here reflects the forms and vocabulary of gnosticism, though he rejects its non-Christian content.

If Christ crucified is power and wisdom this is so only in a paradoxical sense, for he certainly does not represent a divine act of coercion, or a formulated system of theology, metaphysics,
25 or ethics. This paradox Paul underlines. **For this, God's foolishness** (not the abstract noun, as in verses 18, 21, 23, but the neuter of the adjective; this points to a particular act of 'foolishness'; M. iii. 14 is a little beside the point with 'God seeming to be foolish'), **is wiser than men, and this, God's weakness** (neuter adjective again), **is stronger than men.** What God has done in Christ crucified is a direct contradiction of human ideas of wisdom and power, yet it achieved what human wisdom and power fail to achieve. It does convey the truth about God (and man), and it does deliver man from his bondage (though this theme has not yet been developed).

The rhythmical parallel construction of this paragraph (i. 18-25) should be noted. It is not verse, and it is not 'Hebraic'; but it does show some conscious rhetorical polish in its balanced clauses. The same phenomenon appears later in the epistle; see for example verses 27 f., and especially chapter xiii.

The paradox of God's mode of action is illustrated by the
26 make-up of the church. **You can see what I mean** (these words bring out the force of the Greek γάρ, *for*; a variant, *therefore*, οὖν (D G) inverts the argument), **brothers, by looking at** (it makes little difference to the sense whether we take the verb, βλέπετε, to be indicative or imperative; as Schlatter points out, the former is suggested by the γάρ) **your own calling as**

Christians. We have already seen (verses 2, 24) that Christians may be defined as those whom God has called. Paul here uses an abstract noun which most naturally denotes the process of calling, but here means 'the circumstances in which you were called', and thus points forward to the kind of person called and the nature of the community brought into being by the call. It is evident that God employs standards differing from those accepted among men, **for there are among you** (the last two words, not in the Greek, are required by the sense and structure of the English sentence) **not many who are wise by human standards** (literally, *according to the flesh*), **not many who are powerful, not many who are nobly born.** For a note on the social structure of the early church, with reference to this passage, see C. F. D. Moule, *The Birth of the New Testament* (Black's New Testament Commentaries, Companion Volume I, 1962), pp. 156 ff. It is evident from vii. 21 that the Corinthian community included slaves; on the other hand, it included also a synagogue-ruler (Acts xviii. 8) who, though not necessarily wealthy, was presumably (among Jews) of some social standing, and Erastus (Rom. xvi. 23), who can hardly have been poor. There is no doubt that Christianity spread most rapidly among the lower classes, and that this was part of its offensiveness. An interesting comment on Paul's description is provided by Celsus (quoted by Origen, *Contra Celsum* III. 44):

> Their injunctions are like this. 'Let no one educated, no one wise, no one sensible draw near. For these abilities are thought by us to be evils. But as for anyone ignorant, anyone stupid, anyone uneducated, anyone who is a child, let him come boldly.' By the fact that they themselves admit that these people are worthy of their God, they show that they want and are able to convince only the foolish, dishonourable and stupid, and only slaves, women, and little children.

Assuming Celsus's presuppositions, the Christian rag-tag-and-bobtail proved the falsehood of Christianity; assuming Paul's, it demonstrated an important truth about God—not only that God's standards and terms of reference are other than those accepted by the world, but also that he is now engaged in overthrowing the world's false standards. Compare Matt. xi. 25 f.

27 **God chose what the world counts foolish**—taking the genitive (*τοῦ κόσμου*) to mean 'in the world's estimation'; alternatively one might say, 'the foolish element in the world', but this implies a world that is partly foolish and partly wise, and it is doubtful whether Paul intended to be as complimentary as this. God chose (*ἐξελέξατο*; cf. Rom. viii. 33 for the cognate verbal adjective) these unpromising persons in the first instance out of pure love but also **in order to put to shame the world's wise men** (*the world's*, though not in the Greek, seems a helpful, and certainly correct, supplement), that is, by proving them wrong, and also by leaving them outside the scope of salvation, unless they should be willing to become fools (cf. iii. 18). Similarly **God chose what the world counts weak in order to put to shame what it counts** (the last three words are a supplement; see above) **strong.** There is a problem in the genders used in this verse. *Foolish*, *weak*, and *strong* are all neuter plurals; *wise* (*men*) is masculine plural. This makes the sentence look odd (especially in Greek), but probably no elaborate explanation is needed. Paul uses the neuter adjectives in order to generalize (perhaps also in order to spare the Corinthians too blunt a description of themselves, and because he knows that in the next verse he is going to speak of 'things that do not exist'); but the adjective *wise* can hardly be used in the neuter, and therefore stands by itself in the masculine.

28 With **what the world counts base** (the word signifies the opposite of *nobly born* in verse 26), **and despised** Paul continues what is essentially a description of the Corinthian church; the impetus of his rhetoric carries him forward to add **even the things that did not exist God chose, that he might do away with** (cf. 2 Cor. iii. 11; the thought is eschatological—Heim) **what did exist.** But rhetorical though the words are, they are not meaningless (though their meaning bears no relation to the familiar philosophical usage). When God set his plan in motion there was no church in Corinth, save in his intention; notwithstanding opposition (and its own weakness), it now existed. God's wisdom in the Gospel has already been validated by its effect, and will in the end be completely vindicated by the totality of the new creation. If however its purpose outside the church might be stated as humiliating the world's pride in its

wisdom and power, it had a purpose also within the church—
that no one (literally, *no flesh*—an Old Testament expression) 29
might glory in God's presence—'a negative expression of what justification positively states' (Wendland). Here Paul is returning to the immediate point. It is not the world's false boasting in its wisdom and ability that causes him to write 1 Corinthians but the same false boasting within the church, and at Corinth, where Christians were *glorying in men* (iii. 21, in their own apostles and ministers), and wrongly evaluating their gifts (see the notes on i. 5 ff.). They can only do this because they have forgotten that their Christian existence depends not on their merit but on God's call, and the fact that the Gospel is the message of the cross. This Paul brings out explicitly in the next verse.

You (the pronoun is emphatic) **are related to God** not in 30
yourselves but solely **in Christ Jesus.** It would be possible to construct this sentence in reverse, and retain the same fundamental sense: It is from God, as his gift, that you are in Christ Jesus; that is, you owe your Christian existence to God, and not to yourselves. This however does not fit the context, in which Christ is described in terms of those things that relate men to God. Christ is the means, and God the goal (cf. viii. 6; xv. 24). *You are related to God* is literally, You are from God (ἐκ θεοῦ); compare the similar Greek expression (ἐκ πίστεως), which means on the basis of faith, depending on faith, by faith. It is a pregnant way of saying: Not only do your sources of supply—wisdom, strength, and so forth—come from God; your very being comes from him. This describes the proper relation between man and his Creator; in Christ, in whom *things which do not exist* are brought into being (verse 28; cf. 2 Cor. v. 17), this relation is restored by a new creation. In these circumstances, boasting is evidently excluded (cf. Rom. iii. 27).

Paul goes on to define the terms in which man is related to God through Jesus Christ, **who as God's gift** (paraphrasing *from God*, ἀπὸ θεοῦ) **became wisdom for us, and righteousness and sanctification and redemption too.** *Wisdom* (σοφία), which we have already encountered in more senses than one (i. 17, 19, 21, 24), appears now with a new meaning. In Jewish speculation (see especially Prov. viii. 22-31; Wisdom of Sol.

vii. 22-viii. 1) the more or less personified figure of Wisdom had come to occupy a place of increasing importance as a mediator between God and men, both in creation, and in communicating knowledge and salvation. Wisdom was thus a term that lay ready to hand for Christological purposes, and Paul uses it, sometimes directly, as here, and sometimes by appropriating to Christ functions and predicates which in Judaism had been ascribed to Wisdom. The word itself is used (in various senses) so frequently in the opening paragraphs of 1 Corinthians that we may reasonably conclude that Paul knew it to be in popular use in Corinth; this would stimulate his own thought on Wisdom lines. But this observation serves only to underline the importance of what he himself says. True wisdom is not to be found in eloquence, or in gnostic speculation about the being of God; it is found in God's plan for the redemption of the world, which, for all its own wisdom, had fallen away from God, a plan that was put into operation through the cross. Thus Christ crucified himself becomes the personal figure of Wisdom, God's agent in creation (cf. viii. 6), but especially (as far as the present passage is concerned) God's means of restoring men to himself.

Having used the word that is particularly apt in the present context, Paul adds others that express the same essential mediatorship of Christ but belong to the common stock of his vocabulary. For Christ as God's gift of *righteousness* compare for example Rom. i. 17; iii. 21; x. 4. The root of the thought is forensic: man is arraigned in God's court, and is unable to satisfy the judge unless righteousness, which he cannot himself produce, is given to him. In these circumstances his faith is counted to him as righteousness (Rom. iv. 3; Gal. iii. 6, both quoting Gen. xv. 6), Christ himself becomes righteousness for him (2 Cor. v. 21), and God the judge views him not as he is in himself but in Christ. *Sanctification* (holiness) in Paul's usage has more often a moral connotation, but here it is used in a similar way to *righteousness* (cf. vi. 11: You were sanctified, you were justified). Man can draw near to the holy God only if he himself is holy (cf. Heb. xii. 14); this he is not in himself, but Christ becomes for him the holiness which otherwise he does not possess, and though in a moral sense he is neither righteous nor holy in Christ he has the righteousness and holiness which allow him to approach God, and will in the end effect moral purification too. Compare the use of *saint* (i. 2). With *redemption*—an eschatological word, though Paul by relating it to Christ brings it into history—Paul turns to a somewhat different line of thought, though it is one that he connects elsewhere (Rom. iii. 24) with the manifestation of righteousness. When God confers on sinful men the righteousness and holiness of Christ he is not simply carrying out a paper transaction, or operating a magical process. The transference can take effect only in virtue of the act of redemption that was wrought in Christ crucified. The theme of redemption, that is, of liberation, effected normally by the payment of a price, is not developed at this point (cf. vi. 20), but by his use of this word Paul sets the others—wisdom, righteousness, and sanctification—in the only context in which they can be rightly understood. *Wisdom* does not simply arise out of speculative Judaism; *righteousness* is not simply a forensic counter, nor is *holiness* simply a technical religious term; each is a direct product of Christ's self-offering for men, of the work of *redemption* wrought by God through him.

Paul winds up the paragraph by quoting what we may possibly regard (see above, p. 51) as the text of his sermon for Ab 9 – Jer. ix. 22 f., taken from the Haphtorah for this day. If man has no standing before his Maker but that which is given him in Christ, there could be no more striking fulfilment than this of
the written word, 'If anyone is to glory, let him glory in 31
the Lord.' Men cannot boast of themselves, or of their own achievements; they have nothing that they have not received (iv. 7). But in Christ they have all things (iii. 21 ff.), and in him they have abundant scope for glorying.

The quotation is not exact, but the Semitic use of the conditional participle as subject (*If anyone is to glory*..., ὁ καυχώμενος; K. Beyer, *Semitische Syntax im Neuen Testament* I. i (1962), pp. 211 f.) is due to the LXX; cf. 2 Cor. x. 17.

5. ii. 1-5. SIMPLE TESTIMONY

(1) It was in line with this principle, brothers, that, when I came to you, I did not come proclaiming my testimony

about God[1] with preeminent eloquence or wisdom. (2) For I resolved that in the midst of you I would know nothing but Jesus Christ, and him crucified. (3) And I came to you in weakness and in fear and in great trepidation; (4) and my argument and my proclamation were not enforced by persuasive words of wisdom[2] but by a manifestation of Spirit and power, (5) that your faith might not depend on men's wisdom, but on God's power.

The theological principle Paul has stated at the end of chapter
1 i has practical applications, for example to his own ministry. **It was in line with this principle** (this clause draws out the meaning implied by an emphatic κἀγώ, 'And I', at the beginning of the new paragraph), **brothers** (cf. i. 1), **that, when I came to you, I did not come proclaiming my testimony about God with preeminent eloquence or wisdom.** The general sense of this sentence is clear, but some of the details raise difficulties. *Testimony* is the reading of many important MSS., but others have *mystery*. The words are not dissimilar in Greek (μαρτύριον—μυστήριον), and one could easily pass into the other in the course of transmission. It is not easy to decide which Paul wrote; the balance of probability favours *testimony*, (a) because *mystery* is in the context (ii. 7, cf. iv. 1), and could have affected a copyist subconsciously, and (b) because *testimony* is more suitable to the initial proclamation of the Gospel, whereas *mystery* suggests the wisdom Paul was able to speak

[1] Instead of *testimony about God* (μαρτύριον τοῦ θεοῦ), P^{46} ℵ* and other MSS. have *mystery of God* (μυστήριον τοῦ θεοῦ). See the commentary.

[2] The text here is in considerable confusion. The above translation renders πειθοῖς σοφίας λόγοις, which is the reading of B ℵ* D pc vg^{codd}. The majority of MSS. have this reading with the insertion of ἀνθρωπίνης (human) before σοφίας. This insertion is certainly secondary. The most important alternative is given by P^{46} G pc: πειθοῖς σοφίας. Taken as it stands this requires some such supplement as λόγοις (as in the longer text), but it may be regarded as a corruption of πειθοῖ σοφίας, πειθοῖ (which appears in a few MSS.) being the dative of πειθώ (persuasion). Zuntz (pp. 23 ff.) argues strongly for this text ('my discourse was not in persuasion of wisdom but in manifestation of Spirit'). But it was not beyond Paul to invent the adjective πειθός (and to do so in a way that does not quite win the approval of the grammarians—though M. ii. 78 and B.D. §112 (the latter giving a parallel, φειδός) seem not unwilling to allow it); and it would be rash to assume that the word may not yet appear in a new papyrus discovery.

among mature Christians (ii. 6). This reading is accepted by Zuntz (p. 101), not by K. W. Clark (*Studia Paulina*, pp. 57 f.). Commentaries differ among themselves. If the reading *testimony* is accepted our problems are not at an end. Paul's words are literally *the testimony of God*; this could be taken (as in the translation) to mean *my testimony about God* (objective genitive), or *the testimony borne by God* (subjective genitive), or *initiated by God* (genitive of the author). As in i. 6 (the testimony of Christ), and for similar reasons, the first is the most probable construction, though Lightfoot contrasts the two genitives, taking i. 6 as objective, ii. 1 as subjective: 'It is the testimony borne by God (τοῦ θεοῦ) to Christ (τοῦ Χριστοῦ).'

In his proclamation Paul placed no reliance upon *eloquence or wisdom*. For *wisdom* see notes on p. 49. The two nouns are close together in meaning, for *eloquence* (literally, word, λόγος) here is rational talk, and *wisdom* wordy cleverness. They represent the outward and inward means by which men may commend a case, effectiveness of language, and skill of argumentation. Paul's words (καθ' ὑπεροχὴν λόγου ἢ σοφίας; for a very careful discussion see Bachmann) do not mean that Paul employed no kind of speech or wisdom; this would be absurd (cf. ii. 16; xii. 8). But these were not preeminent in his evangelism; rather were they kept in the background. Positively, **I resolved that** 2
in the midst of you wisdom-loving people **I would know nothing** (following Moule, p. 168, in supposing the negative to be misplaced; cf. *Corpus Hermeticum* xiii. 16; the opposite view is put well by Lightfoot) **but Jesus Christ, and him crucified.** According to Acts xviii. 1 Paul moved on to Corinth from Athens, and it is often supposed that after an attempt to marry the Gospel to Greek philosophy in his Areopagus speech (Acts xvii. 22-31), which was attended with indifferent success (Acts xvii. 32 ff.), he determined to change his tactics and preach nothing but the cross. For this imaginative picture there is no evidence whatever. Acts may or may not contain an accurate account of what Paul said in Athens, but we may be confident that Luke did not intend to describe a lapse on the part of his hero, and there is nothing in Paul's own words in 1 Corinthians to suggest a change of plan; rather he intends to describe his normal practice, though this normal practice was bound to

appear the more striking in such a place as Corinth. He is not contrasting his evangelistic method in Corinth with that which he employed elsewhere, but with that which others employed in Corinth (Moffatt).

For the concentration of Paul's Gospel upon *Jesus Christ, and him crucified,* compare i. 18. Paul must have known that he could not surpass or even equal the Greek world in its own kind of eloquence and wisdom, and like wise Christian preachers in every age he focused his attention upon the one theme the world did not share with him. Of all the epistles, those to the Corinthians are most full of Christian paradox—of strength that is made perfect in weakness, of poor men who make many rich, of married men who are as if they had no wives, of those who have nothing but possess all things, who are the scum of the earth but lead it to salvation, who die and yet live; and the heart of the paradox is the preaching of the feeble and stupid message of the crucified Christ, which nevertheless proves to have a power and a wisdom no human eloquence possesses, since it is the power and wisdom of God himself. See below on verse 5.

True as this is, it does not defend the preacher of the Gospel
3 from scorn and attack; no wonder therefore that **I** (*κἀγώ*, emphatic: I as well as my preaching was marked by weakness . . . cf. verse 1) **came** (*ἐγενόμην*) **to you in weakness and in fear and in great trepidation.** The alternative rendering (of *ἐγενόμην πρὸς ὑμᾶς*), 'In my intercourse with you (*πρὸς ὑμᾶς*) I was in weakness' (Lightfoot) does not alter the general sense. It finds some support in Paul's common usage of the verb (*γίνεσθαι*); but compare xvi. 10; 1 Thess. i. 5. On his own showing, Paul was not an impressive speaker (2 Cor. x. 1, 10), though this is a strange comment, for his writing, which always reads like speech, has (quite apart from its content) genuine eloquence, and for all its common touch and occasional Semitic structure rises to the heights of Greek prose. See T. R. Glover, *Paul of Tarsus* (1925), pp. 194-7, with the quotation from E. Norden: 'In these passages (Rom. viii and 1 Cor. xiii) the diction of the Apostle rises to the height of Plato's in the *Phaedrus*.' Even had he been able to do so, however, he had no intention of using his human powers of oratory, whatever they may have been, and his confidence in the power of Christ and of

the Spirit could not conceal from him that Christ was Christ crucified, and that the preacher's role might well be to fill up that which was lacking in the sufferings of Christ. Not that this was the deepest source of Paul's *fear* and *trepidation*; in opposition and success alike he must bear responsibility for the Gospel
(Schlatter). Thus **my argument** (the same word, λόγος, that is 4
translated *eloquence* in verse 1; it has no uniform English equivalent, but suggests 'speech in rational form', with the emphasis lying now on 'speech', now on 'rational', and now on 'form') **and my proclamation were not enforced by** (the last two words represent the preposition ἐν, *in*; this may suggest simply the circumstances that surrounded, and thus characterized, Paul's speech, but probably conveys the thought of instrumentality as well) **persuasive words of wisdom** (cf. verse 1). There is no doubt that the final phrase represents substantially the thought Paul intended to express, but it conceals notorious textual and linguistic difficulties (see note 2 on p. 62). The textual problems were probably caused to a great extent by the fact that Paul appears to coin a word for himself (πειθός), derived from the verb 'to persuade' (πείθειν), and meaning *persuasive*. See M. ii. 78; Robertson, p. 157; B.D. § 112. Copyists not unnaturally made various attempts to ease the difficulty, and also applied the adjective *human* to the noun *wisdom*; this makes good enough sense (cf. verse 13), but is unnecessary. Paul, without further definition, uses *wisdom* in both good and bad senses. The genitive (σοφίας) is subjective: not words about wisdom, but words directed by (worldly) wisdom, not by Christ crucified.

Paul's preaching, with no dependence on rhetorical devices, was enforced (the same construction—literally *in*—as above) **by a manifestation of Spirit and power.** *Manifestation* (ἀπόδειξις) suggests the further thought of *proof*. The supernatural conviction and force that accompanied the preaching furnished a better proof of its truth than any logical process (persuasion—compare the contrasting first clause of the verse) could provide. The genitives (πνεύματος and δυνάμεως) are thus both objective (since Spirit and power are manifested) and subjective (since the manifested Spirit and power bring proof and conviction). *Spirit* and *power* are often mentioned together (e.g. Acts i. 8), and may be regarded as a hendiadys—one concept expressed by means of two words. When Paul preached a divine power gripped his hearers (or some of them; cf. i. 18) and constrained them to penitence and faith; this was the work of the Holy Spirit. Compare e.g. Rom. xv. 19; 1 Thess. i. 5.

Preaching that depended for its effectiveness on the logical and rhetorical power of the preacher could engender only a faith that rested upon the same supports, and such a faith would be at the mercy of any superior show of logic and oratory, and thus completely insecure. Moreover, it would not be Christian in its
5 content. Paul's preaching, however, leads to a **faith** which, like itself, does **not depend on** (again the hard-working preposition *in* is used) **men's wisdom, but on God's power.** This indeed is the reason why Paul's preaching is based as it is. For the contrast of human wisdom and divine power compare i. 18 f. It runs through the opening chapters of the epistle, and is comparable with another contrast even more characteristic of Paul, that between works done in obedience to law, and divine grace accepted in faith (see e.g. Rom. iii. 28; iv. 16; xi. 6). These contrasts are particularly apt to discussion with Greeks and with Jews respectively; each is a special case of the contrast between a man-centred and a God-centred faith. *Men's* wisdom provides a suggestive parallel to *the wisdom of this age* (ii. 6), and *of the world* (i. 20).

6. ii. 6-16. WISDOM, FALSE AND TRUE

(6) We do however speak wisdom among mature Christians, only it is not a wisdom belonging to this age, or to the rulers of this age, who are being brought to nothing. (7) No, we speak God's wisdom in a mystery: the hidden wisdom, which God determined before the course of ages began, and determined for our glory. (8) None of the rulers of this age knew this wisdom, for if they had known it they would not have crucified the Lord of glory. (9) But the hidden wisdom has been revealed. In the words of Scripture:

Things which eye never saw, and ear never heard,

And never entered into the mind of man,
All the things that God prepared for those who love him.

(10) But[1] to us did God reveal them through the Spirit; for the Spirit searches out all things, even the deep things of God. (11) For what human agency[2] knows the inward truths about a man except the man's spirit which is in him? In the same way, no one knows the inward truths about God except the Spirit of God. (12) But we did not receive the spirit of the world but the Spirit that comes from God, that we might know the things that God has freely given us. (13) Further, we speak of these things not in words[3] taught us by human wisdom but in words that are taught us by the Spirit, interpreting spiritual truths by means of spiritual words.[4]

(14) A natural man does not receive the truths revealed by the Spirit of God, for to him they are foolishness, and he cannot know them, because they are investigated spiritually. (15) The spiritual man, however, investigates all things, but he himself is not open to comparable investigation on the part of anyone. (16) For who ever knew the mind of the Lord, so as to instruct him? But we have the mind of Christ.

It might appear from the preceding paragraph that wisdom is something with which a Christian has nothing to do. This would be a false conclusion. Throughout the epistle, but especially in this part of it, Paul is hampered by the fact that he is obliged to use the word *wisdom* in two senses—or rather in four, for he uses it in two distinguishable bad senses, and in two distinguishable good senses. It may be well to recall and summarize these before proceeding with the new paragraph. Wisdom is used in a bad sense when it denotes simply the skilled marshalling of human

[1] *But* (δέ) is read by the majority of MSS. (including the Western Text); *for* (γάρ) is read by P^{46} B 69 1739, and a few others.

[2] Literally, *Who of men . . .?* (τίς ἀνθρώπων). Héring follows A 33 in omitting ἀνθρώπων on the ground that the meaning is not *What man* (among others), but *What part of man.*

[3] Weiss and Héring, without MS. support, omit *words* (λόγοις), and so make the adjective (διδακτοῖς) apply to persons: We speak wisdom not among those who are instructed in human wisdom (but among the truly mature; verse 6).

[4] B 33 have *spiritually* (πνευματικῶς); probably a slip.

arguments, employed with a view to convincing the hearer. This process is by no means evil in itself, and becomes evil only when it is employed as a substitute for true Christian preaching, and veils the power of the Spirit by its show of human persuasiveness. It readily passes over, however, into a more seriously evil kind of wisdom, in which truth, theological and ethical, is evaluated in terms of human standards rather than those which are given in Christ crucified. To reasoning based on such standards, which asks ultimately what *I* wish to believe and to do, the cross is inevitably foolishness. To Paul, this is the most profound error it is possible to conceive, since the word of the cross is the wisdom of God. This, wisdom in the good sense, is also capable of differentiation. It may mean God's wise plan of redeeming the world through a crucified Messiah, a plan which none but he could have prepared, and man can grasp only if he is willing to surrender his natural man-centred values; but the word is also used to denote the actual substance of salvation itself as given through the wise plan of salvation. Wisdom, in Paul's usage, is thus a fairly close parallel to righteousness, which also describes the way in which God acts, and the gift which his action bestows upon man (and has its bad uses too; e.g. Rom. x. 3). The two good senses of wisdom are conveniently represented by two German words, *Heilsplan* and *Heilsgut* (see U. Wilckens, in *T.W.N.T.* vii. 520, note 382); but the simple English equivalents, *plan of salvation* and *substance of salvation* are rather clumsy and inadequate substitutes.

This sketch of Paul's use of the term *wisdom* should lighten the exposition of the new paragraph, which, as Weiss notes, stands out distinctively between ii. 1-5 (the rejection of wisdom) and iii. 1-17 (the rebuke of party spirit). There *is* a Christian wisdom, and there *is* a difference between infant and mature, natural and spiritual, Christians. Stylistically, the paragraph is marked by the use of the first person plural (compare ii. 1, 2, 3, 4; iii. 1, 2; with ii. 6, 7, 10, 12, 13, 16).

There is a kind of wisdom that the Christian preacher can
6 only renounce. **We do however speak wisdom among mature Christians** (τέλειοι). According to M. iii. 264, this should be rendered, . . . *to mature Christians* (ἐν and the dative being taken as equivalent to the simple dative). This is almost

certainly wrong. When Paul uses the verb 'to speak' (λαλεῖν) and mentions the person spoken to, he does so ten times by means of the simple dative, and once with the preposition 'to' (πρός and the accusative). When the preposition 'in' (ἐν) is used with 'to speak' it is in a completely different sense (xiv. 11, 21; 2 Cor. ii. 17; xii. 19; xiii. 3). The point is not trivial; 'we speak *to*' would imply that all the speaking was done by Paul (and perhaps his missionary colleagues); 'we speak *among*' implies that all may speak—and this is confirmed by xii. 8. Christian wisdom is not confined to a group but is given generally at the disposition of the Spirit. The gift however is one for the *mature Christian*. For this word in Paul (as applied to men) see xiv. 20; Phil. iii. 15; Col. i. 28; iv. 12. It is not common in the Greek Old Testament, but its use there suggests ethical perfection (e.g. Wisdom ix. 6; Sirach xliv. 17); elsewhere it is used more generally of those who are full-grown, adult. The sense here is given by ii. 12; iii. 1; compare also the *spiritual man* of ii. 15. By their behaviour the Corinthian Christians show themselves, in general, to be still infants; they are thus not mature, not spiritual, and therefore not ready for Christian wisdom. There is no need to see in Paul's use of this word a direct allusion to, or borrowing from, the mystery cults, though in the paragraph as a whole (see especially verse 10, *the deep things of God*) there is gnostic language (see Bultmann, *Theology*, p. 180 (E.T., 181); and e.g. *Corpus Hermeticum* iv. 4), and some of Paul's words may have received in Corinth a more gnostic content than he himself gave them. For the notion of an esoteric tradition there is no need to go outside Judaism; see J. Jeremias, *Jerusalem zur Zeit Jesu* (1958), II B 106-9, to which the Dead Sea Scrolls (e.g. Manual of Discipline viii. 1) add little fresh. Most societies of any size have their inner groups with their special secrets. The significant point here (see Sevenster, *Seneca*, pp. 144 f.) is that Paul does not have a simple Gospel of the cross for babes (iii. 1), and a different wisdom-Gospel for the perfect (τέλειοι). All Christians are potentially *perfect* or *mature* in Christ (Col. i. 28), though only some are actually what all ought to be. This is not a gnostic distinction between earthly and spiritual men.

The true Christian wisdom is first defined negatively; **it is not a wisdom belonging to** (possibly, originating from) **this age,**

or to the rulers of this age (compare John xii. 31; xiv. 30; xvi. 11). In speaking of *this age*, which is evil (Gal. i. 4), Paul contrasts it, in the manner of Jewish apocalyptic (see *Background*, pp. 239-42), with the age to come, in which God will establish his kingdom and save the elect. A wisdom proper to this age is therefore one that arises out of and is marked by rebellion against God; it represents (however splendid and spiritual—or scientific—it may appear) the creature's attempt to secure his position over against the Creator; in a word, it is (as far as men are concerned) man-centred (compare pp. 67 f.). But more than men are concerned. It is the wisdom of *the rulers of this age* (compare verse 8; and 2 Cor. iv. 4). Paul, like very many of his contemporaries, conceived the present world-order to be under the control of supernatural beings, often represented by or identified with the planets, or other heavenly objects. These (except in so far as the power of God was available to overthrow or hold them in check) controlled the destiny of men. The wisdom they themselves entertained, and perhaps communicated to men, was naturally of the kind described. Non-Christian gnostic wisdom was essentially self-regarding, and it is easy to give it an interpretation that simply reveals the temper of the natural man, and does not involve the real existence of the mythological *rulers* as independent beings. This is important; but there is no doubt that Paul believed in their existence, and believed also that it was coming to an end. He and his contemporaries still lived in this age, and in it the rulers still ruled; but they were **being brought to nothing,** and the powers of the age to come (Heb. vi. 5) were already at work. Paul not merely permits but encourages the demythologizing of the primitive Christian beliefs, in part—but only in part.

True wisdom (which is evidently related to apocalyptic, in that it discloses the age to come; cf. verse 7, *for our glory*) is now defined positively—though indeed it is not capable of easy
7 description. **No, we speak God's wisdom in a mystery.** The last three words may be taken adjectively, as more or less equivalent to 'mysterious'; or they may be adverbial, and refer to the manner in which the wisdom is set forth. The absence of the definite article may slightly favour the latter interpretation, but *hidden wisdom* (see below) is decisive for the former. Paul

uses the word *mystery* to denote a specific Christian truth, or, in the plural, for the Gospel (compare iv. 1; xiii. 2; xiv. 2; xv. 51; also Col. i. 26 f.; ii. 2; iv. 3; it is doubtful whether it ever alludes to the 'mystery' rites into which the *mature*, *τέλειοι*, had been initiated). The main point here lies in the contrast with worldly wisdom, which essentially is and intends to be openly convincing; the preaching of the cross is **the hidden wisdom**. It is *hidden* in the sense that it has only been disclosed at the turning of the ages, in the recent historical event of Christ crucified; hidden also in that it has nothing to do with *persuasive words of wisdom* (ii. 4). Though only now revealed, this wisdom, as God's wisdom, is eternal as God is; **God determined** it **before the course of ages began** (literally, *before the ages*; there is no need to raise the question of pretemporal 'timelessness', nor, in view of verse 6, is it likely that the *αἰῶνες* here are to be understood in a spatial sense—O. Cullmann, *Christus und die Zeit* (1962), p. 67; E.T., 46) **and determined** it **for our glory.** From the beginning, it was God's purpose to redeem mankind through Christ, and paradoxical, self-giving wisdom was always the mark of his purpose. *For our glory* stands between the reference to *the rulers of this age, who are being brought to nothing* (verse 6), and that to Christ as *the Lord of glory* (verse 8). The rulers lose their glory because they rebel against God; Christ achieves his glory precisely in that he is obedient even unto the death of the cross (compare Phil. ii. 6-11; the present passage, however, goes further than the Philippian hymn, in that it is already as *the Lord of glory* that Jesus is crucified). God's wisdom leads to *our glory* in so far as it makes us obedient. Glory is that which awaits men in the age to come (e.g. xv. 43), but it is to some extent anticipated in the present age (e.g. 2 Cor. iii. 18).

None of the rulers of this age (see the note on verse 6) 8
knew (possibly *has known*, or *knows*; but the translation given suits the context best) **this** true, divine **wisdom.** Either: they did not understand God's plan for the salvation of the world, based as it was on the cross; or: they did not recognize Christ crucified as the agent chosen by God for the world's salvation. These two interpretations are distinguishable, but the difference between them is not great. Paul's language is gnostic, and recalls the myth of the redeemer who is unrecognized in his descent to

earth (Bultmann, *Theology*, pp. 174 f. (E.T., 175); Knox, *Gentiles*, pp. 220 f.), but the myth is thoroughly moralized. Whether in outline or in the details of its operation God's wisdom operates through sacrificial and self-giving love, and this was contradictory to the nature of the rulers. Their failure to understand God's purpose is plain: **If they had known it they would not have crucified the Lord of glory.** In the exposition so far the rulers have been taken to be the supernatural forces who control events in this age (until their overthrow by Jesus Christ). Some (e.g. Lightfoot) suppose that they are the earthly rulers (such as Pontius Pilate the procurator, and Caiaphas the high priest; cf. Baruch iii. 16) who were responsible for the crucifixion. This view is possible in verse 8 but much less likely in verse 6; and the gospels represent the ministry, and not least the death, of Jesus as a record of conflict with supernatural powers. On this question, see Héring, p. 26 (E.T., 16 f.). Man may, however, properly recognize himself in the inability of the world-rulers to see God's wisdom in the cross. *Lord of glory*, an expression common in 1 Enoch (xxii. 14; xxv. 3, 7; xxvii. 3, 4; lxvi. 2; lxxv. 3), means primarily 'glorious Lord', but Jesus is glorious because he belongs to the heavenly world and shares in the being of God.

The connection of the next verse is far from clear, for, in the Greek, Paul begins without a main verb: *But, as it is written, Things which* . . . The connection is given by observing that in verse 8 something is hidden from the rulers (cf. verse 6), and that in verse 10 something is revealed to *us*; we thus arrive at a rendering which, though it paraphrases, appears to give Paul's
9 meaning. **But the hidden wisdom has been revealed** (the effect of this insertion is not widely different from Allo's suggestion that verse 9 should be regarded as a further object of *we speak* in verse 6). **In the words of Scripture:**

Things which eye never saw, and ear never heard,
And never entered into the mind (literally, *heart*, though the organ of thought is intended; the expression is Hebraistic, a fact that must bear on the question of the source of the quotation) **of man,**
All the things that God prepared (in secret) **for those who love him.**

But where do these words occur in Scripture? In the form in which Paul gives them, nowhere. We may note Isa. lxiv. 3 (LXX):

> From the beginning we did not hear nor did our eyes see any God but thee, and thy works, which thou shalt do for those who await (thy) mercy;

also lxv. 16:

> They shall forget their former affliction, and it shall not enter into their mind (compare verse 17).

These passages are reminiscent of but by no means identical with Paul's words, nor is their general sense the same as his. According to Origen, Paul was quoting not the Old Testament but the apocryphal Apocalypse of Elijah; this however does not seem to be capable of demonstration; full details are to be found in Weiss. W. D. Davies (p. 307) thinks Paul was using language 'traditional in Judaism' to describe the blessedness of the age to come, but this in itself does not account for the citation formula, 'as it is written' (*καθὼς γέγραπται*). This clause almost certainly means that Paul believed that he was quoting the Old Testament and we must conclude either that he was doing so from memory, and very inaccurately, or that he had a text, perhaps of Isa. lxiv, lxv different from ours. For an elaborate discussion of this see Stauffer.

Whatever its source, Paul uses the quotation to indicate the meaning of wisdom, the hidden, divine wisdom, not the wisdom of this age, in the sense of 'plan of salvation'. In his wisdom, God has prepared for his own such good things as the mind of man has never conceived. Dr W. D. Davies is probably right in thinking that the language is derived from traditional descriptions of the age to come, but as used by Paul the picture is modified by that measure of realization to which New Testament eschatology is regularly exposed. Paul does not say (as no doubt many in Corinth, as elsewhere, would have said) that these treasures are prepared for those who know God, but for those who love him (compare viii. 3). Not *gnosis* but love is the touchstone of Christian maturity and spirituality.

Moreover man does not learn these secrets by any achievement

10 of his own. **To us did God reveal them through the
Spirit (compare Manual of Discipline ix. 17, 22). The connection of this sentence with what precedes is uncertain, but **But**
(δέ), marking a contrast not only with the mysteriousness of
what has been prepared by God, unseen, unheard, unthought,
but also with the ignorance of the rulers, seems to make better
sense than *for* (γάρ; see note 1 on p. 67; Zuntz, p. 205, prefers
δέ). Man cannot himself find out the truth about God and his
purposes; only the Spirit of God can make these things known,
**for the Spirit searches out all things, even the deep things
of God.** It is the Spirit who convinces the hearer of the truth of
the Gospel (ii. 4), the Spirit also who brings out the meaning of
what is given in the Gospel (ii. 12); compare the Johannine
doctrine of the Paraclete (John xvi. 8-15). Commentators often
show embarrassment here in dealing with the relation between
the Spirit and God, and with the reason for the Spirit's search,
or inquiry. Paul is probably taking over language used (perhaps
by his correspondents; cf. viii. 1; for Stoic parallels see Knox,
Gentiles, pp. 116 ff.) in a different sense. Men supposed that they
could by searching find out God, and plumb the depths of his
being (cf. Rev. ii. 24, the deep things of Satan; also the gnostic
emanation Bythos, *Depth*). Paul does not share these gnostic
convictions. For him there is no profounder truth than the word
of the cross, and only the Spirit can of himself know, and then
11 communicate, the truth about God; **for what human agency**
(or, *what man*, or *who among men*) **knows the inward truths
about a man except the man's spirit** (his self-consciousness,
we might say) **which is in him?** This is common human
experience. There is an analogy (located rather in the usage of
the word *spirit* than in the realm of being) between God and
man. **In the same way, no one knows** (or, has ever known,
ἔγνωκεν) **the inward truths about God except the Spirit of
God.** Only God knows and can communicate the truth about
himself (cf. Matt. xi. 25 ff.; Luke x. 21 f.); among men, only any
given man knows the truth about himself, but God also knows
this truth—here the analogy breaks down.

Apart therefore from the Spirit of God, man remains in
12 ignorance of God and of his wise purpose for the world. **But** we
are not in this position. **We did not receive the spirit of the**

world but the Spirit that comes from God. Paul does not explain what he means by *the spirit of the world*; elsewhere in his writings compare Rom. viii. 15; xi. 8; 2 Cor. xi. 4. The first at least of these passages appears to be rhetorical, in the sense that reference to the Spirit of God has given rise to a similar expression describing the character and motivation of those who do not have the Spirit of God, and not necessarily implying the existence of a distinct and personal evil spirit. Dr W. D. Davies (*Christian Origins and Judaism* (1962), pp. 172 f.) is right in thinking that the Qumran parallels are of limited importance; but it is evident that Paul did believe in a spiritual force opposed to God, and connected it with this world (2 Cor. iv. 4), so that conversion meant to pass from its authority to God (cf. Col. i. 13). *The Spirit of the world* can in fact hardly be distinguished from *the wisdom of this age* (verse 6), and each suggests a self-regarding wisdom, a man-centred planning in which man provides for his own interests, a condition in which it is impossible for him to understand the sort of divine truth that is manifested in Christ crucified.

To us, who have become Christians, however, God gave his Spirit, **that we might know the things that God has freely given us** (literally, *that have been freely given us by God*). Paul makes no attempt to define what these things are; indeed, they are the undefinable and undescribable things of verse 9, things proper (in ordinary Jewish eschatological thought) to the life of heaven, but already freely given to Christians. The tense of the verb here (aorist participle, τὰ χαρισθέντα) is important because it shows that in verse 9, and in the passage generally, Paul is not speaking only of the future but also of the present life of Christians.

The Spirit thus enables inward apprehension of profound divine truths; the Spirit also provides language that makes conversation about these truths possible. **Further, we speak of** 13
these things not in words taught us by human wisdom (or, if διδακτός is more than a simple verbal adjective, 'in learned words of human wisdom'; the genitive is subjective—so Moule, p. 40, M. iii. 211, 234, though it is not necessary to see Hebrew influence here, as Turner does), **but in words that are taught us by the Spirit.** That which can only be discerned through the

Spirit, and not by unaided reason, needs more than human reason for its expression. It may however be the theme of Christian discussion. *We* may possibly refer only to Paul, or to Paul and his colleagues; more probably the meaning is that all mature Christians (how many of them there were in Corinth among the many immature Christians we cannot say) could and did speak of profound spiritual truths. In this conversation we use words prompted by the Spirit, **interpreting spiritual truths by means of spiritual words.** This clause has given rise to a variety of translations and interpretations. Two main problems arise: (1) What is the meaning of the verb (συγκρίνειν) here rendered *interpreting*? (2) What is the gender, and what the meaning, of the adjective (πνευματικοῖς—the variant πνευματικῶς can safely be rejected) here rendered *spiritual words*? These are not unconnected. The verb may mean 'to interpret', 'to compose', or 'to combine' ('*montrant l'accord des choses spirituelles pour des spirituels*'—Allo). The adjective may (as far as its form goes) be masculine, in which case it will mean 'spiritual persons', or neuter, in which case it will mean 'spiritual things', or 'spiritual words'. The rendering adopted here is supported by Old Testament usage (e.g. Gen. xl. 8; Dan. v. 7), and by the fact that Paul has just spoken of truths which are first perceived, and then communicated, by the Spirit. But in the context he speaks of the *mature* and of the *spiritual*, and there is thus reason for thinking that his meaning may be 'interpreting spiritual truths to spiritual persons'. The idea of comparison does not seem to occur in the context, but this is the meaning of the verb in 2 Cor. x. 12; and it is not impossible, though perhaps not likely, that Paul means 'putting together spiritual things'—possibly, revelation with the expression of it, or the inspired word of wisdom with the inspired word of knowledge (xii. 8). None of these explanations can be excluded, but the first two are the more probable, and in the end the reader must judge which of the two is the more appropriate to the context.

It would be useless to try to explain spiritual truths to one who was not a spiritual man (a man, that is, who had received
14 the Holy Spirit—not a mystic). **A natural man does not receive the truths revealed by the Spirit of God.** The *natural man* is the counterpart of the *spiritual man* (cf. verses

13, 15). 'Spiritual' (πνευματικός) is an adjective derived from the noun 'Spirit' (πνεῦμα); 'natural' (ψυχικός), a rendering in whose favour there is little to plead but its familiarity, and the difficulty of finding an alternative, is an adjective derived from the noun 'soul' (ψυχή). For the contrast between these words, and their meaning, see especially xv. 44 ff., and the notes thereon. The natural man is most easily defined negatively: he is a man who has not received the Holy Spirit. His natural resources, for example his intellectual resources, are, or may be, complete; he is not in any ordinary sense a 'bad man', or a foolish man, or an irreligious man. But lacking the Spirit of God he cannot apprehend spiritual truths, **for to him they are foolishness, and he cannot know them, because they are investigated spiritually.** This is not simply a matter of inspiration. The Spirit of God is the Spirit of Christ crucified, and the wisdom taught by the Spirit is the word of the cross (i. 18), and to the natural man this is foolishness, for it inverts the values by which he lives. *Investigated* is perhaps not an entirely satisfactory rendering (of ἀνακρίνεται). The same word is used twice in the next verse, and it is these uses that suggest that 'investigate' should be selected as the translation. The word is unusually frequent in this epistle (ten times; once in Luke; five times in Acts; nowhere else in the New Testament), and it has been suggested (Weiss) that it was a word in common use in Corinth among Paul's adversaries, and that in response Paul plays on it
in various shades of meaning. **The spiritual man** (it is just 15
possible that ὁ πνευματικός means the Spiritual One *par excellence*, God; this would fit the next verse, but is not suitable to the context as a whole, **however, investigates all things, but he himself is not open to comparable investigation on the part of anyone.** More than examination is involved: the man who has received the Spirit (which for Paul means divine gift rather than divine substance—Kümmel) is able to consider and appraise all things because he is not only inspired to understand what he sees; he is also furnished with a moral standard by which all things may be measured. This does not ascribe infallibility to the spiritual man. 'A man judges aright and with assurance, according to whether he is born again, and according to the measure of grace bestowed on him—and no more'

(Calvin). But in what sense is the spiritual man himself not open to investigation and appraisal? Commentators say that he is not exposed to investigation by the natural man, and quote Chrysostom, who points out that the man with sight is capable of seeing all things, including those that pertain to a blind man, but that a blind man cannot see the things pertaining to a man with sight. But this is not what Paul says; he says that the spiritual man is not investigated and appraised by anyone. Further, if we may judge from the epistle as a whole, he certainly does not mean that anyone showing the phenomena of inspiration must not be exposed to testing; the contrary is stated in xiv. 29. The solution of the problem is given by iv. 3 f., where Paul makes the point that human condemnation and acquittal are nothing to him; his only judge is the Lord. The same point is probably intended here.

16 Proof from Scripture follows. **For who ever knew the mind of the Lord, so as to** (on the consecutive relative see Robertson, p. 724) **instruct him? But we** (spiritual Christians) **have the mind of Christ.** The word *mind* here replaces *Spirit* because of Isa. xl. 13, which however is not very exactly followed. The Hebrew has *Spirit*; the LXX runs: Who ever knew the mind of the Lord (*νοῦν κυρίου*) . . . Compare Rom. xi. 34. No man can plumb the depths of God's mind (cf. verse 10); no one can put him right. But Paul and his spiritual colleagues have the mind of Christ, and the proposition of verse 15 naturally follows. Verse 16 is thus appropriately introduced by *for* (*γάρ*).

Wendland notes the trinitarian character of the paragraph as a whole, and the observation is just in the sense that it alludes to three divine agencies; it is however right to add that it is difficult to draw out from this passage alone any clear account of the relation between Christ and the Spirit, and that the matter is obscured by the introduction of the word *mind*.

7. iii. 1-4. EVEN TRUE WISDOM UNSUITABLE FOR BABES

(1) As far as my own experience of you goes, brothers, I could not speak to you as to spiritual men, but only as to

fleshly men,[1] as to babes in Christ. (2) I fed you on milk, not on solid food, for solid food you were not yet able to take. And indeed even now you are still unable[2] to take it, (3) for you are still fleshly.[3] For where there are envy and strife[4] among you, are you not fleshly[3]? Do you not conduct yourselves in accordance with human standards? (4) For when one says, 'I belong to Paul', and another, 'I belong to Apollos', are you not men—that and nothing more?

In the preceding paragraph Paul has elaborated the theme of Christian wisdom; not only the contrast between it and the wisdom of this age but also its positive content. He now returns to the present situation. It is true that there is a Christian wisdom that mature Christians can understand and discuss, but
this is not for Corinth. **As far as my own experience of you** 1
goes (this paraphrases, and perhaps over-translates, an emphatic κἀγώ, *and I*), **brothers** (cf. i. 10; Paul's criticisms are not such as to make him drop this mode of address; *spiritual* and *fleshly* mark older and younger, mature and immature, brothers within the same family, not those who are within and those who are outside a gnostic circle), **I could not speak** (the word is λαλεῖν, as at ii. 6) **to you as to spiritual men, but only as to fleshly men.** For *spiritual men* compare ii. 14 f.; the meaning is the same as *mature* (ii. 6). Compare also xiv. 37; Gal. vi. 1. The word does not refer to those who are separated from material life by the practice of asceticism, but to those who have received,

[1] In this verse Paul appears to have written σαρκίνοις, though many MSS. have σαρκικοῖς. There is a distinction between the words (Robertson, pp. 158 f.); the proper sense of σάρκινος (made of flesh) is given by 2 Cor. iii. 3, of σαρκικός (having the character of flesh) by 1 Cor. ix. 11. But σαρκικός is used in verse 3, and it seems most improbable that Paul intends any distinction in this paragraph (so Lietzmann, against Bachmann and Schlatter).

[2] P[46]B omit ἔτι. This short but probably secondary reading (Zuntz, pp. 40, 285) improves the construction, which appears to conflate 'not even now (οὐδὲ νῦν) are you able' and 'even now (ἔτι καὶ νῦν) you are still unable'.

[3] In these places also there is textual confusion between σαρκικός and σάρκινος, as in verse 1. See note 1.

[4] Many MSS., including P[46] D G it, add καὶ διχοστασίαι, *and dissensions.* There was no reason for omitting these words if they stood in the original text; they may well have been added from the 'works of the flesh' in Gal. v. 20 (so Zuntz, p. 170).

and have their existence determined by, the Spirit of God. Correspondingly, *fleshly men* are not those who habitually indulge in sensual sins, but those (cf. the *natural man* of ii. 14) whose existence is determined not by God but by considerations internal to themselves, or internal at least to humanity as distinct from God. See also the distinction of xv. 44; and compare Rom. vii. 14.

The next words introduce a qualification. To call his readers *fleshly* is to imply that they are completely outside the Christian way, and this would go too far. *Mature* provides a better basis of comparison than *spiritual.* Mature the Corinthians certainly are not, but they may be described as **babes in Christ;** that is, they are not heathen, but Christian; but they have only just made a beginning in the Christian life. Compare Paul's use of the word *brothers* (above). Because they are *in Christ* they have been brought into relation with the age to come, and into the realm of the Spirit, but they are not yet determined by the Spirit; they are not yet mature. For a different use of the metaphor see xiv. 20.

Hence one cannot speak wisdom to them (ii. 6); or, as Paul
2 puts it in a natural metaphor, **I fed** (literally, *I gave you to drink*, ἐπότισα, used by zeugma with both *milk* and *solid food*) **you on milk, not on solid food.** The metaphor is found in a large variety of ancient sources (see a long list in Knox, *Gentiles*, p. 111, including Philo, the Mishnah, Macrobius, Sallustius, Epictetus, and the *Corpus Hermeticum*), but there is no need to think that Paul is indebted to any particular one of them; he was quite capable of noticing for himself the kind of food that is usually supplied to infants. Compare a similar but not pejorative use of the metaphor at 1 Pet. ii. 2; also Heb. v. 12 ff. In none of these places is there any occasion to think of the custom of supplying a drink of milk to newly baptized converts. This custom (first attested by Tertullian and Hippolytus) rests on the New Testament (and the Old), not the New Testament on the custom.

Paul's reserve in disclosing Christian wisdom was due not to secretiveness but to concern for his Corinthian brothers, **for solid food you were not yet able to take**—a hard saying for the Corinthians; cf. i. 4-7. The implications of Paul's statement are superficially difficult. Earlier (see pp. 67 f.) we saw reason to think that wisdom was essentially the same as the word of the cross, and this evidently (i. 17 f.; ii. 1 f.) was what Paul communicated to his hearers at the beginning. Here (as in ii. 6) wisdom is described as not good for beginners. It seems that the wisdom Paul spoke with the mature must be further defined. It rests on the word of the cross, but is a development of this, of such a kind that in it the essential message of the simple preaching of the cross might be missed, or perverted, by the inexperienced. Essentially it differs in form rather than content, as meat and milk are both food, though differently constituted.

Moreover, Paul's complaint does not relate only, or chiefly, to the time of his earliest work in Corinth. **And indeed** (ἀλλά; for the intensifying effect of this word see B.D. §448) **even now
you are still unable to take it, for you are still fleshly.** 3
Mere lapse of time does not bring Christian maturity, though one might hope that it would do so, and a rebuke is implied. '*Then* it was reasonable to expect the Corinthians to be babes, but *now* they ought to be mature and ready for true wisdom' (Harris). **For where** (this natural English equivalent seems to bring out adequately the causal use of ὅπου—B.D. §456) **there are envy** (ζῆλος, originally *emulation* in a good sense, but now 'degraded'—Lightfoot) **and strife among you, are you not fleshly?** Other standards than Paul's seem to have been employed at Corinth. Gifts of the Spirit such as speaking with tongues or prophecy were taken to confer the status of 'spiritual'; but such gifts when not accompanied by love (cf. xiii. 1-3) were no more than fleshly, that is, man-centred, spirituality. *Envy and strife*, the opposite of love and clear indications of egocentric living, are a more trustworthy criterion. **Do you not conduct yourselves in accordance with human standards?** This question (a rhetorical repetition of *Are you not fleshly?*) brings out clearly what Paul means by fleshliness, which is life cut off from and opposed to God; self-centred, self-contained, self-directed. The point is brought into still closer relation with
events in Corinth when Paul adds, **When one says, 'I belong** 4
to Paul', and another, 'I belong to Apollos', are you not men—that and nothing more? The last four words have no equivalent in the Greek, but are needed (or, at least, desirable)

in order to bring out the meaning of the question, *Are you not men?*—for of course the Corinthians are men. The trouble is that they are human beings who choose to forget their absolute dependence on God, and to determine their own existence in accordance with their own desires rather than with his command. It is however further possible that Paul's expression reflects a gnostic opinion, current at Corinth, that the true Christian experienced apotheosis, so as to be no longer merely human.

The sentence in verse 4 is to be compared with i. 12; it is more clearly expressed, and also omits two names, Cephas and Christ. The name Cephas is omitted because, as the next paragraph will show, Paul sees the relation between himself and Cephas in a different light from that between himself and Apollos. The juxtaposition of Paul and Apollos in the present verse is particularly significant because there was no difference or competition between the two men; to set Paul and Apollos over against each other was less excusable, more 'fleshly', than to set Paul over against Cephas. The name of Christ may have been omitted because the existence of a Christ-group raises special problems of its own, or (if this view of i. 12 is taken—see the note there) because the words 'I am of Christ' were not those of a group, but Paul's own. The present verse may add some weight to the view (not taken in this commentary) that there were only three groups in Corinth. But the essential point here is that there is nothing wrong with Paul and Apollos; what is wrong is the resounding *ego* with which each slogan begins. By misusing their Christian freedom in exalting their teachers the Corinthians endanger, and in the end will lose it. In defending the apostolic Gospel Paul is defending also the freedom of the church (Schlatter).

8. iii. 5-17. PAUL AND APOLLOS

(5) I have mentioned the names of Apollos and myself. Well then, what[1] is Apollos? and what[1] is Paul? Servants,

[1] Many MSS., including P^{46} and the Western Text, have not *What?* but *Who?* But the neuter (τι) in verse 7 is decisive for *What* in verse 5; since the answer is 'Nothing' the question cannot have been 'Who?' (Zuntz, p. 131).

through whom you became believers; and each one simply performed the service the Lord gave him to do. (6) I planted, Apollos watered the plants; it was not we, however, but God who made them grow. (7) It follows that neither he who plants nor he who waters counts for anything, but only he who causes the growth—God; (8) and he who plants and he who waters are one, and each one shall receive his own pay according to his own labour. (9) For we are fellow-workers in the service of God; you are God's field, God's building. (10) In accordance with God's[1] grace which was given me for the purpose, as a wise master of works I laid a foundation, and someone else builds upon it. Well: let everyone take care how he builds upon it, (11) for no one can lay a different foundation from that which already lies there, namely Jesus Christ. (12) Whatever anyone builds on the foundation, gold, silver, precious stones, wood, hay, straw, (13) each man's work will become manifest, for the Day will show it up, because the Day is revealed in fire, and the fire will test what each man's work is like. (14) If anyone's work, which he has built upon the one foundation, abides, he shall receive pay for it; (15) if anyone's work is burnt up, he will be mulcted of his pay, but he himself will be saved, though only as one who passes through fire. (16) Do you not know that you are God's temple, and the Spirit of God dwells in you? (17) If anyone destroys God's temple, God will destroy him; for God's temple is holy —and that is what you are.

The opening sentence of the translation is a supplement intended to show the link between this and the preceding paragraph. Paul's connecting particle (*οὖν*) is not fully argumentative ('In view of what I have just said, what conclusion do we
draw regarding Apollos and Paul'?), but resumptive. **I have** 5
mentioned the names of Apollos and myself. Well then,

[1] Zuntz (p. 47) follows P^{46} in omitting *τοῦ θεοῦ*, in line with the 'true parallels' in Rom. xii. 3; Gal. ii. 9. It is, however, at least as likely that P^{46} should have assimilated to these passages as that almost all other MSS. should have diverged from them.

what (note the neuter gender, which is more forceful than *who* would be) **is Apollos? and what is Paul?** It might seem that the answer ought to be, Nothing at all. They are completely insignificant, so that the moment attention is focused upon them, fleshliness, the assessing of a situation in purely human terms, appears. But this is not so. Apostles (see the rest of the section and chapter iv) are not to be idolized, but they are not insignificant. Paul and Apollos are **servants** (of Christ, not in the first instance of the Corinthians, but cf. 2 Cor. iv. 5; certainly not masters—contrast 2 Cor. xi. 20)**, through whom** (*per quos, non in quos*—Bengel) **you became believers** (aorist, *ἐπιστεύσατε*; Weiss notes the implication that Apollos as well as Paul had evangelized). The nature of their service is further defined as the paragraph proceeds, and is crystallized in iv. 1, where a different (but not significantly different) word for *servants* is used, and *stewards* is added. In the present verse *servants* translates the word (*διάκονοι*) which later grew into the technical term *deacons*. Evidently it does not have this technical sense here. It was later that the differentiation of ministerial functions in these terms developed (see e.g. 1 Tim. iii. 8-13, and my comment); Acts vi does not describe (and was probably never intended to describe) the institution of the diaconate. Here the word means simply that Paul and Apollos are servants (of no very high standing; *διάκονος* was often *waiter*) who do the bidding of their master, Jesus Christ (to whom alone they owe such dignity and authority as they have); and their carrying out of the tasks assigned to them led to the creation of a company of believers in Corinth. Of this they were not the cause but the instruments: God himself evoked faith in the Corinthian believers, by means of his servants. In this process they had different tasks, **and each one simply performed the service the Lord gave him to do.** The Greek here is very obscure. Literally it runs, 'and to each one as (*καὶ ἑκάστῳ ὡς*) the Lord gave'. This could refer not to the preachers but to those who believed: faith came *to each one as the Lord gave it*. Their faith was no more the Corinthians' own achievement than it was the work of their evangelists; it was the gift of God. This makes good sense, good Pauline sense, and it may be the meaning of Paul's words. The translation offered above, however, has the advantage of leading to the next verse and fitting the context, and may for that reason be preferred. Paul is not here concerned (as he is elsewhere) to make the point that man cannot create his own faith. 'Each one' refers to the preachers, or servants; *to each one* was assigned a task, *as the Lord gave it*, and each performed his own duty.

Thus, **I planted, Apollos watered the plants** (*the plants* is 6
not in the Greek, and must not be taken as an allegorical reference to converts). This must mean that Paul was the first evangelist to work in Corinth (note his principle, stated in Rom. xv. 20: Ambitious to preach the Gospel not where Christ had been named, lest I should build upon someone else's foundation); Apollos arrived later, continued the work of evangelism, and helped in the task of building up the church. Compare Acts xviii. 27–xix. 1. For the metaphor of planting, compare ix. 7; Matt. xv. 13. But merely to put a plant in the ground and pour water over it is nothing. **It was not we, however, but** (these six words are needed to render the Greek ἀλλά, which has the effect of negating the preceding subjects; see B.D. §448) **God who made them grow.** This repeats in terms of the metaphor what was said above (verse 5, and note). The creation and nurturing of faith is the work neither of preacher nor of hearer, but of God. When this comparison is
made **it follows that neither he who plants nor he who** 7
waters counts for anything, but only he who causes the growth—God (*θεός* is in apposition after *ὁ αὐξάνων*). The only significance of planter and waterer is that God accepts their labour and works through them (verse 9); they have no independent importance.

A further truth relevant to the Corinthian situation emerges. Since both planter and waterer draw any significance they have not from themselves but simply from the fact that God makes use of their efforts, it is absurd to try to play one off against the
other (i. 12; iii. 4). **He who plants and he who waters are** 8
one (neuter: *one thing*), in that the aim, result, and motive power of their work are identical. Paul and Apollos have worked in Corinth as allies, not as rivals. Having said this, Paul now characteristically moves back to the other side, and recognizes the distinction, as well as the unity, between himself and his

colleague. **Each one** (that is, planter and waterer, though the proposition is capable of wider application) **shall receive his own pay according to his own labour.** Paul does not develop the thought of the *pay*, or reward (*μισθός*), received by God's gardeners, and it is not clear whether he refers to a recompense in heaven, or to the return for his labours in the growth of his plants that is a gardener's immediate reward. In the present context he is more interested in the work being done, in the workers and their products; that they are paid underlines their
9 responsibility to their Master. **For we are fellow-workers in the service of God.** An alternative rendering is, We are fellow-workers with God (cf. xv. 10; 2 Cor. vi. 1); but this, though entirely satisfactory as a rendering of the Greek (no ground is given in M. iii. 231 for the statement that *θεοῦ* is a possessive genitive) and consistent with Paul's thought in general, is not so apt in the context, which emphasizes that men like Paul and Apollos are not in opposition to each other, but colleagues. Here they are God's paid agents, rather than his colleagues.

A corresponding statement can be made about the Corinthians: **You are God's field, God's building;** that is, the field which God, through his servants, is cultivating, the building which God, through his servants, is erecting. It would be possible to take both nouns as *nomina actionis* rather than as concrete (*tillage, building*): You are the (metaphorical) agricultural and architectural work done by God. We shall however in the next few lines see that (though the horticultural metaphor is dropped) Paul goes on to describe the Corinthian church as a structure.

10 Paul's next step is to develop the building metaphor. **In accordance with God's grace which was given me for the purpose** (this is a common Pauline expression; see e.g. i. 4; Rom. xii. 3; *grace* is primarily God's act on behalf of all mankind in Jesus Christ (e.g. Rom. iii. 24) but it is also crystallized in particular gifts to persons), **as a wise** (*σοφός*; I translate *wise* in order to show the connection with earlier uses of the word and its cognate, but *skilled* would be a better rendering here of a Greek word used in one of its normal senses) **master of works** (*ἀρχιτέκτων*; see the definition worked out in Plato, *Statesman* 259E, 260A—he contributes knowledge, not manual

labour, but also assigns their task to individual workmen) **I laid a foundation, and someone else builds upon it.** In the new metaphor Paul repeats what he had said in verse 6; he was the original evangelist who made the first converts in Corinth and thus laid the foundations of the church (not that the converts are the foundation; see verse 11). In this process it was his firm resolution to know nothing but Christ crucified (ii. 2). The work was not done when the first converts were made; they had to be instructed and built up, and others had to be won. Paul's work was thus the beginning, but there was no reason why it should also be the end. *Someone else* may *build upon* his foundation; and Paul makes it quite clear that this is a proper thing to do, and that he has no objection to it. This is what his friend Apollos has done. One plants, another waters; one lays a foundation, another builds. **Well: let every one take care how he builds upon it.** This can be done well or ill. There are two ways in which it can be done ill. One arises out of an attempt
to tamper with the foundation: **for no one can lay a different** 11
foundation from that which already lies there (τὸν κείμενον, emphasizing that man has no choice in the matter of the foundation of the church), **namely Jesus Christ.** Compare Gal. i. 7; 1 Pet. ii. 5. Paul does not mean that it would be impossible to construct a community on a different basis, only that such a community will not be the church. The foundation is the person of Jesus Christ, not (as has been suggested) the confession that Jesus of Nazareth is the Messiah. Was Paul here asserting in general terms the centrality of Christ in Christianity? Or had he in mind a particular error which threatened to subvert the church in Corinth? Probably the latter. There is good (though not conclusive) reason to think that Peter had been at work in Corinth (see ix. 5, and p. 44). If he had not himself been present, others had, who represented him and pushed his claims. In either case use had probably been made of the tradition (Matt. xvi. 18) that Jesus had renamed Simon as Peter (*Kepha*, the rock), and given the promise that he would build his church on this rock. We may recall also the description (in Gal. ii. 9) of Peter, John, and James as 'pillars' (cf. Eph. ii. 20). We cannot here discuss the meaning, or the authenticity, of the Matthean saying, but it seems probable that (with or

without his approval) Peter had been represented as the true
foundation of the church. In a sense this was true, but what it
meant was that Peter was the primary bearer of the testimony
on which the church rests. This is true also of all the apostles
(cf. Matthew xviii. 18; Acts i. 8, 21 f.). They are not the
foundation of the church in the sense of indispensable administrative authorities, but point away from themselves to Christ.

The second way in which a builder may go wrong is by using
inferior materials in the superstructure. Unworthy material will
12 be exposed. **Whatever anyone builds** (or, *if anyone builds*; but
the effect of the *if* is to generalize; for the construction cf. Rom.
xii. 6 ff.) **on the foundation, gold, silver, precious stones**
(possibly valuable marbles, but cf. Isa. liv. 11 f.; Rev. xvii. 4;
xxi. 18 ff.)**, wood, hay, straw** (for the rhetorical effect of the list
13 in asyndeton, see B.D. §460), **each man's work will become
manifest, for the Day will show it up.** *The Day* (without
further definition, but cf. the Old Testament 'Day of the Lord',
e.g. Amos v. 18) is the day of judgement; compare iv. 3. On this
day God will judge the secrets of men (Rom. ii. 16), and no con-
cealment of shoddy workmanship will be possible. For **the
Day is revealed in fire.** No subject is expressed in Greek, and
it would be possible to take the subject to be (*each man's*) *work*.
But 'day' is nearer, and to render 'each man's work is revealed
in fire' would make the next clause repetitive. The idea of
judgement by fire is by no means uncommon (see below). The
fire is not retributive, but testing: **the fire will test what each
man's work is like.** Combustible material will perish; the rest
will abide. So the day of judgement will reveal the quality of
each man's (in particular here, of each minister's) contribution
to the life of the church. For testing by fire compare 1 Pet. i. 7;
14 also Prov. xvii. 3; Wisd. iii. 6. **If anyone's work, which he
has built upon the one foundation** (the last three words are a
supplement, but in English a necessary one)**, abides** (that is,
stands the test, and remains unharmed by the fire)**, he shall
receive pay for it.** The idea of reward is certainly not absent
from Paul's thought, though the notion that men can put God
in their debt is; compare verse 8, and Rom. iv. 4 f. The thought
is however in this context only touched on in passing; the pay is
not mentioned so much for its own sake as to signify God's

approval. Paul passes on to the opposite case. **If anyone's** 15
work is burnt up (by the testing fire), **he will be mulcted of his pay.** The word thus rendered (ζημιωθήσεται) is not easy to translate with confidence. It might mean, 'he will be punished', but this does not go well with the emphatic *but he himself* (αὐτὸς δέ) that follows. It might mean, 'he will suffer the loss of his work', but this is trite and unnecessary after the statement that the work will be burnt. The translation in the text gives full weight to *but he himself*, and also provides a link with the reference to *pay* in verse 14. The servant of God who uses improper or unworthy materials, though himself saved, will miss the reward he might have had. We have thus already noted the next words, which are clear enough and need little comment: **he himself will be saved** (it is underlined that salvation is to be distinguished from reward, or pay; it cannot be earned). Less clear is the final clause in the sentence: **though only as one who passes through fire** (literally, *but thus, namely as through fire*; the construction, οὕτως . . . ὡς, introduces a metaphor, as at ix. 26, not a fact, as at iv. 1). *Fire* is in the context; see verse 13. The fire is still the fire of judgement, not that of cleansing, though this has been maintained. Unworthy building materials are consumed; worthy remain. There is thus no hint in the context that the fire has the effect of purifying an unworthy workman. It would not be unlike Paul to develop a metaphor in a fresh direction, but there is nothing to suggest that he has here developed it in this direction, for in verse 17 destruction is still threatened. The point appears to be that the day of judgement is marked by conflagration (cf. 2 Thess. i. 8; also Isa. xxvi. 11; xxxi. 9; lxvi. 24; Dan. vii. 9 ff.; Obad. 18; Mal. iii. 1 ff., 19), and that a workman caught in the flames of his own badly constructed house runs the risk of being engulfed in them. In fact, he will escape, but it will be as one who dashes through the flames (διὰ πυρός is to be taken in a local sense), safe, but with the smell of fire upon him. To abandon the metaphor, and say plainly what Paul appears to have had in mind: if Judaizing Christians, such as the disciples of Peter, attempt to build their old Jewish exclusivism into the structure of the church (cf. Gal. ii. 11-14) they will fail; this rotten superstructure will perish. They themselves, however, will not be excluded from salvation,

though the destruction of their work will involve them in pain and loss.

16 The theme of building carries Paul further. **Do you not know** (a Pauline expression; it is implied that they ought to know, perhaps that Paul himself had told them) **that you are God's temple, and the Spirit of God dwells in you?** There is no logical connection, but it may be taken that the building erected on the one foundation of Jesus Christ is a meeting-place for God and man, a setting in which man offers to God the glory due to him. This building is not made of bricks and mortar, but consists of those who do so glorify God by believing and obeying him. The language Paul uses here was not uncommon in the Hellenistic world, where religious and moral philosophers reminded their hearers of the indwelling God who found his temple and dwelling-place not in buildings made of stone, but in the human heart. Epictetus, for example, exhorts his hearers: If an image of God were present you would not dare to do any of the things you do. But when God himself is present within, and sees and hears all things, are you not ashamedto be pondering and doing these things . . .? (II. viii. 14). The thought was borrowed in various forms by Christian writers (notably in 1 Pet. ii. 5), and indeed is used by Paul himself later in the epistle (vi. 19). Here (cf. 2 Cor. vi. 16 f.), however, he does not think of the individual Christian as the shrine inhabited by God, but of the church; this is the theme of the context as a whole, and it is perhaps related to the Jewish apocalyptic notion of a new or renewed temple to be established in the last days (cf. e.g. Isa. xxviii. 16 f.; 1 Enoch xci. 13; Jubilees i. 17). This eschatological temple the church is, and the sign, or mode, of the divine presence within it is *the Spirit of God*. Later in the epistle (especially chapters xii-xiv; cf. i. 7; ii. 5, 10-16) we are to hear much more about the ways in which the presence of the Spirit is made known. There is no need for enumeration here; no Corinthian Christian (however inadequate his understanding of the Spirit's work) doubted that his church was the home of the Holy Spirit, and Paul is therefore free to draw the necessary
17 inference at once. **If anyone destroys God's temple, God will destroy him.** Paul's thought has shifted since verses 12-15, where the fault in mind was not that of destroying the holy

building (and of being destroyed in punishment), but that of putting unworthy material into its construction (and of losing one's pay as a builder in consequence). Probably Paul himself found it hard, in the situations with which he had in practice to deal, to distinguish between the two possibilities. Judaizing Christians, for example (and these, in the 'Cephas-group', Paul probably has in mind here), might introduce certain Jewish customs into the church, or at least plead for their retention, without committing an intolerable offence; their observance of *kosher* food regulations, for example, could be tolerated by better instructed consciences (viii. 7-13; x. 28–xi. 1; cf. Rom. xiv. 1–xv. 6), though they added nothing of value to the structure of the church. But an attempt to import legalism wholesale would be, not an undesirable and unnecessary addition to Christian faith and practice, but a destruction of the whole sacred building, a complete transformation of it, which would leave no church, no meeting-point between God and man, at all. This would be the destruction of the church, and must lead to the destruction of the offender also, not as an act of vindictive retribution but because he has already in his offence rejected the possibility of salvation. It seems better to understand *destroy* in this way than to suppose that Paul is already thinking of the scandals to be mentioned in chapters v and vi (Héring).

It is sometimes said that Paul's verb (φθείρειν) cannot be translated 'destroy', because the church, God's temple, cannot be destroyed. In a sense this is true: even the gates of hell (much less human legalism) cannot prevail against the church (Matt. xvi. 18). It must be remembered, however, that Paul is thinking of a local manifestation of God's temple, a local church: and it is a matter of fact that local churches have, under various pressures, including that of heresy, simply gone out of existence (cf. Rev. ii. 5; iii. 16—not to mention the historical fact of the disappearance of all seven churches of Rev. ii, iii). Further, Paul is thinking not only of false doctrine but of factious behaviour. It may be that his present tense (φθείρει) should be given a conative sense ('sets out to destroy'), but this is not demanded by the context.

Destruction of the temple is inevitably punished, **for God's temple is holy—and that is what you are.** The words recall primitive conceptions of holiness, operating almost like an electric charge; compare for example the fate of Uzzah, who stretched out his hand to touch the sacred Ark (2 Sam. vi. 6 ff.). Paul is not thinking of the profanation of a cult object; the temple of which he speaks (as the final clause underlines) is not a material building at all. But it does involve (and this is the root idea of holiness) relation with God, and if a man wrecks the relation of the church with God (e.g., by substituting legalism for grace), this can only mean that he has rejected grace for himself; he has denied his own relation with God.

The general sense of the last words of the verse is clear, but it is not easy to explain their form. The Latin of the Vulgate is straightforward: *quod estis vos*, which (namely, the temple) you are. This (The temple is what you are, not, Holy is what you are) is probably Paul's meaning; but the Greek has not the neuter singular of the relative, but the masculine plural of a compound relative (οἵτινες). The number of the relative is probably due to assimilation to the number of 'you' (ὑμεῖς). In Hellenistic Greek the distinction between the simple and the compound relatives was wearing thin. Allo may make too much of this distinction in suggesting that Paul's word refers to each one *and* to the entire category—'which you *all* are', but the word may suggest the quality in respect of which the persons addressed are God's temple—'which *as Christians* you are'; and their Christianity has both an individual and a corporate aspect. The rendering adopted attempts to bring this out in the same allusive way as Paul's Greek.

9. iii. 18-23. PAUL, APOLLOS, CEPHAS, AND CHRIST

(18) Let no one deceive himself. If anyone among you supposes that he is wise by the standards of this age, let him become foolish by the standards of this age, in order that he may become truly wise. (19) For the wisdom of this world is foolishness with God. For in Scripture God is described as 'He who catches the wise in their own

craftiness'; (20) and again, 'The Lord knows that the thoughts of the wise are vain.' (21) So let no one make his boast in men: for all things are yours—(22) Paul, Apollos, or Cephas, the world, or life, or death, things present or things to come—all belong to you, (23) and you belong to Christ, and Christ belongs to God.

The discussion of wisdom and folly, which has proceeded intermittently since i. 18, now moves to a close, though it will be illustrated in chapter iv, and picked up again occasionally (vi. 5; viii. 1 ff.; x. 15; xii. 8; xiii. 8-12). At the same time Paul brings to a head the discussion of the Corinthian party conflict, which has proceeded concurrently with that of wisdom, and
shows the ultimate absurdity on which the conflict rests. **Let** 18
no one deceive himself. Paul writes in the style of the Cynic-Stoic diatribe (see *Romans*, p. 43). Self-deception is the common fate of those who mistakenly fancy themselves wise; deluded in this, they are deluded in many other matters also. Compare vi. 9; xv. 33; Gal. vi. 7; and especially Gal. vi. 3, which states the matter in general terms. In Corinth the particular danger is that men (even within the church) may delude themselves into thinking that they are wise, because they estimate wisdom by the wrong standards. Such men need to take new standards and reverse their judgements. **If anyone among you** (that Paul writes ἐν ὑμῖν and not ὑμῶν does not prove that the person in question was not a Corinthian but an outsider; Paul is in any case generalizing) **supposes that he is wise by the standards of** (or, perhaps, with a simple reference to time, *in*) **this age, let him become foolish by the standards of this age** (the last six words are interpretative addition, though some apply the words ἐν τῷ αἰῶνι τούτῳ, which occur once only in the Greek, not to the first clause, as in the present translation, but only to the second)**, in order that he may become truly wise.** *Truly* also is an interpretative addition. For the wisdom prevailing in this age (αἰών) compare ii. 6; it is not to be distinguished from the wisdom of the world (κόσμος), in the next verse, and i. 21. It matters little whether one thinks of the period or of the space within which men choose to live out their lives without reference to God. We have already seen that this determination

is the essence of the world's wisdom, which may be expressed
both in a way of arguing that depends wholly upon human persuasiveness, and in a way of living and a form of religion that are
rooted in man and self. If a man conceives himself to be wise in
such terms he cannot advance from human to divine wisdom by
becoming wiser; he must negate the old wisdom in order to
acquire the new (cf. Rom. x. 3; Phil. iii. 6-9, which state precisely the same truth in a different field; if a man is to be truly
righteous, that is, righteous before God, he must despise and
abjure his own righteousness). The wisdom of this world cannot be improved or developed into the wisdom of God; it must
19 be destroyed (cf. i. 19; ii. 6). **For the wisdom of this world**
(note the change from *age*) **is foolishness with God** (for the
construction cf. Rom. ii. 13). The contradiction is stated in the
sharpest possible terms. The next verse however shows that
the thought is here taking a new turn. The world's wisdom is
foolishness in God's estimation because human and divine
wisdom are opposites; but, further, the exponents of worldly
wisdom are no more than fools in God's hands. Even when they
suppose that they can banish him from the world he remains
their master. **For in Scripture God is described as** (literally,
For it is written) **'He who catches the wise in their own
craftiness'** (the construction—article and participle—means
that we have here a description of God). The *wise* are like
cunning beasts, for whom the hunter is nevertheless too clever.
Craftiness suggests that Paul may at least suspect some under-
20 hand activities in Corinth. **And again, The Lord knows that**
(restoring the order of the words, inverted in Greek) **the
thoughts** (διαλογισμούς: thought-out plans, or even plots; possibly also philosophical thinking; cf. Rom. i. 21) **of the wise
are vain'**, that is, ineffectual, futile. The Old Testament quotations are from Job v. 13; Ps. xciv. 11. The use of *wise* and
wisdom in the Old Testament manifests the same diversity of
good and bad senses as the New Testament. The quotation from
Job (like that in Rom. xi. 35) differs markedly from the LXX
rendering; there is much to be said for the view that Paul had a
different translation of this book.

Since all men, even the wisest, are mere children in God's
21 hands, the conclusion follows. **So let no one make his boast**

in men. This boasting in 'men' is precisely what the Corinthians, in their party-conflict, had been doing. One had boasted in
Paul, another in Apollos, another in Cephas. But only in the
Lord, not men, may one boast (or glory; cf. i. 31; also Gal. vi. 14;
Phil. iii. 3). Moreover (and here is the line of development that
will take Paul into the next chapter), boasting in, and glorifying,
human leaders is not only dishonouring to God but also de-
grading to those who boast, for it mistakes the relationship
between the Christian and the leader. Those who gloried in the
church leaders said (i. 12), I belong to Paul, I belong to Apollos,
I belong to Cephas. This inverts the truth. You do not belong
to this or that minister, **for all things are yours—**the ministers,
Paul, Apollos, or Cephas (that there is no reference in this 22
context to Christ can prove nothing with regard to the existence
of a 'Christ-group'), and all things else—**the world, or life, or
death, things present or things to come.** The apostolic
messengers are *yours* in the sense already given in iii. 5 (*Servants,
through whom you became believers*), and to be elaborated later in
iv. 1-5. They are not lords over God's people, but helpers of
their joy (2 Cor. i. 24); they preach not themselves but Christ as
the Lord; they are servants of Christ, and thus of the church
(iv. 5). To attach oneself devotedly to one minister is thus not a
proper expression of Christian humility, but a denial of the
sovereignty of Christ. Naturally, when Christian teachers differ
(as Paul and Cephas certainly differed on occasion) the Christian
must choose between them, but he will do so in accordance with
the truth, and not on the personal grounds that he has decided
to attach himself to one rather than another.

Paul is led on from this to a point that does not immediately seem strictly coherent with the context. The ministers belong to you because they are servants of Christ and the church; yours also are the *world, life, death, things present, things to come—all things.* It is evident that *all things* are not yours in the same sense, and that the world, for example, is not a servant of the church as the apostles are. Paul's thought has moved on, by a natural transition, to the general sovereignty of the church as the people of God. It is in Christ, and in the community that is in Christ, that humanity recovers its lost lordship, and because Christ is the Lord over the world, over life and death (through his crucifixion and resurrection), and over both this age and the age to come, that his people are no longer the servants of destiny and corruption, but free lords over all things. Thus the Christian lives in the world but the world does not dominate his attitude to life—in other words he does not think in terms of the wisdom of the world (ii. 2, 6; also vii. 29 ff.). He is subject to the vicissitudes of life, and ultimately to death (unless, as Paul conceives to be possible, he survives till the dawn of the age to come), but none of these experiences can separate him from the love of God (cf. Rom. viii. 38 f., where a very similar train of thought occurs, in which it is made even clearer that Paul is thinking of the certain triumph of the Christian over opposed spiritual and cosmic forces). He lives in this age, and its inimical rulers (ii. 6, 8) will injure him if they can; but they cannot do so in any final sense, and he will in his due order (xv. 23) enter the age to come, for Christ is Lord now, and will continue to be Lord.

The last observation underlines the source and nature of the Christians' lordship; it is never free and independent, but rests
23 entirely upon Christ's: **you** (all of you; not—as in i. 12—one group of you only) **belong to Christ.** As Dr Sevenster (*Seneca*, p. 119) points out, by Christian freedom and lordship Paul means something entirely different from Seneca's *omnia illius* (the wise man) *esse dicimus* (*De Beneficiis* VII. viii. 1; Zeno (Diogenes Laertius VII. i. 25), Cicero (*Academicae Quaestiones* ii. 44), and other Stoics had said the same thing). The Christians' sovereignty over the world rests only upon the renewal of humanity in the order of creation as willed by God (cf. Gen. i. 26, 28; Ps. viii. 6-9), and this renewal takes place only through and in Christ. The moment Christians seek to escape from the sovereignty of Christ they lose their own partially recovered status among God's creatures, and become once more enslaved to created things that ought to be their servants (cf. Gal. iv. 9). For example, when the church ceases truly to belong to Christ, the apostles are bound to exercise their authority against it, as we see Paul doing in his dealings with Corinth (for the inverse situation see 2 Cor. x-xiii: when an apostle, or his representative, uses authority for the sake of using it, he loses all claim to it); when the Corinthians turn the Lord's Supper into their own

supper (xi. 20 f.), and thus throw off the yoke of Christ, they become subject to death (xi. 30); when they forget that they were bought with a price (vi. 20), they lay stress on the fact that all things are lawful and ignore the fact that not all things are expedient, and thereby lose the freedom they abuse. Thus, if at first it may have seemed that Paul was wandering from his main point, he here comes sharply back to it, for 'all things belong to you, and you belong to Christ' expresses succinctly his message to Corinth. It has been held that *all things belong to you* is Paul's concession to the 'spiritual' party in Corinth (cf. *all things are permitted* in vi. 12); he allows the proposition to be true, but qualifies it by adding *You belong to Christ.* Weiss however seems to be right in saying, 'It seems impossible that Paul should have intended so inspired a description of Christian lordship over the world merely as a concession, taken out of the thought of his adversaries. If anywhere, he himself is speaking here; this is his own conviction' (p. 88, note 1).

The practical position now stated needs further theological grounding. It has been pointed out that the Corinthian Christians owe their restored freedom and sovereignty not to themselves but to Christ. But **Christ** achieved this benefit for them only because he **belongs to God.** It was the obedience of Christ unto death that won their freedom for them, and it is in him that they enjoy their new relation with God.

We should avoid a difficulty if we stopped at this point, and thought of Christ's belonging to God as something that refers only to his earthly life and humanity (so, e.g., Calvin, and most earlier commentators), in which he practised sacrificial obedience, as the Corinthians also must. We are however forbidden to do this not only by Paul's thought in general, but by the explicit statement of xv. 28 (*When all things shall have been subjected to him, then the Son himself also shall be subjected to him who subjected all things to him, that God may be all in all*). There is eternally a relation of superordination and subordination between the Father and the Son. This does not however mean (if we may use language that did not arise till many years after Paul's time—though Lightfoot notes that to take this phrase with reference to the divine nature of Christ 'is necessary for the proper understanding of the Nicene Creed') that the Son is not of one substance with the Father, and belongs to a different order of being; it means rather that the Son, being of one substance with the Father, is differentiated from him precisely in this, that he renders the obedience of perfect love to the perfectly loving will of the Father. This language is indeed much too formal for Paul, whose thought moves in terms of function rather than essence. For him, Jesus is the willing agent of God. The obedience the Corinthians owe to God, and render to him so far as they receive and share in the righteousness of Christ, which they express (or ought to express) in constantly developing and advancing ethical achievement, Christ offered completely, perfectly, and actually in history. Hence *you belong to Christ* because *Christ belongs to God.*

10. iv. 1-5. SERVANTS OF CHRIST, AND THEIR WORK

(1) How then should a man think of us? As Christ's servants, and stewards of God's mysteries. (2) Well now, what is required[1] in stewards is that a man be found trustworthy. (3) But to me it is a matter of the smallest importance that I should be examined by you, or by any human assize; nay, indeed, I do not even examine myself. (4) For though I have nothing on my conscience it is not by that that I am justified. He who examines me is the Lord. (5) So do not judge anything before the Time, until the Lord shall come, who shall throw light upon the things that are hidden in darkness, and make known the plans of men's hearts. Then each man shall get his meed of praise from God.

In the new paragraph Paul winds up his treatment of the arrogant and divided Corinthian church so far as its troubles arise out of and are reflected in its relations with its apostolic

[1] *ζητεῖται*, third person singular passive, is in the majority of Greek MSS., also in B, and the Latin and Syriac. Others (including P^{46} A D G) have *ζητεῖτε*; ℵ* has *τί ζητεῖτε;*. See the commentary.

leaders. **How then should a man** (ἄνθρωπος: Greek would 1
more naturally have had τις; it may be that the Semitic background of Paul's style shows through here, but genuine Greek parallels, e.g. Epictetus III. xxiii. 15, can be adduced; see M. ii. 433 and cf. xi. 28) **think** (λογίζεσθαι: Weiss notes that this word occurs no fewer than six times in 2 Cor. x-xii, and thinks that it was a word used by Paul's adversaries; see especially 2 Cor. x. 7, 11) **of us?** There is no question in the original, which runs literally, *Thus let a man think of us, namely as* . . . Compare Eph. v. 28. The question is used in the translation in order to bring out as clearly as possible the fact that with *Thus* (οὕτως) Paul is drawing, from what he has already said, conclusions about the proper attitude of Christians to their ministers. *Us* signifies at least Paul and Apollos; possibly Cephas also, but possibly (in view of iv. 6) these two only. Compare iii. 5. If there is restriction it is historical only; what Paul says may, *mutatis mutandis*, be applied generally to the role of ministers within the church.

Paul answers the implied question: We are to be thought of **as Christ's servants.** The word (ὑπηρέτης) is different from that of iii. 5 (διάκονος), but there is little difference in meaning. For the new word compare Luke i. 2; Acts xiii. 5. According to Schlatter, the word of chapter iii suggests the service done by the servant, that of chapter iv his subordination to his master It is doubtful whether this fine distinction would have been in the minds of Paul and his readers. The *servant* in any case has no significance of his own; the work done is not his but his master's; apostolic ministry is marked by the fact that it makes no claims for itself, but points from itself to Christ. This does not depreciate it. Paul and his colleagues are **stewards** (οἰκονόμοι; cf. the picture of the church as God's οἶκος, household, in 1 Tim. iii. 15) **of God's mysteries.** The word *mystery* as used in Greek generally refers to sacred rites (e.g. Euripides, *Suppliants* 173, Δήμητρος μυστήρια, the mysteries of Demeter), and later the word came naturally to be used of the Christian sacraments. *Stewards of God's mysteries* might on this showing be taken to mean, 'dispensers of the sacraments', but this is not Paul's use of 'mystery'; see especially ii. 7, and in addition ii. 1(?); xiii. 2; xiv. 2; xv. 51; Rom. xi. 25; xvi. 25; 2 Thess. ii. 7;

and compare Col. i. 26, 27; ii. 2; iv. 3. This is not an easy list from which to generalize, but the sense suggested by most passages is of secret knowledge of God's purpose, disclosed in the Gospel. The apostles are thus to be thought of primarily as preachers of the Gospel, 'teachers of the revealed truths' (Lightfoot). A *steward* is a household administrator, and there might thus be implied a reference to administrative authority exercised by the apostles within the church. Paul is however probably seeking a synonym in order to provide verbal variety after *servant*, and this administrative sense of *steward* cannot be pressed; so far as it is present it is evidently conditioned by and operates in terms of the Gospel. The chapter as a whole (see especially iv. 9-13) makes it impossible to think of the apostolate as an ecclesiastical civil service. Epictetus describes the Cynic preacher as a servant of Zeus (ὑπηρέτης τοῦ Διός, III. xxii. 82, 95), and as a steward (οἰκονόμος, 3). Paul may well have been aware of the use of the words in this setting.

Steward, however, gives Paul the necessary connection as he proceeds. If he and Apollos are stewards, what is required of them? This is clearly the sense of the developing argument, but both the text and the translation of the words that follow are uncertain. The first word of Paul's sentence (ὧδε) has a variety of meanings: *thus*, *as it is*, *hither*, *here*. It may suggest 'in this world'—that is, a human illustration is to be presented; or, 'in the realm of thought suggested by stewards', 'taking up the notion of stewardship'. Or it may be taken more closely with the next word (λοιπόν), which itself may mean simply, 'Well now', or may be taken more strictly as, 'for the rest', 'in addition'; according to Moule, p. 161 these meanings may be extended as far as 'it follows'. If the two words are taken together the meaning could be something like, 'Now to pursue the present theme', 'Now to take the matter a stage further'. These suggestions however may well read rather too much into the text. If the opening particle (ὧδε) is taken to mean *here*, *in the realm of stewardship*, it makes *in stewards* redundant, and we may be content to give the combined particles (ὧδε λοιπόν) a simple
2 resumptive sense, and adopt the rendering, **Well now, what is required in stewards is that a man be found trustworthy.** On the whole question see M. E. Thrall, *Greek*

Particles in the New Testament (1962), pp. 25-30. A textual problem however remains, for there is a variant which contains the rougher form, Well now, what you require (or, taking ζητεῖτε as imperative, What you ought to require) in stewards is that a man be found . . ., and one MS. has a more forceful variant still, with the question, Well now, what do you require in stewards? That a man be found . . . The difference between the third person singular passive of the verb (ζητεῖται) and the second person plural active indicative or imperative (ζητεῖτε) is small, and was not pronounced in ancient Greek. The second person perhaps fits better with the next verse, but may for that reason be secondary. The general proposition about stewards is in fact preferable. Fortunately there is no great difference in sense, and Paul's point is sufficiently evident. It is not expected that a steward should exercise his own initiative, still less his own personal authority (though this, Schlatter notes, is what the Corinthians seem to have looked for in an apostle); it is expected that he should do his master's bidding, and be trustworthy in looking after his affairs. The question is, By whose standards of trustworthiness is he to be judged? Who is the master to whom he stands or falls (Rom. xiv. 4)?

Paul answers for himself. **To me it is a matter of the** 3
smallest importance that I should be examined by you, or by any human assize. If Paul had attended to all the criticisms of himself and of his work made within his own churches (to go no further) he would have given up his apostolate. He was not thick-skinned, but simply recognized the truth (see Rom. ii. 1, 19 f.; xiv. 4) that man is not qualified to act as his brother's judge. It is a reasonable inference that that criticism of the apostle, which in 2 Corinthians will appear as a full-scale attack, had already begun. The last words of the verse are literally *by any human day*. Some (see B.D. §5) have seen here a Latinism (*dies forensis*; cf. *diem dicere*); it is much more probable that we should recall iii. 13, where *the day* is the day of the Lord's judgement. Here we have to do with man's feeble attempt to imitate God's judgement, and to behave as if he himself were judge. Rabbinic Judaism knows the contrast between 'judgements of men (or, of flesh and blood)' and 'judgements of heaven' (S.B. iii. 336). Paul is not interested in

human attempts to do God's work for him; **nay, indeed** (ἀλλά; cf. iii. 2), **I do not even examine myself.** 'A good conscience is an invention of the devil.' Paul has one, but sets no
4 store by it. **For though I have nothing on my conscience** (we must either say, with Calvin, that Paul means only 'in respect of my apostolic duties', or agree with Lightfoot that this 'is simply a hypothetical case . . . The sentence means "on the supposition that I am not conscious, though I am" ') **it is not by that that I am justified.** Paul does not in the original use the noun *conscience* (συνείδησις) but the verb (σύνοιδα) from which the noun is derived; this signifies literally 'knowing with', in the sense of sharing a guilty secret. Paul has no such guilty secret to share with himself, but this fact speaks of human ignorance rather than human innocence, and justification is an act of God, not of man, an act based not on man's sinlessness but on God's grace: God justifies not the good but the ungodly (Rom. iv. 5). Paul disagrees here with Cephalus (and doubtless Plato), though in part he uses their language: To him who has no sin on his conscience (μηδὲν ἑαυτῷ ἄδικον ξυνειδότι) sweet hope is present . . . (*Republic* 331A). Paul's verdict on himself is of no consequence.

For a note on Paul's use of *conscience* see *Romans*, p. 53, and especially Sevenster, *Seneca*, pp. 99 ff., where it is made clear that whereas for the Stoic Seneca conscience passes the final judgement (see *De Ira* III. xxxvi. 2 ff.), for Paul 'only the Lord is in a position to pass the last judgement'. **He who examines me** (brings me before his court for interrogation) **is the Lord,** that is, Christ, the judge of all men (cf. 2 Cor. v. 10). *The Lord* could signify God the Father (cf. Rom. xiv. 10), but the next verse makes this unlikely (see however p. 104). In Greek, *Lord* (κύριος) has no article. This can hardly be brought out in English, but may suggest that Paul is thinking of Christ as the competent authority—the only competent authority—for judging.

It is not the business of Christians to judge their brothers (cf. Rom. xiv. 4). **So do not judge anything before the Time.** *Judge* is the simple form (κρίνειν) of the compound verb (ἀνακρίνειν) translated *examine.* If the two are to be distinguished it will be by the fact that judging presupposes the process of examination (ἀνάκρισις was used in Greek of a preliminary inquiry), and lays stress on the verdict reached at the end of it. The distinction however is a small one. One might have expected Paul to write not 'Do not judge any*thing*', but, 'Do not judge any*one*'. It may be that we should render his sentence, 'Do not reach any verdict'. This would have the effect of underlining the distinction noted above between the verbs *examine* and *judge*.

There is indeed a moment when verdicts will be reached. In the translation the word *Time* is printed with a capital to bring out the fact that Paul is not simply condemning precipitate and untimely verdicts, but is thinking of the judgement that will take place at the last day, when **the Lord shall come.** In view of this *last* judgement, all human verdicts must be *pre*-judice, though at vi. 3 he notes that Christians will join in the judgement of angels, and also allows, for practical purposes, Christian courts in this age. For the coming of the Lord (Jesus Christ) to judgement compare Rom. ii. 16; 1 Thess. iv. 16; 2 Thess. ii. 8; and especially 1 Cor. xi. 26, where the context shows that judgement is in mind. The meaning of the Lord's coming to judgement is made clear in the following clauses. The first is metaphor: **who** (ὃς καί; if καί is to be pressed we must say either, 'who when he comes will also ...', or 'who will both throw ... and make ...' but this is doubtful) **shall throw light upon the things that are hidden in darkness.** This is common biblical language; compare for example Ps. cxxxix. 11, 12. The coming of Christ to judgement will have the effect of throwing light on all those things that men have kept secret, 'kept dark', as we say. They will no longer be concealed, but clearly known. These, *the hidden things* (τὰ κρυπτόμενα) are the object of the verb (φωτίζειν), not 'the darkness which hides' them, as M. iii. 14 appears to suggest. Weiss quotes a good parallel from Epictetus I. iv. 31: ... To him who has found the truth and brought it to light (φωτίσαντι) and brought it forth to all men. The truth (in the present context, the truth about men's conduct and character) is hidden in a dark place; the Lord throws a beam of light upon it. The next clause states the same fact without metaphor: Christ will **make known the plans** (or, intentions) **of men's hearts:** not only their acts (which may be concealed and therefore unknown), but their inward thoughts (which may, for good or ill, be concealed even behind their public actions). When this is done we shall have passed by all human opinions, favourable and unfavourable. **Then each man shall get his meed of praise from God.** The emphasis lies upon the first word and the last. *Then*, at the judgement, not now; from *God* himself, not from men. Clement of Rome (1 Clement xxx. 6) is not quite right in his interpretation when he says *αὐτεπαινετοὺς μισεῖ ὁ θεός*; it is not self-praise alone that Paul attacks, but any praise that is simply human in origin. He says nothing here about those who will receive not praise but blame; he is still thinking in terms of the Corinthian situation, in which some have praise for Paul, some for Apollos, some for Cephas. But compare iii. 5: the Lord appointed the gifts and the duties of his servants, and it is for him, not for the Corinthians, to give or to withhold praise for duty done.

It has been suggested, on the basis of their parallel structure, that the two clauses

> Who shall throw light upon the things that are hidden
> in darkness,
> And make known the plans of men's hearts,

were quoted by Paul, perhaps from some apocryphal book, in which *the Lord* was not the Messiah but God. If however Paul is quoting, his quotation might equally well be taken from a Christian hymn (cf. Eph. v. 14). But there is no need for such a hypothesis; Paul is writing in a style suggested by his biblical theme and his own Semitic cast of mind (though indeed parallelism of structure is by no means un-Greek).

11. iv. 6-13. THE CORINTHIANS AND THEIR APOSTLES

(6) Now, my brothers, I have for your sake made these things seem to apply to Apollos and myself, in order that by our example you may learn the meaning of 'Nothing beyond what stands written', so that you may not be puffed up, each on behalf of one and against another. (7) For who makes you different from your neighbour? And what have you that you did not receive? But if you

received it, why do you boast as if you had not received it? (8) Already you have reached satiety; already you have become rich; apart from us you have come to your kingdom. Yes, and I wish you had come to your kingdom, that we too might be crowned with you. (9) For I think God has put on us the apostles as last in the show, as men under sentence of death, for we became a spectacle to the whole world, angels and men alike. (10) We are fools for Christ's sake, you are sensible in Christ. We are weak, you are strong. You are held in honour, we in dishonour. (11) Up to this very moment we go hungry, thirsty, and naked, we are cuffed, we are homeless, (12) we toil, working with our own hands. When we are abused, we bless; when we are persecuted, we are forbearing; (13) when we are slandered, we speak kindly. We have become as it were the world's scapegoats, the scum of the earth, to this day.

It is clear that the new paragraph continues in the same line that Paul has pursued through most of the epistle up to this point. The Corinthians must not exaggerate the importance of such teachers as Paul and Apollos; they must not be puffed up and conceited; they must not go beyond what is commanded them; they must recognize that whatever they have and are they owe entirely to the gracious activity of God. Many of the details of the opening verse, however, are far from clear.

Now, my brothers, I have for your sake made these 6
things seem to apply to Apollos and myself. In this sentence it is the verb (μετεσχημάτισα) that is difficult. This verb is used, in the active voice, in a straightforward and simple sense at Phil. iii. 21: Christ will *transform* our body to make it like his. In 2 Cor. xi. 13, 14, 15 it is used in the middle voice with the sense of changing one's own appearance, of disguising oneself: False apostles disguise themselves as (make themselves look like) apostles of Christ; Satan disguises himself as an angel of light; his servants disguise themselves as servants of righteousness. There are no other uses of the verb in the New Testament. Some draw attention to the use of one of the components (σχῆμα, form) of the compound verb, with the meaning 'figure of

speech'. This leads to the view that *these things* are the figures of gardener, builder, and stewards, which Paul has applied to himself and Apollos. It is however more probable that Paul means that he has made the argument of the last few paragraphs (apart from iii. 22; but iii. 5-17 is especially in mind) look as if it applied (or applied only) to himself and Apollos. He has deliberately omitted other names (notably Peter's; but it may be that 'false apostles' were already at work in Corinth).

Paul and Apollos, then, have been used as the figures by whom the Corinthians may learn their lesson. They have been mentioned **in order that by our example you may learn the meaning of 'Nothing beyond what stands written'.** *By our example* is literally *in us* (ἐν ἡμῖν); perhaps 'in our case', or 'by means of us'. The use of the definite article in the Greek (τὸ Μὴ ὑπὲρ . . .) shows that the following words are a quotation (perhaps not from a book but from a current saying, possibly but not necessarily current at Corinth); but their translation is difficult and their reference obscure. *Stands written* (γέγραπται) is a regular formula introducing Old Testament quotations (e.g. i. 19), and it probably refers here to the Old Testament, so that the saying enjoins life in accordance with Scriptural precept and example. If this however is the general sense, 'nothing beyond' remains a far from obvious way of expressing it. There is no verb in the principal clause, which literally is *Not beyond*; the *nothing* of the translation paraphrases with a view to producing tolerable English, but less freely than the addition of a verb (e.g., Do not go beyond) would do. We can only guess at the original application. It may be that the Corinthians were in danger of treating their own party slogans and traditions as if they were on the same level as Scripture. Schlatter saw in 'going beyond Scripture' the characteristic and watchword of the Christ-group. 'In the church, the message was being preached, "Everything is permitted"; this was the fundamental step beyond Scripture; the Law with its prohibitions, which separate what is permitted from what is forbidden, lay for Christians in the past' (p. 154). According to Stauffer, 'Nothing beyond what stands written' was a Jewish formula, brought to Corinth by the Cephas-group, rejected by Hellenist Christians, and defended by Paul in his own sense. In view of the fact that we are reading an intimate letter, full of allusions to circumstances well known to writer and readers but unknown to us, we may be content with some such interpretation; there is no need to resort to conjecture, or to suppose (as e.g. Moffatt does) that the text is hopelessly corrupt. It is possible that *what stands written* may be a reference not to Scripture in general but to the Old Testament passages adduced in chapters i-iii; so Dr Hooker, whose detailed discussion of the problems of this verse (*N.T.S.* x. 127-32) should be consulted. It is not however easy to see how one could go *beyond* the quotations in question.

The new dependent clause may look back to the main sentence (*I have made these things seem to apply*), but is more probably dependent on the foregoing (. . . *that you may learn* . . . *so that* . . .). Again, the meaning is obscure: **so that you may not be puffed up, each** (εἷς) **on behalf of one and against another.** The translation is offered with reserve. Being 'puffed up' (φυσιοῦσθαι) was a standing and characteristic danger of the Corinthians: see iv. 18, 19; v. 2; viii. 1; xiii. 4; 2 Cor. xii. 20 (elsewhere in the New Testament only Col. ii. 18). It took different forms: boasting against Paul, and moral indifference (v. 2), for example. Here it seems best (in view of the preceding verses) to suppose that *one* and *another* refer to the leaders whom the Corinthians have chosen for themselves. How foolish to stir up strife by exalting Paul against Apollos, or *vice versa*, when each recognizes the other as a servant of Christ, and the two work in harmony! Indeed, not only foolish; it is an example of inflated pride, even when the subject fancies that he is being humble before his leader. Alternatively, Paul may refer to the exaltation of a teacher over those who, though they lack his gifts, are nevertheless his Christian brothers; this would be equally deplorable, but it seems less probable as an interpretation of Paul's words.

Paul now generalizes the theme of pride, and in doing so provides its antidote. **For** (introducing the reason why you should 7
not be puffed up) **who makes you different from your neighbour?** The verb (διακρίνειν) is used in different senses elsewhere, but there can be little doubt of its meaning here; compare Acts xi. 12; xv. 9. It is not however certain what answer Paul expects to his rhetorical question. The answer may

be 'No one; for in fact you are not different from your neighbour; you are and can be nothing more than a pardoned sinner.' Alternatively it could be, 'So far as you differ from your neighbour, by possessing special gifts, it is God (not you yourself) who made you differ, since the gifts were given by him; you have nothing therefore to boast of.' The former alternative seems to make better sense, but if it is accepted it must be recognized that later in the verse Paul's mind goes on to work in the sense suggested by the latter.

And what have you that you did not receive? Of course, nothing; Christian virtues and Christian wisdom are not self-made. **But if you received** (*καὶ ἔλαβες*; the *καί* underlines the verb) **it** (whatever gift you may have), **why do you boast as if you had not received it** (but possessed it in your own right)? Paul is thinking here of gifts received from God, not of instruction received from teachers; compare iii. 5. It is well known that this verse played a decisive part in the development of Augustine's thought about total depravity, the irresistibility of grace, and predestination. Augustine was not wrong, at least in the general drift of his inferences; but Paul was not writing with high theological intention of this kind. His motive was strictly practical, and this is rightly recognized by Calvin, who makes no attempt to wring out of the text more theology than is intended. 'The true basis of Christian humility is, on the one hand, not to be self-satisfied, for we know that we have no good in ourselves at all; and, on the other hand, if God has implanted any good in us, to be, for that reason, all the more indebted to his grace.'

From straightforward argumentation Paul turns to irony. Of course, the Corinthians are already prepared to sit in judgement on their apostles and put everyone in his place! Paul's words may well reflect what some were saying in Corinth in all serious-
8 ness. **Already you have reached satiety** (that is, you have not only received *a* gift from God; you have received all the gifts); **already you have become rich** (in a sense this was true, and Paul had himself said so at i. 5; but see the notes there); **apart from us** (that is, without the assistance of such nonentities as Paul and Apollos) **you have come to your kingdom.** It would be possible to take these sentences, or at least the first

two, as ironical questions, and this may be right; the change in manner after verse 7 however suggests that the questions have ceased. It may be that Paul is here using language that he (or the Corinthians before him) had borrowed from the Stoics; see Weiss, who quotes many passages (not only from Stoics), including for example Horace, *Epistles* I. i. 106 ff.: The wise man is only less than Jove, rich, free, honoured, handsome, and indeed a king of kings. But, though some connection of this kind is not impossible, the keyword is *already* (note also the aorist tenses, ἐπλουτήσατε, ἐβασιλεύσατε, which suggest not 'indecent haste' (Lightfoot) but eschatological fulfilment; cf. 2 Tim. ii. 18, and, for its possible connection with 1 Cor. xv, see pp. 347 f.), and thought and language are both eschatological. The Corinthians are behaving as if the age to come were already consummated, as if the saints had already taken over the kingdom (Dan. vii. 18); for them there is no 'not yet' to qualify the 'already' of realized eschatology. In this they are simply mistaken. 'They misinterpret Gospel and faith, and change both into *gnosis* and enthusiasm, by believing that the consummation is already realized' (Wendland). It is true that the Holy Spirit has already been given as an earnest (2 Cor. i. 22; v. 5) of their inheritance, but even so they must still live by faith, not by sight (2 Cor. v. 7). The End (1 Cor. xv. 24) has not yet arrived, and the time for fullness and wealth is not here (cf. Rev. iii. 17).

Certainly it would be a happy thing if this time had come. **Yes, and I wish you had come to your kingdom, that we too might be crowned with you.** 'Crowned' is a paraphrase; 'that we might reign with you' would however miss the tense of the verb (aorist, συμβασιλεύσωμεν), which suggests entering upon the kingdom. This (with its implication that the End had come, and that the reign of sin, suffering, and death was over) would indeed be a pleasant change for apostles like Paul. The next few verses provide a grim though triumphant sketch of what apostolic ministry was like; cf. 2 Cor. vi. 4-10. To sit on a throne
would be a new experience for Paul, **for** (this word introduces 9
the reason why Paul wishes the Corinthian boasting were based on fact) **I think God has put on us the apostles as last in the show, as men under sentence of death.** It is the last six words (ὡς ἐπιθανατίους, in Greek), not, as is sometimes said, the

verb (ἀπέδειξεν, though with this compare the Latin *edere*) that determine the metaphor (Weiss): the apostles (contrast xii. 28, *first apostles*) are presented by God to the world like the wretches brought on at the close of a display in the arena, men who are already condemned to death, and are sure to perish by combat with one another, or with gladiators, or with wild beasts (cf. xv. 32). This is indeed a position of privilege, though not when estimated by worldly standards, for it is the position of Christ himself: by their human fortunes as well as by their preaching the apostles placard Christ crucified (Gal. iii. 1) before the eyes of the world, **for we became a spectacle to the whole world, angels and men alike.** *Spectacle* (θέατρον) is normally the place (*theatre*) where spectacles are presented; there can be no doubt that its sense is slightly different here. The last three nouns in the sentence could be coordinated, 'to the world, and to angels, and to men', but they make better sense when taken as in the translation, which also does justice to the fact that only *world* has the definite article (Robertson, p. 788). *Angels* and *men* between them constitute the world's population. The Stoic also could think of himself as forming, in his struggle against destiny, a universal spectacle. Thus for example Seneca: Behold a worthy spectacle (*spectaculum*; cf. θέατρον), fit for God . . . to look at, a spectacle worthy of God, a brave man matched with evil fortune . . . I cannot think, I say, what nobler thing Jove has on earth than to look at Cato . . . (*De Providentia* ii. 9). There is, however, a profound difference in motive and intention, for the Stoic thinks with pride of the spectacle of courage and strength that he presents; Paul glories in his weakness and humiliation. See Sevenster, *Seneca*, pp. 115 f.

Paul proceeds with the contrast between himself and his
10 fellow-missionaries, and the self-satisfied Corinthians. **We are fools for Christ's sake** (cf. 2 Cor. v. 13), **you are sensible in Christ.** Throughout this verse Paul speaks *ad hominem*. The Corinthian letters themselves show that there is a sense in which it is right to be a *fool* (see iii. 18) and that it is also right to be sensible (x. 15); but here, notwithstanding the *for Christ's sake* and the balancing *in Christ*, it is clear that Paul means that he has become foolish by worldly standards in order to be wise in a Christian sense, and that the Corinthians' common sense comes

very near to worldly wisdom. At least, his foolishness gives him a very uncomfortable existence, whereas the Corinthians' common sense enables them to look down on him from a supposedly superior position. He continues in the same vein. **We are weak, you are strong. You are held in honour, we in dishonour.** Again, Paul knows well that in his weakness divine strength is manifested (2 Cor. xii. 9); it is in Christ that he is weak (2 Cor. xiii. 4), and this makes him formidable to his antagonists (2 Cor. x. 4), whereas the strength of the Corinthians is likely to evaporate in mere talk (iv. 19). If they are *held in honour* (ἔνδοξοι) and he is *held in dishonour* (ἄτιμοι; for this pair of contrasting words cf. xv. 43), the standard of reference is not God's. The irony of this verse is more subtle than that of verses 8, 9; and the more devastating.

Paul drops irony, and proceeds to give a plain account of the life of an apostle. Compare 2 Cor. iv. 7-12; vi. 4-10; xi. 23-33. It is a concrete expression (Bultmann, *Theology*, p. 346, E.T., 350)
of the sufferings of Christ, which he shares. **Up to this very** 11
moment: compare verse 13. These words may hint at a particularly acute period of suffering at the time of writing; xv. 32 might point to such a moment; cf. xvi. 9. More probably however Paul simply means to point out that the apostolic story has no happy ending in this age. No relief from labour or suffering is expected; contrast the *already* of verse 8. **We go hungry, thirsty, and naked**—on journeys, no doubt, through the depredations of robbers, and through sheer lack of supplies (cf. Phil. iv. 14). **We are cuffed,** not simply struck, but in an insulting manner (like slaves, 1 Pet. ii. 20, or a condemned man, Mark xiv. 65). **We are homeless:** the verb (ἀστατεῖν) is so used at Isa. lviii. 7 (Aquila). From the beginning of his missionary
activity Paul had no settled residence. **We toil, working with** 12
our own hands. This may be no more than a reference to Paul's practice (cf. Acts xviii. 3; xx. 34; 1 Cor. ix. 6, 12, 15-18; 2 Cor. xi. 9; xii. 13; 1 Thess. ii. 9; 2 Thess. iii. 8) of supporting himself by his craft without appealing to the generosity of his converts; if this is so, the participle *working* (ἐργαζόμενοι) simply expands the meaning of the verb *toil* (κοπιῶμεν). The latter word, however, in Paul's use often suggests specifically Christian work, the labour of preaching, of founding and caring for

churches (see xv. 10; xvi. 16; Rom. xvi. 6, 12; Gal. iv. 11; Phil. ii. 16; Col. i. 29; 1 Thess. v. 12). If this sense is accepted here the meaning will be: We do our Christian service, and at the same time for our support engage in secular work. A Greek would despise such behaviour in a teacher, and it is evident that the Corinthians shared this view; for the different rabbinic attitude see S.B. iii. 338.

Paul passes to moral relationships. His behaviour as he describes it recalls clearly the teaching of Jesus, especially in the Sermon on the Mount (Matt. v. 5, 10 ff., 44; Luke vi. 21 ff., 35), of which there are fairly clear echoes; Paul, however, characteristically gives no indication that he is aware that he is using the language of Jesus, or acting in obedience to his precepts. Com-
13 pare Rom. xii. 14; xiii. 1-10; and see *Romans*, p. 241. **When we are abused, we bless; when we are persecuted, we are forbearing; when we are slandered, we speak kindly.** All this is clear, apart from the last verb (παρακαλοῦμεν). This verb is used by Paul in two senses: (a) 'to exhort', weakening to 'to ask' (i. 10; iv. 16; xiv. 31; xvi. 12, 15; 2 Cor. ii. 8; v. 20; vi. 1; viii. 6; ix. 5; x. 1; xii. 8, 18—to give only Corinthian references); and (b) 'to comfort' (2 Cor. i. 4, 6; ii. 7; vii. 6, 7, 13; xiii. 11). 'We ask (pray to) God on their behalf' seems an impossible rendering; 2 Cor. ii. 7 is the closest parallel: we speak kindly to those who speak harshly. To sum up: **We have become as it were the world's scapegoats, the scum of the earth, to this day.** For the last three words see the note on verse 11. It is very difficult to assess the precise meaning, and especially the precise nuance, of the words *scapegoats* (περικαθάρματα) and *scum* (περίψημα). The former is built upon the root meaning 'to cleanse', and may refer simply to the filth cast out in the process of cleansing. The word (or a simple form of it—κάθαρμα; see parallels in Lucian given by Betz, p. 67, note 7) was also used however to denote the means by which a people or city might be morally or religiously cleansed, thus for a human sacrifice (details are given by Lietzmann); but since it became customary for the most worthless of men (cf. verse 9, *men under sentence of death*) to be used for this purpose the word in this connection also became a term of abuse; Epictetus (III. xxii. 78), for example, says that Priam 'begot fifty rascals (περικαθάρματα)'. Its one use

in the LXX (Prov. xxi. 18; Hebrew, *kopher*) suggests that it did not altogether lose its sense of sacrificial cleansing; *scapegoats* may perhaps convey the double meaning of despised persons who nevertheless perform a vicarious service for the community. This would accord with Paul's view of his mission (cf. Col. i. 24). *Scum* is a word with similar meaning, though the sense of sacrifice and atonement is perhaps not so easy to establish (it may occur at Tobit v. 19, but this is disputed); hence the rendering here. It should also be noted however that Ignatius uses the word in another sense. At *Ephesians* viii. 1 he uses it to say to his readers, 'I am your meanest, most devoted servant'; at xviii. 1, 'My spirit is an abject and devoted servant of the cross' (see Lightfoot's notes). Ignatius may have derived his use of the word from Paul, and it would suit the context of 1 Cor. iv if Paul were here to describe himself in his apostolic office as the servant of all men (taking *πάντων* as masculine); on the whole, however, though with some hesitation, we may retain *scum of the earth* (taking *πάντων* as neuter).

Whatever the precise sense of this verse may be, it is clear enough to permit an instructive comparison between Paul and his understanding of apostleship, and some of his contemporaries (see e.g. 2 Cor. xi. 20, and the commentary on 2 Corinthians),—and, it may be, some of his would-be successors in the Christian ministry. There can be little doubt which conception of ministry corresponds more closely to the Lord's command (e.g. Mark viii. 34 f.; x. 42-5; Matt. xxiii. 8-11).

12. iv. 14-21. THE CORINTHIANS AND THEIR APOSTLE; PAUL'S PLANS

(14) I am not writing these things with the intention of shaming you; no, I am admonishing[1] you as my dear children. (15) For if you have thousands of tutors in Christ, yet you have not many fathers; for it was I who in Christ Jesus begot you, through the Gospel. (16) I beg you, then,

[1] Reading not the participle (*νουθετῶν*, a smoother variant) but the finite verb, *νουθετῶ*, with P^{46} B D G and the majority of MSS.

be imitators of me. (17) For this[1] reason I have sent you Timothy, who is my dear and faithful child in the Lord. He will remind you of my ways in Christ Jesus, as I teach them everywhere in every church. (18) But some people have become puffed up, as if I were not coming to you; (19) but I will come to you, and quickly, if the Lord will, and then I shall know not how eloquent but how powerful these puffed up people are; (20) for the kingdom of God does not operate in eloquence but in power. (21) What would you like? Am I to come to you with a rod? or in love and a spirit of gentleness?

Paul brings to a close the long opening section of the epistle. He has dealt with a situation that had its roots in Corinthian preference for the wisdom of the world over against the wisdom of Christ, the loving, sacrificial wisdom that the world esteems foolish. Because of this wrong (but very natural and very common) choice of a human outlook on life the Corinthian Christians had developed an arrogant attitude in which (perhaps subconsciously) they patronized their missionaries and ministers and attempted to play them off against one another. Paul's answer is in a theology and a way of life both rooted in the cross. He has written with vehemence and power, and a Corinthian with a spark of humanity (not to say Christian conviction) left in him must have blushed to see held up before him, especially in chapter iv, the picture of himself in his conceited self-importance and the picture of Paul (and his apostolic colleagues), the despised, scorned, suffering, but undaunted servants of Christ, the church, and mankind. The blush will have done him good; yet this was not Paul's intention (except
14 perhaps in the indirect sense of 2 Cor. vii. 8). **I am not writing these things with the intention of shaming you.** Contrast vi. 5; xv. 34. The present participle (*ἐντρέπων*) is not easy to translate satisfactorily; the future would express purpose more naturally. We may think of the present as conative: I am not trying to shame you. For a somewhat similar use of the present participle compare 1 Pet. v. 12. **No, I am admonishing** (see

[1] Some MSS. have 'for this *very* (*αὐτό*) reason'; but it is better to omit *αὐτό*, with P[46] B C D G and many others. Cf. Zuntz, p. 63.

note 1, on p. 113) **you as my dear children.** To *admonish* (Rom. xv. 14; Col. i. 28; iii. 16; 1 Thess. v. 12, 14; 2 Thess. iii. 15) is characteristically the act of a father (cf. Wisdom xi. 10, to which Paul may allude here; Schlatter notes Josephus, *War* i. 481: Herod, as king, gave them some stern threats, as father, many admonitions, ἐνουθέτησεν): positive and creative correction, performed in love. The emphasis is on *as my dear children*, and Paul goes on to emphasize the parental relationship between
himself and the Corinthians. **For if you have thousands** 15
(literally, tens of thousands, μυρίους, but this is rhetoric, not arithmetic) **of tutors** (cf. Gal. iii. 24; the stress is on guardianship rather than instruction, and the word is not one of esteem) **in Christ** (that is, Christian leaders who inculcate Christian behaviour—and perhaps teach 'wisdom'), **yet** (ἀλλά; at least, at any rate: B.D. §448) **you have not many fathers.** In the construction of the protasis (ἐάν with the subjunctive) Robertson-Plummer (cf. Bachmann) see an element of futurity that suggests 'you will never have had but one father' for the apodosis. This perhaps reads too much into the Greek. The father-child relationship is unique, and corresponding to it is the relationship between the convert and the preacher responsible, under God, for his conversion. **For it was I** (the pronoun, ἐγώ, is emphatic; and in Greek ὑμᾶς stands next to it) **who in Christ Jesus begot you, through the Gospel.** It was Paul's missionary work that made them Christians. According to *Sanhedrin* 19 b, If a man teaches his neighbour's son Torah, Scripture counts it to him as if he had begotten him. Compare similar passages in S.B. iii. 340 f. Here, as in i. 14 ff., Paul is careful that this relationship shall not be taken too far. If he has begotten them (it is worth noting that Paul does not use the metaphor of regeneration; contrast e.g. John iii. 3, 5; Titus iii. 5), it is not in his own right but *in Christ Jesus* and *through the Gospel.* Christ is the agent and the Gospel the means by which men are brought to new life. Paul does not use the title 'father' for a Christian minister (cf. Matt. xxiii. 9), but keeps the metaphor for the special purpose of describing the relation between an evangelist and his converts, and introduces it for a
particular purpose: **I beg you, then** (οὖν: in view of the 16
relationship just described), **be imitators of me** as your father.

This is expected of a son. The theme of imitation recurs at xi. 1 (*Be imitators of me—as I am of Christ*); compare Gal. iv. 12; Phil. iii. 17; 1 Thess. i. 6; ii. 14; 2 Thess. iii. 7, 9. Behind it lies the fact drawn out above (p. 110) that the life of an apostle is a particularly clear reflection of Christ crucified. There is no reason why Christian men should not imitate Christ directly; but there is no reason to think that the Corinthians knew much about the life and behaviour of Christ, whereas Paul had lived for months under their eyes, and not merely the details but the whole pattern of his life (as depicted in this chapter) provided an immediate example. If the Corinthians were as ready as he to be humble servants of their church problems would disappear. But they need help.

17 **For this reason** (that is, because I wish you to imitate me, and wish to provide assistance for you in the task) **I have sent** (or, *am sending*) **you Timothy.** The verb (ἔπεμψα) is in the aorist tense, which normally (in the indicative) refers to action in past time, but is sometimes used in letters (the epistolary aorist) from the point of view of the recipient, so that from the point of view of the writer it is equivalent to a present. Timothy was sent either before the letter (this is probable since he is not mentioned at i. 1), or at the latest at the same time as the letter. This raises a difficulty in view of xvi. 10 f. Some see here an argument for the composite structure of 1 Corinthians; probably it is better to suppose that Timothy (who cannot on this view have been the bearer of the letter) was sent by a different route, with other visits to make. See Introduction, pp. 5, 16. It may be that *I have sent* means, 'I have sent word to Timothy, who has already set out for a different destination (Macedonia), that he should go on from there to visit you'. Timothy was a trusted member of Paul's staff, who had taken part in the evangelization of Corinth; see (in addition to 1 Corinthians) Rom. xvi. 21; 2 Cor. i. 1, 19; Phil. i. 1; ii. 19; Col. i. 1; 1 Thess. i. 1; iii. 2, 6; 2 Thess. i. 1; Philem. 1; also Acts xvi. 1; xvii. 14, 15; xviii. 5; xix. 22; xx. 4; and Heb. xiii. 23. The two epistles to Timothy bear witness to the continuing tradition, which linked his name with Paul's. In the present passage he is commended as Paul's **dear and faithful child in the Lord;** that is, he is a convert of Paul's (see above, and cf. Philem. 10), he has stood by the faith

he adopted, and has earned Paul's affectionate regard. He is therefore fitted for the purpose Paul has in mind: **He will remind you** (since you appear to have forgotten; perhaps we should connect with the previous sentence and translate, *I have sent Timothy* . . . to remind you, but ὅς and the future indicative as a final construction is not common in Greek; see however Robertson, pp. 960, 989) **of my ways in Christ Jesus, as I teach them everywhere in every church.** For the word *church* see the notes on i. 2. In the present context it must refer to local assemblies of Christians, but *every church* shows a sense of the interdependence and unity of all such local assemblies. Paul's *ways in Christ Jesus* are moral standards, expressed to some extent in recognized patterns of behaviour (cf. vii. 17; xii. 31; xiv. 33; 2 Thess. ii. 15), which can be taught. The word *way* may suggest Paul's Jewish, rabbinic background (cf. the word *halakah*); it seldom has a moral significance in Greek. This verse may indirectly bear witness to the love of novelty and forced originality, and the waywardness of the Corinthian church.

At verse 14 Paul began to moderate his tone towards his readers; he did not wish to humiliate them, only to see that they were soundly instructed in Christian principles. When however he recalls the actual (though not the universal) state of the Corinthian church he feels obliged to end his paragraph on a
firmer note. **But some people have become puffed up** (cf. 18
iv. 6; a characteristic word of this epistle, as the fact was characteristic of Corinth), **as if I were not coming to you** (cf. 2 Cor. x. 14). It is evident that, during his ministry in Corinth, Paul had kept his hand on the development of the church, and, against pressure, had prevented some of its members from running wild—not from giving up their faith, but from exercising the freedom it gave them in unrestrained fashion. When his back was turned, their freedom became licence; in his absence they became so used to pleasing themselves without restraint that they overlooked the possibility of his return. They were
masters of the situation now. **But** they were mistaken; **I will** 19
come to you, and quickly, if the Lord will. In xvi. 5-9 Paul explains why his coming to Corinth must be delayed. This contradiction, like that in regard to Timothy (iv. 17; xvi. 10 f.) has led some to think that the two passages cannot originally have

belonged to the same letter (see Introduction, pp. 12-17). This is not a necessary conclusion. This epistle may well have taken some time to write, and there may have been a change of plan (but no revision of the text) between the writing of chapter iv and chapter xvi; more important, there is a completely different motivation in the two chapters. In chapter xvi, Paul is setting out something of a timetable; in chapter iv he writes heatedly, Anyone would think I was never going to appear in Corinth again; but I shall be there, and sooner perhaps than you think. Even so, it may be noted, his plans are subject to the Lord's will; compare xvi. 7; Jas. iv. 15. They were subject to many variations. Phrases such as *if the Lord will* were widely used, not only by Jews and Christians.

Paul, then, plans another visit to Corinth; **and then I shall know not how eloquent but how powerful these puffed up people are** (literally, ... *not the word but the power of* ...; for the contrast of λόγος and δύναμις see ii. 4, 13; cf. 2 Cor. x. 5). There was a good deal of talking in Corinth (cf. i. 5, and the note); much of it amounted to little. In fact, though, at a later stage the situation got so far out of hand that a visit by Paul proved sorrowful and ineffective; see Introduction, p. 5. Their
20 loud words, however, are insignificant; **for the kingdom of God does not operate** (no verb is expressed in Greek; *is* would be the natural supplement, but seems tame in English) **in eloquence but in power.** *The kingdom of God* is an expression much less common in Paul than in the synoptic gospels; see the note on xv. 24. It is always an eschatological concept (though sometimes brought forward into the present), and the *power* with which it works is the power of the Holy Spirit (cf. Rom. xiv. 17), by which God's purpose is put into effect and the future anticipated in the present. In contrast, *eloquence* (λόγος) is often though not always the human art of speech; it can however be the vehicle of the power of the Spirit (see ii. 4; xii. 8). It is implied that the claim of iv. 8 may be little more than empty talk.

It is for the Corinthians to decide. Paul will certainly (if God wills) visit them. Is it to be a visit in which the mutual confidence of father and children is expressed in mutual love, or one in which the father must punish and discipline his children

because they have disgraced the family? **What would you like?** 21
Am I to come to you with a rod? or in love and a spirit of gentleness? (cf. Gal. vi. 1). Certainly, if Paul comes armed with (ἐν and the dative; possibly but not necessarily a Semitism; M. i. 12; ii. 23) *a rod*, he will nevertheless come *in love*, for love must sometimes wield a rod. The question is whether love is to be expressed in gentleness or in violence, and this will depend not on Paul's mood but on the Corinthian response to his admonition (verse 14). The antithesis, though like that of verse 14 (where shaming and admonishing are not mutually exclusive) it is not quite logical, is clear enough.

(b) FORNICATION

13. v. 1-13. FORNICATION INSIDE AND OUTSIDE THE CHURCH

(1) There is actually reported to be fornication among you, and such fornication as is not practised even among the Gentiles, so that one is living with his father's wife. (2) And are you in these circumstances puffed up? Did you not rather go into mourning, that he who had committed this deed might be taken away from you? (3) For, as far as I am concerned, absent in body as I am, but present in spirit, I have already reached my decision, as if I were present, in regard to the man who has thus done this thing. (4) When you have been gathered together, with my spirit, in the name of the Lord Jesus, we should, with the power of our Lord Jesus, (5) hand over such a man as this to Satan for the destruction of his flesh, in order that his spirit may be saved in the day of the Lord.

(6) No, this boasting of yours is no good thing. Do you not know that a little leaven leavens the whole lump of dough? (7) Purge out the old leaven, that you may be a fresh lump of dough—as indeed you are unleavened; for besides, our Passover lamb, Christ, has already been sacrificed. (8) So let us celebrate the feast, not with old

leaven, not with the leaven of malice and wickedness, but with unleavened loaves of sincerity and truth.

(9) I wrote to you in my letter that you should not mix with people guilty of fornication—(10) not in the absolute sense that you should avoid contact with the fornicators of this world, or the rapacious and thieves, or idolaters, since then you would have to come out of the world. (11) No: what I now write to you is that you should not mix with anyone known as a Christian brother who is a fornicator, or rapacious man, or idolater, or abusive man, or drunkard, or robber; with such a man you ought not even to eat. (12) For what business is it of mine to judge those who are outside? Do not you yourselves judge those who are inside?[1] (13) And those who are outside God will judge. Exclude the wicked man from your company.

The Corinthians' tendency to the divisive pursuit of high-flown but essentially worldly wisdom was perhaps the most fundamental and significant expression of their arrogance before God and self-opinionatedness, the quality which Paul describes as being 'puffed up'. This could, however, find other expressions (there is an important parallel in second-century gnosticism), of which one was laxness in regard to moral questions, and in the following paragraph Paul proceeds to deal not simply with a case of fornication but with the Corinthian reaction to it, which had been marked by levity and arrogance and was perhaps as blameworthy as the deed itself. It may be that it is in this reaction that we should see the enthusiastic antinomianism that Schlatter finds in the fornication. The paragraph includes, allusively, a reference to the grounds for moral purity, and also instructions in regard to church discipline. In fact, 'the instruction about the limits of Christian freedom extends from v. 1 to xi. 34' (Schlatter).

1 **There is actually** (this appears to be a late development of meaning for ὅλως (see L.S. *s.v.* III 4), but makes good sense here; Weiss, Héring, and others, take it to mean *universally, everywhere*—an equivalent to ἐν ὅλῳ τῷ κόσμῳ) **reported to be**

[1] P46 (alone) has, *Judge those who are within* (ἔσωθεν, not ἔσω), *yourselves.* This can hardly be anything but a free paraphrase.

fornication among you (taking ἐν ὑμῖν with πορνεία; grammatically it could be taken with ἀκούεται (Lightfoot), but this makes inferior sense). Paul's word (πορνεία) means, if strictly taken, prostitution, or traffic with prostitutes; in the New Testament however it is regularly used for unchastity and sexual irregularity of almost any kind. Its meaning here is defined by the following sentence. It is **such fornication as is not practised** (no verb is expressed; late MSS., borrowing from Eph. v. 3, have 'is not mentioned') **even among the Gentiles, so that one is living with his father's wife.** The sentence is awkward because *such* (τοιαύτη) is followed first by a relative (ἥτις), and then also by a conjunction (ὥστε). Paul does not call the offence adultery, so that we may probably infer either that the offender's father was not living, or that he had divorced his wife; he does not describe it as incest, so that the woman was probably the offender's stepmother. Nothing more is said of her; she was probably not a Christian; compare verses 12, 13. The practice is forbidden in Lev. xviii. 8; xx. 11 (cf. *Sanhedrin* vii. 4), and Paul adds that it was not to be found among the Gentiles, evidently meaning not that no Gentile had ever committed it, but that the Gentiles themselves condemned it. This is true; thus Lightfoot quotes Cicero, *Pro Cluentio* v. 14: *nubit genero socrus . . . O mulieris scelus incredibile, et praeter hanc unam . . . inauditum.* Compare Gaius, *Institutes* i. 63: *Item amitam et materteram uxorem ducere non licet. Item eam quae mihi quondam socrus aut nurus aut privigna aut noverca fuit.* It is, however, possible that Paul is also alluding to the so-called Noachian decrees, taken by the Rabbis to express the minimum divine requirements laid upon non-Jews. There was a difference of opinion on the question whether, under the Noachian decrees, the marriage of a proselyte with a widowed step-mother was permissible. Evidently Paul (like Akiba) condemned the practice (for details of Jewish opinion see Daube, p. 113; also S.B. iii. 353-8). But it is not certain, and Paul certainly does not say, that the point at issue was whether conversion, becoming a Christian 'proselyte', set a man free to have sexual relations with a woman who stood in what would otherwise be a forbidden relationship with him; the sin may have arisen directly out of Corinthian libertinism (cf. iv. 6). On the question of the

Noachian decrees and Paul's use of them see *Adam*, pp. 23-6. The tense of Paul's verb (ἔχειν, present infinitive) shows that the case is one of marriage or concubinage, not of a single incident. This inference is not contradicted by the aorists of verses 2, 3, which are constative, summing up the affair as a whole.

To Paul, the relationship was inexcusable; not so, however,
2 to the Corinthians. **Are you** (καὶ ὑμεῖς, emphatic) **in these circumstances puffed up?** Paul's words do not necessarily imply that the Corinthians were *puffed up* simply in regard to the act of fornication, proud that it should have happened; he may refer to their general state of inflation, a bubble that this pin at least should have pricked. But in any case the Corinthians' arrogance was sufficient to carry them over, if not actually to evoke, the fornication Paul describes. It could be regarded as an example of the freedom (cf. vi. 12; x. 23) of which they were proud. They were now spiritual persons, and what they did with their bodies was no longer significant, except in so far as it could demonstrate how completely they had transcended the old moral restrictions of conventional religious life, Jewish and pagan alike. Their reaction could not have been more mistaken. **Did you not rather go into mourning** (to bring out the aorist tense, ἐπενθήσατε)**, that he who had committed this deed might be taken away from you** (literally, *out of your midst*, possibly a Latinism—B.D. §5)? An alternative translation (according to M. iii. 95 the only one that makes good sense) would place the question mark after *mourning*, and continue, Let him who committed the deed be taken away from you (imperatival ἵνα). This way of construing the sentence corresponds with the instructions Paul gives in the following verses; it may be right. The construction involved is however less common in the New Testament than is sometimes supposed (see Moule, pp. 144 f.), and the sentence as translated here also makes good sense if we may understand a natural, and characteristically Pauline, ellipse: *Did you not rather go into mourning*, and show the sincerity of your mourning by taking the necessary action in order *that he that had committed this deed might be taken away . . .?*

It has been pointed out (e.g. by S. E. Johnson, in *The Scrolls and the New Testament* (1958), ed. K. Stendahl, p. 139) that this removal of the erring member has a parallel in the discipline of the Qumran community (1 QS v. 26–vi. 1), but the point is not of great importance. Any community inculcating moral standards (such as the primitive church and the Qumran sect) is bound to recognize a degree beyond which transgression of its code becomes intolerable because destructive of the foundations on which the community itself rests, so that exclusion becomes necessary. There may well have been some sort of relationship between primitive Christianity and the Qumran sect, but it cannot be proved by generalizations of this kind. What is important is Paul's insistence that the circumstances call not for arrogance but for lamentation. Sin can and does invade the church, but this, when it happens, is something unnatural, which can only be mourned.

The next three verses are both difficult and important. There are many possible variations in translation (not all of which can be noted here); the precise significance of some of Paul's simplest words is in dispute; and the bearing of the whole on Paul's understanding of Christian life and communal discipline calls for evaluation.

For (bringing out the grounds on which the preceding clause 3
rests), **as far as I am concerned** (the sentence opens with a very emphatic ἐγὼ μέν, corresponding to the ὑμεῖς of verse 2—*you* may be puffed up, but *I* take a completely different view), **absent in body as I am, but present in spirit, I have already reached my decision, as if I were present.** The meaning of *absent in body* is clear enough: Paul's physical body is not in Corinth but in some other place (presumably Ephesus; see Introduction, p. 5). But what does *present in spirit* (παρὼν δὲ τῷ πνεύματι) mean? In Paul's usage 'spirit' more often than not refers to the Spirit of God, and the presence of the article might seem to support the view that this is intended here; but it is more probable, in view of the contrast with 'body' (which also has the article) that Paul is using the word in a 'quite popular sense' (Weiss), that is, psychologically rather than theologically. Compare Col. ii. 5. Paul refers to his thoughts, and his concern for the Corinthian church; certainly it is true that these operate in the sphere of the Holy Spirit, but this is not the primary thought.

Paul is well informed about the situation, and therefore, *as if* he *were* actually *present*, he has *reached* his *decision*. This takes the verb (κέκρικα) in an absolute sense which requires no direct object; alternatively, it may be given the meaning 'judge' (I have already judged . . .), the next words—**the man who has thus** (in the circumstances described) **done this thing**—being taken as the direct object. This would however leave the infinitive (παραδοῦναι) of verse 5 without any connection in the sentence, and should not be preferred. Paul has reached a decision, given judgement, *in the case of* the offender, namely that we should hand over . . .

Paul thus knows his own mind quite clearly, and does not
hestitate to declare it. This does not mean however that he
intends to impose it on the church (cf. iv. 1, and the notes on
chapter iv; 2 Cor. i. 24). Before action is taken certain conditions
4 must be fulfilled. **When you have been gathered together**
(the verb, συνάγειν, became a technical term for the meeting of
the Christian assembly), **with my spirit, in the name of the**
Lord Jesus, we should, with the power of our Lord Jesus,
5 **hand over** (παραδοῦναι; this infinitive is taken to be dependent
on κέκρικα in the original; in the translation the sentences are
separated for convenience and clarity) **such a man as this to**
Satan (cf. 1 Tim. i. 19 f.). Paul envisages a church meeting in
Corinth. The local members will naturally be present. He cannot himself be present in the same sense, but he can (as he said in verse 3) be present in spirit; that is (and this confirms the interpretation of verse 3: *spirit* is in this context an aspect of Paul's personality), not his body but his spirit will be in their meeting. He will make his contribution, as the Corinthians reflect on what they remember of his convictions, character, and ways, and on what they know of his mind in the present matter. It goes without saying that the assembly, being a Christian body, will meet *in the name of the Lord Jesus*—under his authority, and with the intention of acting in obedience to him. Under these circumstances the act contemplated will be the act of the whole church, not of the apostle only. Later the Corinthian church was to encounter false apostles (2 Cor. xi. 13) who would act in a different way, with a view to enforcing their own will. However influential, these men could not act, as Paul and

an obedient church could act, *with the power of our Lord Jesus.* These words do not simply reduplicate *in the name of the Lord Jesus*, but refer to the supernatural power granted to the obedient people of God. 'The name' may sometimes have a similar meaning (e.g. in cures and exorcisms, as in Acts iii. 6), but here, and in Paul's writings generally, it is used differently. Bultmann (*Theology*, p. 126, E.T., 126 f.) suggests that the *power* operates through the invocation of the *name*; this may be so, if the *name* is understood in the fundamentally moral sense referred to above. The phrase *with the power* . . . is to be taken adverbially with *hand over*; *with* (σύν) is sometimes used of the instrument or means, but in the present phrase it is more personal, and means 'with the help of' (as in for example σὺν θεῷ, with God's help, or blessing; the existence of this Greek idiom makes it unnecessary to resort to the magical contexts in which also σύν is used—Robertson, p. 628; M.M., *s.v.*).

It seems best to take the sentence in this way—assembled in the name, to hand over with the power; but other arrangements have been proposed (Allo has a very full account): (a) assembled in the name and with the power, to hand over; (b) assembled, to hand over in the name and with the power; and (c) assembled with the power, to hand over in the name. For (c) it may be said that *with* goes naturally with *assembled* (σύν, with συναχθέντων); but it forces the order of the words. There is little to be said for (a) and (b), and the rendering given here may be accepted with confidence. It should be noted that the power of the Lord Jesus lies behind the act of the assembled church. Paul does not claim to exercise it on his own, but urges the community (as a whole, not its leaders, or presidents, προϊστάμενοι, as Allo suggests) to act. He has no doubt what it ought to do, or of his place in its counsels, but he does not seek to by-pass it. He 'is obviously striving to establish the Church as the real bearer of responsibility' (Schweizer, 23e).

Such a man as this (cf. 2 Cor. ii. 6, 7) simply restates, in Pauline fashion, the object of 'to hand over', earlier anticipated at *the man who has thus done this thing*. The man is to be handed over to Satan **for the destruction of his flesh, in order that his spirit may be saved in the day of the Lord,** that is, at the last day, the day of judgement. From the rest of the chapter (especially verses 7, 13) it seems that the practical step Paul wished the Corinthian church to take was to exclude the offender from their society, to excommunicate him (though this word must not be taken in an anachronistic way). This was a proceeding already known to Judaism; see a very full note in Weiss. Its effects in its new Christian setting were even more damaging than they had been thought to be in the old, for the new community rested upon the preliminary defeat of Satan by Jesus (see xv. 24-7; Phil. ii. 10 f.; Col. ii. 15). To be excluded from the sphere in which Christ's work was operative was to be thrust back into that in which Satan still exercised authority. 'While Christ reigns within, so Satan reigns outside, the Church' (Calvin). This authority, however, was limited. If a man was handed over to Satan it was not that Satan might have his way with him, but with a view to his ultimate salvation; Satan in fact was being used as a tool in the interests of Christ and the church. There is thus, as well as a real verbal parallel, a substantial difference in the papyrus quotation adduced by Deissmann (*Light from the Ancient East* (1910), p. 304): Daemon of the dead . . ., I deliver (παραδίδωμι) to thee so-and-so, in order that (ὅπως) . . . (*London Magical Papyrus* 46. 334 ff. = K. Preisendanz, *Papyri Graecae Magicae* i, p. 192). Satan's power, though limited, was nevertheless real. He would destroy the offender's *flesh*. This does not mean only the flesh as a source of moral evil (see e.g. Rom. vii. 5, and *Romans*, p. 137), but the physical flesh itself, a realm in which Paul himself received Satan's attentions (2 Cor. xii. 7). Suffering at least is meant (cf. Acts xiii. 11), probably death (cf. Acts v. 5, 10; also 1 Cor. xi. 30). This dreadful process is intended (ἵνα, denoting purpose) to lead to the salvation of the man's spirit (see verses 3, 4 for this use of πνεῦμα to denote the human spirit, the essential, inward self—it is not Paul's customary use, but it is too common for us necessarily to associate it with Qumran). It is not clear how the destruction of the physical side of man's nature can effect the salvation of the immaterial side. Suffering may indeed be remedial, but nothing in the context suggests this thought. In Judaism, death was sometimes thought of as the means of atonement for sins not dealt with by the Day of Atonement (see e.g. *Sanhedrin* vi. 2, where even the criminal about to be executed is instructed to say, May my death be an atonement for all my sins), but for Paul atonement is not through our death, but through Christ's. The thought may be that the devil must be given his due, but can claim no more; if he has the flesh he has no right to the spirit, even of the sinner. The thought may be simply that of iii. 15: the man's essential self will be saved with the loss not only of his work but of his flesh.

Paul's first concern is thus for the salvation of the erring member. He is also concerned for the purity of the church as a whole. This is another reason for excommunication (see Calvin, *Institutes* IV. xii. 5, where the matter is dealt with more clearly than in his commentary). He comes to this point by way of another reference (cf. verse 2, φυσιοῦσθαι) to Corinthian arrogance. **No, this boasting of yours is no good thing;** not 6
simply because a church with a rotten spot in its structure was in too perilous a position to boast, but because even the good things the church enjoyed were gifts which it had received (iv. 7), and thus no ground for boasting. The present situation, however, was particularly dangerous, and a church exposed to corruption would do well to sing in a lower key. **Do you not know** (implying that they certainly ought to know) **that a little** (probably the Corinthians had minimized the affair) **leaven** (*yeast*, ζύμη, but the old word must be used because *yeast* provides no equivalents for 'to leaven' and 'unleavened') **leavens the whole lump of dough?** The same proverb is used at Gal. v. 9. In Jewish circles leaven was a natural image for evil (the comparison in Matt. xiii. 33; Luke xiii. 20 f. with something good is exceptional) because all leaven (*ḥameṣ*, fermenting material) had to be removed from the house before the Passover could be celebrated. Paul (conceivably using a saying attributed in *Orlah* ii. 12 to his teacher Rabban Gamaliel the Elder—see Schoeps, *Paulus*, p. 27, note 3; E.T., p. 37, note 3) employs the metaphor in several ways. The first is evident enough—a small quantity of yeast is sufficient to impregnate a whole lump of dough, and one corrupt member is sufficient to corrupt a whole church. The church must therefore exercise discipline in order to maintain its purity; in terms of the metaphor, **Purge out the old leaven** (that is, the leaven used in the 7
period before Passover; after the feast of Unleavened Bread new

leaven would be introduced into the house), **that you may be a fresh lump of dough,** without leaven. Here a direct imperative is addressed to the church: evil influences must be banished. But the imperative rests upon an indicative: **as indeed you are unleavened** (or perhaps the adjective is used as a substantive: *you are unleavened loaves*). This combination of imperative and indicative is the fundamental structure of Paul's ethical thought (see especially Rom. vi. 11-14, 19, and the comment on it; also Col. ii. 20–iii. 14). The people of God have in fact been freed from sin; because this is so, they must now avoid sin and live in obedience to God's command. The imperative is unthinkable without the indicative, which makes the otherwise impossible obedience possible; the indicative is emasculated if the imperative, which gives it moral bite, is wanting.

Paul continues: **for besides, our Passover lamb, Christ, has already been sacrificed.** This clause gives an additional reason (*καὶ γάρ*) for purging out the old leaven, though it is not wrong to see in it also the ground for the statement that *you are unleavened*. The analogy with the Jewish Passover is not perfect, for in ordinary Jewish practice it would have been necessary to dispose of the leaven before the feast could take place. In the Christian application, God has been beforehand in providing the lamb for sacrifice (Gen. xxii. 8; John i. 29), and it remains for men to catch up with the initiative that he has taken. It is also true that the sacrificial death of Christ is the only means by which sin can be removed. Paul nowhere works out in detail a theory of Christ's sacrifice, but as in Rom. iii. 25 he alludes to one great Jewish festival (the Day of Atonement), so here he alludes to another. The great theme of Passover was deliverance: the deliverance from Egypt was commemorated, deliverance was enjoyed as a fact in the present, and deliverance was hoped for in the future. Christ as the Lamb of God summed up God's action for the deliverance of his people; and the context suggests (though much less explicitly than John i. 29) that he delivered them by bearing for them the burden of their guilt and thus removing their sin. For discussion of the rationale of this process we must look ahead to other passages, especially to 2 Cor. v. 21. The fact that Paul could speak of Christ as the

Passover lamb does not imply that (with John, and against the synoptic gospels, which date the crucifixion a day later) he believed Jesus to have died on Nisan 14, at the time when the Jewish lambs were being slaughtered in the Temple (though it is consistent with this belief). Acceptance of Jesus as the Lamb of God is independent of chronology; and the idea could have grown out of the belief that the Lord's Supper is the new, Christian Passover—though this belief in turn is independent of the synoptic identification of the Last Supper with the Passover meal.

The Passover theme is now developed in a new direction: **So** 8
let us celebrate the feast (Lightfoot renders 'Let us keep perpetual feast', but the context shows that the stress lies not on the continuous tense of the verb, ἑορτάζωμεν, but on its adverbial accompaniment), **not with old leaven, not** (literally *and not*, but the new description of the leaven is parallel, not additional, to *old*) **with the leaven of malice and wickedness, but with unleavened loaves of sincerity and truth.** Since Christ's sacrifice of himself, Christians live in the festival he founded, and Christian life consists in thanksgiving to God for his mighty act of love and deliverance, thanksgiving expressed at least as much in action as in speech. If however this is to be taken seriously it means that Christians must not only rejoice (which, it appears, the Corinthians were willing to do) but must also observe suitable paschal purity, banishing leaven in its transferred, moral, sense as the Jews at Passover season banished leaven from their houses. It is evident not only that leaven lingered in the household of faith at Corinth, but also that some Corinthians at least were happy that it should do so. This to Paul was intolerable. *Malice and wickedness* (cf. Rom. i. 29) must be replaced by *sincerity and truth.*

Paul's purpose in using this paschal imagery is clear: the sacrifice has been offered, potentially Christians are participating in a feast which involves perfect purity of character and conduct, and they must make every effort to realize this potentiality. This statement of fact, and this exhortation, are perfectly apt to the situation disclosed in this chapter. But why does Paul cast his argument in this form? It has often been suggested, and may well be true, that he does so because he was writing at

Passover time. If we may assume the unity of 1 Corinthians (see Introduction, pp. 12-17), he was writing in Ephesus (xvi. 8), and intended to stay on there some little while, until the feast of Pentecost. It is not unreasonable to reckon back seven or eight weeks, and suppose that Paul was at the time of writing engaged in preparations for, or in the celebration of, Passover, and was thereby prompted to use the figure of the new Passover. *Our Passover has already been sacrificed* refers, however, to the historical event of the crucifixion, not to a repeated liturgical representation of this (Lietzmann). It is hardly more probable that (as Héring thinks) there is in *Let us keep the feast* an allusion to the Lord's Supper. Paul's use of Old Testament and Jewish material seems to be confined to Passover; there is no good reason to see here (as Schoeps, *Paulus*, pp. 144-52 (E.T., 141-9), does) a reference to the 'Binding of Isaac' (cf. *Adam*, pp. 26-30).

Paul now begins to work back to affairs at Corinth, which need firm and practical treatment. There is however a point to clear up on the way: this was not Paul's first letter to Corinth, or his first attempt to deal with the problem of immorality, and his previous letter had been misunderstood. 'We may suspect that the misunderstanding was in part deliberate—that they had raised the objection of the impossibility of being entirely separate from evil to excuse themselves from making a serious attempt to deal with evil' (Harris). For a further account of Paul's correspondence with Corinth, and attempts to find the
9 'lost letter', see the Introduction, pp. 12-17. **I wrote to you**
in my letter (the last three words determine that ἔγραψα is a genuine past tense, *I wrote*, not an epistolary aorist, *I am writing*) **that you should not mix with people guilty of fornication**—in the broad sense explained above in the note on verse 1. In the sense in which Paul (as we shall see) meant this injunction he had already given a special application of it in the current letter when he advised the excommunication of the offender. But it had been taken in another sense, which Paul
10 states, and immediately corrects: **Not in the absolute sense**
(πάντως; cf. Rom. iii. 9) **that you should avoid contact with the fornicators of this world,** those who, never having become Christians, continue unchecked to follow the lusts which are natural when life is thought to be confined to the here and

now (cf. xv. 32; for *this world* cf. e.g. iii. 19). For full measure Paul adds (possibly quoting from the earlier letter) other classes of sinner: **the rapacious** (cf. Rom. i. 29, and the note) **and thieves, or idolaters.** For the whole list compare vi. 9 f., and see the notes there. Clearly Paul can have given no such impossible injunction, **since then** (*ἐπεί*, 'otherwise', as at vii. 14; xiv. 16; xv. 29; Rom. iii. 6; xi. 6, 22) **you would have to come out of the world** (to which the fornicators belonged). Such offenders were too numerous to avoid in Corinth (see Introduction, pp. 2 f.), and it seems unthinkable to Paul that Christians should withdraw from common life into monastic or conventual solitude, though this practice was by no means unknown in the ancient world. He implies also the theological truth that Christians cannot (even if they retire to solitude or religious community life) escape this world; decisive as the work of Jesus is, it does not mean that the old age has now completely passed and the new fully come. See xv. 25 f. If the Corinthians thought
he had said this, they had mistaken his meaning. **No: what I** 11
now write (*νῦν ἔγραψα*, probably epistolary aorist; contrast verse 9; alternatively, *but in fact what I wrote was* . . ., or (M. iii. 73) the reference is 'to an earlier place in the same letter') **to you is that you should not mix with anyone known as a Christian brother** (*ὀνομαζόμενος*: he bears the *name* of Christian but by his behaviour shows that in truth he is one no more—Weiss) **who is a fornicator, or rapacious man, or idolater, or abusive man** (*λοίδορος*, added to the previous list; such people were not uncommon in Greek public life; Apollonius of Tyana encountered one in Bassus of Corinth; see Philostratus, *Life of Apollonius* iv. 26, using the cognates *λοιδορεῖσθαι* and *λοιδορία*—Bassus also taught a bogus wisdom, *σοφία*), **or drunkard, or robber; with such a man you ought not even to eat.** Christians must take the world as they find it, as Jesus himself had done, eating freely with publicans and sinners (e.g. Mark ii. 15). No more for them than for him should this social freedom deny prophetic freedom to criticize and when necessary to condemn; but criticism is not to be exercised by the easy device of withdrawal. What happens in the church itself, however, is another matter, and here it is essential that purity should be sought. Paul uses simply the word *brother* (as e.g.

at i. 1); he means one who is recognized as a member of the church, even though events show him to be unworthy. If such a man falls into open sin he must, in his own interests (see above, verse 5) as well as in those of the church, be separated from the main body. The only ground given for this exclusion from Christian fellowship is that of moral failure. His former companions should not mix with him, and Paul adds the particular example that they should not eat with him. This prohibition will evidently include (though it will not be confined to) his exclusion from the church's common meal (cf. Gal. ii. 12; and see x. 16-21; xi. 17-34), as well as from private entertainment. It is implied that Christians retained their freedom to eat with non-Christians, and this will at least sometimes have meant the eating of foods sacrificed to idols; see the discussion of this matter in chapters viii and x.

Strict discipline within the church; complete freedom of association outside it. This twofold principle is based as follows.

12 **For what business is it of mine to judge those who are outside** (the church)? On the construction see B.D. §299; Robertson, p. 736; and compare Epictetus II. xvii. 14; III. xxii. 66. For *those who are outside* in rabbinic usage see S.B. iii. 362. The statement as it stands is clear enough, and is consistent with Paul's explanation that he does not require the church to isolate itself from non-Christians of bad character. Rather, judgement is God's prerogative, and when men undertake to sit in judgement on their neighbours they are prone to fall into their neighbours' sins (cf. Rom. ii. 1; xiv. 4, 10, 13). Difficulty arises when this verse is compared with vi. 2. There however the reference is to judgement at the time of the end; here Paul is dealing not with final judgement but with discipline, which by definition is limited to the community. Conversely, **Do not you yourselves** (emphatic) **judge those who are inside** (the church)? Both object and subject are important. Judging is directed inwards, and means not censoriousness but church discipline. This is a vital part of church life, and though the church cannot claim infallibility for its judgements it must in obedience to Christ condemn, and exclude from its midst, action that involves disobedience to Christ. The whole church in fact stands under this judgement; and the whole church is

judge—for Paul does not claim that he judges the church members. Responsibility for judgement is in the hands of the whole body of believers, not of a small group of ministerial authorities.

What then of the outsiders? **Those who are outside** (such 13
as, apparently, the woman of verse 1, who is not judged in this chapter) **God will judge,** presumably, that is, at the last day, whose verdict is not to be anticipated by men, and may indeed bring to the orthodox Christian a number of surprises (ix. 27; x. 12; Matt. vii. 22 f.). This (see above) is why no Christian, not even an apostle, has the right to judge those who stand outside the organized framework of the church. The verb translated *will judge* could be taken as a present tense, *judges*; the only difference between the two tenses (in the third person singular) lies in the accents, and these are not used in the oldest New Testament MSS. (κρινεῖ, future; κρίνει, present; the same problem occurs at Rom. iii. 6). It is possible to decide between the tenses only on the basis of the general sense of the passage. It makes good sense, and is true, to say that God judges the world here and now ('The verb is certainly to be accented as a present: it states the normal attribute of God'—Robertson-Plummer), but it makes perhaps better, and more Pauline (cf. Rom. ii. 5; cf. Acts xvii. 31), sense to say that he will judge it hereafter.

Finally Paul returns to emphasize once more what is the central point in the passage as a whole. Judgement of the outsider may safely be left to God, but the church must keep itself pure by excising corrupt members. **Exclude the wicked man** (probably the fornicator of verse 1; possibly a reference to the wicked in general; very improbably the Wicked One—Satan) **from your company.** These words are a quotation from Deut. xvii. 7; there are similar expressions in xix. 19; xxii. 21, 24; xxiv. 7. It is notable that wherever they occur in the Old Testament the verb is in the singular; here it is plural. This corresponds with what Paul has said throughout the paragraph; excommunication is not an apostolic prerogative; if it is to be exercised at all, it must be exercised by the whole community, in whose hands (under Christ) authority lies.

(c) LITIGATION

14. vi. 1-11. THERE SHOULD BE NO LITIGATION —OR GROUNDS FOR IT

(1) Does any of you dare, when he has a suit against his fellow, to go to law before the unrighteous, and not before the saints? (2) Or do you not know that the saints shall judge the world? And if it is by you that the world is judged, are you unworthy to sit in the lowest courts? (3) Do you not know that we shall judge angels, not to mention everyday affairs? (4) So, if you do have courts for everyday affairs, do you appoint as judges those who have no standing in the church? (5) I say this to your shame. Has it come to this, that there cannot be found among you one wise man, who can decide between his brothers, (6) but brother goes to law with brother, and that before unbelievers? (7) In fact it is already nothing but a failure on your part that you have lawsuits with one another. Why do you not rather allow yourselves to be wronged? Why do you not rather allow yourselves to be robbed? (8) But you wrong and rob, and your brothers at that.

(9) Or do you not know that unrighteous men shall not inherit the kingdom of God? Do not be misled. Fornicators, idolaters, adulterers, catamites, sodomites, (10) thieves, rapacious men, drunkards, abusive men, and robbers—none of these shall inherit the kingdom of God. (11) And that is what you were, some of you; but you were washed, you were sanctified, you were justified, in the name of the Lord Jesus Christ and in the Spirit of our God.

Paul has not finished with the theme of church discipline in regard to sexual life; see vi. 12 and chapter vii; but in v. 12 f. he had spoken of judgement, and this brings to his mind another feature of Corinthian life of which he had heard (perhaps by way of Chloe's household, i. 11; or through Stephanas and his colleagues, xvi. 17; hardly by letter, vii. 1). This must be treated at some point in his letter, and is appropriately introduced here. It appears that lawsuits between Christians have been brought before secular, pagan, courts. Such actions Paul deprecates on two grounds: (1) Christians ought to be able to settle their own disputes in their own courts (verses 1-6); (2) they ought not to have disputes at all (verses 7 f.).

Does any of you dare (a strong word; cf. Rom. v. 7; xv. 18; 1
Paul implies that to act in this way insults God and the church), **when he has a suit** (Paul uses a word often used in public affairs, πρᾶγμα) **against his fellow** (the word could mean any other person, but the context shows that a fellow-Christian is intended), **to go to law before the unrighteous, and not before the saints?** Neither *unrighteous* nor *saints* is a satisfactory translation; possibly 'non-Christians' and 'Christians' respectively would be preferable. By *unrighteous* Paul does not imply that the Roman courts were unjust; for his view of the Roman state and its magistrates see Rom. xiii. 1-7—and he had special reason for gratitude to Gallio's impartiality in Corinth (Acts xviii. 12-17); the word is to be taken not in a moral but in a religious sense—not justified, not rightly related with God through Christ. Similarly *saints* (cf. i. 2) has no necessary moral connotation; it refers to the people of God, who ought to be morally good, as God is, but often are not. The point is simply that cases that arise within the people of God should be kept there. This is partly (but not wholly, as the next verses show) a matter of not sending out the dirty linen; Christians inherited from Jews a desire to make a good impression on their heathen neighbours (for the importance of this as an ethical motive cf. x. 32, and see W. C. van Unnik, 'Die Rücksicht auf die Reaktion der Nicht-Christen als Motiv in der altchristlichen Paränese', in *Judentum-Urchristentum-Kirche, Festschrift für Joachim Jeremias* (1960), pp. 221-34; for the comparable attitude of the Qumran sect, who made full provision for legal processes within their own community, see M. Burrows, *The Dead Sea Scrolls* (1956), p. 235). T. W. Manson (*Studies*, p. 198) suggests that the point had been raised by the Jewish group in Corinth; Paul agrees with them, though he goes beyond them. It was the Jewish custom to settle disputes within the Jewish community (S.B. iii. 362 f.), and there were also Greek and Roman social

and religious groups who followed the same practice. A pity if Christians, with much stronger grounds (see below), could not do the same!

2 **Or do you not know** (that is, If you disagree with my initial proposition, can this possibly mean that you do not know) **that the saints** (cf. i. 2; as Heim points out, all Christians, not a special class of judges or rulers) **shall judge** (or, *judge*, present tense; there is the same ambiguity as at v. 13, but here verse 3 shows conclusively that the future is intended) **the world?** This follows awkwardly upon v. 12, where Paul disclaims the right to judge those who are outside the church. The explanation is that v. 12 refers to a censorious kind of criticism practised by church members in the present, whereas vi. 2 refers to the participation of the people of God in the judgement at the last day. This is referred to in many apocalypses (C. H. Dodd, *According to the Scriptures* (1952), p. 68, sees here a reference to Dan. vii. 22; cf. Wisd. iii. 7 f.; 1 Enoch i. 9, 38, and other passages; Jubilees xxiv. 29; see also Matt. xix. 28; Luke xxii. 30; Rev. xx. 4), but it is here given a new application by Paul. **And if it is by you** (literally, *among you*, ἐν ὑμῖν, recalling perhaps a technical use of the preposition, found in the papyri, *in your department*—see M. i. 103; but the usage, of courts and tribunals, is classical—see Lightfoot) **that the world is judged, are you unworthy to sit in the lowest courts?** A simple *a majori ad minus* argument: Christians have no right to plead their own (or their brethren's) unworthiness to judge such cases as can be brought before them in this world. The future assessors at the last judgement are already competent to deal with trials in this age.

3 **Do you not know that we shall judge angels, not to mention** (μήτι γε; see L.S. for the developing meaning of this word; also M. i. 240) **everyday affairs?** *Angels* as well as men will appear in God's court at the last day; the general category of angels, in Paul's usage, includes bad as well as good (e.g. 2 Cor. xii. 7, an angel of Satan). It must be considered doubtful whether Rom. xiii. 1 (see my note, and the references) means that angels are the true authority behind the state, but if this view is accepted it sharpens Paul's argument that Christians, who are to judge angels, ought not to submit themselves to secular courts, since these are under the authority of the angels

whom Christians are to judge. *Everyday affairs* means matters relating simply to the present life; in the next verse the adjective
qualifies the noun *courts*. **So, if you do have courts for every-** 4
day affairs (possibly, *cases concerning every day affairs*, but as just noted, the noun, *κριτήριον*, is that used in verse 2; it is unlikely to change its meaning so quickly; for *βιωτικὰ κριτήρια* see Bauer, under both words)**, do you appoint as judges** (literally, *cause to sit*) **those who have no standing in the church?** The object is perhaps not given sharply enough in the translation: 'those who count for nothing' might be better. The point is that a society consisting of potential judges in God's tribunal stultifies itself when it appears before even a Roman proconsul, who, whatever his legal training and experience, and natural virtue, stands outside the people of God. The verb *appoint as judges* (*καθίζετε*) has here been taken as indicative and interrogative. It is possible to take it as imperative. The sense would then be: If it is absolutely necessary to have suits dealing with everyday affairs, show your contempt for them by singling out the meanest and most despised members of the church and appointing them as judges. Though possible grammatically (and fitting *καθίζειν* better than the translation given since in the strictest sense it was not within the power of the church to *appoint* the secular judges of Corinth) this rendering cannot be accepted, for Paul does not speak in this slighting, or (taking the words differently) ironical, way even of the lowliest members of the church (the description in i. 26 is in a quite different vein), and Corinth was the last place in which he would have exposed himself to misunderstanding by doing so. Every Christian 'counts for something' in the church. There is nothing to suggest that the ironical description is being quoted from the puffed up members of the church. The next words confirm our
interpretation: **I say this to your shame:** it is to be hoped that 5
when you read what I say you will feel ashamed of yourselves and of your resort to heathen courts. Contrast iv. 14; Paul speaks more freely here because he is not personally involved (as an injured and neglected apostle). If it is right to take *appoint* as an imperative, and *those who have no standing* to mean insignificant Christians, the point will be: I do not say this with the intention that you should actually set up such

courts, but that you may be ashamed (so Allo; cf. Bachmann); but this is less probable.

Paul rubs in his complaint. **Has it come to this that there cannot be found** (οὕτως οὐκ ἔνι) **among you one wise man** (possibly an ironical reference to boasted Corinthian wisdom —cf. e.g. viii. 1; but Paul may have in mind the Jewish *ḥakam*, a scholar of lower grade than a rabbi, capable of acting as judge), **who can** (literally, *shall be able*, but this is Greek rather than English idiom) **decide between his brothers** (cf. i. 1, but
6 the word is specially significant here), **but brother goes to law with brother, and that before unbelievers?** There is much uncertainty in the latter part of this sentence, though the general drift is clear. Thus it would be possible to put a question mark after *brothers*, and begin a new sentence, which might be either a question or a statement, with *But brother goes to law*... The word rendered *decide* is not the simple verb 'to judge' (κρίνειν), but a compound (διακρίνειν); for the use of this verb compare iv. 7; xi. 29, 31; xiv. 29. It is doubtful whether much difference is intended in this passage; the compounded preposition (διά) is probably introduced because the following phrase suggests the making of a decision *between* two brothers, but here too there is difficulty since *his brothers* is a paraphrase rather than a translation of the Greek, which literally is *his brother* (singular). This does not make sense (but cf. Sirach xxv. 18; Rev. vii. 17). The text may be corrupt (so M. i. 99; not so Robertson, pp. 409, 648), or possibly Paul himself hurried on and left his sentence incomplete (cf. M. iii. 23 (following B.D. §139): the singular is 'less likely to be generic than a combined result of Semitic influence and abbreviation thereof'). There can be little doubt that the translation represents substantially the meaning Paul intended. A church has come to a pretty pass when its members believe that they are more likely to get justice from *unbelievers* than from their own brothers.

7 Paul now turns to an even more serious indictment. **In fact** (μὲν οὖν) **it is already** (ἤδη—before we get to the question where the case should be adjudicated) **nothing but** (ὅλως) **a failure** (or *defeat*, in the sense of moral defeat—ἥττημα; 'From the truest Christian standpoint you have already lost the case by bringing it to the courts at all'—Harris) **on your part that you have**

lawsuits (not the word of verse 1: πρᾶγμα there, κρίμα here; the former is in itself more general, but given a legal determination by the context, the latter is necessarily forensic) **with one another.** The existence of contention that calls for decision by a third party (whoever he may be) proves that love (see chapter xiii) has been overthrown and replaced by selfish desire, either to acquire or to retain. So far as this is true, the Christians involved have ceased to be Christian; they have suffered defeat. There is a better way, though a hard one. **Why do you not rather allow yourselves to be wronged? Why do you not rather allow yourselves to be robbed** (or defrauded)? M. iii. 57 takes the verbs *wronged*, *robbed* (ἀδικεῖσθε, ἀποστερεῖσθε) as middles that are 'intransitive active in idea' (*submit to* fraud, loss); B.D. §314 reaches a similar conclusion, but takes the verbs to be passive. Paul could here have appealed to the teaching of Jesus: see for example Matt. v. 39-42. The fact that he does not do so raises questions too large to be handled in the course of this commentary. Did he not know the teaching of Jesus? Did he assume that the Corinthians knew it so well that they needed no reminder of it? Had Paul some good reason for not appealing to the Lord's authority (as he does at vii. 10; ix. 14)? See *Romans*, p. 241. It is not only the New Testament that contains teaching of this kind. 'It is only right to point out that Greek moral philosophy too was not unaware that it was better to suffer evil than to do it' (Héring). See for example Plato, *Gorgias* 509 C, We say that to do wrong is the greater evil, to suffer wrong the less.

Paul can point to the Christian ideal; it is not being pursued,
much less achieved, in Corinth. **But you wrong and rob** (or 8
defraud)**, and your brothers at that.** We have no particulars of the cases brought against one another by the Corinthian Christians, and of the injuries they inflicted. A lawsuit could have arisen out of the events alluded to in v. 1; compare 2 Cor. vii. 12. Paul develops his argument by showing the fatal consequences of the Corinthians' behaviour. The connection is easier to see in Greek than in English, for *unrighteous* in verse 9 is the adjective (ἄδικος) corresponding to the verb *to wrong* (ἀδικεῖν) used in verses 7 f. The connection of thought is important, but it does not seem to go so far as to show, as Barth

(*C.D.* III. iv. 429) supposes, that those who are involved in *defensive* litigation are as such unrighteous and equally excluded from the kingdom with fornicators, idolaters, and so forth. The new subparagraph is introduced by the form of words Paul not infrequently uses to remind his readers of truths he feared they had forgotten.

9 **Or do you not know that unrighteous men shall not inherit the kingdom of God?** The term 'kingdom of God' is not frequent in Paul (for 'kingdom of Christ' see xv. 24). In four places (vi. 9, 10; xv. 50, Gal. v. 21) out of ten (counting xv. 24 as referring to the kingdom of God as well as to the kingdom of Christ) he speaks of inheriting (or failing to inherit) it. In these passages at least (cf. Matt. vi. 10; Luke xi. 2, to mention no other New Testament passages) it must refer to a future good, the time of blessedness when God is all in all, the forces of evil having been overcome (cf. xv. 28). In this future kingdom of righteousness, by definition, the unrighteous will have no share. Paul here (contrast verse 1 above) understands *unrighteous* in a strictly moral sense, and goes on to specify examples, chosen no doubt on the basis of his own observation, not least in Corinth, but formulated in close parallel with contemporary pagan and Hellenistic-Jewish lists of vices; see the parallels quoted in W. L. Knox, *Some Hellenistic Elements in Primitive Christianity* (1944), p. 5. **Do not be misled** (a charge common in the Greek diatribe; but cf. xv. 33; Gal. vi. 7; also Luke xxi. 8; James i. 16; it is precisely in such matters as this that men deceive themselves, persuading themselves that God cannot mean his moral demands seriously). **Fornicators** (to be taken broadly; see v. 1 and the notes), **idolaters, adulterers, catamites, sodomites** (the passive and active partners re-
10 spectively in male homosexual relations), **thieves, rapacious men** (cf. v. 11 above, with the notes), **drunkards, abusive men, and robbers** (if the *robber*, ἅρπαξ, is to be distinguished from the *thief*, κλέπτης, it may be by the addition of violence to his crime)—**none of these shall inherit** (in the Old Testament sense of *acquire possession of*; cf. Gen. xv. 7; also e.g. Matt. v. 5; 1 Pet. i. 4) **the kingdom of God** (see above). Notwithstanding the parallels noted above Paul is not writing in merely literary or in imaginary terms, but addressing the greatest of miracles,

a church of redeemed sinners, won from their old life by the power of God. **And that is what you were, some of you** 11
(ταῦτά τινες ἦτε). Calvin takes the *some* (τινες) to be superfluous, but the sentence would make much less good sense without it. Not all the Corinthians had been fornicators, not all thieves, and so on, but in the Corinthian congregation a good assortment of such immoral and criminal persons was to be found. Their background must be remembered before the modern Christian hastens to condemn the failings of the saints in Corinth. This is what they had been. **But** (the *but* is repeated before each verb; this is impressive and effective in Greek but seems impossible in English) **you were washed, you were sanctified, you were justified** (δικαιοῦν takes up ἀδικεῖν, ἄδικος)**, in the name of the Lord Jesus Christ and in the Spirit of our God.** Of the three verbs, the second and third are in the passive voice; the first is in the middle voice, which normally, though not simply the equivalent of a reflexive, denotes an action performed with reference to the agent, and may sometimes be best rendered by a reflexive. It may be so here (and in English the intransitive 'You washed' could in this case be used), but the passive form of the verb (λούειν and its compounds) is rare, and it is perhaps better to suppose that the middle is used for the passive (so A. Oepke, in *T.W.N.T.* iv. 306). The same verb is used, in the same voice, in Acts xxii. 16, where Ananias exhorts Paul, at the time of his conversion, Arise, and be baptized, and wash away your sins, calling upon his [Christ's] name. In the present verse the reference to *the name of the Lord Jesus Christ* makes it probable that baptism is in mind, though the use of the non-technical word (when 'you were baptized', ἐβαπτίσθητε, would have been as easy to use) shows that it is the inward meaning rather than the outward circumstances of the rite that is important to Paul. Baptism is elsewhere connected with the name of Jesus (e.g. Acts ii. 38; Paul writes 'into Christ', e.g. Rom. vi. 3) and with the gift of the Spirit (xii. 13). Baptism is certainly thought of as the chosen act of an adult believer (this may be the reason for the middle ἀπελούσασθε—the Corinthians themselves had chosen to be baptized (so Bachmann); it would go too far to assert that the verb shows that baptism was self-administered—cf. i. 14, 16); but behind the believer's decision lies the

act of God in Christ by which, through the gift of forgiveness, men are released from guilt and so cleansed. If *you were washed* brings into prominence the consent of the Christian, the other two verbs emphasize the essential and self-motivated work of God. *You were sanctified* does not refer to the process of ethical development, or it could scarcely have preceded *you were justified*; it means rather, You were claimed by God as his own and made a member of his holy people—in Paul's language, a saint (ἅγιος). *You were justified* however probably does have its technical Pauline sense (You were acquitted in God's court), though some think that Paul has here taken over the primitive use of the word (Bultmann, *Theology*, p. 135 (E.T., 136)) and that it means, You were made morally righteous. In the verse taken as a whole, however, Paul is not saying that the Corinthians have been made good men, perfectly holy and righteous; it is evident from the context that they have a long way to travel along the road of moral virtue. He claims that, gross as their sins have been, they have for Christ's sake been freed from guilt, united to God, and acquitted. The verse, however, is full of ethical overtone and implication. Because of what God has done, the possibility of new life is open to them; they are (in the language of v. 7) 'unleavened', and they must now purge out the old leaven and keep the Christian feast in sincerity and truth. That Paul is referring here to the moral effects of conversion *in nobis*, rooted in the work of Christ *extra nos* and *pro nobis*, and sealed in baptism, is more in keeping with the context (which is not that of chapter x) than to suppose that 'in this allusion to the change made in them by baptism he is not seeking to console them, but smiling ironically at their idea that now as baptized persons they have become, without any inner effort on their own part, entirely different from what they were before' (Schweitzer, *Mysticism*, p. 261). They were adulterers, and so forth; this, since their conversion, they are no longer, but they show their imperfection by the fact that they are conducting lawsuits aginst one another; they must now become as perfectly holy and righteous morally as they already are theologically by participation in the holiness and righteousness of Christ.

Formally, *in the name of the Lord Jesus Christ* is based upon baptismal usage; substantially, it indicates that the whole work of grace done in the Corinthian Christians depends upon the work of God in Jesus Christ, and on their relation with him. Similarly, *the Spirit of our God* may suggest the gift of the Spirit at baptism, but in fact the Spirit is the agent of sanctification (see Rom. viii. 8 f.; Gal. v. 22-5), and is connected with justification (see Rom. viii. 4; xiv. 17). As *that is what you were* confirms, Paul is in this verse describing, in not too orderly a way, the conversion experience that had changed his readers' lives. Arrested and convinced by the work of the Spirit in Christian preaching they had expressed in baptism the faith created within them, their sins were washed away, they were brought to God and made members of his people, and became justified believers, living by the power of the Spirit.

The quite unconscious Trinitarianism of the concluding words should be noted: *the Lord Jesus Christ*, *the Spirit*, *our God*. Trinitarian theology, at least in its New Testament form, did not arise out of speculation, but out of the fact that when Christians spoke of what God had done for them and in them they often found themselves obliged to use threefold language of this kind.

(d) THE ROOT OF THE TROUBLE

15. vi. 12-20. THE ROOT OF THE TROUBLE

(12) 'All things are permitted me'; but not all things are expedient. 'All things are permitted me'; but I will not be overpowered by any of them. (13) 'Foods are for the belly and the belly is for food; and God will do away with both the one and the other.' But the body is not for fornication, but belongs to the Lord, and the Lord belongs to the body; (14) and God by his power both raised the Lord and will raise up[1] us. (15) Do you not know that your bodies are members of Christ? Shall I then take away the members of Christ and make them members of a harlot? No!

[1] The MSS. are fairly evenly divided over the tense of this verb. Some (including the first hand of P46) have the present, some (including the first corrector of P46) the future, and some (including the second corrector of P46) the aorist (past). See the commentary.

(16) Or do you not know that he who unites himself to a harlot is one body with her? For, says Scripture, the two shall become one flesh. (17) But he who unites himself to the Lord is one spirit with him.

(18) Flee from fornication. Every sin a man may commit is outside his body; but he who commits fornication sins against his own body. (19) Or do you not know that your body is the temple of the Holy Spirit, who is in you, whom you have from God, and that you are not your own? (20) No, for you were bought at a price; very well, then, glorify God[1] in your body.

Verses 9-11 provide Paul with a suitable way of working back to the theme of sexual licence which he left at the end of chapter v, a theme which he intends to handle positively in his discussion of marriage in chapter vii. Whereas however in chapter v the discussion started from a particular moral act, here it starts from a proposition or principle, which Paul appears to quote from a Corinthian source; this makes it possible for him to deal with Corinthian libertinism at a deeper level. He will carry the discussion of the principle further still in viii. 1-3; x. 23.

12 **'All things are permitted me.'** There is fairly general agreement that these words are quoted by Paul, and that they were in use at Corinth; see for example Moule, p. 196. As we shall see, Paul gives qualified agreement to the words themselves but not to the conclusions drawn from them. What was their source? The most probable view (in view of their recurrence at x. 23, where the whole context, including viii. 7-13, should be noted) is that they were the watchword of a gnostic party in Corinth (see the note on i. 12; also 'Christianity at Corinth'). We know that developed gnosticism in the second century moved sometimes in the direction of asceticism, sometimes in

[1] There is no doubt that the translation renders the original text of this verse, but there are some interesting variants. For *glorify God* the Latin has *glorify and carry* (*et portate*) *God*. It is an interesting conjecture that this arose from a Greek variant, ἄρα γε in place of δή, which was later misread as ἄρατε. At the end of the verse many MSS. add, *and in your spirit, which belong to God*, notably weakening Paul's reference to the *body* as the sphere in which God must be glorified. See the commentary.

that of libertinism. Its disparagement of the material (see verses 13, 18 f. below) could already have led to the moral indifferentism of 'All things are permitted me'—nothing done in the body really matters, and therefore anything may be done. An alternative view is that the Corinthians are quoting words Paul had himself used in anti-Judaizing polemic; so for example Hurd (see Introduction, pp. 6 ff.). Against those who wished to bind the primitive church in the bonds of Jewish legalism he had asserted Christian freedom (cf. e.g. ix. 1; Gal. v. 1), conceivably in these words; here they come back to him. This view is possible, and could be combined with the other, since Corinthian gnostics could have used in their sense words that Paul had uttered in another. But in its Corinthian setting the sentence is not specifically anti-Jewish. Note the gnostic or quasi-gnostic context in which freedom is discussed, both here and in chapters viii and x; also the ground given for bodily freedom—the body is perishable, and its acts are therefore insignificant. Schlatter may well be right in connecting the implied claim to the right to make use of a harlot with the Corinthian attitude to marriage which appears in chapter vii—marriage is to be avoided if possible, and married people would do well to avoid intercourse. It could have been argued in Corinth (especially, Schlatter suggests, by Christian women) that the right course was for a husband to keep his wife 'pure', and, if necessary, find occasional sexual satisfaction in a harlot.

'*All things are permitted me.*' Paul does not disagree, but adds, **but not all things are expedient** (συμφέρει; as many quotations in Weiss show, the word was common in popular philosophy; in Paul cf. x. 23; xii. 7; 2 Cor. viii. 10; xii. 1). Christian existence is dependent not upon the observance of rules, whether Jewish, pagan, gnostic,—or Christian—in origin, but solely and entirely on the free gracious activity of God, who out of pure love accepts even those who break his own laws. It does not follow, however, that it is a good and profitable thing for a Christian to exercise his freedom in an irresponsible way (cf. Gal. v. 13; also 1 Pet. ii. 16). In truth, only love, and actions based on love, are expedient for the people of God, since only these build up (viii. 1), and though obedience to law is now completely discounted as a means of justification God's law still stands (ix. 21), or rather has been simplified and reinforced in Christ (the *law of Christ*, Gal. vi. 2), and may be regarded as marking out for men not a way of salvation but ways that are inexpedient, because they will lead inevitably to the collapse of society and the ruin of men's lives. Christian freedom must be limited by regard for others.

Christian freedom must also be limited by regard for the true well-being of the self. **'All things are permitted me'; but I will not be overpowered by any of them.** One might retain, but perhaps also exaggerate, a small play on words by rendering 'All things are in my power, but I will not put myself in the power of any of them'. In both these renderings the pronoun *any* (ὑπό τινος) has been taken as neuter—that is, as one of the *all things* (πάντα). It could, though less probably, be taken as masculine: I will not put myself in anyone's power, for example, by placing my members at the disposal of a harlot. But Paul's thought goes deeper than this, for he sees that it is possible in the name of freedom to enslave oneself, to pass under the authority of inexpedient practices, and of one's own desires. The Corinthian who fancies himself, as a superior spiritual person, free to have dealings with harlots will find himself confined under a sterner authority than the commandment 'Thou shalt not commit adultery'. Paul is thus prepared in a sense to accept the watchword, 'All things are permitted', but he will not let it go without strict qualification. Christian liberty is not licence, for licence is not more but less than liberty.

The next words probably, though not certainly, continue the
13 quotation. **'Foods are for the belly and the belly is for foods; and God will do away with both the one and the other.'** This is a rational, one may perhaps say gnostic, argument for freedom to eat without restraint by food laws. Paul probably did not frame it, and does not note its relation with the teaching of Jesus (Mark vii. 19), but he appears to accept it; at least he does not qualify it as he does the earlier proposition (though he does make a significant addition), and in the discussion of food sacrificed to idols (viii. 8; x. 25 ff.) he adopts essentially the same position. Whatever I eat passes into my stomach and is there broken down into its constituents; and, in due course, at death, my stomach will be dissolved into its

elements. It is God himself who has ordained both the process of digestion and the dissolution of the body at death; how can we think it a matter of eternal significance that we should eat only this or that food? One might have expected, in view not only of the next verse but also of chapter xv, that Paul would qualify this argument, since he believed in the resurrection of the body. But he does not qualify it, and we must recall that he believed that the resurrection body would be a transformed body (see xv. 35-44; 2 Cor. v. 1-5; Phil. iii. 21). Moreover, as we shall see, by *body* Paul means much more than a physical complex of such organs as the *belly*. It may nevertheless be true that the original context of the unbelief referred to in xv. 12 was the argument that the acts of the body had no eternal value; see below.

The Corinthian argument, then, is valid as far as food laws are concerned. Christians are not bound by them. It is at this point that Paul diverges from his correspondents. The paragraph as a whole is about relations with harlots, and we must assume that there were some at Corinth who had argued that just as the transiency of the body and of foods made it legitimate for a Christian to satisfy one physical appetite without regard to food laws, similar considerations would justify him in satisfying his sexual appetite in the most convenient way available. To this proposition (which he probably felt he could not put on paper, though it might have clarified his discussion if he had done so) Paul puts no qualification, but a direct negative. 'It is not forbidden; it is intrinsically impossible' (Barth, *C.D.* III. ii. 305). **But the body is not for fornication, but belongs to** (or, *is for*) **the Lord, and the Lord belongs to** (or, *is for*) **the body.** Belly and eating, yes; but not, body and fornication. The change in wording is significant. The belly is matter pure and simple, and has no permanence; but in Paul's usage *body* (σῶμα) means more than animal tissue. Even the 'natural body' is matter informed by soul (ψυχή); and if there is a natural body there is also (xv. 44) a spiritual body, matter informed by spirit (πνεῦμα). *Body* in fact is one of several terms used by Paul to denote not one part of man's nature but man as a whole. The *belly* is a material organ which I use for a short time; the *body* is myself. The argument therefore which the Corinthians appear to have

employed is fallacious; there is no valid analogy between the use of the stomach for digestion and of the body for fornication. The body is intended for the Lord's service (cf. Rom. vi. 12, 13, 19; xii. 1), and the Lord has given himself for the body, and it is intended that the two should be permanently united, both in the weakness and suffering which the believer shares with Christ in this age (2 Cor. vi. 10; xii. 9 f.) and in the glorious state into which he will be transformed (xv. 51; 2 Cor. v. 1-5; Phil. iii. 21). Here, and through the remainder of the paragraph, Paul may be answering the libertine claims of the Christ-group by bringing out what it really means to 'belong to Christ' (Schlat-
14 ter). He proceeds to make the point explicit. **God by his power both raised the Lord and will raise up us.** Sexual intercourse, unlike eating, is an act of the whole person, and therefore participates not in the transiency of material members but in the continuity of the resurrection life. In this verse Paul uses two verbs, a simple form rendered 'to raise' (ἐγείρειν), and a compound, rendered 'to raise up' (ἐξεγείρειν). It is doubtful whether he intends to indicate any greater difference than the English word 'up' suggests. A more important question is raised by a group of various readings at the end of the verse (see note 1 on p. 143): *will raise up, raised up, raises up*. Each of these has support numerous and early enough to be taken seriously, but Zuntz (pp. 256 f.) rightly compares 2 Cor. iv. 14; only the future provides the argument that Paul needs. It is because *the body* will not simply pass away but will be raised up that men must avoid using it for fornication.

15 The next verse repeats and emphasizes the argument. **Do you not know** (as usual—cf. e.g. vi. 2—Paul implies that his readers ought to know, but tend to behave as if they did not) **that your bodies are members of Christ?** Compare Rom. xii. 5; Col. i. 18, 24; Paul uses the metaphor of the body in various ways. In xii. 12-27 there is one body of Christ; here the many human bodies are members of Christ, each several one united to him, and (ideally) at his disposal for use as he wills. The consequence follows: **Shall I then take away the members of Christ and make them members of a harlot?** The imagery shifts slightly, for Paul, writing now in individual terms, thinks of the members that make up one human body. All belong to Christ,

and are (though in one sense mine) in fact his. Am I to deny him the use of what is his, and hand over his members for the use of a harlot? Put like this (as it rightly is), it is an unthinkable proposition. **No!** But perhaps the Corinthians will deny Paul's premise, affirming that to have relations with a harlot involves no transference of the members from Christ. They should know
better, for Scripture proves them wrong. **Or** (cf. vi. 9, and the 16
note) **do you not know that he who unites himself** (taking *κολλώμενος* as middle; the word is used in the Old Testament both for sexual union, and in a religious sense) **to a harlot is one body with her?** The last two words are not in the Greek but seem an inevitable addition in English. **For, says Scripture** (the verb has no expressed subject in Greek, and it would be possible, without difference in meaning, to supply *God* rather than Scripture; or the verb may be impersonal—The saying is)**, the two shall become one flesh.** The word *body* might seem at first sight to have suited Paul's argument better than *flesh*, but he quotes Gen. ii. 24, and in fact derives from it the means of taking an important step forward. In his anthropology, *body* is a neutral term in that it represents the human self at the place of decision. It may be the servant of sin, or the servant of righteousness. If one places his body at the disposal of a harlot, and so becomes one body with her, the body has taken the wrong turning, and becomes flesh, which for Paul has often (there are exceptions) a bad sense, signifying human nature perverted—not perverted because it is material but because as a totality it has fallen away from God and is living anthropocentrically. The body is also capable, however, not in its own strength but by the operation of the Holy Spirit, of turning in the right direction, and living theocentrically; if this happens it moves into the realm not of flesh but of spirit—not because it has ceased to be material but because as a totality it is controlled by the Spirit of
God. The use of Gen. ii. 24 thus enables Paul to continue: **But** 17
he who unites himself (*κολλώμενος*, as in verse 16) **to the Lord is one spirit with him.** As in verse 16 the last two words are a supplement to help the English. *The Lord* (Christ) provides the means by which man may achieve the God-centred existence which means life in the Spirit. In view of the change from *flesh* to *spirit* it is difficult to see how Schweitzer (*Mysticism*, p. 127) can

use this passage to prove that 'being in Christ' is a *physical* union, of the 'same character' as 'bodily union between man and woman'. To say this is not to say that union with Christ is merely (in the modern sense) 'spiritual'. Union with him is possible in the first instance through his initiative, expressed in physical action and suffering (cf. verse 20 below, *bought at a price*); secondarily through faith, and the surrender to him of the members which are his by right since he has bought them. Paul proceeds to develop this point, beginning a new paragraph however with a round imperative.

18 **Flee from fornication** (φεύγετε τὴν πορνείαν; cf. x. 14, where the construction is φεύγειν ἀπό; according to Robertson, p. 471 there is a difference, but he does not say, and it is not easy to see, what it is); not merely avoid, but run away from. Temptations to fornication were so common in Corinth that mere disapproval was likely to be inadequate; strong evasive action would be necessary. The same was true of idolatry (x. 14).

The next words raise a difficult exegetical problem. **Every sin a man may commit is outside his body; but he who commits fornication sins against his own body.** A distinction is made between fornication and all other sins in respect of their relation to the body. Is the distinction valid? 'In fact, gluttony, drunkenness, self-mutilation, and suicide also are crimes against one's own body' (Lietzmann). To overcome this difficulty Moule (pp. 196 f.) suggested that the sentence *Every sin ... outside his body* might be regarded as a slogan of the Corinthian libertines, to which Paul replies with the assertion that fornication is not a deed committed outside the personality and in such a way as not to affect it, but is a sin against the body itself, and must therefore be avoided. This attractive explanation is not entirely satisfying, because Paul's reply seems to accept the general proposition, and make an exception to it (cf. verses 12 f.), which leaves us with the original problem. It is perhaps best to suppose that Paul is writing rather loosely, and not in the manner of a textbook of moral philosophy. This interpretation goes back to Calvin: 'My explanation is that he does not completely deny that there are other sins, which also bring dishonour and disgrace upon our bodies, but that he is simply saying that these other sins do not leave anything like the same filthy stain on our bodies as fornication does.' Comparatively speaking, they are *outside the body* (the word is used here for the sum of the members (cf. verse 15), the physical apparatus provided by God as a means whereby a man may express his ego). Fornication is a sin not only against God, and not only against the other person involved, but against the fornicator's own body, which is designed to belong not to a harlot, but to the Lord (verse 13), and is wronged if devoted to any other end. It may be that Paul's argument here reflects the Jewish belief that man as originally created was androgynous (Daube, pp. 79 ff., 84), but it is not dependent on this belief, and though there are Stoic parallels to Paul's conclusion they are reached by different reasoning from different presuppositions.

Paul can go on to write in even more precise and forceful terms, since he is writing to Christians, for whom the destiny of the body has already been partially and in a preliminary
manner achieved. **Or do you not know** (for this 'Paulinism' 19
cf. verse 16) **that your body is the temple** (or, *shrine*; cf. iii. 16) **of the Holy Spirit, who is in you, whom you have from God, and that you are not your own?** Though the language at iii. 16 f. (see the notes) is similar the thought is different; there Paul thought of the community as the dwelling-place of the Spirit, whereas here, in closer agreement with the hellenistic parallels (for many examples see Weiss), he thinks of the individual. There is no inconsistency between the two ways of using the metaphor; both are correct, and each is used in an appropriate context. When the unity and purity of the church are at stake Paul recalls that the church is the shrine in which the Spirit dwells; when the unity and purity of the moral life of the individual are threatened, he recalls that the Spirit dwells in each Christian, who ought not therefore to defile the Spirit's shrine. Stoic moralists argued very similarly (e.g. Epictetus, quoted on iii. 16); when the divine Spirit is understood to dwell in man not by nature but by grace, and is conceived in terms of the moral holiness of Christ, the argument gains reality and force.

There is much to be said for putting the question mark after *God*, and starting a new sentence with, *And you are not your own*. On the whole however it seems unlikely that Paul would

have begun such a sentence with a simple *and* (*καί*), and it is better to continue the question, which recalls to the Corinthians what they ought never to have forgotten: (a) the Holy Spirit dwells within them; (b) they are not proprietors of their own bodies, or indeed of their own selves. They were made and destined for Christ, not for harlots, and have not the right to bestow their members where they will. Nor is this a matter of
20 creation only. *You are not your own*: **No, for you were bought at a price.** When man sought to be free from God and his own master (see the treatment of Adam in Rom. i. 20-23; v. 12-21) he became the slave of sin, who reigned with death (Rom. v. 17; vi. 23). From this bondage (essentially, as verse 19 shows, bondage to self) he could be freed only by becoming again what he had been created to be—the son and servant of God; hence the limitations imposed on Christian freedom in verse 12. His freedom in service to God was restored to him through the work of Christ, which Paul is therefore able, here and elsewhere (Rom. iii. 24; Gal. iii. 13; iv. 5), to describe as ransoming, or purchasing. The process of sacral manumission, by which a slave was bought 'for freedom' (cf. Gal. v. 1) in the name of a god may well have served as an analogy and have supplied him with useful terminology, but the fundamental idea of ransoming Paul derived from the Old Testament, where the words are used in a wide variety of senses (e.g. Exod. vi. 6; xiii. 13; Ruth iv. 4 ff.; Ps. ciii. 4; Isa. xliii. 1). *At a price* is probably intended to emphasize not the magnitude of the price paid (though the Vulgate, with *pretio magno*, took it so) but the fact that the transaction has been duly carried out and completed.

In accordance with the context Paul lays stress here not on the freedom which results from the payment of the ransom price but on the fact that those who have been redeemed are free for the service of God. *You were bought with a price*; **very well, then** (δή), **glorify God in your body.** This carries the negative implication, Do not use your body for fornication, but in itself it is positive. Whatever they do, Christians must act for the glory of God (x. 31). It is characteristic of Paul (cf. e.g. Rom. xii. 1) to add *in your body*. 'It is inconceivable that such a statement should come from Seneca. For him the soul, the spirit, could glorify the gods, but this is impossible for the contemptible body which always threatens the purity of the spirit' (Sevenster, *Seneca*, p. 76). For Paul, however, it is in the concrete circumstances in which the physical members operate that God is to be served. The failure of later generations of Christians to grasp this truth is reflected in the variant readings (see note 1 on p. 144).

C. A LETTER FROM CORINTH

(a) MARRIAGE AND RELATED QUESTIONS

16. vii. 1-7. BEHAVIOUR WITHIN MARRIAGE

(1) About the things you wrote. 'It is a good thing for a man not to touch a woman.' (2) Yes, but because cases of fornication occur let each man have his own wife, and let each woman have her own husband. (3) Let the husband render his wife her due,[1] and in the same way let the wife render his due to her husband. (4) It is not the wife but the husband who has authority over the wife's body; and in the same way it is not the husband but the wife who has authority over the husband's body. (5) Do not rob one another, unless it be by agreement and for a limited time, in order that you may be free for prayer, and then be together again, that Satan may not tempt you on account of your incontinence. (6) But I say this by way of concession, not by way of command. (7) I desire all men to be as I am myself; but each man has his own gift from God, one in one direction, another in another.

The theme of sexual irregularity has occupied much of Paul's attention since he first turned to it at v. 1; he now moves on to the related theme of marriage, though as verse 2 quickly shows he is obliged to see marriage in the light of the perversions of it that were all too common at Corinth. It also appears immediately that though the matters discussed in chapters i-iv, and

[1] That is, the sexual relations to which she is entitled. This was too much for many copyists, who substituted 'the kindness to which she is entitled'.

probably those of chapters v, vi, were brought to Paul's notice indirectly the themes of this chapter (and the following chapters) were raised by the Corinthians themselves in a letter.

1 **About the things you wrote:** a similar form of words (περὶ δέ) introduces particular subjects at vii. 25; viii. 1; xii. 1; xvi. 1. It is a very probable view (see the Introduction, p. 4) that the Corinthians had written to Paul, asking his advice on certain problems of conduct and the like. He appears to quote the letter occasionally, and at least some of its substance can be reconstructed from Paul's replies; on this see especially the work of Hurd, though with the qualifications noted in the Introduction, pp. 6 ff. **'It is a good thing for a man not to touch a woman.'** Some difficulty is alleviated if these words are regarded as a quotation from the Corinthian letter, and this is a hypothesis that may very probably be accepted (cf. vi. 12 f., and the note; and Jeremias, *Studia Paulina*, p. 151). The difficulty is not wholly removed, however, for even if Paul did not himself coin the sentence he quotes it without immediate indication of disapproval, and yet goes on not merely to sanction marriage but to disapprove abstinence within marriage. If he affirms (as he appears to do) the Corinthian statement, it is necessary to explain it in some such way as Calvin's, who points out that the proposition 'It is a good thing for a man not to touch a woman' does not logically imply 'It is not a good thing, that is, it is a not-good, evil, sinful thing, for a man to touch a woman'. Sexual relations expressed within marriage are not wrong; yet (for various reasons to be brought out below) it is a good thing not to engage in them. See also Lightfoot on the limitations within which celibacy is approved here. The limitations, given by the context, are more likely to be Paul's than the Corinthians'.

As S.B. (iii. 367) point out, with reference to the statement taken over by Paul, 'This fundamental proposition did not correspond to the ideas of the ancient synagogue.' Paul did not learn his views of marriage from the Jewish environment in which he had been brought up. There marriage was regarded as obligatory for men. More important, his views do not appear to correspond with those of the Old Testament; see especially Gen. ii. 18, which provides a verbal counterpart to 'It is a good thing for a man not to touch a woman' in 'It is not a good thing for the man to be alone' (οὐ καλὸν εἶναι τὸν ἄνθρωπον μόνον; cf. Tobit viii. 6). It is only a partial answer to say (with Calvin) that the passage in Genesis refers to the time before the Fall, when sin had not yet corrupted the divine institution of marriage, for the Old Testament writers probably did not make this distinction, but related the creation narrative with a view to vindicating marriage, as they knew it in the sinful world, as ordained by God. In later verses Paul so strongly qualifies the statement that it is good for a man not to touch a woman that it is impossible to describe his attitude (as Bultmann, *Theology*, p. 199 (E.T., 202), does) as ascetic and dualistic, and thus in contradiction with the Old Testament. Parallels (see Betz, p. 75) are afforded by philosophers, who abstained from marriage, but the Corinthian attitude probably arose in a Christian setting. 'The longing for celibacy breaks off every connection with Judaism, but it is not for that reason Greek. It is thinkable only under the protection of the proposition, "All things are permitted me", and this proposition has nothing to do with the Greek traditions, but was the Christian answer to the Jewish service of the law' (Schlatter). For Paul the issue is one of expediency; *good* is not used in a moral sense (Héring compares Jonah iv. 3, 8; also Gen. ii. 18, pointing out that 'for the Christian, as member of the church, the solitude of the first Adam exists no longer'). The unmarried state is, for a number of reasons of a pragmatic kind, a very fine thing, and happy are they who can maintain it; but marriage is at worst troublesome, is in no way wrong, and is a divine institution.

More than that. It is not wrong for the Corinthians to assert
that *it is a good thing for a man not to touch a woman.* **Yes, but** 2
because cases of fornication occur let each man have his own wife, and let each woman have her own husband ('an incidental prohibition of polygamy'—Lightfoot). The word *fornication* is in the plural, and it is best to interpret it as in the translation (M. iii. 28 speaks of a *pluralis poeticus*, but without good reason; he adds however that the plural 'may imply *cases of* . . .'). We have already been informed of one case of fornication (in the broad sense of the term; v. 1), and the drift of the letter suggests that a good deal of disreputable behaviour penetrated even the church in Corinth. Paul does not

say that marriage serves no purpose but that of acting as a prophylactic against fornication, but it does serve that purpose. Men and women have sexual urges, and if they are expressed within the institution that God himself has appointed they are less likely to be expressed in ways that God has forbidden. Marriage moreover must be real, and not 'spiritual' marriage.
3 **Let the husband render his wife her due, and in the same way let the wife render his due to her husband.** Here (contrast verse 1) Paul is entirely at one with Jewish opinion. He expresses it in a neatly phrased sentence in chiasmus, which is imitated rather than precisely reproduced in the translation. His parallel counsel to husband and wife is given further
4 emphasis and grounding in a similar parallel clause. **It is not the wife but the husband who has authority over the wife's body; and in the same way it is not the husband but the wife who has authority over the husband's body.** It is the exact parallelism that is most striking here. Conjugal rights are equal and reciprocal. If the husband has authority over his wife, his wife has equal authority over him. This striking assertion must be borne in mind as we follow Paul's arguments about the
5 relations between man and woman. **Do not rob one another, unless it be** (there is no serious doubt about the meaning, but the Greek, *εἰ μήτι ἄν*, is unusual; see M. i. 169; B.D. §376) **by agreement and for a limited time, that you may be free for prayer, and then be together again.** Paul repeats in negative form (and in terminology that recalls that of the rabbis; see Daube, p. 365) the commandment of verse 3. Marriage is to be real marriage, and any attempt to spiritualize it by one partner means that the other is being robbed. This precept is qualified: abstinence may be permitted if it is *by agreement* (in which case it is not robbery) and *for a limited time*, which would minimize the danger, and for a religious purpose. It was recognized in Judaism (see *Berakoth* ii. 5) that a newly married man was excused from the obligation of saying the Sh^{e}ma,—for the evident reason that his mind would be otherwise occupied, so that he could not give proper attention to his prayer. This means that there is no need to draw the conclusion that, in Paul's view, intercourse was defiling, so that it made prayer impossible or improper. A second purpose clause (*ἵνα*) is

attached: *and* (*that you may*) *then be together again.* According to some (e.g. Lietzmann) this does not follow in strict logic ('The purpose of the agreement is to pray, not also "to be together again" '), and some grammarians propose that the connecting word (ἵνα) should here be taken as imperatival: Then you must come together again. But it is the objection that is illogical. The separation is made in order that you may be free for prayer, and it is made *by agreement and for a limited time* in order that, your religious purpose achieved, you may again be together. On 'imperatival ἵνα' see p. 176.

The return to normal conjugal relations is an important part of the matter, **that Satan may not tempt you on account of your incontinence.** *Incontinence* (in the sense of irrepressible desire for sexual relations) must be presupposed; if the couple did not have this incontinence they would presumably not be married (cf. verses 1 f.). If it does not find its legitimate outlet, Satan (see v. 5; here however Satan is less a destroying agent than one who seduces to evil) will tempt the married but unsatisfied partners to express it in fornication.

But I say this by way of concession, not by way of com- 6
mand. To what does *this* refer? Various suggestions have been made. (a) It may refer to verse 2, or rather to the whole section, verses 2-5, which enjoins, or appears to enjoin, marriage, with at most temporary abstention from sexual relations. On this view Paul means, I am not *commanding* you to marry, when I say 'Let each man have his own wife . . .', but merely conceding that you may marry. (b) *This* may refer only to verse 5b, the resumption of marital relations after an interval for prayer: I concede that you may resume your former cohabitation, but I do not say that you must. If we are confined to these possibilities (a) is to be preferred. Another suggestion however seems to fit the context better (see the exposition of the next verse). We may suggest (c) that *this* refers to the whole of verse 5, where *unless* itself introduces a concession of some kind. You should (Paul's advice runs) not rob one another of your rights, but I will make this concession to the ascetics among you (whose voice is heard in verse 1): If husband and wife both wish, they may agree not to cohabit for a short time, in order to give themselves without distraction to prayer. But note: this is concession,

not command, and if you do practise abstinence in this way it must be for a limited time, and with a view to returning to each other. We must now examine the next verse, and its connection with verse 6.

7 **I desire** (θέλω) **all men to be as I am myself.** This verse is often mistranslated, as in the New English Bible (I should like you all to be as I am myself). When Paul intends to express a wish he knows to be unattainable he (rightly) uses the imperfect tense of the verb (e.g., Gal. iv. 20, ἤθελον δὲ παρεῖναι—he knows he cannot be present; cf. Rom. ix. 3, ηὐχόμην); when he uses the present tense (as here) he intends to express a wish that is capable of realization, and ought to be realized (examples are numerous; see xi. 3; xiv. 5), almost a command. The right sense is given by Bachmann, though he does not adopt the exegesis suggested here: 'What he wishes cannot be mere celibacy in itself, but only that all might possess the capacity for resistance to sensual allurements, such as he indicates that he enjoyed for himself, and made it possible for him to live without marriage'. In verse 8, as will be seen, both the language and the thought take a somewhat different turn; in the present verse however Paul begins by stating his unqualified Christian desire that all men should live in obedience to God (see the notes on vii. 29), and in freedom from fornication, the inordinate and disobedient expression and release of the urges within them. This he can, in God's name, require absolutely. But he recognizes that there are more ways than one in which the claim can be fulfilled. **Each man has his own gift from God, one in one direction, another in another.** That is, one expresses his obedience to God within marriage, another by remaining unmarried. For *gift* (χάρισμα) see i. 7; elsewhere Paul speaks of such gifts as conferred by the Holy Spirit, and his meaning here (*from God*) is not different. Modern interpreters (e.g. Barth, *C.D.* III. iv. 144-8) show an understandable desire to reach the conclusion that Paul teaches that just as a celibate life requires a special gift from God so also does marriage, but (though it would certainly not be true to suggest that Paul ascribes only negative significance to marriage—see xi. 11 f., and cf. 2 Cor. xi. 2, not to mention material in epistles that may not have been written by Paul) his point here seems rather to be that some have the gift

of celibacy, and others, who lack this gift, and are therefore well advised to marry, have some other compensating gift or gifts.

So far, then, Paul has given very sharply qualified approval to the Corinthian proposition, 'It is a good thing for a man not to touch a woman'. If men can express their obedience in such complete self-control and abstinence (and Paul himself, as appears later if not already in verse 7, can do this), this is well; but marriage is no sin (cf. vii. 28, 36), and if it is entered into it must be full marriage, physically consummated.

17. vii. 8-24. CHRISTIAN AND MIXED MARRIAGES, SLAVERY AND FREEDOM

(8) For those who are unmarried, and for the widows, this is what I say: it is a good thing for them if they remain as they are, as I do myself. (9) But if they are not living continently, let them marry, for it is better to be in the married state[1] than to burn. (10) To the married I give this charge (though it comes not from me but from the Lord), that the wife is not to separate from her husband—(11) and if a separation does take place let her remain unmarried, or be reconciled to her husband—and the husband is not to divorce his wife. (12) To the rest, this is what I say (and it is I that speak, not the Lord). If a Christian brother has an unbelieving wife, and she is content to live with him, let him not divorce her. (13) And a Christian woman, if she[2] has an unbelieving husband, and he is content[3] to live with her, let her not divorce her husband. (14) For the unbelieving husband has been sanctified through his Christian wife,[4] and the unbelieving wife has been sanctified through the Christian brother.[5]

[1] *To marry* (γαμῆσαι) has the strong support of P^{46} B D G, but is to be rejected on internal grounds; see the commentary.

[2] Reading εἴ τις, with P^{46} ℵ D G, and the Latin; ἥτις is a smoother, secondary reading.

[3] Probably εὐδοκεῖ should be read, with P^{46} B.

[4] τῇ πιστῇ (D G, Latin and Syriac) is correct interpretation.

[5] ἀδελφῷ; the variants are due to parallelizing assimilation to the preceding clause.

Otherwise your children would be unclean, whereas in fact they are holy. (15) But if the unbeliever separates, let him go. In such cases the Christian brother or sister is not enslaved. But God has called you[1] in peace. (16) Wife, it may be that you will save your husband; husband, it may be that you will save your wife.

(17) Only let each one walk according to the lot the Lord has apportioned him, as God has called him. This is the charge I give in all the churches. (18) Was anyone called in a state of circumcision? Let him not undo his circumcision. Has anyone been called uncircumcised? Let him not be circumcised. (19) Circumcision is nothing; uncircumcision is nothing: what matters is that we keep God's commandments. (20) Let each man continue in that calling in which he was called. (21) Were you a slave when you were called? Let not that trouble you, but even though you should be able to become free, put up rather with your present status. (22) For the slave who has been called in the Lord is the Lord's freedman; and similarly the freeman who has been called is Christ's slave. (23) You were bought at a price: do not become slaves of men. (24) Let each man, brethren, remain with God in that state in which he was called.

After general observations, evoked by the proposition (probably quoted from a Corinthian source) that it is a good thing for a man not to touch a woman, Paul proceeds to give more detailed instructions (though in vii. 5 he had already dealt with one matter of detail) to particular classes.

8 **For those who are unmarried** (the Greek words are masculine, but probably intended—according to Greek idiom—to cover both sexes)**, and for the widows** (the article suggests that Paul has in mind the members of the Corinthian church who are widows, though naturally his remark is capable of generalization)**, this is what I say: it is a good thing** (cf. verse 1, and contrast verse 7a, *I desire*) **for them if they re-**

[1] ἡμᾶς (P^{46} B D G, and many others) is a natural easing of the text, but *you* brings out the fact (see the commentary) that this clause connects with the next verse.

main as they are, as I do myself. Here is no positively expressed desire that the persons addressed should be like him, but the advice (in their own interests; see below, vii. 28, 35) that they should stay as they are. Paul himself had presumably no wife at the time of writing (ix. 5 is consistent with this, though it does not prove it). He may never have married; it is however more probable that he was a widower. Unmarried rabbis were few, and marriage appears to have been obligatory for a Jewish man (S.B. ii. 372), though one cannot suppose that this rule was universally observed. Whether as bachelor or widower, Paul was now remaining unmarried; indeed he would have found it difficult to combine marriage with his missionary work. Others would do well to imitate him—provided they had the gift (vii. 7)
of continence. **But if they are not living continently** (there is 9
no ground for watering this down into 'if they find it difficult to live continently'—cf. vii. 2, *cases of fornication*), **let them marry, for it is better to be in the married state** (reading the present infinitive, *γαμεῖν*; the aorist, *γαμῆσαι*, *to marry*, though it has excellent MS. support, is probably due to assimilation to the aorist imperative, *γαμησάτωσαν*) **than to burn.** *To burn* does not mean actually to flare out in lustful acts (it would hardly be necessary at this stage to point out that marriage was preferable to fornication), but to be consumed with inward desire, even if one does not yield to it. In such a state it is impossible to 'wait upon the Lord with decorum and without hindrance' (vii. 35, cf. 5), and it is better to marry (cf. 1 Tim. v. 11). Paul's language 'may derive from a Rabbinic argument' (Daube, p. 369).

It is clear from these verses that, in Paul's view, the most fortunate state is that of the unmarried person who is under no pressure to marry; less desirable is that of the person who must express his sexual nature and does so within marriage; least desirable is that of the person who needs marriage as such a means of expression, but attempts (or possibly is compelled) to do without it. This relative evaluation raises a question. What of those who, being married, feel that they do not need marriage? Should they dissolve their union and live separately? Paul has the best of grounds for his answer.

To the married (the context shows that Paul is speaking to 10

Christian husbands and wives) **I give this charge (though it comes not from me but from the Lord), that the wife is**
11 **not to separate from her husband . . . and the husband is not to divorce his wife.** Not even the higher evaluation of the celibate life should lead to the dissolution of a marriage once it has been contracted; an *a fortiori* argument will lead to the conclusion that no other ground will suffice. This *charge* Paul gives not on his own authority, but on that of the Lord himself; see Mark x. 2-12 and the parallels. Since 1 Corinthians is earlier in date than any of the gospels this passage gives additional support to the claim of Mark x (rather than the Matthean parallel) to give the original form of Jesus's saying on divorce. Paul's specific references to the teaching of Jesus are notoriously few (see above, p. 112); in this Commentary it is our duty not so much to explain this general paucity of sayings of Jesus, as to explain why Paul does quote Jesus here. One possibility is that he always quoted the sayings of Jesus when he could, but knew very few of them; this verse would give one of the few. If Paul knew more but selected only a few, it may be that he chose only those where the teaching of Jesus differed sharply from that prevailing in Judaism: on divorce, the school of Hillel differed from the school of Shammai, but neither agreed with Jesus, who in his absolute prohibition of divorce differed from the Old Testament (Deut. xxiv) itself. It may be that it was this disagreement with the Old Testament that led Paul to claim the Lord's authority here. Paul's use in this verse of different words —*separate* (χωρίζεσθαι, of the wife), and *divorce* (ἀφιέναι, of the husband)—may reflect the fact that in Judaism only the husband had the right to divorce; but the rabbis were familiar with the different conditions of the Gentile world (Daube, pp. 362-5), and Paul, who had travelled widely, must have known them better than most of his Jewish contemporaries. Later, in verse 13, he uses *divorce* of the wife. In verse 15 he uses *separate* of both husband and wife, possibly not meaning legal divorce. See the notes.

The prohibition of separation and divorce (between Christians) seems absolute; but Paul includes a parenthesis that shows awareness that marriages could and did break up. **If a separation does take place** (the English *does take place* is an attempt to bring out the force of the Greek *καί* and the aorist *χωρισθῇ*) **let her remain unmarried, or be reconciled to her husband.** This (cf. vii. 6) shows that even where Christian legislation exists it is not to be interpreted, and was not interpreted by Paul, in a legalistic manner. Separation does not put the separated partners outside the church; they remain part of the fellowship, and subject to its discipline. For the woman in question this means that a second marriage, while her husband is living, is impossible. She must either remain unmarried, or restore the previous relationship. It must be remembered (see above, pp. 154 ff.) that Paul is dealing (perhaps not exclusively) with marriages that are threatened by an ascetic view of sexual relations. The parenthetical clause deals with the wife who separates, and there is no corresponding clause to state the duty of the husband who divorces his wife. The general run and balance of the paragraph suggest that Paul expects him to remain unmarried or be reconciled to his original partner.

These are the duties of Christian couples. For marriages of non-Christians Paul makes no attempt to legislate. There remain however the important cases of Christian men with non-Christian wives, and Christian wives with non-Christian husbands. To these Paul now turns, though it is the content rather than the introduction of the paragraph that makes this clear. That it is undesirable to contract mixed marriages appears from 2 Cor. vi. 14–vii. 1 (which some regard as part of the 'Previous Letter'—see Introduction, p. 4), but this does not answer the question what is to be done when a mixed marriage comes into being through the conversion of one partner but not the other.
To the rest (this is very vague; Paul must mean, To married 12
Christians other than those whom I have just addressed—that is, married, and having in marriage unbelieving partners), **this is what I say (and it is I that speak, not the Lord).** Compare verse 25; Paul distinguishes sharply his own judgement from a pronouncement traceable to Jesus, but this does not mean that he regards his charge here as having no authority, or even significantly less authority than that of verse 10. Jesus, whose ministry was cast almost exclusively within Judaism (see J. Jeremias, *Jesus' Promise to the Nations* (1958)) did not have occasion to deal with mixed marriages between the people of

God and others. The instruction follows, again in closely parallel clauses for husband and wife respectively. **If a Christian brother** (the Greek has simply ἀδελφός, *brother*, but see i. 1; it would be perverse to see here, and in the following verses, the current *koine* Greek use of 'brother' as a term of endearment from a wife to a husband) **has an unbelieving** (that is, a non-Christian) **wife, and she is content** (possibly we should translate 'is quite content', allowing perfective force to the preposition in the compound verb συνευδοκεῖν—M. ii. 325) **to**
13 **live with him, let him not divorce her. And a Christian**
woman (the Greek has *woman*, but the context, and analogy with verse 12, make the meaning unmistakable), **if she** (see note 2 on p. 159) **has an unbelieving husband, and he is content** (see note 3 on p. 159; but the simple form of the verb will hardly differ in meaning from the compound used above) **to live with her, let her not divorce her husband.** The point is clear: in a mixed marriage the Christian partner is not to take the initiative (cf. verses 10 f.; the stronger word, ἀφιέναι, is now used of both partners) in a move towards separation. This is
14 partly in the general interests of peace, partly also because **the**
unbelieving husband has been sanctified through (literally, *in*, but some measure of instrumentality is implied; see below) **his Christian wife** (*Christian* is interpretative addition; cf. note 4 on p. 159), **and the unbelieving wife has been sanctified through** (*in*) **the Christian** (see above, verse 12) **brother.** In Paul's usage, to be holy (ἅγιος), or sanctified (ἡγιασμένος), is normally the distinguishing mark of the Christian. The Christians are the saints (ἅγιοι), and as such radically distinguished from the rest of mankind. To them he writes (vi. 11) that notwithstanding their wicked past they have been sanctified in the name of Jesus Christ, and through the Spirit of God (ἡγιάσθητε). By definition, the persons referred to in the present verse have not been sanctified in this sense, for they are unbelievers; as verse 16 shows (see below) they stand at present outside the realm of salvation, though there is reason to hope that they may be brought within it. The verb 'to sanctify' (ἁγιάζειν), and the adjective 'holy' (ἅγιος), must therefore be used in this verse in a sense differing from that which is customary in Paul. The majority of commentators (some

illustrating from the Jewish, others from the Hellenistic background) suppose that Paul is treating the idea of holiness in a physical or quasi-physical way; it is true that it is so used in many primitive religions, and in parts of the Old Testament. It is however unlikely that Paul uses it so, since it is evident that the holiness shared in marriage does not of itself 'save' the partner who is sanctified by it (verse 16). The clue to the problem is to be found in the fact that Paul is still dealing with the antipathy, felt by at least some in Corinth, to sex and marriage in general. If marriage between Christians may be permitted, they argue, mixed marriages at least must be forbidden, for the Christian partner will be defiled by the non-Christian, and the children issuing from the marriage will be unclean. Paul answers that the truth is the reverse of what is suggested. The Christian partner has the effect of sanctifying the relationship (which, on his part, is the divine institution of marriage), and his partner in it. 'The godliness of the one does more to "sanctify" the marriage than the ungodliness of the other to make it unclean' (Calvin). Paul adds, **Otherwise** (for the construction—ἐπεὶ ἄρα with the indicative—cf. v. 10), if the Christian partner did not sanctify the relationship, **your children would be unclean, whereas in fact they are holy.** Paul uses this truth, which he regards as self-evident, to clinch the matter. He is probably dependent on Jewish usage and conviction here. The children are within the covenant; this could not be so if the marriage itself were unclean.

It does not seem possible to draw any conclusion from this passage about the practice of baptism in the Corinthian church. Some have argued (partly on the basis of the Jewish analogy in *Yebamoth* 78a, where it is said that if a pregnant woman becomes a proselyte and receives baptism her child when it is born does not need further baptism) that the custom reflected is one in which the children already born to converts were baptized with their parents but that children subsequently born were not baptized, since they were born holy; others think that the holiness of the children born in a Christian, or even a half-Christian, marriage would constitute a ground for their baptism as infants. Kümmel gives a good summary of opinions on this point. It can only be said that neither of these propositions is stated, or necessarily implied, by the text. There seems to be no indication in 1 Corinthians, or in any other Pauline letter, that baptism was administered except to believers.

These considerations confirm the injunction that the Christian partner should not take the initiative in dissolving a mixed marriage. There is however another case to consider. The condition Paul mentions may not be fulfilled. The unbelieving partner may not be content to live with one who has committed the social *faux pas* of becoming a Christian, and thereby incurred
15 (it may be) suspicion and dislike. **If the unbeliever separates** (see the note on verse 10; more than the refusal of conjugal rights, but less than legal divorce is probably intended)**, let him go** (literally, *let him separate*)**. In such cases** (possibly, but less probably, *to such persons*—ἐν τοῖς τοιούτοις) **the Christian brother or sister is not enslaved,** that is, to a mechanical retention of a relationship the other partner wishes to abandon. The prohibition of divorce does not apply here—a further indication that Paul is not using the precept he quotes from the teaching of Jesus in a legalistic way. He now returns to his main theme, that mixed marriages are essentially Christian marriages, and are not to be broken by Christians. Verse 15c is to be linked with verse 16 (and 14) rather than with 15ab (which contain 'a parenthetical limitation'—Lightfoot).

God has called you in peace (or, better perhaps, taking ἐν with the dative to be used for εἰς with the accusative, *into peace*, into a state of peace; or perhaps, with Moule, p. 79, *into* a peace *in* which he wishes you to live.) It is the will of God that men and women should live in harmony, and this aim will not be furthered if a Christian partner withdraws from marriage on religious grounds; such a separation could only engender strife. The Christian partner must continue the union 'for the sake of the ways of peace' (Paul's words recall this rabbinic expression; Daube, p. 127). This seems the more probable interpretation, but it would be possible to reverse it: If the non-Christian partner objects to living with a Christian partner the latter ought to separate, rather than stay and fight the matter out. This however would require not *But God has called* . . ., but 'For God has called . . .'.

There is a further reason why the Christian partner should if

possible continue to live with the non-Christian. **Wife, it may** 16
be that you will save your husband; husband, it may be that you will save your wife. *Save* is here used in the sense that it has in for example Rom. xi. 14; 1 Cor. ix. 22; not in that of for example Rom. v. 9 f.; that is, it means 'bring to conscious participation in Christian faith and life', 'convert'; it is a 'missionary term' (Weiss, who compares *κερδαίνειν* in ix. 19-22). Salvation in this sense may be the result of the witness—spoken and lived (cf. 1 Pet. iii. 1 f.)—of a partner in marriage, and as long as this possibility exists the Christian should pursue and cultivate it. This at least is one possible interpretation of a difficult phrase, which is literally, What do you know if (or, whether) you will save . . .? (*τί οἶδας εἰ . . .;*). This has often been taken to denote resignation in the face of a hopeless situation: It is of course not impossible that you may save your husband (wife), but how can you possibly know this? The next verse (see below) would then continue: All we do know is that we should continue in the position in which God has called us, and thus—for example—should not break up our marriages. This however does not really do justice to the context. Paul has already (verse 14) asserted that the unbelieving partner has been brought within the sanctity of Christian marriage; there is therefore good reason to hope that he may be led to conscious acceptance of his partner's faith. The Greek fathers all interpret the passage in this sense, and J. Jeremias has shown (*Neutestamentliche Studien für Rudolf Bultmann* (1954), pp. 255-60) that good linguistic considerations suggest that the difficult phrase should be rendered *perhaps*. Compare 2 Sam. xii. 22; Epictetus II. xx. 28-31; xxv. 2. The sentence means, How do you know that you will not? that is, Perhaps you will.

Thus to retreat from a (possibly difficult) mixed marriage would be to withdraw from a missionary situation, in which at least a reasonable possibility existed of achieving the salvation of another.

In the rest of the paragraph (up to verse 24) Paul generalizes on the conclusions he has reached and stated in regard to
marriage in general and mixed marriages in particular. **Only** 17
(*εἰ μή*; this looks back to verse 15, which contemplates the possibility in certain circumstances of separation) **let each one**

walk according to the lot the Lord has apportioned him, as God has called him. The construction of the verse is difficult, though its general drift is sufficiently clear. It would be easier if the clause *as God has called him* (relegated in the translation to the end of the sentence, but in the Greek in the middle of it) were not present. It could, without this clause, be literally translated, Only, as the Lord has appointed his lot (*μεμέρικεν*) to each one, so let him (each one) walk. This metaphorical use of *walk*, Jewish in origin, is not uncommon in Paul: iii. 3, and frequently in other epistles. There is a similar use of the verb 'to appoint one's lot' (elsewhere in Paul simply 'to divide') at 2 Cor. x. 13. Paul inserts 'as God has called each one' because the idea of calling is an important one which he will develop in the course of the paragraph; see verses 18, 20, 21, 22, 24. These verses show that Paul is not thinking primarily of a vocation *to* which a man is called, but of the condition *in* which a man is when the converting call of God comes to him and summons him to the life of Christian faith and obedience. There is at least a presumption that the Lord will wish the convert to stay where he is. **This is the charge I give** (*διατάσσομαι*: cf. xi. 34; xvi. 1; possibly, This is the arrangement I make) **in all the churches.** *This* refers to what has just been said; what follows illustrates it by a number of particular examples. Compare iv. 17; xiv. 33. Paul is not making a special case of the Corinthians, nor is there good reason why he should do so. There is no suggestion that his apostolic authority is geographically limited.

18 **Was anyone called** (to become a Christian) **in a state of circumcision? Let him not undo his circumcision** (as the Hellenizers did before the Maccabean revolt: 1 Macc. i. 15; Assumption of Moses viii. 3; *Aboth* iii. 15; etc.). **Has anyone been called** (a different tense of the verb *to call*, but it is hard to see any point in the change) **uncircumcised? Let him not be circumcised.** Paul is thinking of more than surgical operation, of one kind or another. The converted Jew continues to be a Jew, with his own appointed way of obedience. It does not appear that the demand that Gentile Christians should be circumcised caused a major problem in Corinth; contrast Gal. ii. 3; v. 2-12; vi. 12 f. This has sometimes been taken to show

that Judaizers cannot have been at work at Corinth. All that can be rightly said however is that Judaizing propaganda took a different form in Corinth from that which it took in Galatia. See the Introduction, pp. 20 f.; also 'Things Sacrificed to Idols', pp. 147-50. It may be that Paul's point, that the Jerusalem church itself had not insisted on the circumcision of Titus (Gal. ii. 3), had gone home. We know, moreover, that apart from Christian influence, some Jews were more, others less, stringent in regard to circumcision. In fact, it matters not at all whether a
man is circumcised or not. **Circumcision is nothing; un-** 19
circumcision is nothing: what matters is that we keep God's commandments. Compare Gal. v. 6; vi. 15. From the Jewish point of view this is a paradoxical, or rather an absurd, statement. A Jew would reply, Circumcision is one of God's commandments; if therefore we are to keep God's commandments we cannot say that circumcision is nothing; we must be circumcised. It is further to be noted that the commandment of circumcision is not one that arises in the Jewish oral tradition, but is firmly rooted in the Old Testament (Gen. xvii. 10-14; *et al.*). Paul here hints at a distinction he will work out more fully at ix. 20 f. (see the notes there); see also Rom. ii. 25-9 (and the notes). It is possible, in his view, to be circumcised and not to keep God's commandments, and equally to keep God's commandments without being circumcised. He sees God's commandments now as the 'law of Christ' (cf. in addition to the passages above Gal. vi. 2; also Rom. xiii. 8-10). *That we keep God's commandments* means an obedience to the will of God as disclosed in his Son far more radical than the observance of any code, whether ceremonial or moral, could be. If a man's life has been determined by the obedience of faith (Rom. i. 5; xvi. 26) conversion to or from Judaism becomes irrelevant.

The main proposition is now repeated before Paul proceeds
to a further example. **Let each man continue in that calling** 20
in which he was called. Compare verses 17 f., 24. Elsewhere (Rom. xi. 29; Phil. iii. 14; 2 Thess. i. 11) Paul gives the word *calling* (κλῆσις) an important theological content; it would be wrong to introduce this content here; compare i. 26. *Calling* in this verse is not the calling *with* which, *to* which, or *by* which a man is called, but refers to the state in which he is *when*

he is called by God to become a Christian. Since Paul in the same sentence, and repeatedly in the context, declares that it is the will of God that the Christian should continue in this state, it acquires new meaning: the slave, for example, becomes the Lord's freedman. But it is misleading to import into this passage modern ideas of, for example, vocation to missionary service, and still more misleading to speak, as the medieval church did, of Christian vocation as exclusively vocation to monastic life. A man is not called (so far as this passage is concerned) to a new occupation; his old occupation is given new significance. Barth, it is true, finds more theological meaning in *calling* here. 'Each man must obey his given calling as it has come to him, whether as circumcised or uncircumcised, free or slave. He is not called to be circumcised or uncircumcised, free or slave; he is called precisely in the state in which he is. He must always be true, not to the state, but to his calling within it, as this man with this background and history. It is not important that he is one thing or the other . . . What counts is the *τήρησις ἐντολῶν θεοῦ*, the obedience which he must render whether as circumcised or uncircumcised. This obedience, however, is to be rendered at this point, i.e., within what is proper to him, in the place where God has found him and he must respond' (*C.D.* III. iv. 605; see the whole discussion, pp. 600-7, 645 f.). But, though Barth's words are in themselves true, the verses 21-4 seem to fix the meaning of our verse beyond doubt.

21 **Were you a slave when you were called?** See i. 26 for the low social standing of many Corinthian Christians. **Let not that trouble you, but even though you should be able to become free** (emancipation could take place in a variety of ways, and was not infrequent) **put up rather with your present status.** A number of grammarians (e.g. M. i. 247; ii. 165; Moule, pp. 21, 167; M. E. Thrall, *Greek Particles in the New Testament* (1962), pp. 78-82), and many commentators, prefer to render, If you actually (*εἰ καί*) have an opportunity of becoming free, by all means (*μᾶλλον*, elative) seize it. This finds some support in the aorist tense of the imperative (*χρῆσαι*), but does not make sense in the context; see especially the discussion, with references, in Sevenster, *Seneca*, pp. 189 f. (and the same context for a discussion of the Pauline and Stoic attitudes to slavery).

Particularly important is the *for* (γάρ) with which the next verse begins: You need not hesitate to put up with your servile condition, **for the slave who has been called in the Lord** (that is, 22
to be a Christian, one who is in Christ) **is the Lord's freedman; and similarly the free man who has been called is Christ's slave.** For the paradox compare vii. 29 ff. below. The ground of the slave's Christian emancipation is stated in the next verse: Christ has bought him, at the cost of his life. In becoming free, however, he did not become a completely independent figure, but the freedman (*libertus*) of a protector (*patronus*), to whom he had at least a moral obligation, and owed loyalty and service. The slave who becomes a Christian, though he retains his social status, has been freed from bondage to sin and death, and to the evil powers of this age (cf. ii. 6, 8); he owes his freedom to Christ, and it is on this gift of freedom that Paul here lays stress, though the thought that the emancipated slave now owes loyalty and service to his patron is not far below the surface. The freedman in any case was a humble rather than a dignified figure (see J. Jeremias, *Jerusalem zur Zeit Jesu* (1958), II B 210). In the corresponding clause the stress is naturally reversed, The man who begins, and continues, on the social level of the free man has been bought by Christ, and thus becomes Christ's slave, owing him loyalty and service. Both slave and free man stand in the same twofold relation, of freedom and service, to Christ, and their differing social ranks become irrelevant.

You were bought at a price (cf. vi. 20, and the note there): 23
do not become slaves of men. This corresponds to the command to slaves in verse 21b. Free men sometimes, for a variety of reasons (see the note on xiii. 3), sold themselves into slavery. To do this would be to shirk Christian responsibility, and to obscure the truth that a Christian has been set free by Christ, and owes absolute obedience to him only. It is better to take Paul's words thus than to suppose that he here gives the word *slave* 'a religious sense' (Héring); it is not however wrong to paraphrase the verse, with Bultmann (*Primitive Christianity in its Contemporary Setting* (1956), p. 185), 'Do not make yourselves dependent on the value judgements of men'. In his discussion of slavery and freedom Paul often speaks like a Stoic

(see references in Sevenster, as above, Weiss, and Lightfoot); but there is nothing Stoic in the foundation of the argument (*You were bought at a price*), and the paradoxical theme that it is in service that perfect freedom is found is for Paul focused not upon an impersonal and pantheistic *logos*, but upon the personal and historical Redeemer, Jesus Christ.

24 Paul sums up finally: **Let each man, brethren, remain with God** (the language suggests a slave who remains in the same service) **in that state** (or condition; no substantive is expressed in Greek) **in which he was called** (to be a Christian). This state, whatever it may have been, is now transformed by the fact that man is in it *with God*, and uses it as the channel of his service to Christ.

18. vii. 25-40. VIRGINS

(25) About the virgins I have no charge from the Lord, but I give my opinion, as one who, by the Lord's mercy, is trustworthy. (26) I consider that, on account of the present necessity, 'this is a good thing', namely, that 'it is a good thing for a man to stay as he is'. (27) Are you bound to a wife? Do not seek release. Are you free from a wife? Do not seek one. (28) But if you do marry, you have committed no sin; and if the virgin marries, she has committed no sin; but such people will get affliction for the flesh, and I am trying to spare you. (29) This is what I am saying, brothers: the time is short; henceforth let those who have wives be as though they had none, (30) and those who weep as though they did not weep, and those who rejoice as though they did not rejoice, and those who buy as though they did not possess, (31) and those who use the world as though they had no full use of it; for the outward show of this world is passing away.

(32) I desire you to be free from anxiety. The unmarried man is anxious about the things of the Lord, how he may please the Lord; (33) the married man is anxious about the things of the world, how he may please his

wife; (34) and so he is divided. And the unmarried woman and the virgin[1] is anxious about the things of the Lord, 'in order that she may be holy both in body and in spirit'; but she that is married is anxious about the things of the world, how she may please her husband.

(35) I am saying this to you for your own advantage, not in order to put a halter round your necks, but that you may wait on the Lord with seemliness and without hindrance. (36) But if anyone considers that he is not behaving in a seemly way towards his virgin, if he is over-sexed, and so it must be, then let him do what he wishes; he commits no sin; let them[2] marry. (37) On the other hand, he will do well who stands firm[3] in his own mind, and is under no necessity, but has authority over his own will, and has made up his own mind to this decision, namely, to keep his virgin as she is. (38) So that he who marries his virgin does well, and he who does not marry her will do better.

(39) A wife is bound as long as her husband is alive; but if her husband falls asleep she is free to marry anyone she chooses—remembering only that she is a Christian. (40) But she is happier if she stays as she is, in my opinion; and I think that I too have the Spirit of God.

About the virgins: compare vii. 1, etc. Paul turns to a new 25
subject, probably following the Corinthians' letter. Who *the virgins* are does not immediately appear, for after passing references in verses 28, 34, they are not mentioned till verses 36 ff., where the meaning of the term in its Corinthian setting will be discussed. For the present it may be observed that there is so far nothing to suggest that the word has any other than its customary meaning, that is, a woman (or man; used here in the

[1] This is the reading of P^{15} B, the Vulgate and the Sahidic. Alternative readings are *the unmarried virgin*; *the virgin*; *the unmarried woman and the unmarried virgin*. See the commentary.

[2] The singular γαμείτω is read by D* G *al.* But the plural (which makes it more difficult to think of a father giving his daughter in marriage—see the commentary) is certainly original.

[3] ἑδραῖος occurs in various places, and is omitted by P^{46} G, and the Old Latin, rightly. Zuntz's defence of the word (pp. 96 f.) is not convincing. ἕστηκεν alone can mean 'stand firm'.

genitive plural, τῶν παρθένων, there is nothing to indicate gender; according to M. Black, *The Scrolls and Christian Origins* (1961), p. 85, verses 25 ff. are 'best understood as referring primarily to a class of *male* celibates'—this is unlikely, (a) because it means distinguishing *virgin* here from *virgin* in verses 36 ff., and (b) because of verse 28, on which see the note) who has not had sexual experience. Having dealt with the duties of married persons, Paul begins to instruct (though with much reference back to what he has already said) the unmarried. He is careful to define the nature of his advice. **I have no charge from the Lord** (contrast vii. 10)**, but I give my opinion** (cf. vii. 12)**, as one who, by the Lord's mercy** (Robertson, pp. 1128, 1140, describes the participle ἠλεημένος as causal)**, is trustworthy.** The last word (πιστός) usually has this meaning with Paul (cf. especially iv. 2). It is sometimes applied to God, when also it means trustworthy, and occasionally (especially at 2 Cor. vi. 15) it means 'a believer' (as its opposite, ἄπιστος, means an 'unbeliever', as at vii. 12-15). Here Paul means that he is one whose advice can be trusted (not on his own account, but by God's mercy—cf. 2 Cor. iv. 1; 1 Tim. i. 12 f.), even when he has no direct command of the Lord to quote. Dr Black (loc. cit.) thinks that the word reflects the Syriac *mehaimena*, in the technical sense of *male celibate*. It is true that this word can mean *eunuch*; but why Paul should attach a variant of this meaning (which is not the usual meaning of the Syriac) to a Greek word, which neither he elsewhere nor any other Greek writer uses in this sense, is not apparent. If he means *virgin* (παρθένος) why does he not say *virgin*? Did the Corinthians know Syriac?

26 **I consider** (the verb corresponds to the noun *opinion*—he does not say 'I know') **that, on account of the present necessity, 'this is a good thing', namely, that 'it is a good thing for a man to stay as he is'.** There is good reason (see J. Jeremias in *Studia Paulina*, p. 151) to think that, as at vi. 12, 13; vii. 1, Paul is quoting words used by the Corinthians. Again, he does not disagree with them but he qualifies them; and again we may distinguish between 'it is a good thing for a man to do so-and-so' and 'a man is under obligation to do so-and-so'. In view of *the present necessity* a change of state is likely to bring

more trouble than happiness. The *necessity* is probably to be interpreted in terms of verse 29 rather than verse 37; that is, Paul is thinking not of the inward urge that drives men into marriage (this operates in the opposite direction), nor of the troubles of a married woman (Gen. iii. 16), nor even of persecution as such, but of the eschatological woes that are impending over the world, and are already anticipated in the sufferings of Christians. In view of these, men have already troubles enough, and will have more, without allowing themselves to enter into domestic tangles of one kind or another. It is probable that the Corinthians employed this maxim in one direction only: a single man is wiser if he does not marry. Paul adds the converse: a married man ought not to seek release from marriage; compare his earlier advice in vii. 10-16. He goes on at once to this twofold application.

Are you bound (the Greek verb is in the perfect tense, but 27
this implies, Have you been bound so that you now continue to be bound?) **to a wife? Do not seek release. Are you free** (literally, Have you been freed?, but it is scarcely possible to suppose that Paul is speaking only to widowers and the separated, and not to bachelors) **from a wife? Do not seek one** (in Greek, Do not seek a wife, but in English it is awkward to repeat the substantive). On the lively asyndeton of this verse see B.D. §§464, 494. It contains Paul's advice on what, in the present circumstances, it is a *good thing* for a man to do; but it is
in no sense a strict ruling which all must obey. **But if you do** 28
marry (the English auxiliary brings out the emphasis of the Greek *καί*), **you have committed no sin; and if the virgin marries, she has committed no sin.** *You* is evidently any male member of the Corinthian church who reads or hears Paul's words. It is evident from the fact that Paul takes up this side of the situation that the tendency in Corinth was to insist not so much that the married remain married (see above), as that the unmarried should remain single. There is, Paul allows, much good sense in this, but no question of Christian discipline. If you seek to lose your freedom in marriage you may be foolish, but you are not sinful. It is not so clear who is meant by *the virgin.* It is possible that the article is generic (cf. verse 25), and that we should render *a virgin*; this would almost certainly seem

the correct rendering, were it not for verses 36 ff., where the word *virgin* (παρθένος) evidently has a special meaning, which it will be necessary to discuss in due course. If the present verse is taken alone, it is most natural to understand it in the simple sense: If you (a man) marry, you have committed no sin; if a girl (referred to in the third person because male members of the congregation would be the primary recipients of the letter, and would also take the initiative in regard to marriage) marries, she has committed no sin. This it may be well to recall when we reach the latter passage. Dr Black (loc. cit.) thinks the *virgin* here to be a male celibate (see above); but on this view, which fits badly with verses 36 ff., the verse is grossly tautologous.

Man and woman alike are free to marry; **but such people** (acting against Paul's advice) **will get affliction for the flesh, and I am trying** (the present tense, φείδομαι, is conative) **to spare you** (cf. 2 Cor. i. 23; xiii. 2). The word *flesh* does not here have the special theological sense that it often has in Paul (see *Romans*, pp. 137, 146, 148), but refers simply to the physical sphere, within which marriage inevitably means obligations. If wars and rumours of wars, earthquake, pestilence, and famine (cf. Mark xiii. 7 f., and especially 17) are at hand, marriage can only have the effect of multiplying affliction. In the circumstances of the last days men must sit loose to all earthly relationships.

29 **This is what I am saying, brothers: the time is short,** that is, the time before the End. *Short* translates not an adjective but a participle (συνεσταλμένος), and we ought perhaps to render, The time has been shortened (cf. Mark xiii. 20). The context, however, does not suggest a special shortening of the time, only (as in Rom. xiii. 11 f.) that time is running out and there is little left. **Henceforth** (the meaning of the Greek, τὸ λοιπόν, is disputed; see M. E. Thrall, *Greek Particles in the New Testament* (1962), pp. 25-30; it may, as at iv. 2, be simply *now*, but the context suggests the sense given in the translation) **let those who have wives be** (here we have a genuine example of the imperatival ἵνα; see p. 157, and cf. Robertson, p. 994; Moule, p. 145; M. iii. 95) **as though they had none.** Verses 2-5 prove conclusively that by these words Paul did not mean that husbands and wives should live a celibate life within the framework of

marriage. He allowed that abstinence from marriage was advantageous for those who had the gift for such an unnatural kind of life, but, as a general rule, advised marriage, and insisted that it should be true marriage. What then did he mean? If the meaning of his 'as if not' can be established for this clause it should be possible to understand it in the following clauses too. Two points must be anticipated from the remainder of the paragraph. In verse 31b Paul says that *the outward show of this world is passing away*, and in verses 32 f. he contrasts *the unmarried man* whose thought is concentrated on pleasing the Lord with *the married man* whose thought is concentrated on pleasing his wife. From these two points two further points are to be deduced. First, the married man must recognize that the institution which he has allowed to shape his life belongs, notwithstanding its divine appointment, to an order which is passing away, and indeed will pass away soon (since *the time is short*). In a very little while he will share the life of heaven in which there is no marrying or giving in marriage (Mark xii. 25), and it will be well for him to prepare for this heavenly existence now—not by divorcing his wife, or ceasing to cohabit with her (still less, we may add, by ceasing to love her and enjoy her society; contrast the use of *as if not*—*ὡς μή*—in the *Acts of Paul and Thecla* 5 (Lipsius-Bonnet i. 238. 16)), but by recognizing that very soon their relationship will be on an entirely different basis. Secondly, the married man must (and in giving the command Paul presupposes that it is capable of fulfilment) wait on the Lord with single mind, as if he had no wife to distract his attention. Verse 32b does not mean that every single man gives undivided heed to the Lord, simply because he is single (and we shall see that Paul can be critical of the single man's 'anxiety'); conversely, in the paradox of the *as if not* the married man (though not without difficulty) is able to share the same concentration of devotion to the Lord. He who can thus live, in service to God and in detachment from the world, is a free man (Bultmann, *Theology*, p. 347 (E.T., 351), also Schoeps, *Paulus*, p. 222 (E.T., 211)), though his freedom is not that of the Stoic (cf. e.g. Epictetus III. xxiv. 60; IV. i. 159 f.), but of the slave of Christ (cf. vii. 22).

The other clauses may now be added. Let **those who weep** 30

be **as though they did not weep, and those who rejoice as though they did not rejoice, and those who buy as though**
31 **they did not possess, and those who use the world as though they had no full use of it.** Two points may be mentioned in regard to the translation. *Though* is an unfortunate English word in this context, for its common usage suggests an atmosphere of pretence and unreality, *as though* Paul were asking for a hypocritical show of sorrow or rejoicing. It is however difficult to see how the word can be avoided, and one can only hope by noting the danger to minimize it. *As though they had no full use of it* is sometimes rendered, As not abusing it, but both the context and the usage of the word (καταχρᾶσθαι) suggest the translation given. As in his advice to husbands Paul does not advocate asceticism, so here he does not advocate Stoic apathy. In Rom. xii. 15 he tells his readers to rejoice with those who rejoice and to weep with those who weep, and his advice here is not inconsistent. The point is that neither laughter nor tears is the last word; a man should never allow himself to be lost in either. Paul, again, no more forbids trade than marriage, but allows it under the same conditions; and the 'use of the world' is a general statement that will cover both social relations (such as marriage), and commerce. Christians may use the world (for the significance of the word see for example i. 21) but must not be absorbed in it; **for the outward show** (a not uncommon meaning of the word σχῆμα) **of this world is passing away**—indeed the world itself is passing away, but Paul's point is not the transiency of creation as such, but the fact that its outward pattern, in social and mercantile institutions, for example, has no permanence.

The transition to the next point is clear enough, though, as will appear, it contains a difficulty that is seldom observed. Those whose whole life is wrapped up in, for example, marriage or commerce, in a world where all possessions and relationships are passing away, can scarcely hope to avoid anxiety. But, says
32 Paul, **I desire you to be free from anxiety** (ἀμερίμνους). Jesus himself commands his followers to be free from anxiety: Do not be anxious (μεριμνᾶν) for your life, what you shall eat or what you shall drink, or for your body, what you shall put on . . . (Matt. vi. 25-34). And the rest of the New Testament echoes the

same thought, for example 1 Pet. v. 7; for Paul himself see Phil. iv. 11. It is moreover the essence of Paul's Gospel that man no longer needs to feel anxiety before God. Justified by faith he has peace with God (Rom. v. 1), and Paul's criticism of Judaism and of Judaizing Christianity is that they lead to bondage and fear (e.g. Rom. viii. 15); men engage in good works and religious practices because they are not confident of God's grace, but now that he has proved his love beyond doubt in that while we were still sinners Christ died for us such anxious religiosity is out of place, and is indeed a slight upon God's grace. The next sentence therefore appears to be anything but a commendation of the unmarried man. *I desire you to be free from anxiety* (ἀμερίμνους); **the unmarried man is anxious** (μεριμνᾷ) **about the things of the Lord, how he may please the Lord.** He ought not to be anxious; apart from any effort to please on his part, the Lord already loves him. If taken in this way the sentence is a criticism of the ascetic tendency in Corinth, a tendency that is evidence of an anxiety to win God's favour by pleasing him through the performance of meritorious religious works. The ascetics who decry marriage (cf. vii. 1, above) are not rising above but falling below the Christian standard. It is against this interpretation that Paul can elsewhere use the expression 'to please God' in a good sense (Rom. viii. 8; 1 Thess. ii. 15; iv. 1): one who is aware of the unmerited love of God will for that reason endeavour to please God who first loved him. If however we are to accept this alternative interpretation we must draw the conclusion that within one verse Paul uses *anxiety* in two senses: first in a bad sense—Christians ought not to be anxious; and then in a good sense—the unmarried man does well to be anxious about the things of the Lord. This is possible, for the argument could be that a good anxiety (about the things of the Lord) casts out a bad anxiety (about the things of the world); but it must be acknowledged that there are difficulties in both interpretations.

We come to firmer ground with the next sentence. **The** 33
married man is anxious about the things of the world,
how he may please his wife; and so he is divided—for we 34
are dealing with a Christian husband, who equally with the unmarried man, desires (in a good sense) *to please the Lord.* If he

did not, he would not be a Christian; just as, if he did not take thought for his wife, he would be unfaithful to his marriage vow (Schlatter). Hence his divided interest. *And so he is divided* (καὶ μεμέρισται) is here taken as the end of the sentence begun in verse 33. Some editors attach it to the following sentence, and there are variant readings (see note 1, on p. 173) in which this connection is necessary. The punctuation adopted in the text, however, makes better sense. The prime misfortune of the married man is not that he is married and involved thereby in a relationship rooted in the material world, but that his mind is divided.

What Paul has said about men, married and unmarried, can equally be said about women; and, as was noted above (p. 156), it is significant that he treats the two sexes in the same terms and on the same level. **The unmarried woman and the virgin is anxious about the things of the Lord, 'in order that she may be holy both in body and in spirit'; but she that is married is anxious about the things of the world, how she may please her husband.** Notwithstanding the general resemblance to what has been said above, this verse raises several problems. Is it possible to distinguish between *the unmarried woman* (ἡ ἄγαμος) and *the virgin* (ἡ παρθένος)? The fact that the verb following the double subject is singular (μεριμνᾷ) is not decisive. An *unmarried woman* clearly might be a virgin; it is possible that the word might refer to a widow (though in this case it is difficult to know why Paul does not use the word widow, χῆρα), or to a woman separated from her husband by divorce, or indeed to a single woman who was not a virgin—Schlatter rightly refers to the presence in the church of slaves, who might have had little choice in the matter. In each of these cases, however, *unmarried* seems scarcely the right word to use; this (with the singular verb) may in part account for the variant readings referred to above. The problem is further complicated by the difficulties which the word *virgin* causes in the following verses. It may be that Paul is thinking only of one group, *virgin* being added as a further explanation of *unmarried*: The unmarried woman, by which term I really mean not a woman who has lost her husband but the virgin . . . Alternatively, we might take *virgin* in the ordinary sense, to denote a woman unmarried and without other sexual experience, and *unmarried* to mean a woman (and it seems probable that there were such women in Corinth) who had renounced marriage. But this is guesswork; evidence cannot be cited to prove this meaning of *unmarried* (ἄγαμος).

Where the unmarried man is said to be anxious *to please the Lord*, the unmarried woman's aim is given in the words, *that she may be holy both in body and in spirit*. The parallelism gives some superficial support to the view that 'pleasing the Lord' in verse 32 should be taken in a good sense. It must however be assumed that holiness is the aim of all Christians, whether married or unmarried. The unmarried woman's special aim is presumably therefore to be holy not only in spirit but in body; she wishes to sanctify her body by abstinence from sexual relations. But this is not consistent with Paul's teaching in general, for he believes that all Christians, married or unmarried, must be holy in body; see Rom. vi. 12; xii. 1; 1 Cor. vi. 13, 15, 19, 20; xv. 44; 2 Cor. iv. 10; Gal. vi. 17; Phil. i. 20; iii. 21; 1 Thess. v. 23. It is true that Paul's usage is not wholly consistent, but it cannot be maintained that in all these passages, which speak of the holiness of the body (or in similar terms) he is addressing holy bachelors and spinsters only. Moreover, in the present chapter he has told married men and women that through their marriage they *sanctify* their unbelieving partners, and that the children born of these marriages are *holy*. We must conclude therefore that in *that she may be holy both in body and in spirit* we have words quoted from the Corinthian ascetical party. Paul approves the sentiment, though he would not himself confine it to the unmarried. Again, he is making the point that though in the present circumstances the unmarried state is desirable, it is not intrinsically better.

For the latter part of the verse, compare verse 33.

With a further word of caution Paul moves on to a point of notorious difficulty, which he appears to have had in mind since
verse 25. **I am saying this to you for your own advantage** 35
(cf. verses 26, 28 above; his argument is not a matter of what is right or wrong, but of what is or is not expedient and profitable in particular circumstances), **not in order to put a halter round your necks** (and so to direct you, like a domesticated

animal; cf. 2 Cor. i. 24), **but that you may wait on the Lord with seemliness and without hindrance.** The last clause is a paraphrase; close translation is scarcely possible. In Greek, the whole clause is parallel to what is expressed by the adjective 'that which is advantageous' (*τὸ σύμφορον*). There are two adjectives, meaning 'that which is seemly' (*εὔσχημον*; cf. verse 36), and 'that which is suitable for waiting' (*εὐπάρεδρον*, possibly coined by Paul; cf. ix. 13, where the verb *παρεδρεύειν* is used for 'waiting upon the altar'). An adverb, 'without hindrance, or encumbrance' (*ἀπερισπάστως*), follows. The neuter adjectives are used by Paul as abstracts, thus: with a view to seemliness, and due attention to the Lord, without hindrance. Kümmel compares Epictetus III. xxii. 67 ff.: the Cynic in carrying out his vocation must be without hindrance (*ἀπερίσπαστος*). The drift is clear: if you avoid marriage you avoid encumbrances, and you can devote yourself to the Lord's work without incurring problems, difficulties, and anxieties, which married people incur. But this is no rule, and indeed seemliness may be transgressed by celibacy as well as by marriage (a concession the Corinthian ascetics would probably find it very difficult to
36 allow). **If anyone considers that he is not behaving in a seemly way** (the verb, *ἀσχημονεῖν*, 'to behave in an unseemly, or dishonourable, way', is related to the adjective, *εὐσχήμων*, 'seemly', in verse 35) **towards his virgin** (the normal meaning of the noun *παρθένος*; see verses 25, 28, and below), **if he is over-sexed** (*ὑπέρακμος*), **and so it must be, then let him do what he wishes** (M. iii. 75, 'let him go on doing what he wants', which fits the tense of the present imperative, *ποιείτω*, but not the sense of the context, where the problem arises because he is not doing what he wishes); **he commits no sin; let them marry.** This translation retains most of the ambiguities of the Greek, but by using the rendering *over-sexed* it determines the meaning of a difficult and ambiguous sentence in what seems the most probable but is certainly not the only possible sense. Who is the, unexpressed, subject of the sentence? And what is meant by *his virgin*? The following suggestions have been made. (1) The man in the sentence is a father, and *his virgin* is his daughter. If this view is taken the clause I have translated *if he is over-sexed* must be taken to mean 'if she (the

adjective can be masculine or feminine, and there is no pronoun) is at (or, perhaps, passing) the age of marriage'. We thus have to do with one who is in the position to exercise the *patria potestas* over his daughter, who cannot marry without his permission. If he thinks that by restraining her from marriage he is not treating her fairly he should have no scruples about permitting her to do what she wishes (again, in the absence of pronouns, this is a possible rendering), let them (the virgin daughter and the chosen bridegroom) marry. This interpretation is subject to three disadvantages: (a) it involves some awkward changes of subject; (b) 'at the age for marriage' is a less probable rendering of the Greek (ὑπέρακμος; the fact that Jews—see S.B. iii. 376 f.—recognized a 'marriageable age', and thought that a father was well advised to give his daughter in marriage as soon as she reached it, is not in any way conclusive); (c) the word *virgin* does not mean 'daughter'. To the last point Schlatter answers not unreasonably that though the person under whose authority a marriageable girl stood would normally be her father there were other possibilities. If the father were dead, his place might be taken by the girl's brother, or a guardian. If the girl's parents were slaves, the authority would lie in the hands of their master. Even so, however, *his virgin* remains a surprising expression. (2) The man and the woman (*his virgin*) have entered upon a spiritual marriage, that is, they live together but without having physical relations. We know that the practice of permitting *virgines subintroductae* existed (though never with full approval) later in the history of the church (perhaps as early as the second century); it is suggested that it, or something like it, originated in Corinth as early as the middle of the first century. Within this practice it might well happen that a man (or woman) found the strain greater than he could bear; possibly some in Corinth were in favour of insisting that the *status quo* be maintained, but Paul advises that in these circumstances the marriage should become an ordinary marriage. This would be no sin. It is against this interpretation that we have no other evidence that the custom of 'spiritual marriages' arose as early as it must have done if it is to be found here, and that in view of vii. 2-5 Paul could hardly have countenanced it to the extent he appears to do here. (3) A recent suggestion, made by Miss J. M.

Ford (in *N.T.S.* x. 361-5), is that in these verses Paul is dealing with a possible case of levirate marriage (see Deut. xxv. 5-10). Paul's word for the woman (παρθένος) means here not ***virgin*** but 'young widow'. The adjective (ὑπέρακμος) more naturally, from its position, qualifies the woman, and means 'of marriageable age'; 'it may refer to the passage in the Mishnah [*Niddah* v. 6, 7] which states that the levirate law only applies when the girl has reached the age of puberty' (*op. cit.* 364). Here too at least three serious difficulties arise: (a) the Greek noun (παρθένος) means virgin (so e.g. in the only other place, 2 Cor. xi. 2, where it is used by Paul) and does not mean widow; (b) the Greek adjective (ὑπέρακμος) does not mean 'at the age of puberty'; (c) there is nothing in the paragraph to suggest that the point under discussion is a rather obscure piece of Jewish law, which could only arise in a Jewish community and would probably have been incomprehensible to the Corinthian church. See also the note on verse 39. (4) Fewest difficulties are raised by the fourth possibility, which has been argued convincingly by Kümmel (in Lietzmann-Kümmel, and in *Neutestamentliche Studien für Rudolf Bultmann* (1954), pp. 275-95). The man and woman are an engaged couple, in doubt (under the influence of the ascetic party) whether to carry out their planned marriage. 'His virgin' remains a somewhat odd expression in this case also, but the woman in question is a virgin, and the colloquial English 'his girl' provides a close analogy. The adjective (ὑπέρακμος) is used in a natural sense, and the advice given is obviously sensible. To renounce marriage may seem to be a fine and spiritual act, but in some circumstances it may be unfair to the girl and impossible to the man.

So far, interpretation (4) seems the most probable; the rest of the paragraph will confirm this. One possible case has been
37 considered; there is another. **On the other hand, he will do well who stands firm in his own mind** (literally, *heart*, καρδίᾳ), **and is under no necessity, but has authority over his own will, and has made up his own mind** (literally, *heart*, καρδίᾳ) **to this decision, namely, to keep his virgin as she is** (the last three words are not in the Greek, but probably give the sense; to omit them would depict a very different situation, which, as Dr Black and Dr Chadwick point out,

would be much like that of the later *virgines subintroductae*—so much like it that it would incur the criticism of vii. 2-5). It is very difficult to apply this advice to the case of a father with his unmarried daughter, or to levirate marriage. The picture, however, of a young man who is able to master his natural desire to marry his fiancée is perfectly clear. Paul maintains his point consistently. There is no evil in marriage, but it is well to avoid
it if you can. He sums up both sides of the matter: **So that he** 38
who marries his virgin does well, and he who does not marry her will do better. It is in this verse that the strength of the case for interpretation (1) resides, for here a different word for 'marry' is used from that which occurs in verses 28, 36; its form (*γαμίζειν*) suggests that it means 'to give in marriage' and should be used of the father (cf. Mark xii. 25). Most commentators (with Allo, Bachmann, and Heim as notable, and vigorous, exceptions), grammarians, and lexicographers, however, seem agreed that there is no insuperable difficulty in supposing that Paul could use it in the sense 'enter into the relationship of marriage' (the strict distinction between verbs in -*έω* and verbs in -*ίζω* was breaking down in the Hellenistic age; for the use of 'marriage' verbs see, in addition to the dictionaries, B.D. §101; M. ii. 409 f.; iii. 57).

It seems therefore that under the heading *virgins* the Corinthians in their letter (perhaps it is significant of their point of view that a fiancée should be described as a *virgin*—the implication being that this is the important thing about her and that she would do well to remain what she is) had raised the question whether it might not be better for an engaged couple to refrain from going on to marriage. Paul replies that it would indeed be better; but that if they marry they not merely do not sin, but do well.

One further point within the field of marriage relations arises.
Should widows remarry? **A wife is bound as long as her** 39
husband is alive. Compare Rom. vii. 2. This was common law before it was Christian ethics. Paul believed that a man was equally bound (verses 11, 27); he does not say so here, probably because he was answering a specific question. **But if her husband falls asleep** (*κοιμηθῇ*; Paul uses this euphemism always, or almost always, of Christians, so that there may be an

implication that the deceased husband was a Christian; cf. his use of *καθεύδειν* at 1 Thess. v. 10; this conclusion is however by no means certain) **she is free to marry anyone she chooses** (that is, the law of levirate marriage does not hold among Christians; cf. p. 184)—**remembering only that she is a Christian** (literally, *only in the Lord*). The last clause is usually taken to mean, 'She may marry anyone she pleases, provided he is a Christian', but, as Lightfoot points out, this narrows Paul's meaning—'She must remember that she is a member of Christ's body; and not forget her Christian duties and responsibilities'; similarly Schlatter. It is reasonable to add that, in view of the difficulties caused by mixed marriages (see vii. 12-16), a widow exercising her right to second marriage would no doubt be wise to choose a Christian husband. In 1 Tim. v. 14 younger widows are urged to marry.

As throughout the chapter, Paul asserts against all ascetics that there is no evil in marriage; a Christian may indeed be married more than once. Marriage is permitted, but is not
40 therefore necessarily advisable. **But she is happier if she stays as she is, in my opinion** (for the word cf. verse 25). It is trouble, rather than happiness, that marriage brings, in Paul's view; and it is a view not to be disregarded. **I think that I too have the Spirit of God.** Compare verse 25; also ii. 16. With perhaps a touch of irony, Paul seems here to claim (and to allow that other Christians may also claim—perhaps he expected to be contradicted in Corinth) to possess the Spirit who leads men into all the truth and instructs the Christian conscience; he does not claim any unique (*I too*) kind or degree of authority in the application of the Gospel to specific situations (Schweizer, 26b). *I too* probably means that the Corinthians claimed the authority of the Spirit for their opinions; they seem to have been unwilling to consider views and practices that obtained elsewhere (cf. iv. 17; vii. 17; xiv. 33). Such claims are always dangerously exposed to contradiction and can have no authority.

It is worth noting that, though the thought of verses 39 f. coheres with that of the chapter as a whole, their formal attachment to it is loose; they seem to be almost an afterthought. This probably reflects the way in which the epistle was written (cf.

Introduction, p. 15), and should make the student hesitant to accept theories of dislocation and composition. Paul was probably not in a position to write a perfectly connected work.

(b) FOOD SACRIFICED TO IDOLS

19. viii. 1-13. THE SOURCE OF THE TROUBLE—EXALTATION OF KNOWLEDGE OVER LOVE

(1) About things sacrificed to idols: we know[1] that 'we all have knowledge'. Knowledge puffs up, but love builds up. (2) If anyone thinks he has achieved some piece of knowledge, he has not yet attained the knowledge he ought to have; (3) but if anyone loves God,[2] he has been known by God.[2] (4) So, with regard to the eating of things sacrificed to idols, we know[1] that 'there is no idol in the world', and that 'there is no God but one'. (5) For indeed though there are so-called gods, whether in heaven or on earth, as there are in fact many 'gods' and many 'lords', (6) yet for us there is one God, the Father, from whom come all things and to whom our own being leads, and one Lord Jesus Christ, through whom all things, including ourselves, come into being.

(7) But it is not everyone who has this knowledge. Some, through their familiarity[3] up to the present with the idol, eat their food as something sacrificed to an idol, and their conscience, which is weak, is defiled. (8) 'Food will not commend us to God': if we do not eat we go short of nothing; if we do eat, we gain no advantage.[4] (9) But beware lest this authority of yours becomes a

[1] *οἴδαμεν*; it is possible, and may be preferable, to read this as *οἶδα μέν*, *I know*. See Jeremias, *Studia Paulina*, p. 151.

[2] P[46] and Clement omit *τὸν θεόν* (*God*), and, supported by, ℵ* 33, *ὑπ' αὐτοῦ*, *by him* (in this translation, *by God*). Zuntz, pp. 31 f., thinks the longer reading 'ruinous' of the sense; a different view is taken in the commentary.

[3] Instead of *συνηθείᾳ* the majority of MSS., including D G and the Latin, have *συνειδήσει*; see the commentary.

[4] The order of these clauses is reversed by ℵ D G and the majority of MSS., whose text is approved by Zuntz, pp. 161 f.

stumbling-block to those who are weak. (10) For if someone sees you,[1] who have knowledge, sitting at table in an idol-shrine, will not his conscience, this weak man's conscience, be fortified to eat things sacrificed to idols? (11) For the weak man perishes by your knowledge, your brother, for whose sake Christ died. (12) And so, by sinning against your brothers, and wounding their conscience, weak as it is, you sin against Christ. (13) Therefore, if food offends my brother, I will never eat flesh again, that I may not offend my brother.

1 **About things sacrificed to idols:** Paul turns to a fresh theme raised (it appears) in the Corinthians' letter (cf. vii. 1, and the note). Much though not all (for this and other facts about food sacrificed to idols, and much detail concerning the matters discussed in this chapter, see 'Things sacrificed to Idols') of the food offered for sale in ancient towns had, in whole or part, passed through sacred rites in heathen religious establishments. It was commonly described as 'sacrificed for sacred purposes' (*ἱερόθυτον*, used by Paul at x. 28; *θεόθυτον* was also used), but Jews and Christians, who had their own estimate of such sacred purposes, preferred to call it 'sacrificed to idols' (*εἰδωλόθυτον*). Such food was prohibited to Jews, on three grounds: (a) it was tainted with idolatry; (b) it could not be supposed that the heathen would have paid tithe on it; (c) if it was meat, it could not be supposed that it had been slaughtered in the proper way. No doubt there were in Corinth local or travelling Jews who urged the same prohibition as binding on the church. Against them, Christian gnostics, whose presence is betrayed not only by the claim to possess knowledge (see below) but also by the freedom and authority enjoyed in consequence of it (Bultmann, *Theology*, p. 180 (E.T., 180 f.)), submitted the argument to an analysis that showed that it had no validity. What then ought to be done? Paul deals with the question in two places, here in chapter viii, and again in x. 14-33. It is sometimes held that the two treatments of the same question are not

[1] *σε*, *you*, is omitted by P^{46} B G and the Latin, so that we should have to render, '... sees one who has knowledge, sitting...'. This generalizes and weakens a more forceful statement.

consistent with each other, and that they must originally have formed parts of two different letters. This would also account for their being separated in 1 Corinthians as it now is. The reason why chapter ix intervenes is discussed below (pp. 199 f.); only detailed exegesis can decide the question whether or not Paul is consistent throughout the two parts into which his discussion falls. For a summary of the results to which the exegesis leads see the Introduction, pp. 16 f.

We know that 'we all have knowledge'. As at vii. 1, and other places, Paul appears to quote the Corinthian letter, and allows the claim that all have knowledge, because his first step is to show the limitations of knowledge in itself, and in doing this shows that he shares the knowledge of the 'gnostics'. In verse 7, considering the matter from another angle, he denies that all have knowledge, and asserts that those who do not have it nevertheless have rights, and make claims on the charity of their brethren which must not be ignored or denied. For *knowledge* (*γνῶσις*), see above on p. 18, cf. pp. 67 f. The term was probably (at this stage) a wide one, and the next few verses show that it included Christian speculative theology in general, and drew conclusions with regard to Christian social and moral behaviour. It seems, however, to have been focused upon the doctrine of God; evidently the gnostics claimed to know God (cf. 1 John ii. 4). We shall see that though Paul was critical of the gnostic movement he nevertheless shared many of its views. His main criticism appears in his first comment. **Knowledge puffs up, but love builds up.** It was characteristic of the Corinthians to be puffed up (cf. iv. 6, 18, 19; v. 2; contrast xiii. 4), and of Paul to be concerned with the building up of the church (iii. 9, 10, 12, 14; x. 23; xiv. 3, 4, 5, 12, 17, 26). The present paragraph goes on to demonstrate the consequences of a loveless *gnosis* (verses 9-13). It may be asked if there is a necessary tension between knowledge and love. Was it impossible to have a loving gnostic? Paul himself is evidence that the two were not altogether incompatible; he held substantially gnostic opinions together with loving concern for the church as a whole. But Corinthian gnosticism had an essentially self-regarding element which was incompatible with Christian love; it was not merely a body of doctrine (which Paul himself might hold) but

an approach to life and to religion which was acquisitive (*erotic*,
in the broadest sense of the term) and therefore inconsistent with
love (ἀγάπη; see chapter xiii). The next verse shows the termino-
2 logical difficulty in which Paul finds himself. **If anyone thinks
he has achieved some piece of knowledge** (literally, *thinks
himself to have come to know something*), **he has not yet attained
the knowledge he ought to have** (literally, *he has not yet
come to know as he ought to know*). The distinction which it seems
that these rather cumbersome clauses seek to express is between,
on the one hand, the collection of pieces of information (*gnosis*)
about God, and, on the other, the state of being personally, and
rightly, related to him. Being a Christian, and building up the
life of the Christian church, does not consist in acquiring and
teaching a number of propositions about God, even when they
happen to be true, and to be such that an apostle himself must
not only share but repeat and teach them, and (with qualifications) act upon them. To possess and to preen oneself upon
such sound doctrine is quite different from that knowledge of
God of which Christianity consists (e.g. John xvii. 3); this is the
knowledge that man *ought to have*; there is a true Christian
gnosis, even if the Corinthians have not yet achieved it as fully
as they think. Even so, however, it is not knowledge but love
3 that is the key-word. **But if anyone loves God, he has been
known by God.** The apodosis of this sentence is obscure;
literally it runs, 'this person has been known by him', and it
would be not impossible to take it to mean, 'God has been
known by him'; that is, if you love God (instead of speculating
about him), you know God (cf. 1 John iv. 7). Compare however
xiii. 12; xiv. 38; and Gal. iv. 9; also 2 Tim. ii. 19. Paul's fundamental reply to the characteristically gnostic idea of the spiritual
ascent of the soul to God is to assert the primacy of God's
initiative in taking knowledge of man, and acting on his behalf
by sending his Son. The sentence does not mean (for this would
be contrary to Paul's clearly expressed thought elsewhere), If
a man loves God, God rewards him by recognizing him. The
sense rather is, If a man loves God, *this is a sign that* God has
taken the initiative. It is more characteristic of Paul to describe
man's response to God as faith rather than love. For love to God
however see ii. 9; Rom. viii. 28; and compare Rom. v. 5; 2 Thess.

iii. 5; this expression is probably chosen here because Paul is contrasting love with knowledge, and sees that a Christian's love for his fellows (which, rather than *gnosis*, should determine his actions) arises out of his grateful love to God. The language of mutual knowledge between God and man is gnostic in formulation, but it is the language alone that Paul borrows from gnostic sources; the content is the biblical doctrine of election and acceptance with God (Exod. xxxiii. 12, 17; Amos iii. 2; Jer. i. 5; see Lietzmann; also Bultmann in *T.W.N.T.* i. 709 f.). Compare verse 6.

But what is the—substantially correct—gnostic position with
regard to food sacrificed to idols? **With regard to the eating of** 4
things sacrificed to idols, we know that (cf. verse 1; the words again introduce a quotation from the Corinthian letter) **'there is no idol in the world', and that 'there is no God but one'.** The first proposition presumably means that no idol in the world has any real existence, though in view of x. 20 f., not to mention verse 5, this affirmation needs careful statement. Paul himself undoubtedly believed in the real existence of demonic beings, and that these beings made use of idolatrous rites; the fact that they had been defeated, and were ultimately to be completely put down, by Christ, did not remove their threat to Christians, nor did the fact that the object of worship was in itself no more than a piece of wood or stone. It is easy to use loose language in such a context as this, and probably the Corinthians did so, meaning that the proposition that a statue is, or is the residence of, for example, Zeus or Athena, is not true. In particular, it is not true that either the statue, or the mythical figure it represents, is what a Christian means by God. Of what Christians mean by God there is and can be no more than one. This conviction is already to be found in the Old Testament (e.g. Deut. vi. 4; Isa. xliv. 8; xlv. 5); the Corinthians may also have owed something to the monotheistic tendency in Greek speculation (notably among the Stoics, not without earlier precedent; but also others—see e.g. the eloquent argument of Plutarch's tract *On the Delphic Ei*). What Paul means by the uniqueness of God he sets forth in the following verses.

For indeed though there are (εἴπερ concessive, as in Homer 5
—B.D. §454) **so-called gods, whether in heaven or on**

earth, as there are in fact many 'gods' and many 'lords',
6 **yet for us there is one God.** It would have been foolish to deny
that the word *god* was in common use; in common opinion the ancient world was thickly populated with divine beings, who, though their natural home was *in heaven*, acted freely and from time to time also appeared *on earth*. Paul seems to go further than this. The word *god* as used by the heathen certainly does not denote the God of the Old Testament, the God and Father of the Lord Jesus Christ, but it does not follow from this that it denotes nothing, and that those beings whom the heathen call *god* have no existence. The Old Testament itself presupposes their existence, for example in Deut. x. 17, which, like the present verse, puts *gods* and *lords* together. In this verse Paul appears to express no definite opinion on the question; it would exaggerate in one direction to suppose that he denied the existence of beings neither truly God nor human, but it would exaggerate in the other direction if we were to take his *there are* to affirm the reality of the beings mentioned. Later discussion of the problem of sacrificial food (see x. 20 f.) shows Paul's view on this matter. He speaks not only of *many gods* but also of *many lords* in view of the double statement that is about to follow about God the Father and the Lord Jesus Christ; this statement was therefore probably a formula Paul had used before, and not coined on the spur of the moment.

The drive of his argument is towards the assertion that, whatever other spiritual or demonic beings there may be, *for us* there is only one whom we recognize as God, whom we trust and obey in a unique sense as the source of life and redemption. This recognition takes place on the basis not of speculation but of the act of this God in history, through his Son. He is therefore described as **the Father** (primarily of his only Son, Jesus Christ; secondarily also of those who through Christ have a derivative sonship)**, from whom come all things** (that is, he is the Creator) **and to whom our own being leads** (literally, *and we unto him*; that is, we exist in order to serve him, and our destiny is to be found in him)**, and one Lord Jesus Christ, through** ('This διά has its exegetical basis in the b^e of Gen. i. 26, *b*^{e}*ṣalmenu*'—Schlatter) **whom all things, including ourselves, come into being** (this rendering, in bringing out the relation tends to obscure the distinction between *all things* and *ourselves*—Christ is the agent of creation, and also the agent of redemption, and it is as the product of redemption that we come into being; cf. Bultmann, *Theology*, p. 131 (E.T., 132)). As at an earlier point (see pp. 90, 151), Paul makes use of the terminology of Hellenistic religious philosophy. Compare also Rom. xi. 36. See, as one among several passages that might be quoted, M. Aurelius iv. 23: From thee [nature, φύσις] are all things, in thee are all things, to thee are all things.

Jesus Christ is not described as God, and the fact that *Lord* (κύριος) serves very frequently in the Greek Old Testament as an equivalent of the Hebrew name of God (YHWH) loses some force from the fact that it was also used in a variety of other senses; for example, it might be no more than 'Sir', used as a polite form of address. It is always important to note the context in which *Lord* is used. Here it evidently stands in close relation, but is not identical, with God. *Christ*, in Paul's usage, is seldom more than a second personal name, but its use means that Paul accepted the belief that Jesus was the Messiah whose coming Judaism awaited; in him the promises of the Old Testament were fulfilled (cf. 2 Cor. i. 20). To the Hellenistic world *Lord* was a more meaningful way of expressing the divine kingship of Jesus than messianic terminology could provide. As was noted above, Jesus Christ the Lord is related to both creation and redemption. As O. Cullmann (*Christologie des Neuen Testaments* (1957), pp. 2, 253, 336 f. (E.T., 2, 241, 326), cf. *Christus und die Zeit* (1962), p. 110 (E.T., 114)) rightly points out, the Father and the Son are distinguished not by their spheres of operation (creation and redemption), but by the prepositions, *from* and *to* of the one, *through* of the other. In creation and redemption Jesus occupies a place held in Judaism by personified Wisdom and personified Law (see W. D. Davies, pp. 147-76, though without specific reference to this passage). This observation, though useful and important, does not in itself bring out the full meaning of what is said, which is indeed independent of Wisdom and Torah speculation. Jesus Christ is the divine agent in whose action God is perceived; he would be visible in his work of creation were it not that creation had been defaced. As it is, it is in the work of restoration that he, and in him God, can be perceived and encountered (see *Adam*, pp. 87 f.).

So far Paul's representation of the Corinthian *gnosis* (which he may have improved as he quoted and expanded it—cf. Col. i. 15-20). It is not so irrelevant to the main theme as some commentators have held, since reflections on the reality of idolatrous worship and belief must bear upon the question of food sacrificed to idols, and Paul has no difficulty in returning to the practical question of what the Corinthians might and might not eat. If all recognized the essential unreality of idols (as was claimed in verse 1—*we all have knowledge*) there would be no
7 problem; but it is not so simple. **It is not everyone who has this knowledge.** Compare verse 1, and the note there; there is no need to suppose (with Héring) that Paul uses the word *knowledge* (γνῶσις) in different senses in the two verses. It is easy for 'enlightened' Christians to forget the existence of their weaker brothers, who, though as Christians they believed in the one God and one Lord, had not drawn the inference that so-called gods and lords, and demonic beings of every kind, were now unable to separate the Christian from God (Rom. viii. 38 f.). **Some, through their familiarity up to the present with the idol, eat their food** (the last two words are not in the Greek, but in English *eat* needs an object; it is assumed that what is eaten has come from an idolatrous source) **as something sacrificed to an idol, and their conscience, which is weak, is defiled.** A well attested reading (see note 3 on p. 187) gives: 'Some, through their awareness (συνειδήσει) of the idol, . . .', but this has probably arisen through the resemblance between *familiarity* (συνήθεια) and *awareness* (*conscience*, συνείδησις), and because *conscience* occurs in the next line. There are in Corinth men who have eaten sacrificed food all their lives, and have always thought of it as sacrificed to an idol having real existence, and thus bearing real spiritual significance and force. In becoming Christians they have not ceased to believe in the reality of the spiritual beings behind idols, and have accordingly not ceased to think of the food itself as having religious meaning. They are *weak* (cf. ix. 22; also Rom. xiv. 1, 2, 21; but note that in the present passage the 'weak' cannot be of Jewish origin, since they have been familiar with idolatry), *weak* in *conscience*, for they are scrupulous where scrupulosity rests on

pure error; to eat food sacrificed to idols is contrary to their conscience, and if they do eat their conscience is defiled. All this is foolish, and Paul does not defend it, though he will go on to defend the weak man's place in the church and his interest in his strong brother's behaviour. He does this by quoting again from the Corinthians' beliefs (and presumably from their
letter), and then qualifying as well as approving it. **'Food will** 8
not commend us to God' (that is, to observe food laws does not constitute a claim on God; cf. Rom. xiv. 17): **if we do not eat, we go short of nothing; if we do eat, we gain no advantage.** The first clause is clearly consistent with the position of the strong Christians in Corinth, who see no objection to eating sacrificed food, and Paul agrees with it. An alternative interpretation is, Food will not bring us before God's judgement seat (cf. Rom. xiv. 10; 2 Cor. v. 10); we shall be neither rewarded nor punished for eating or not eating. There is little difference in meaning. The second and third clauses begin Paul's correction of the Corinthian position. The strong Corinthian would have worded them differently: If we eat sacrificial food we lose nothing of our Christian status or Christian reward; if we do not eat, but abstain as the weak Christians do on rigorist grounds, we gain no advantage. This is certainly true; but Paul is concerned to point out that the converse is equally true. No man is saved because he is an 'advanced' Christian with liberal views, or damned because he follows the dictates of an over-scrupulous conscience. Serious application of their own theological principle provides a check to the gnostics. An even more important consideration follows. Christians must walk in love, and consider the needs of their
brothers. **Beware lest this authority of yours** (*ἐξουσία*—not 9
explained here, but clearly authority to eat any kind of food is meant, or included; the word probably occurred in the Corinthian letter, and etymologically recalls the 'all things are permitted me' of vi. 12; x. 23; cf. ix. 4, 12, 18; according to Lietzmann it is a gnostic term) **becomes a stumbling-block** (*πρόσκομμα*; cf. Rom. xiv. 13, 20) **to those who are weak** (cf. verse 7, those who have weak consciences), as it may if they are thereby induced to do what is contrary to their consciences. The
point is made clearer by concrete example. **For if someone** 10

sees you, who have (see note 1 on p. 188) **knowledge, sitting at table** (literally, *reclining*) **in an idol-shrine** (as chapter x shows, there were many ways short of this in which sacrificial food might be eaten), **will not his conscience, this weak man's conscience** (an attempt to imitate the unusual word-order of the Greek), **be fortified** (literally, *built up*; see above, p. 189—the word is commonly used by Paul in a good sense) **to eat things sacrificed to idols?** Many Greeks (as Schlatter points out) who on rationalistic grounds had given up belief in the gods and in the efficacy of sacrifice continued to take part, for social reasons, in rites in which they now saw no meaning. Could not a Christian, with stronger reason, not only accept invitations to private houses (x. 27) but also dine with his friends in heathen temples, in the setting of idolatrous rites? What harm would he do? Would he not even do good? This verse probably reflects a claim made by the strong Corinthians: If I set a good example by publicly taking part in an idolatrous feast, knowing that the food is just food and nothing more, our less advanced Christian brothers will be encouraged, built up, edified, to do the same thing. True, Paul comments; but unlike you they will be acting against their consciences, and therefore sinning, since whatsoever is not of faith is sin (Rom. xiv. 23). This will be their destruction, whatever the theological truth about idols may be. '*Une belle édification . . . qui les pousse à*
11 *leur perte!*' (Héring). **For** (what happens is that) **the weak man perishes by your knowledge, your** (Greek, *the*; cf. i. 1) **brother, for whose sake Christ died.** Because you act out of knowledge (γνῶσις) rather than love, and see fit to exercise your strong conscience, your brother, whom you lead into sin,
12 perishes, and Christ in respect of him suffers in vain. **And so, by sinning against your brothers** (Greek, *the brothers*, the community as a whole, but especially the weak), **and wounding their conscience, weak as it is, you sin against Christ** (cf. Matt. xxv. 40). So mistaken can the possessors of knowledge be; perhaps we should add, so sinful can those who profess to be the most spiritual members of the church be. Paul does not dictate to others (an interesting sidelight on his understanding
13 of his ministry), but his own conclusion is clear. **Therefore, if food** (notably idolatrous food, but, as the rest of the sentence

shows, other kinds of scrupulosity about food are in mind too) **offends** (*makes to stumble*, but the verb is not etymologically related to the noun in verse 9; see rather i. 23) **my brother** (drives him away from the Christian faith), **I will never eat flesh again, that I may not offend my brother** (Rev. ii. 14). *Flesh*, not sacrificial food; for Christian vegetarians compare Rom. xiv. 2. We can scarcely infer from this verse that the same kind of vegetarianism was current in Corinth; Paul simply widens and generalizes the situation. Schlatter notes Josephus, *Life* 14: certain Jewish priests, sent to Rome, lived on figs and nuts to avoid defilement. Paul is willing to abridge his liberty (see ix. 1, and the note, for the connection) to any extent in the interests of his brethren. He does not consider the possibility that this curtailment might in some circumstances give a false impression of Christian truth; no doubt there was no danger that the position of the strong might go by default in Corinth.

It is worth while to note, before leaving the paragraph, that by putting together the quotations that have been noted in verses 1, 4, 8 a full account of the Corinthian position can be obtained. 'We all have knowledge (viii. 1): there is no idol in the world, there is only one single God (viii. 4). Therefore the eating of meat offered to idols is an adiaphoron (viii. 8). Hence there applies here also: πάντα ἔξεστιν (x. 23). That is a clear, compelling sequence of thought, which is entirely in accord with the mind of Jesus (Mark vii. 15a)—apparently!' (Jeremias, *Studia Paulina*, p. 152).

It may also be noted that in discussing the question of food offered to idols Paul neither here nor in chapter x makes any reference to the so-called Apostolic Decree (Acts xv. 20, 29; xxi. 25). See Introduction, p. 8.

20. ix. 1-27. EVEN AN APOSTLE WILL RENOUNCE HIS RIGHTS FOR THE SAKE OF THE GOSPEL

(1) Am I not free? Am I not an apostle? Have I not seen Jesus our Lord? Are you not my work in the Lord? (2) If I am not an apostle to others, yet at least to you I am, for you are the seal of my apostleship in the Lord. (3) My

defence against those who would like to examine me is this. (4) Have we not the right to eat and drink? (5) Have we not the right to take about a Christian sister as wife, as do the other apostles, and the Lord's brothers, and Cephas? (6) Or are Barnabas and I the only ones who do not have the right not to work for our living? (7) Who ever goes to war at his own charges? Who plants a vineyard and does not eat its fruit? Or[1] who tends a flock and does not drink some of the milk the flock yields?

(8) You don't suppose, do you, that I am saying these things with no more than human authority? Does not the law say these things too? (9) For in the law of Moses it stands written, 'You shall not muzzle the ox when it is threshing'. Does God care about the oxen? (10) Or is he not speaking simply on our account? Yes, it was written on our account, for he who ploughs ought to plough in hope, and he who threshes ought to do so in hope of partaking of the crop. (11) If we have sown spiritual things for you, is it a great thing if we reap material things from you? (12) If others share in authority over you, do not we the more? But we have made no use of this authority, but endure all things in order that we may put no obstacle in the way of the Gospel of Christ.

(13) Do you not know that those who officiate in holy things eat the things that come from the holy place? that those who attend upon the altar have their share together at the altar? (14) In the same way too the Lord gave charge for those who preach the Gospel, that they should live by the Gospel. (15) But I have made use of none of these privileges. Nor have I written these things in order that in my case things may be done in this way. For I would rather die than—no, no one shall make this boast of mine an empty thing.[2] (16) For if I preach the Gospel, that gives me no ground for boasting;[3] for I am under com-

[1] ἤ is omitted by B D G, other Greek MSS., and the Latin VSS. See an interesting note in Zuntz, pp. 104 f.

[2] There are several variants, of which *ἵνα τις κενώσει* (-η) has most numerous support. All were intended to smooth a difficult text.

[3] ℵ* D G and the Old Latin have *χάρις* (*thanks*) instead of *καύχημα* (*ground for boasting*).

pulsion—for woe is me if I fail to preach the Gospel! (17) For if I do this of my own will, I have a reward, but if without choice of my own I have been entrusted with an office, (18) what then is my reward? That when I preach the Gospel I should present it without charge, so as not to make full use of my authority in the Gospel. (19) For though I am free from all men I have made myself a slave to all men, in order that I might win the more of them. (20) To the Jews I became as a Jew, in order that I might win Jews; to those who were under the law I became as if I were under the law (though I am not myself under the law), in order that I might win those who are under the law; (21) to those who were outside the law I became as if I were outside the law (though I am not free of legal obligation to God but under legal obligation to Christ), in order that I might win those who are outside the law; (22) to the weak I became weak, in order that I might win the weak. I have become all things to all men, in order that at all events I might save some. (23) But whatever I do, I do for the sake of the Gospel, that I too may have my share in it.

(24) Do you not know that all the competitors in the stadium run, but only one of them receives the prize? Run in such a way that you may win it. (25) Everyone who takes part in the contests disciplines himself in every way. They do it to receive a perishable crown, we to receive an imperishable one. (26) So, for my part, that is how I run—not as if I did not know where I was going; that is how I box, not as though I were beating the air. (27) But I buffet my body, and bring it into slavery, lest, when I have preached to others, I should myself prove to be rejected.

At the end of chapter viii Paul undertook to abstain from eating meat for the rest of his life, if eating meat should prove to be prejudicial to the interests of his Christian brother. Since there is nothing in the Christian faith, rightly understood, to prevent a Christian from eating meat (the humanitarian motive apart) this means that Paul himself was willing, and by implication invited his readers, to impose a serious limitation on his Christian liberty. He had, it seems, good reason to suspect that this attitude would not only provoke opposition among the Christians at Corinth whose watchword was spiritual liberty, but also lead to questioning of his own authority. 'If this man were a true apostle, and enjoyed an apostle's authority, he would not allow himself to be restricted in this way—and in other ways, which we have observed in his behaviour in Corinth itself.' It is to this sort of complaint that Paul immediately proceeds to reply in chapter ix, and there is therefore no reason to see this chapter as an intrusion between two separate and distinct treatments of the question of food sacrificed to idols. There is no ground here for the partition of the letter, though there is certainly evidence of a mind that was ready to digress, perhaps also of composition over an extended period—which is in any case likely; see the Introduction, p. 15. It is also true that Paul would hardly have spent so long on the question of apostolic rights if his own apostolic status had not been questioned in Corinth.

Paul assumes the objection, and counter-attacks in the vigorous debating style of the diatribe (cf. the words of the Cynic in Epictetus III. xxii. 48: Am I not free from sorrow? Am
1 I not free from fear? Am I not free?). **Am I not free?**—as every Christian is (though there is good ground for suspecting a special gnostic emphasis on freedom in Corinth). Do you suppose that because I limit my freedom out of love my freedom does not exist? If any Christian can claim to be free I can do so, for **am I not an apostle?** See i. 1, with the note and references; also xv. 8-10. In the following verses Paul shows what are the grounds of apostolic office, and the privileges attached to it; it is clear however that the latter in particular were differently understood by different apostles. The point is developed much more fully (and under pressure of sterner necessity) in 2 Corinthians, especially in chapters x-xiii, but Paul was already aware, when he wrote 1 Corinthians, of the difference.

Have I not seen Jesus our Lord? Compare xv. 8, where the appearance of the risen Jesus and the call to apostleship are combined, as they should be understood to be here. Luke also took over the principle that such a commission, carrying with it

the ability to bear witness at first hand to the fact of the resurrection, was the indispensable foundation of apostleship (Acts i. 22). Not all who saw Jesus after the resurrection became apostles (but see xv. 6 and the note—it is possible that Paul thought that all the 500 became apostles), but those whom he commissioned for the purpose. How could such persons be distinguished? Apart from their own claim (made e.g. by Paul in Gal. i. 1, 16), by the results of their apostolic activity. A true apostle was a successful evangelist, who had no need to build on foundations laid by others (cf. Rom. xv. 20) but himself established new churches. Thus Paul's next rhetorical question is part of his demonstration of his apostolic office. **Are you not my work in the Lord?** Compare iii. 6, 10; iv. 15: Paul planted, or founded, the church in Corinth; he was its father—in the sense that he was the instrument used by God (iii. 7). Compare also 2 Cor. x. 13-16; xii. 12. The existence of the church authenticates, as nothing else could do, the apostolic ministry of its founder. **If I am not an apostle to others** (that is, in 2
their estimation; the epistles give adequate evidence of the querying of Paul's status)**, yet at least to you** (*ἀλλά γε ὑμῖν*; as the grammarians, e.g. Robertson, p. 1148, B.D. §439, point out, *ὑμῖν γε*, or *ἀλλ' ὑμῖν γε*, would have been better; *yet* is an attempt to represent Paul's *ἀλλά*, which was presumably intended to have strong adversative force) **I am, for you are the seal of my apostleship in the Lord.** For *seal* compare 2 Cor. i. 22, and especially Rom. iv. 11. It is a visible token of something that already exists; thus the Corinthian church does not make Paul an apostle, and his apostleship does not depend on it (any more than on the Jerusalem church—cf. Gal. i. 1), but its existence is a visible sign of his apostleship.

The evidence (a commission from the risen Jesus; manifest success as an evangelist) for his apostleship having now been stated, Paul proceeds, using technical legal language, to defend himself against his opponents (whose existence so far we have only been able to infer; the inference is now vindicated). **My** 3
defence (*ἀπολογία*, used elsewhere of defence in a lawcourt—Acts xxii. 1; xxv. 16; Phil. i. 7, 16; 2 Tim. iv. 16; cf. 1 Pet. iii. 15; in 2 Cor. vii. 11 it is the Corinthians who must offer a defence) **against those who would like** (treating the present participle

as conative) **to examine** (cf. iv. 3f.; perhaps *cross-examine*) **me is this** (the position of the pronoun at the end of the sentence suggests, as does the sense of the passage, that the defence now follows, but it would be possible to refer *this* to what precedes in verses 1 f.). Evidently there were some in Corinth (whether of local origin, or visitors) who wished to put the apostle to the test—with some presumption that examination would expose his lack of authority. He continues his reply.

4 **Have we not the right** (ἐξουσία, *authority*) **to eat and drink?** It is usual to take this in the sense, *Have we not the right to eat and drink* at the expense of the community, that is, to be maintained by it? Compare verse 6. This view is supported by the fact that in verse 6 the 'we' of the subject is explained as 'Barnabas and I', who are thus contrasted with other apostles, so that the right in question clearly becomes one that is peculiar to apostles and not common to all Christians, who (as Paul agrees) have the right to eat and drink what they choose. There is much force in this argument; it is worth recalling that the philosopher who taught for pay was often attacked (there is a good selection of evidence in Betz, p. 114, note 3). When however the theme of chapter viii, which led directly to the present development is considered, it appears that there is also much weight in the view that Paul is claiming here the right to eat and drink without regard to the idolatrous or other origin of his food—the right denied by the weak in Corinth, but claimed and exercised (in spite of opposition) by the strong; see viii. 9, where the same word (ἐξουσία, there translated *authority*) is used. Perhaps the most likely view is that though Paul (as verse 1 already shows) is moving on to the theme of apostleship he begins where he does because the question of idolatrous food is fresh in his mind. 'I am speaking of the voluntary relinquishing of rights in the interests of others. Well: have not we the right to eat and drink what we please—*and* to do so at the expense of the community?' The authority (ἐξουσία) that the gnostics claim is (in the right place) a fine thing; and who should be more likely to have it than the apostles? On the meaning of *we*, see below.

5 The next clause has a similar double meaning. **Have we not the right to take about a Christian sister** (ἀδελφή; see vii. 15, and i. 1 for 'brother') **as wife** (according to M. iii. 246 γυναῖκα

is predicative, but it may be questioned whether this is the best sense; the alternative is 'a wife who is a Christian sister'), **as do the other apostles, and the Lord's brothers, and Cephas?** Here the first point is that apostles, like other Christians, have a right to be (and many of them are) married (thus the argument of chapter vii is confirmed); the second, that apostles, unlike other Christians, have the right to have their wives (it strains the text to see here, with Allo, a reference to female assistants, who might but need not be the apostles' wives) maintained by the communities in which they are working. This is not only apostolic theory but apostolic practice. Who the *apostles* are will depend on the view taken of the constitution of the apostolate in Paul's time. In Acts it is assumed that the apostles are the twelve disciples of Jesus (Judas Iscariot being replaced by Matthias), together with Paul and possibly one or two more (see Acts xiv. 4, 14). It must not however be assumed that Luke's view was held a generation or two earlier. For the meaning of xv. 1-11 see the notes; elsewhere Andronicus and Junias appear to be apostles (Rom. xvi. 7), and in 2 Corinthians Paul speaks not only of false apostles (xi. 13), but also of 'super-apostles' (xi. 5; xii. 11). Apostles are the most important servants of the church (1 Cor. xii. 28), but it would be unwise on the basis of the Pauline evidence to say more than that they were travelling evangelists and pastors who had received a commission from the risen Jesus. That in addition to himself only the twelve were apostles Paul never says or implies; how many of them there were (in his view) we do not know. Presumably the majority were married, and took their wives with them on their journeys. So did *the Lord's brothers*: see Mark iii. 31; vi. 3; Acts i. 14; Gal. i. 19. Paul's expression is most naturally taken to refer to sons of Mary and Joseph; conceivably to sons of Joseph by a former wife. Apparently some of these brothers travelled among the churches. We have no other evidence for this; James, the only brother of whom we have serious information, appears to have concentrated his work in Jerusalem. Paul however would have had no reason to mention the brothers here if the fact alleged were not secure, and at least possibly known to his readers, though the brothers may have confined their journeys to Palestine. Finally *Cephas* is mentioned alone; see above on

i. 12. He is certainly included among *the other apostles*, and it is hard to see why he should have been singled out for special mention here if he had not himself visited Corinth, presumably bringing his wife with him. See 'Cephas and Corinth'. Perhaps it was those who 'belonged to Cephas' who had questioned Paul's apostleship.

6 Paul continues the argument. **Or are Barnabas and I the only ones who do not have the right** (ἐξουσία, as at verse 4) **not to work for our living?** The last three words are a supplement necessary to bring out the sense in English. See above on verse 4, and compare Acts xx. 33 ff.; 1 Thess. ii. 9; 2 Thess. iii. 8. Apostles had a right to maintenance from the churches, but the fact that Paul and Barnabas had made no use of this privilege did not mean (though probably some asserted this; see 2 Cor. xi. 7-11) that they were not apostles, or were only second-rate apostles. There were other reasons for their attitude, which will be brought out later. It seems probable that when in verse 4 Paul turned from the use of the first person singular (used in verses 1-3) to the plural this was because he began to associate another (or others) with him; a plural of majesty loses its point if it is not consistent throughout a passage. Paul's association with Barnabas is mentioned in Acts ix. 27–xv. 39; by the time the epistles were written the defection described in Gal. ii. 13 (perhaps a more accurate version of Acts xv. 37-40) had taken place, and we hear of Barnabas again only indirectly at Col. iv. 10. The present verse however is probably to be taken as evidence that he rejoined the Pauline mission, though we know nothing whatever of any contact he may have had with Corinth. Apparently Paul thought of him as an apostle; compare Acts xiv. 4, 14.

Though Paul and Barnabas had not made use of it the custom of providing for the maintenance of apostles was a reasonable one, grounded in common sense as well as common practice.
7 **Who ever goes to war at his own charges?** A soldier on service expects to be maintained; why not an apostle? **Who plants a vineyard and does not eat its fruit?** Compare iii. 6. A vinedresser expects to be nourished from that on which he bestows his labour; why not an apostle? **Or who tends a flock and does not drink** (the verb, ἐσθίειν, is usually rendered 'eat';

'consume' would be stilted, and 'drink' is the only possible alternative) **some of the milk the flock yields?** A herdsman reaps advantage from the flock he cares for; why not an apostle? The parataxis of the first two questions is claimed by K. Beyer (*Semitische Syntax im Neuen Testament* I i (1962), p. 281) as much commoner in Semitic languages than in Greek; this should perhaps be taken as a reason for omitting *or* before the third (see note 1 on p. 198).

These are human analogies, useful within their limits but not compelling. There are stronger grounds—indeed, the strongest
of all, Scripture. **You don't suppose do you,** (μή), **that I am** 8
saying these things with no more than human authority (κατὰ ἄνθρωπον, at the beginning of the sentence in Greek, is emphatic; for an important discussion of the phrase see Daube, pp. 394-400)? **Does not the law** (that is, the Old Testament, though this passage is in the Pentateuch—Deut. xxv. 4) **say these things** (or, *the same things*, if we write ταὐτά for ταῦτα—there is little difference in meaning) **too?** It is always of the greatest importance to Paul to be able to quote the Old Testament in support of his view. **For in the law of Moses it stands** 9
written, 'You shall not muzzle the ox when it is threshing' —and naturally the animal takes the opportunity of satisfying its hunger by taking mouthfuls of the material it is working on. 'The law affords another example of the humanity which is characteristic of Deuteronomy, and which is to be exercised even towards animals' (S. R. Driver, *A critical and exegetical Commentary on Deuteronomy* (1895), p. 280). Paul does not share the modern commentator's view. **Does God care about the oxen?** Compare Philo, *De specialibus legibus* i. 260: The law is not made for irrational beings, but for those that have mind and reason; but contrast *De Virtutibus* 146: . . . I have mentioned the kindly and beneficent regulation for the oxen when threshing. Attempts to show that Paul did not mean that God did not care
about the animals break down on the next clause: **Or is he not** 10
speaking simply (πάντως) **on our account?** The only interpretation that is not forced is that in the Old Testament law God had in mind not oxen, but Christian preachers and their needs. This does not mean that Paul would have denied the truth (quoted here by Calvin; see also Barth, *C.D.* III. iii. 174) that

God is concerned even over the fall of a sparrow; but it was a quite different truth that he found in the Old Testament and expressed here. His argument is not of the *a minori ad maius* (*qal waḥomer*) kind to which there are rabbinic parallels (S.B. iii. 385): God cares for oxen, therefore so much more for men (Weiss).

Paul continues by answering his own question. **Yes** (*γάρ*, used to introduce the answer to a question; B.D. §452), **it was written on our account, for** (or *that*; see below) **he who ploughs ought to plough in hope, and he who threshes ought to do so** (the last four words are supplied in order to complete the sense) **in hope of partaking of the crop** (the last three words are supplied). For the forward reference of the Old Testament compare 1 Pet. i. 12. The Greek word (*ὅτι*) here rendered *for* also means *that*, and the clause it introduces may *either* give the reason why the figurative command was given by God, *or* repeat the substance of the command in other words (declaratory, or explicative, *ὅτι*—Bachmann, Allo). It has been pointed out that the ox who threshes also ploughs the field; he is the one who ploughs and the one who threshes, and the command in Deut. xxv. 4 allows him to perform both operations with the hope of getting some reward for his labours. This seems far-fetched; *for* is to be preferred. A third possibility is that Paul here introduces a quotation from a non-canonical source: It is written, He who ploughs. . . . But this is unlikely. Paul means that the command was given in order to support the true principle that the workman (including the apostle) should
11 reap some reward for his labour. This is not much to ask. **If we have sown spiritual things for you,** and thus by bringing you the Gospel and making possible the bestowal of spiritual gifts (see e.g. i. 4-7) given you the greatest of all gifts, **is it a great thing if we reap material things** (literally, *things of the flesh*, *σαρκικά*; the word as used here does not carry the theological overtones that *flesh* sometimes has in Paul) **from you?** The argument needs no further elucidation: an apostle's keep is a small price to pay for the Gospel. There is another way of
12 arguing. **If others share in authority over you** (genitive after *ἐξουσία*, as at Matt. x. 1; Robertson, p. 500), **do not we the more?** It was through Paul that the Corinthians were converted

and their church founded. For this reason he had a greater, not a smaller, share of the authority some missionaries made use of in order to provide for themselves. **But we have made no use of this authority** (cf. verse 15; and for *authority* verses 4, 5, 6), **but endure** (the same verb, *στέγειν*, is used at xiii. 7) **all things** (hardship, hunger, and the like; cf. iv. 11 ff.) **in order that we may put no obstacle in the way of the Gospel of Christ.** Here appears the fundamental motive for Paul's habitual behaviour (cf. verse 23, *Whatever I do, I do for the sake of the Gospel*). His service in the Gospel conferred rights upon him, but he forwent them in the interests of the Gospel itself. Put at the lowest level, this meant the consideration that potential converts might think twice about accepting the Gospel if they saw that it would lead to financial commitments on behalf of the missionaries. More important was the fact that Paul would wish there to be no misrepresentation in regard to the collection (xvi. 1); most important of all, that the Gospel, which turned upon the love and self-sacrifice of Jesus, could not fitly be presented by preachers who insisted on their rights, delighted in the exercise of authority, and made what profit they could out of the work of evangelism. An outstanding example of this non-Pauline understanding of apostleship is provided by the Peregrinus whose story Lucian told (*De Morte Peregrini*—it is interesting that Peregrinus in the end fell foul of the Christians by eating forbidden food). But study of 2 Corinthians is enough to show examples much closer and more dangerous.

Nevertheless, Paul continues to vindicate the rights of preachers by a new line of argument. He was as anxious that apostolic rights should be recognized as he was determined himself to make no use of them. Further illustrations follow. **Do** 13
you not know (cf. iii. 16; the implication is that the Corinthians ought to have known what is about to be said, and this suggests that the reference may apply to pagan practice, though it does apply to Jewish also—see J. Jeremias, *Jerusalem zur Zeit Jesu* (1958), II A 21, 29) **that those who officiate** (the word—*ἐργάζεσθαι*, used at verse 6—is general, but in this context it must take some such sense as this) **in holy things eat the things that come from the holy place?** The next sentence generalizes somewhat: **that those who attend upon**

(cf. vii. 35 above, and the note; they serve *God*, *at* the altar: τῷ θυσιαστηρίῳ is 'pure locative'—Robertson, p. 521) **the altar have their share together at the altar** (scarcely, *share with the altar*, though the construction would bear this)? The customs Paul refers to were widespread in antiquity. Those who held sacred offices on behalf of others might reasonably expect to be
14 provided for. This Jesus himself recognized. **In the same way too the Lord gave charge for** (rather than *to*, which is linguistically possible, because of the sense) **those who preach the Gospel** (such as the apostles, but it is not implied that the practice is to be confined to them), **that they should live by the Gospel** (that is, that their converts should support them). See Matt. x. 10; Luke x. 7; also 1 Tim. v. 18. As noted above (p. 162), it is seldom that Paul quotes words of the Lord. He refers to them here because he means to build up a particularly strong case for a practice which he himself does not apply (so far is he from taking the teaching of Jesus as a new *halakah*). Reason and common experience; the Old Testament; universal religious practice; the teaching of Jesus himself: all these support the custom by which apostles (and other ministers) are maintained at the expense of the church which is built up by their
15 ministry; **but I** (in an emphatic position in Greek) **have made use of none of these privileges.** For Paul's practice of following an ordinary employment in order to keep himself see iv. 12. **Nor have I written these things** (in the immediately preceding lines) **in order that** henceforth **in my case** (literally, *in me*, ἐν ἐμοί) **things may be done in this way.** Paul has already (see verse 12) given a reason for rejecting the privileges he might have enjoyed. He returns to passionate reiteration of his decision, and to give (unfortunately, in obscure language) further reason for making it. His language breaks down under the stress of his emotion. **For I would rather die than—no, no one shall make this boast of mine** (that I take no pay for being an apostle) **an empty thing.** The broken construction is characteristically Pauline (cf. e.g. Rom. i. 11 f.; v. 6 f.; 1 Cor. xv. 1 f.; 2 Cor. xii. 6 f., 17; Gal. ii. 3 ff.). It is mended in the great majority of MSS., which read 'I would rather die than that anyone should make this boast of mine an empty thing' (see note 2 on p. 198): but the text which causes anacolouthon is the

more difficult, and (notwithstanding B.D. §§369, 393) should be preferred. There is no difference in sense; only in intensity. *Boasting* (glorying) is always a difficult subject with Paul: man has no business to boast, or glory, except in the Lord (see above, i. 31). C. H. Dodd has noticed the present passage and, contrasting it with others that occur in later epistles, suggested that a crisis in Paul's life occurred between the writing of 1 and 2 Corinthians (see *New Testament Studies* (1953), pp. 79-82). At a later stage (after a 'second conversion') Paul gave up his desire to have some ground of boasting. The present verse, however, hardly supports this reconstruction, for it betrays already the paradox of glorying in weakness which is said to characterize his later references to the subject. Not only will Paul glory in circumstances that must have meant hunger and weariness, he will glory in a situation that can have brought him little but mockery and insult. He goes on to explain his point.

For if I simply **preach the Gospel, that gives me no** 16
ground for boasting. It goes too far to read out of this clause a compulsive desire for some ground of glorying (C. H. Dodd, op. cit. pp. 79 f.). All Paul says is that preaching is no credit to him, because he has no choice about it. He cannot but preach. **For** (as far as this is concerned) **I am under compulsion—for woe is me if I fail to preach the Gospel** (cf. Jer. xx. 9). He has been arrested by Christ Jesus (Phil. iii. 12) and is now Christ's
slave (Rom. i. 1; et passim). **For if I do this** (preaching) **of my** 17
own will, I have a reward, but if without choice of my own I have been entrusted with an office (the language recalls the appointment of imperial secretaries, who as a rule
were either slaves or freedmen), **what then is my reward?** 18
The first clause appears to mean that if Paul, master of his own lot, had voluntarily undertaken to preach he could legitimately claim not only pay from his churches but a reward from God, whom he would be doing a kindness. This involves us in taking the conditional sentence as one implying an unfulfilled condition—If I *were doing* this . . . I *should have* . . .; this is not impossible, since at least in theory the question is an open one. The second clause puts the alternative possibility, which is in fact true. Paul is not a free workman, contracting to hire out his labour (to God). He is a slave whom God has acquired, and put

to work as he, God, decides. This means that he is in no position to claim pay, or reward, and the question is naturally raised, *What then is my reward?* the implied answer being, I have no right to one. This seems to be the best way of taking verses 17, 18a; it is however more usual to place a full stop at the end of verse 17. The meaning then becomes: If I do this of my own will, I have a reward: but if I do it not of my own will, I have been entrusted with an office. 'I have a reward' and 'I have been entrusted with an office' now become alternatives; the difficulty is that there seems to be no good reason why they should be alternatives. Why, if I am entrusted with an office, should I not be rewarded for carrying it out? It is better to take 'I do this' and 'I have been entrusted with an office' as synonymous (or nearly so), as in the text.

We return to Paul's question. Preach he must; and he can claim no credit or reward for doing what he must. At best he will be an unprofitable servant (Luke xvii. 10). *What then is my* reward? **That when I preach the Gospel I should present it without charge** (cf. Matt. x. 8; 2 Cor. xi. 7)**, so as not to make** (or, in order not to make) **full use of my authority** (*ἐξουσία*; Paul continues to insist that he possesses as much authority as anyone to enjoy apostolic privileges) **in the Gospel** (that is, as a preacher of the Gospel). Paul does not mean that his practice of taking no pay from men will lead to his being rewarded by God; the preaching without charge (the parallel with verse 16 shows that *without charge* is emphatic) is itself the reward, because it means that he is putting no stumbling-block in the way of the Gospel (verse 12), and thus has a better chance of seeing the Gospel flourish than would otherwise be possible.

The question raised here is a wider one than that of taking pay for preaching the Gospel. It is more consistent with the role of an apostle or evangelist that he should renounce his rights than that he should claim them. It is not his own advantage, or even his desires and inclinations, but those of his hearers that
19 should govern his actions. Thus: **though I am free from all men** (or perhaps, *things*; he is free because, having been made free as a Christian, he cannot become the slave of men: vii. 23) **I have made myself a slave to all men** (cf. 2 Cor. iv. 5, *ourselves your slaves*) **in order that I might win** (that is, as

Christians) **the more of them** (or perhaps *the majority of them*: for τοὺς πλειόνας cf. x. 5: xv. 6: B.D. §244). The word *win* reflects Jewish usage (Daube, pp. 352-61: Schlatter also compares the gospel phrase, 'fishers of men', Mark i. 17), and Jewish missionary practice was aware of the place of accommodation, service, and humility in its methods (Daube, pp. 336-51), though naturally not in such radical form as Paul displays in the next few verses. Where Jews were willing to make the law no more offensive and burdensome than necessary, Paul was prepared to abandon it altogether. It is impossible to understand Paul if this fact is not grasped. It is true and important that, as recent research has emphasized, Paul remained in many respects not merely a Jew but a Pharisee and a Rabbi: yet he differed from all non-Christian Pharisees in that he was ready (in the interests of the Gospel, verse 23) to cease to be a Jew.

Paul does not begin at this point, but his opening words are
no less striking. **To the Jews** (τοῖς Ἰουδαίοις; according to M. 20
iii. 169, the use of the article, which is unusual with Paul, shows that he must be referring to a particular occasion, perhaps that of Timothy's circumcision; B.D. §262, virtually quoted by Turner though without acknowledgement, notes the same fact but interprets it more probably—'to those, with whom on each occasion I had to do') **I became as a Jew, in order that I might win Jews.** But Paul (as he himself affirms elsewhere, notably 2 Cor. xi. 22; Phil. iii. 5) was a Jew. He could *become* a Jew only if, having been a Jew, he had ceased to be one and become something else. His Judaism was no longer of his very being, but a guise he could adopt or discard at will. His adoption of Judaism is illustrated in Acts xxi. 23-6: but Acts is scarcely aware of Paul's radical un-Jewishness. This was not a matter of indifference to the law, or impatience with the inconvenience which life under the Torah must have involved. It rested on the conviction that in Jesus Christ Judaism had been fulfilled and the law brought to its intended goal (e.g. Rom. x. 4). For when Paul speaks of 'being a Jew' he is certainly not thinking of an allegiance determined simply by racial descent. To *win Jews* seems to mean that Paul conducted a mission to Jews (Weiss); contrast Gal. ii. 7 ff. Judaism is defined further in terms of law. **To those who were under the law I became as if I were**

under the law (though I am not myself under the law), in order that I might win those who are under the law. To be a Jew is to be under the law and thereby related to God in legal terms. Paul is no longer related to God in this way; at the most he may pretend to be so related. He is *not under the law*; he behaves *as if* he *were under the law. The law* here means the law of Moses; but if this is repudiated, by an *a fortiori* argument all less important and directly divine laws are repudiated. Paul is now related to God through Jesus Christ (cf. i. 30), and no room is left for law.

It would be natural to take this to mean that Paul no longer owed to God the obedience which the Jew acknowledged as his debt and sought to express by means of conformity to Torah. This would be a misunderstanding. If Paul is no longer a Jew neither is he a Gentile, though he is related to Gentiles in terms
21 of the Gospel. **To those who were outside the law** (the law of Moses: Gentiles are intended, though as Paul argues elsewhere they were not without a kind of law—Rom. ii. 14) **I became as if I were outside the law (though I am not free of legal obligation to God but under legal obligation to Christ), in order that I might win those who are outside the law.** This is one of the most difficult sentences in the epistle, and also one of the most important, for in it Paul shows how the new relation to God which he has in Christ expresses his debt of obedience to God. Compare Rom. vi, where Paul answers the question (verses 1, 15), Why, if a Christian is related to God not by law (which forbids evil and enjoins virtue) but by grace (which means God's love for man in his present sinful state), should he not continue to sin as much as he pleases? Why, that is, should a Christian trouble to be good?

Just as, in the preceding verse, Paul says that in certain circumstances he behaved *as if* he were under the law, so here he says that in certain circumstances he behaves as if he were outside the law. Just as there it is implied that he is not one whose life is determined by law, so here it is implied that he is not outside the law; and this Paul proceeds explicitly to affirm. He is not *free of legal obligation to God* (ἄνομος θεοῦ) but *under legal obligation to Christ* (ἔννομος Χριστοῦ). The precise interpretation of these Greek phrases is disputed. It is possible (Moule,

p. 42; B.D. §182; M. iii. 215 reproduces B.D.'s references but does not explain the phrase) to emphasize the genitives in relation to the implied *law* (νόμος) and render, 'not subject to the law *of God*', 'under obligation to the law *of Christ*'; see C. H. Dodd, ΕΝΝΟΜΟϹ ΧΡΙϹΤΟΥ, in *Studia Paulina*, pp. 96-110. It is in favour of this view that Paul elsewhere refers explicitly to the *law of Christ*: Gal. vi. 2, Fulfil the law of Christ. Compare Rom. viii. 2; also xiii. 8 ff., where Paul refers to the commandment of love, quoting Lev. xix. 18 in similar terms to Mark xii. 31. It is also in favour of this view that one of Paul's words (ἄνομος) when used earlier in the verse undoubtedly refers to those who, being Gentiles, stood outside the range of the law (of Moses), but against it that his positive word (ἔννομος) is not one that he ever uses of Jews, who were under the law. The linguistic difficulty arises out of the theological difficulty of understanding Paul's teaching about the law, which, though not inconsistent (as is sometimes said), is nevertheless many-sided and complex. The subject can only be outlined here; see further discussion in *Romans*, especially pp. 140-53. The law, given by God, was holy, righteous, and good, a precious gift, in no way contrary to God's gracious promises, but consistent with them, and able to keep a well-intentioned man in the way of life. It expressed man's dependence on the goodness of his Creator, and his debt of obedience. This good gift was seized and perverted by sin, and thus became an instrument not of life but of death. We might say (using a word which unfortunately was not in Paul's vocabulary) that the law was perverted into legalism. It was as legalism that Paul himself encountered the law, both in his life as a Jew and in the activities of Jewish Christians who (perhaps with excellent motives) subverted his churches. Man's situation had however been completely changed by the coming of Christ; not because Christ had brought an entirely new message—he still spoke in terms of God's free mercy, and his absolute claim for obedience—but because he achieved that towards which the law could only point. He was the end of the law in that he fulfilled it, and thus made the written code otiose. He had declared God's love in a form that could not be turned into a ground of boasting for men; and he had representatively on behalf of mankind as a whole (as the last Adam—see xv. 45) offered to God a perfect obedience. Moreover, through his work the Holy Spirit was now available to renew men in the image of God. This, superficially, makes a coherent and complete story. But was a written code in fact otiose? A glance at the Corinthian church is sufficient to show that not all Christians know by inspiration what things they ought to do, and that even when they know them they do not necessarily do them. It was necessary to reiterate that redemption in Christ did not bring to an end man's obligation to be God's obedient child; it was also necessary to give guidance to those who desired to be obedient but did not know what to do.

This discussion has now made clear the difficulty in which Paul found himself. He must direct the Corinthians' obedience in the way of Christ, but he must do this without permitting Christianity to become a new law. Study of post-Pauline Christianity (from the second century to the twentieth) shows how dangerous this possibility was, and is. It seems probable that in Gal. vi. 2 Paul (perhaps unguardedly) falls into a rabbinic expression (for such evidence as there is see W. D. Davies, *Torah in the Messianic Age and/or the Age to Come*, 1952, pp. 50-83); here in 1 Corinthians he seems carefully to avoid it; he does not say that he is 'under the law of the Messiah' (*ὑπὸ τὸν νόμον τοῦ Χριστοῦ*). Yet he is not 'God's lawless one' (*ἄνομος θεοῦ*, taking the genitive to be governed, as the grammar suggests, by the subject—Paul himself); he is 'Christ's law-abiding one' (*ἔννομος Χριστοῦ*; for this use of *ἔννομος* cf. Plato, *Republic* 424E). Thus Paul can adopt his varying attitude—to the Jews as a Jew, to the Gentiles as a Gentile—because he recognizes not a smaller but a greater debt to God than legalism implies. He is not related to God by legal observance, but by grace and faith, and in Christ, only; but precisely in this non-legal relationship he is Christ's slave, who owes absolute obedience not to a code (though on occasion, and with due caution, he can give precepts to his converts) but to Christ as a person, and to the absolute principle of universal love, which Christ both taught and exemplified.

This seems to be the run of Paul's thought; whether the translation offered here, or any other, or indeed Paul's own Greek, adequately and explicitly represents it, is another question. It is also another question how far, and how long, Paul's attitude proved to be practicable within Judaism. He himself may well have claimed (see not only Acts xxii. 3; xxiii. 6; xxvi. 5, 22 but also Phil. iii. 3; Rom. iii. 31; iv. 13; x. 4-13; et al.) that his Christian faith and practice were what Judaism had always been intended to be, but Judaism as a whole, and in its official representatives, did not accept this view, and though Paul's alternating attitude, aimed at conformity with the social and religious customs of his environment, no doubt served its turn, it soon ceased to provide a reasonable way of life for Jews who had become Christians. The troubles and perplexities of such men cannot be pursued here (see J. Jocz, *The Jewish People and Jesus Christ* (1949)).

Paul completes, but also complicates, his theme by adding;
To the weak I became weak, in order that I might win the 22
weak. *The weak* (and weak consciences) we encounter elsewhere; see viii. 7-13; compare Rom. xiv, xv. They are Christians not yet fully emancipated from legalism. How then can Paul speak of *winning* them? Either he uses the word from force of habit, not noticing that it is inappropriate; or he gives it a new sense, meaning no longer 'win them from paganism (or Judaism) to Christianity' but 'win them from an inadequate to an adequate understanding of Christianity'; or, better because more likely to be Paul's attitude though more loosely as far as the word is concerned, '*keep* them for the church, instead of driving them out by wounding their consciences'; compare Matt. xviii. 15. It is to be noted that in this verse Paul does not say *as if* (cf. verses 20, 21); he abstained from sacrificed food, or flesh, or wine, or whatever it was they abstained from. The absence of the phrase, however, must not be stressed, since Paul undoubtedly represents himself as one of the strong (Rom. xv. 1; as well as 1 Cor. viii. 1-13; x. 23-33). Alternatively, but less probably, we may with Heim understand *the weak* in terms of Rom. v. 6; they are non-Christians, whether Jewish or Gentile.

Setting aside particular cases Paul sums up: **I have become all things to all men** (this rendering fails to bring out the Greek article—τοῖς πᾶσιν—which groups together all the examples previously given; 'to all the lot of them'—B.D. §275), **in order that at all events** (attempting to bring out the verbal play in the Greek; πᾶσιν—πάντα—πάντως) **I might save some** (cf. verse 19). *Save* is here a synonym for *win* (verses 19-22; cf. vii. 16), and rather more, for it states, what *win* can only imply, that what is at stake is not simply the failure or success of human persuasion, and a human group, but man's eternal destiny in the will of God. This use of the word, however, is to be distinguished from that in which it stands for the final act of God in gathering together the redeemed (e.g. Rom. v. 9, 10; xi. 26). The gathering of pardoned sinners into the church is a real but partial anticipation of final salvation. Whether he was a universalist or not, Paul does not expect all men to be saved in the sense in which he uses the word here.

It is his concern for the divine activity of salvation that moti-
23 vates all his practice. **But whatever I do** (literally, *all things*), **I do for the sake of** (or, *on account of*) **the Gospel, that I too may have my share in it.** The last clause runs literally, that I may be a fellow-participant (συγκοινωνός) in it. This is sometimes wrongly understood. Paul does not mean, 'a partner with the Gospel' (in the work of salvation; this would require αὐτῷ, not αὐτοῦ); nor does he mean 'one who shares in the work of (preaching) the Gospel'. His word means participation in (the benefits of) the Gospel; and his participation is not guaranteed (cf. verse 27). He addresses his readers, and those whom he would win for Christ, as one who stands with, not over against them. The Gospel has been entrusted to him (verse 17; cf. iv. 1; Gal. ii. 7), but it has not been put under his control. It is in fulfilling his own vocation as an evangelist that he appropriates the Gospel himself. This observation provides the transition to the last sub-paragraph in this chapter.

Less well grounded in Christian truth than Paul, and less modest in their attitude, the Corinthians were disposed to think that, because they were believers, and participants in the sacraments, their salvation was assured. We shall see in the next chapter that this conviction gave rise to their risky attitude to the eating of sacrificial food. Paul did not share their kind of assurance. Absolutely confident of the love of God (e.g. Rom. viii. 38 f.) he had little confidence in himself. Like many preachers of his day, Jewish (e.g. Philo, *Legum Allegoriae* ii. 108) and pagan (see references in Weiss, and Betz, p. 120, note 4; and

e.g. Seneca, *Epistle* lxxviii. 16), he turned to the games for a metaphor. It would be understood universally in the Greek world, not least at Corinth; see Introduction p. 2. **Do you not know** (cf. 24
verse 13) **that all the competitors in the stadium run, but only one of them receives the prize?** That is, entry does not in itself guarantee a prize: it does so neither in athletics, nor in Christianity. You have entered the Christian life through baptism: this does not guarantee your final perseverance. **Run in such a way that you may win it.** Compare Phil. iii. 12 ff. The metaphor creaks a little, for Paul does not mean that only one Christian, or one out of each group, or indeed any arbitrarily limited number, will achieve the prize appointed by God. The weight of his argument is directed simply against the notion that there is an automatic connection between running and winning. There is none. The Christian must not only start but continue in the right way; it is implied that he must put forth all his strength. The process also implies self-discipline—not a strong point with the Corinthians. **Everyone who takes part** 25
in the contests (not only running but other sports—e.g. boxing, as verse 26 suggests—are now in mind) **disciplines himself in every way.** The word (ἐγκρατεύεσθαι) is used at vii. 9, where it is rendered *to live continently*. It takes varying senses in different contexts, but its root meaning is 'to exercise mastery over oneself'. Compare Gal. v. 23; and for athletic training 2 Tim. ii. 5. **They** (the pronoun is emphatic, and refers of course to athletes) **do it to receive a perishable crown, we to receive an imperishable one.** For the metaphor compare 2 Tim. iv. 8; 1 Pet. v. 4. A victorious athlete in the Isthmian Games received a crown of pine; the Christian, after his life of self-discipline, gains his share in the Gospel (verse 23).

The metaphor shifts from that of discipline in training to controlled effort in the race or boxing match itself. **So, for my** 26
part, that is how I run—not as if I did not know where I was going (ὡς οὐκ ἀδήλως: cf. the use of the adjective at xiv. 8 to describe a sound whose meaning remains unknown to the hearer—perhaps the meaning is that the onlooker cannot tell where the runner is going); **that is how I box, not as though I were beating the air** (dealing ill-directed and ineffectual blows). Paul acts purposefully, to save himself and his listeners

(1 Tim. iv. 16). He now however reverts to the theme of self-
27 discipline, retaining the metaphor of the boxing match. **But I buffet my body, and bring it into slavery, lest, when I have preached** (κηρύξας; many commentators see here a reference to the work of the herald, κῆρυξ, in the games, but Paul uses the verb κηρύσσειν for the work of preaching too frequently for us to see more than at most a passing allusion) **to others, I should myself prove to be rejected.** This does not mean that man's material body is an enemy; the sense is that of Rom. vi. 13, 19. The physical members may be offered to sin for use in its employment; or they may be offered to God, for use in the service of righteousness. Here Paul recognizes the need to beat his body out of its all too ready obedience to sin, in order that it may be brought into the service of God. The body is not evil, but it must be made to serve the right master, not the wrong one. This moreover is not something that may be done once, without necessity of repetition. Paul clearly envisages the possibility that, notwithstanding his work as a preacher, he may himself fall from grace and be rejected (for his word, ἀδόκιμος, cf. Rom. i. 28; 2 Cor. xiii. 5, 6, 7; for the sense, Sirach xxxvii. 19; Schlatter aptly quotes *Tosephta Yoma* v.10: . . . that his disciples may not inherit the age to come while he himself goes down to Hades). His conversion, his baptism, his call to apostleship, his service in the Gospel, do not guarantee his eternal salvation. By repeating this truth (cf. above verse 24, and below, x. 5-12) he begins to work back to the dangerous situation in which the Corinthians had placed themselves in relation to idolatry. In speaking of his life of self-discipline, too, he is not far away from the theme on which he set out at the beginning of chapter ix: Christian life involves the limitation as well as the enjoyment of freedom.

21. x. 1-13. EVEN BAPTIZED COMMUNICANTS ARE NOT SECURE

(1) I do not wish you to be ignorant, brothers, that all our fathers were under the cloud, and all passed through the

sea; (2) they accepted baptism[1] into Moses in the cloud and in the sea, (3) and they all ate the same[2] spiritual food, (4) and they all drank the same[3] spiritual drink; for they drank from a spiritual rock that accompanied them; and this rock was Christ. (5) Nevertheless, with the majority of them God was not pleased, as is shown by the fact that they were laid low in the desert. (6) These things happened as examples for us, to warn us not to be men lusting after evil things, as some of them were. (7) Again, do not become idolaters, as they did: as it is written, The people sat down to eat and drink, and rose up for sport. (8) Again, let us not commit fornication, as some of them did, with the result that in one day there fell 23,000 of them. (9) Again, let us not try the Lord,[4] as some of them did, with the result that they were destroyed by the snakes. (10) And do not complain, as some of them did, with the result that they were destroyed by the Agent of Destruction. (11) These things happened to them by way of example, and they were written down as a warning for us, who are confronted by the end of these past ages of history.

(12) The moral is: Let the man who thinks he is standing fast beware lest he should fall; (13) no testing has fallen upon you beyond what is the common lot of men. But God can be trusted not to allow you to be tested beyond your power; on the contrary, along with the trial he will provide also the way out, so that you may be able to endure.

It will be remembered that at the end of chapter viii Paul interrupted his discussion of the eating of sacrificial food by entering on a digression dealing with the voluntary disuse of privilege and freedom; by the end of chapter ix this had moved

[1] The MSS. divide fairly equally between ἐβαπτίσαντο (P46 B, and the majority of later MSS.) and ἐβαπτίσθησαν (א A C D G). See the notes below; Zuntz (p. 234) argues strongly in favour of the middle voice.

[2] αὐτό is omitted by P46 A; א* omits τὸ αὐτό.

[3] αὐτό is omitted by P46 A.

[4] For *the Lord*, P46 D G and many other MSS., Greek and Latin, have *Christ*; a few have *God*.

on to the related theme of self-discipline, but the main subject has not completely disappeared from Paul's mind. The Corinthians took an easy view of sacrificial food (a view that was not the same as what Paul understood by Christian freedom) because they did not take idolatry seriously; and they did not take idolatry seriously (so the present paragraph suggests) because they believed that the Christian rites of Baptism and the Supper secured them from any possible harm. This was a mistake, which Paul, who had just acknowledged (ix. 27) the peril in which he himself stood, exposed by the use of Old Testament analogies. His material had already been to some extent used in the Wisdom speculation of Hellenistic Judaism. See below; also Knox, *Gentiles*, pp. 122 ff.; Schweitzer, *Mysticism*, pp. 20 ff., 258 ff.; and *Adam*, pp. 47-50.

1 **I do not wish** (Paul prefixes 'for', γάρ, but the connection is loose) **you to be ignorant** (he is in fact reminding them of what they should have known and were in danger of forgetting; cf. xii. 1; 2 Cor. i. 8; Rom. i. 13; xi. 25; 1 Thess. iv. 13), **brothers** (cf. i. 1), **that all our fathers were under the cloud, and all passed through the sea.** It is evident that Paul is referring to the story of the Exodus (see Exod. xiii. 21; xiv. 21 f.; Ps. cv. 39); but it is surprising that he should refer to *our fathers*, since the majority of the Corinthian Christians seem to have been Gentiles. By *our* he may have referred to himself (and his fellow-Jews) as distinguished from his readers; more probably he considered that his Gentile readers were now, as Christians, so completely integrated into the people of God that they shared with Jews a common ancestry. Compare Rom. iv. 1; xi. 17-21; also 1 Clement iv. 8 (our father Jacob). Jewish proselytes, on the other hand, continued after conversion to speak of 'your fathers' (see *Bikkurim* i. 4). Another possibility is that Paul was quoting, without modification, an existing Exodus midrash.

2 The events described had religious significance. **They accepted baptism into Moses in the cloud and in the sea.** The verb is given in two forms in the MSS. (see note 1 on p. 219): in the middle (ἐβαπτίσαντο, translated here), and in the passive (ἐβαπτίσθησαν, they were baptized). The middle is to be preferred, (a) because it was less common in Christian usage (but see vi. 11 and the note), and there would therefore be a

tendency to change it into the more common passive, and (b) because the middle corresponds better to Jewish practice, in which the convert baptized himself; so for example Lietzmann and Héring. It should be noted however that B.D. §317 prefer the passive, and that Turner (M. iii. 57) thinks the two voices to be practically indistinguishable here (and that both are equivalent to an intransitive active). For parallels to Paul's use of the Old Testament here see Lietzmann-Kümmel.

There is some evidence that Jews also regarded the passage through the Red Sea as a kind of baptism (analogous to proselyte baptism). If this interpretation of the Old Testament story had already been given Paul's argument is easier to understand, for in fact the Israelites are represented by the Old Testament as having crossed the sea on dry land, so that the comparison with baptism is not one that would readily come to mind. Once however the analogy had been suggested the details would present less difficulty than some commentators (e.g. Héring) suppose; there was enough water in the Red Sea to satisfy the requirements of analogical baptism. Yet it is also true that 'the analogy does not consist in moisture, in getting wet. It is rather a matter of sharing the destiny of a leader' (Heim). *Into Moses*, however, has no Jewish parallel; it was presumably made up by Paul on the basis of the Christian formula, *into Christ*. Lietzmann rightly points out, therefore, that we must not attempt to explain 'into Christ' on the basis of a supposed Jewish formula 'into Moses'. There is no evidence for the existence of such a formula. Granted the analogy with which Paul was working it was natural for him to coin the phrase 'into Moses', not only because it had been Moses who (under God) had delivered his people at the time of the Exodus, but also because of the Jewish belief that the 'latter Redeemer' (the Messiah) would be as the 'former Redeemer' (Moses); see S.B. i. 69.

Not only did the ancient Israelites have their own version of baptism, they also had a sacred meal analogous with the
eucharist. **They all ate the same** (see note 2 on p. 219; *same*, 3
αὐτό, may have been omitted by copyists who found themselves unable to identify the manna with the eucharistic bread, but Paul's point is probably that *all* the Israelites, good and bad, those who would be saved and those who would be rejected,

enjoyed the *same* privileges—so Héring) **spiritual food** (the
4 manna, Exod. xvi. 4, 14-18), **and they all drank the same**
(see note 3 on p. 219, and above) **spiritual drink** (Exod. xvii. 6; Num. xx. 7-13). It is hardly likely that Paul would have denied that the manna eaten and the water drunk by the Israelites were material food and drink; by *spiritual* he may mean that (like the bread and wine of the eucharist) they had a further significance in addition to their material function as food and drink for the body, or that they were symbolical, or typical, of the Christian sacrament. The word (πνευματικός) is usually employed by Paul to denote some thing (or person) that is the bearer or agent of the Holy Spirit (ix. 11; xii. 1; xiv. 1; xv. 44, 46; Rom. i. 11; vii. 14; xv. 27). If this is so here, both interpretations are possible: the food and drink actually conveyed spiritual (as well as material) sustenance to the Israelites, and at the same time were used by the Spirit as visible prophecies of what was still to be established. Moffatt renders *supernatural*. See further on the next verse.

The Israelites enjoyed spiritual drink, **for they drank from a spiritual rock that accompanied them; and this rock was Christ.** The references to the well of water in Num. xx. 11; xxi. 16 seem to have led to the belief (within Judaism) that the well (provided by the rock) accompanied Israel on their journeys; see for example Pseudo-Philo, *Biblical Antiquities* x. 7: A well of water following them brought he forth for them. See fuller references in Lietzmann. Such a well necessarily calls for the adjective *spiritual*, since it was no natural phenomenon. 'Allegorical' would misrender Paul's word (πνευματικός) here, for the well was not a mere representation of Christ but a scene of his activity; it means 'that which comes from God and reveals him'—Schlatter; compare Rom. vii. 14. This defines Paul's meaning. Here too there is Jewish material to help to explain the origin of his thought. Philo (*Legum Allegoriae* ii. 86) declares: The drought of the passions seizes upon the soul, until God sends forth the stream from his strong Wisdom and quenches with unfailing health the thirst of the soul that had turned from him. For the flinty rock is the Wisdom of God, which he marked off highest and chiefest from his powers, and from which he satisfies the thirsty souls that love God. And when they have been given water to drink, they are filled also with the manna, the most generic of substances, for the manna is called 'somewhat', and that suggests the *summum genus*. But the primal existence is God, and next to him is the Word of God. Compare iii. 162, and *Quod Deterius Potiori Insidiari Soleat* 118.

In Philo's allegorical interpretation of the law, the miraculous food and drink (or source of drink) are taken to mean the word and wisdom of God, which themselves are at least partially hypostatized beings. By adapting these identifications Paul interprets Christ in terms of the wisdom of Hellenistic Judaism. This does not mean that he wished to say about Christ all that Hellenistic Judaism said about wisdom. Indeed his thought is rather of the work than of the person of Christ, and his primary meaning is that as wisdom was believed to be the source of understanding, virtue, and salvation, so in truth was Christ; more than that, it was Christ himself who, in the form of a rock and in the person of wisdom, gave life to the people of God, in the past as in the present. See S.B. iii. 406 ff.

Israel, then, in past ages was supplied by God with visible agencies which conveyed to them the benefits of Christ and the Spirit, just as the church had its visible water, bread, and wine in its analogous sacraments. But Israel's privilege did not
guarantee Israel's moral or religious security. **Nevertheless,** 5
with the majority of them God was not pleased, as is shown by the fact that (this clause represents the elliptical use of γάρ) **they were laid low in the desert.** See Num. xiv. 16. Notwithstanding their sacraments, the Israelites fell into sin, and having sinned they perished in the wilderness and were thus not permitted to enter the promised land. Let the Corinthians take warning. Lietzmann illustrates the similar philosophical attack on non-ethical sacramentalism, quoting for example the complaint of Diogenes, Pataecion the thief will after death have a better fate than Epaminondas, because he has been initiated (ὅτι μεμύηται; Plutarch, *Quomodo adulescens Poetas Audire Debeat* 4). Paul's argument is essentially simple: 'If God did not spare them, he will not spare us, for our situation is the
same as theirs' (Calvin). **These things happened as examples** 6
for us, to warn (the notion of warning is taken out of the word τύπος, used here in the sense of *awful, warning* example; cf. iv. 6)

us (the first person plural is not simply a mark of modesty and tact; Paul believed that he too needed to heed and act on the warning: ix. 27) **not to be men lusting after evil things, as some of them were** (literally, *as some of them lusted*, but the transition from noun, ἐπιθυμηταί, to verb, ἐπιθυμεῖν, is harsh). Compare Num. xi. 4-34, where the people desire the flesh-pots of Egypt; it was natural to think of these as connected with idolatry. Paul did not write these words in a vacuum, and it is possible to infer from them some account of those with whom he was dealing. From viii. 1 ff., 11 it appeared that a free attitude with regard to sacrificial food was based on *gnosis*. Knowledge that idols had no real existence, because there was only one God, led to indifference to the idolatrous rites through which the food had passed. This was an attitude Paul shared, though he qualified it by the application of the principle of Christian love. Here, still in connection with the practical question whether a Christian may eat food sacrificed to idols, we meet an attitude which (though it may have been combined with the other) was essentially different. Some Corinthians believed that their participation in the Christian sacraments guaranteed them against any possible loss of future salvation. They might commit idolatry (verse 7), and fornication (verse 8), they might tempt God (verse 9), and complain against him (verse 10), with impunity because they had been baptized and received the eucharist (verses 2 ff. show that these are the only rites in mind). Paul admits no such *ex opere operato* sacramental efficacy, though the notion is to be found (together with protests against it—see above, p. 223) in paganism, Judaism, and in developing catholic Christianity. For him there could be no escape from the perpetually renewed decision of faith and obedience into a once-for-all, or frequently repeated, sacrament, though the sacraments rightly understood were among the vehicles in which faith and obedience might be expressed.

Men lusting after evil things is a general expression, and its meaning is brought out in the following verses. It suggests, first, lusting after forbidden food, but then also sexual lust, and rebellious lusting after false gods.

7 **Again, do not become idolaters, as they did: as it is written** (Exod. xxxii. 6, cf. 19), **The people sat down to eat**

and drink (that is, to idolatrous meals), **and rose up for sport** (that is, either for 'amorous play'—the rendering L.S. suggest for παίζειν—, or for idolatry, as S.B. iii. 410, and, for example, Calvin, suggest; the latter is perhaps more probable, since fornication is dealt with in the next clause). Paul did not condemn (except when it offended against the law of love) the eating of food sacrificed to idols; what he condemns here is the actual participation in idolatrous worship, which he never condones, since he sees it to result in communion with demons (x. 20 f.). It was in such worship that the Israelites engaged in the wilderness; they did not simply buy and eat food that had been sacrificed to idols, but themselves performed the sacrifices. For some account of the Jewish complex of thought which brought together idolatry, the eating of forbidden food, and fornication, see 'Things sacrificed to Idols'; the New Testament and other early Christian literature reflects the connection that undoubtedly existed in popular thought and practice between idolatry and sexual vice. Paul takes up the new theme explicitly in the next verse.

Again, let us not commit fornication, as some of them 8
did, with the result that (expanding Paul's καί) **in one day there fell 23,000 of them.** According to Num. xxv. 1, 9, the number of those punished for their fornication with the Moabite women was 24,000. There is no more probable explanation of Paul's figure than that it was simply due to a lapse of memory; and it is not a bad guess that the lapse was due to the fact that Paul had in mind not only the story of the Moabite women who led Israel into both fornication and idolatry (for the connection between these see also *Romans*, pp. 38 ff. and *Adam*, pp. 17 ff.) but also that of the Golden Calf, in which about 3,000 of the Israelites were killed (Exod. xxxii. 28).

Again, let us not try (ἐκπειράζειν) **the Lord** (see note 4 on 9
p. 219; the well supported variant *Christ* may well be original, since it could have been changed into *Lord*, as more suitable to an Old Testament passage; see Zuntz, pp. 126, 232), **as some of them did, with the result that** (καί, as in verse 8) **they were destroyed by the snakes.** See Ps. lxxviii. 18, summing up Num. xxi. 4 ff. In the Old Testament story the people *try* the Lord by challenging his ability (and will) to provide the food

needful for them, instead of waiting in faith for his provision. This does not seem to be the attitude that Paul has in mind; in Corinth men were trying, or testing, the Lord by seeing 'how far they could go', in idolatry. It is however reasonable to see in both the Israelites and the Corinthians an irritable refusal to accept conditions which God had laid down for their own good. It will be observed that, though Paul believes the Old Testament situation to be one full of significance for his own contemporaries, he makes no attempt to allegorize every detail of it: *the snakes* do not appear in Corinth.

10 **And do not complain** (second person plural; Paul now addresses the Corinthians directly)**, as some of them did** (not infrequently, in the record of the Exodus and wanderings in the wilderness, but the reference here is probably, in view of what follows, to Num. xvii. 6)**, with the result that** (*καί*, as in verse 8) **they were destroyed by the Agent of Destruction** (*ὁ ὀλοθρευτής*; this word occurs nowhere else in the Greek Bible, but there are similar expressions at Wisdom xviii. 20-25; Exod. xii. 23 (cf. Heb. xi. 28); 2 Sam. xxiv. 16; 1 Chron. xxi. 15; see S.B. iii. 412). Paul seems here to be driven forward by the momentum of his Old Testament material; there is nothing to suggest that *complaining* was a special failing of the Corinthians. Some have seen here a reference to Num. xiv. 2 ff. or xvii. 6 ff., but in these passages other agents of punishment seem to be at work. The passages mentioned above were taken by the Rabbis as evidence for the existence of a special destroying angel, and Paul's noun, with the definite article, suggests that he shared this belief. It would be possible to take his Greek noun as a proper name equivalent to the Hebrew *Mashḥith* (literally, *destroyer*, but used as the name of a destroying angel; see S.B. iii. 412-16), but this is not necessary, and is perhaps unlikely. In Corinth also, however, abuse of the sacraments has received physical punishment (xi. 30); and Satan is referred to as an agent of destruction in v. 5.

The list of Old Testament warnings is now at an end, and
11 Paul proceeds to indicate its significance. **These things happened to them by way of example** (cf. verse 6; here the adverb *τυπικῶς* is used, and would be rendered 'by way of *warning* example' if the word *warning* were not introduced in the

next clause in the rendering of νουθεσία), **and they were written down as a warning for us.** Here, and at verse 6, it is a mistake to read a great deal into Paul's words (τύπος and τυπικῶς; his use of τύπος at Rom. v. 14 is exceptional; see the notes there). Paul was not elaborating a typological exegesis of the Old Testament. He could see that his Corinthian readers were riding for a fall; confident of their own security, guaranteed, as they thought, by sacrament and spiritual experience, they not only displayed a foolish pride that was likely to be disillusioned, but betrayed a radical failure to understand the nature of Christian life, whose security is, by definition, in Christ only, and is apprehended by faith only. The same truth, that the people of God have no security of their own and must live by faith, is written in the Old Testament, where it is delivered in concrete terms, in stories in which the reader should be able to recognize himself and his own circumstances. Further than this the present passage does not entitle us to go. Paul does not attempt to deduce Christian doctrine from the passages he cites by typological methods; to him the Old Testament is a book of fundamental and unique importance, but his doctrinal use of it is as a rule direct.

There is however a special relation between the present generation and the Old Testament. We are those **who are confronted by the end of these past ages of history.** This is a paraphrasing translation. A literal rendering would run: Upon whom the ends of the ages have come, or arrived. *Ends* is plural, and this fact has given rise to the suggestion that Paul's meaning is, Upon whom the ends of the ages (that is, the termination of the age of past and present, and the beginning of the age to come) have met each other. Christians (according to this statement) would be living at the meeting-point (or overlap) of the old age and the new. This might not be an inaccurate account of Paul's eschatological beliefs, though he never (unless he does so here) expresses them in this way; it is scarcely admissible as a translation, for (a) *end* (τέλος) means termination, or goal, not beginning, and (b) *arrive* (καταντᾶν) must be constructed not with an unexpressed 'each other' but with *upon whom* (εἰς οὓς). 'The ends (attracted by *ages* into the plural) of the ages' seems to represent 'the end of the days' (Dan. xii. 13, and often in rabbinic usage (S.B. iii. 416 ff.; Schoeps, *Paulus*, p. 101 (E.T., 99), and *Aus frühchristlicher Zeit* (1950), p. 222). The same Greek expression is used with reference (apparently) to the time of the death of Jesus in some texts of Testament of Levi xiv. 1, and a similar one (τέλος αἰώνων) at *Sibylline Oracles* viii. 311, in parallel with 'the last day'. Paul believes that he and his correspondents are living in the last days of world history before the breaking in of the messianic age. Schweitzer (p. 53) is only a little too free with '. . . will outlive the end of time'; Cullmann, more cautiously, says, 'With Christ has broken in the end phase of the delimited age of this world' (*Christus und die Zeit* (1962), p. 58 (E.T., 48). Paul's view of the eschatological situation is developed further in chapter xv.

Its setting in the letter as a whole, and a number of hints thrown out from time to time and noted in the commentary, have made clear the purpose of the preceding paragraph; Paul
12 now proceeds to make this purpose explicit. **The moral is** (this paraphrases one Greek word, ὥστε, which is intended to draw out the consequences of what has been said): **Let the man who thinks he is standing fast beware lest he should fall.** Moule (p. 199) notes that the verse (without ὥστε) is rhythmical, 'an anapaest and cretic twice repeated'. There is no reason to think this intentional on Paul's part, or that he is quoting. The Israelites, as God's elect, equipped with sacraments, fancied themselves secure. They were not; they fell into sin, condemnation, and destruction. Some at least of the Corinthians, possibly gnostics of a sort, fancy themselves secure; they are God's elect, and they too are equipped with sacraments. But they are no more secure than Paul himself (ix. 27). Moment by moment, the Christian life is lived by faith only, without any human guarantee. As the Israelites were lured by the Moabite women into fornication, idolatry, and so into destruction, so the idolatry, which apparently the Corinthians, secure in their sacramental life, thought they could safely trifle with, could lead them into fornication and destruction.

Looking at the matter from a different angle Paul reflects that the Corinthians, if indeed they are still secure, have nothing to boast about. They have not withstood exceptional temptations.
13 **No testing has fallen upon you but what is the common**

lot of men. They need not therefore claim that they themselves (or their prophylactics) have proved exceptionally resistant. It is implied by Paul's words that more severe trials are to be expected; he himself seems to feel the implication, and goes on to reassure his readers that though no human device can afford them security they may trust to God's faithfulness. **But God can be trusted not to allow you to be tested beyond your power** (yet if they do not exert all their power they may succumb)**; on the contrary, along with the trial he will provide** (literally, *make*) **also the way out, so that you may be able to endure.** Sevenster (*Seneca*, p. 40) notes the contrast with the superficially similar words of Seneca, *Epistle* lxxviii. 7; No man can suffer both severely and for a long time; Nature, who loves us most tenderly, has so constituted us as to make pain either endurable or short. Seneca does not share Paul's confidence in the faithfulness of a personal God. The Christian has no security, but he may be completely confident, not in his own resources but in God. This does not mean that God will not permit him to be tested (by circumstances, or temptation, or the like), but that God will never allow it to become impossible for him to resist. He must resist, and he must not put his trust in false securities; this would be to court and ensure disaster. The *way out* is for those who seek it, not for those who (like the Corinthians) are, where idolatry is concerned, looking for the way in. The connection with the next paragraph makes this clear.

22. x. 14-22. CHRISTIANITY INCONSISTENT WITH IDOLATRY

(14) The conclusion of this, my dear friends, is: Flee from idolatry. (15) I am speaking as to sensible men: judge for yourselves what I say. (16) The cup of blessing, over which we say the blessing, is it not a common participation in the blood of Christ? The loaf which we break, is it not a common participation in the body of Christ? (17) Because there is one loaf, we, many as we are, form one body, for we all partake of the one loaf.

(18) Consider historic Israel: are not those who eat the sacrifices partners in the altar? (19) Well; what do I mean by this? That food sacrificed to an idol is anything? or that an idol is anything?[1] (20) No; but the things they sacrifice, they sacrifice to demons, not to God, and I do not wish you to be partners with the demons. (21) You cannot drink the cup of the Lord, and the cup of demons; you cannot partake of the table of the Lord, and of the table of demons. (22) Or are we to provoke the Lord? Are we stronger than he?

The history of Israel proves that even God's elect, fortified by the means of grace provided by God himself, cannot consider themselves automatically and permanently secure against temptation, and in particular against the worship of other gods.
14 **The conclusion of this** (expanding διόπερ, an argumentative conjunction Paul uses only here and at viii. 13), **my dear friends, is: Flee from idolatry.** Compare vi. 18. It is not enough to express disapproval of idolatry; the Christian must run away from it, that is, he must avoid occasions (such as feasts in heathen temples, if these had a markedly religious content—verses 20 f.; contrast viii. 10; x. 27) that would bring him into direct contact with it. M. iii. 173 lays stress on the definite article that appears (in the Greek) with *idolatry* (τῆς εἰδωλολατρείας), and takes it to mean, 'that worship of idols which you know so well', but the inference is hardly legitimate. Greek idiom demands the article, though English does not. This indeed is not to say that the Corinthians did not know a good deal about idolatry. Their understanding of the situation was something on which they prided themselves. This is why
15 Paul continues: **I am speaking as to sensible men** (φρονίμοις; cf. iv. 10, and see below): **judge for yourselves what I say.** It seems that the Corinthians made much of their common sense, as they undoubtedly did of their charismatic wisdom and *gnosis*. Compare 2 Cor. xi. 19. It gave them a convenient vantage ground from which they could on occasion despise the suffering and humiliation experienced by the apostle; here he appeals to it.

[1] The second question (ἢ ὅτι εἴδωλόν τί ἐστιν;) is omitted by P⁴⁶ ℵ* A C and a few other MSS.

Sensible men can surely not fail to see the point. *Sensible men*, which here has a touch of irony in it, does not in itself mean gnostics; but they were those who claimed to know, as others did not, the truth about God and idolatry (viii. 1-6, 7). If they reflected they would see that it pointed in a direction different from what they supposed. *Judge for yourselves* is not a testimony to the power of the unaided human intellect to think God's thoughts after him; it merely presupposes an ordinary measure of common sense, and willingness to use it. Perhaps Paul's point is that (unlike some at Corinth) he is appealing not to (supposedly) inspired discourse but to reasoned argument (Heim). Compare xiv. 19. He does not utter commands, but wishes to take the Corinthians with him.

The cup of blessing, over which (for the construction cf. 16
Mark vi. 41; viii. 6 f.; xiv. 22 f., noting the parallels) **we say the blessing** (that is, the thanksgiving to God): this verse with the next forms one of Paul's two references to the Lord's Supper. See also xi. 23-6, with the notes. It is impossible in this Commentary to give an account of the Supper, from its origins in the ministry of Jesus to its later New Testament developments. It must be remembered that Paul gives at most allusions to, and not comprehensive accounts of, the meal as he knew and understood it. The present allusion is made for one purpose only, to reinforce Paul's warning against idolatry, but it does make possible a few inferences about the way in which the Supper was interpreted in Paul's time.

The *cup of blessing* (see S.B. iv. 72, 628; see also similar expressions in *Joseph and Aseneth* viii. 5, 9; xv. 5; xvi. 6; xix. 5) was a technical Jewish term for the cup of wine drunk at the end of a meal as its formal close (cf. xi. 25). Over it the thanksgiving or grace for the wine was said: Blessed art thou, O Lord our God, who givest us the fruit of the vine. In the Passover meal, this cup was the third of the four that had to be drunk. In Paul, it acquires a new meaning. **Is it not** (the question implies that the Corinthians should have known and remembered the truth stated, which is thus not a newly minted argument) **a common participation** (both English words are needed to render *κοινωνία*) **in the blood of Christ?** These words are evidently related to those which Paul will quote in xi. 25 from the tradition of the sayings of Jesus at the Last Supper: *This cup is the new covenant in my blood*. In this verse, Paul, unlike Matthew and Mark (Matt. xxvi. 28; Mark xiv. 24; cf. John vi. 53), does not identify the cup, or the wine contained in it, with the blood of Christ. This must be borne in mind in the interpretation of *common participation*, which would be oversimplified if we took its meaning to be that all, by drinking the same cup of wine, drink together the blood of Christ. As the parallel in verses 16a, 17 shows, Paul is thinking of the share all Christians enjoy, and enjoy together, in the benefits secured for them through the blood of Christ. The whole expression means 'that the Christian through taking the wine in the cup, receives an interest in the death of Christ, which, according to Rom. iii. 25; v. 9, mediates to man the justification and atonement God provides' (Kümmel). Compare i. 9; *fellowship with his Son* means not simply being with him, but sharing in the benefits that he confers. *Christum cognoscere, beneficia eius cognoscere*. As we shall see, it is not possible to argue back from verses 18, 20 to the interpretation of verse 16, since Paul is not interpreting the Christian Supper by means of Jewish and pagan sacrifices; yet the use in these verses of the related word *partners* (κοινωνοί) is significant. The Jews do not have fellowship with their altar; they participate in the benefits that come from it (verse 18). In verse 20 it is possible to think of men as having fellowship with demons, since these are spiritual though evil beings, consideration of the whole chapter however suggests that Paul is thinking also of the (evil) influences, in the realm, for example, of sexual morality, that proceed from them. Thus the cup, *over which we* (it will be noted that Paul does not appear to confine the saying of the thanksgiving to a limited group of Christians) *say the blessing*, is a means by which Christians participate together in the benefits of Christ's passion; the participation however is not impersonal, since both Christ and Christians are persons, and are related in personal terms.

The loaf which we (see above on *we say the blessing*) **break, is it not a common participation in the body of Christ?** In view of the order of chapter xi, in which the loaf is mentioned first and then the cup, as in Matthew and Mark (there are special problems in Luke—see Dr Leaney's Commentary in this series), it is surprising to find that Paul here mentions the cup first, and then the loaf. The view that Paul bears witness to a mode of celebrating the Supper in which drinking preceded eating seems untenable in view of xi. 23 ff., though there appears to be an isolated parallel in *Didache* ix. 2 f. It is indeed probable that in Paul's time the observance of the Supper had not reached an invariable liturgical form, but the order of verse 16 is sufficiently explained by the connection of thought that leads into verse 17. Only reference to *the body* could lead Paul to the conclusion he wished to establish, and it would have been awkward to mention this first, and then introduce what could have been only a parenthetical reference to *the blood*. Accordingly Paul, who is neither composing nor reproducing a liturgy but conducting a theological argument, reverses the familiar sequence in order to strengthen the connection.

For the breaking of the loaf, compare xi. 23 f. It was a natural act at any Jewish meal, and particularly so in the Passover meal. The sharing of the bread is taken to be a means of sharing in *the body of Christ*. It is very improbable that this is a reference to the human body of Christ in its physical aspect, since this is described by Paul in other terms (using the word *flesh*; see especially Col. i. 22), whereas for him 'the body of Christ' (e.g. xii. 27), or 'the body (which is) in Christ' (e.g. Rom. xii. 5) refers to the church. To eat the loaf means to share (with others) in that company of men which, through its union with Christ, has by anticipation entered upon the new age which lies beyond the resurrection. Only if the words are taken in this sense can Paul proceed to his next point, which it is probably right to see as his own development of the beliefs he shared with the Corinthians. The material in verse 16 can be introduced with the words 'Is it not?' (see above, p. 232); not so verse 17 (see Bultmann, *Theology*, p. 145 (E.T., 147); E. Käsemann, *Essays on New Testament Themes* (1964), pp. 109 f.). **Because there is** 17
one loaf, we, many as we are, form one body, for we all partake (it does not seem possible to distinguish μετέχειν from κοινωνεῖν) **of the one loaf.** This verse can be punctuated and translated differently; Because we, many as we are, are one loaf, one body; for we all partake of the one loaf. The opening 'because' (ὅτι) is now to be connected with verse 16. This way

of taking the verse is however not to be preferred (M. iii. 303; commentators are divided). That given here lacks grammatical connection with verse 16, but this is understandable and natural if in verse 16 Paul is quoting commonly accepted belief, and in verse 17 sets beside this his own freshly thought out deduction from it. Compare xii. 13 for the relation between baptism and the one body.

Paul's argument is analogous to that of v. 7 f. There it was argued that, since the Christian passover sacrifice has been offered, in the person of Christ, Christians are not only celebrating the feast, but are themselves (by a kind of metonymy) the unleavened loaves with which it is celebrated. It now remains for them to *be* unleavened, to make themselves so by purging out the leaven (*malice and wickedness*) that remains within them. Here Paul argues from the fact that one loaf was broken and distributed to the consequence that those who partake of the one loaf are notwithstanding their plurality one body (cf. *Didache* ix. 4). The reality behind the argument (which may seem speculative enough) is in each case that the men in question have been actually united with Christ. Because he is sinless, they are ideally sinless, and must become so in practice. Because he is one, they are ideally one, and must become so in practice. As in chapter v (which deals with sexual morality), so here, Paul is writing in the most practical terms. The Lord's Supper comes into the discussion of food offered to idols, and thus of idolatry, in three ways. (a) It provides no guarantee against falling into sin, or against divine rejection and punishment. It is not to be taken (as it seems many of the Corinthians did take it) as an *opus operatum* behind which they could shelter, while consulting their own convenience in regard to pagan sacrifices and idolatrous practices in general. (b) It was a means by which they were united to Christ in faith and loyalty. In the light of this, actual participation in idolatry (as distinct from merely eating food that had been sacrificed) became unthinkable treachery. (c) The one loaf broken at the Supper represented the reality of the one body of Christ; all who partook of it were united to one another because they were united to Christ. This unity of the Christian body could be adequately expressed only in love, and love for one's brother (however tiresome he might be) involved respect for his conscientious scruples (cf. verses 28 f., and viii. 7, 10 ff.).

Having made his main points Paul looks round for analogies to clarify them (not arguments to prove them). Having earlier in the chapter (x. 1-10) referred to error and sin in Israel's past he now turns to Israel's legitimate religious activities. Compare
ix. 13. **Consider historic Israel** (literally, *Israel according to* 18
the flesh; cf. Rom. i. 3; iv. 1): **are not those who eat the sacrifices partners** (i.e. with one another) **in the altar?** It was the priests' privilege to consume parts of certain sacrifices (see e.g. Lev. x. 12-15). Of others the non-priestly worshippers also consumed part (see e.g. 1 Sam. ix. 10-24). In this material sense there was joint participation in the benefits arising from the altar; in addition, the worshippers naturally share in the spiritual benefits that the sacrifice made available. This, needless to say, was the rationale of sacrifice: those who shared in the act shared in its benefits. As Paul says, they were *partners in the altar*. To this expression there is a striking parallel (discussed by S. Aalen, 'Das Abendmahl als Opfermahl im Neuen Testament', in *Novum Testamentum* vi (1963), pp. 128-52; see p. 137) in Philo (*De Specialibus Legibus* i. 221), who says that he to whom sacrifice has been offered makes the group of worshippers 'partners in the altar, and of one table (with it)' (*κοινωνὸν . . . τοῦ βωμοῦ καὶ ὁμοτράπεζον*). The meaning of this passage however appears to be that God the bountiful benefactor shares with his worshippers the good gift that they have offered him, by inviting them, as it were, to sit down at table with him. They thus have fellowship with him, and derive benefit from their meal. Again, it seems more probable that the statements of verse 18 (and, though in a different sense, of verse 20) are dependent on those of verse 16 (*common participation in the blood*, and in *the body*, *of Christ*) than *vice versa*. If this is so one can scarcely conclude, with Allo, that the parallelism 'proves that Paul considered the eating of the eucharist as a sacrificial meal'.

The analogy drawn from the sacrifices of Israel is up to a point illuminating, but it has to be handled with care; it might
prove too much if applied too widely. **Well: what do I mean** 19
by this? (literally, *What am I saying?*). **That food sacrificed to**

an idol is anything (other, that is, than mere food)? **Or that
an idol** itself **is anything?** See note 1 on p. 230. Though
omitted by some old and good MSS. the last six words should
be read. They may have been dropped through homoeoteleuton
(τί ἐστιν . . . τί ἐστιν), or because the implied denial of the
existence of idols seemed to conflict with the next two verses
(20 f.). These may, conversely, be taken to suggest (Clark in
Studia Paulina, pp. 59 f.; cf. Kümmel) that Paul would not have
written the omitted words; but the paradox—I am not saying
that an idol is anything, but you had better beware of it all the
same—is very characteristic of his argument here. See further
Zuntz, p. 229. The whole text is consistent with viii. 4. In fact, the
idol is not what the heathen worshipper believes it to be; it is a
material object, but it does not correspond to any spiritual
reality. This is why the food sacrificed to the idol *is* not *anything*.
Nothing happens to it in the moment of sacrifice: it is the same
after as before. It follows that no religious harm, or benefit,
happens to the eater simply through the process of physical
eating; for this reason Paul will tell his readers that they may
buy and eat anything sold in the market (x. 25), and that when
invited out they may eat anything their host sets before them
20 (x. 27). All this is true; **but** (a classical use of ἀλλά: What do I
mean? No, but rather . . .; B.D. §448) the question has another
aspect. **The things they** (P^{46} and other old MSS. have *the
Gentiles* as subject; this is correct interpretation, for Paul
certainly does not mean the Jews, but the interpretation is
secondary to the text given here) **sacrifice, they sacrifice to
demons, not to God.** Paul alludes here to a number of Old
Testament passages, especially Deut. xxxii. 17, in the LXX,
They sacrificed to demons and not to God. Other passages in
the Greek Old Testament reflect the belief that non-Jewish
sacrifices, and those imitated by the Jews from the heathen, are
carried out for the benefit of demons: Ps. xcv (xcvi). 5, All the
gods of the Gentiles are demons; cv (cvi). 37, They sacrificed
their sons . . . to the demons. Particularly interesting in the present
context (cf. verse 21) is Isa. lxv. 11, Preparing a table (τράπεζαν)
for the demon. Compare also 1 Enoch xix. 1; xcix. 7; Jubilees
i. 11; and for the same belief in the Clementines see Schoeps,
Aus frühchristlicher Zeit (1950), pp. 73-81. The word *demon*

provides Paul, as it had provided other Hellenistic Jews before him, with a convenient shorthand way of expressing a truth which otherwise would not have been easy to put into words. He was convinced that the image used in idolatrous worship was a block of wood or stone and nothing more; it was not *anything in the world*. At the same time he believed in the reality of an unseen spirit-world (the evidence is to be found in chapter after chapter; e.g. ii. 6, 8; iv. 9; v. 5; vi. 3; viii. 5), and that idolatry was not merely meaningless but a positively evil thing. It was evil primarily because it robbed the true God of the glory due to him alone (cf. Rom. i. 23), but it was evil also because it meant that man, engaged in a spiritual act and directing his worship toward something other than the one true God, was brought into intimate relation with the lower, and evil, spiritual powers. Thus the harmful effect of idolatry was not the eating of food contaminated in a quasi-physical sense, but in the worshipper's committing himself to an evil though subordinate power. It was thus in effect a crime against man as well as against God, a perversion of man's own true nature. Accordingly Paul adds, **I do not wish you to be partners with the demons.** For the language compare verses 16, 18. The effect of sacrifice lies not in the eating (as Kümmel points out, Paul does not think that the Corinthians will eat demons), but in personal relations, and in the consequences that flow from them. Aalen (op. cit.) thinks of a sharing with the demons in the corruption of the sacrifices, and Schweitzer (p. 269) emphasizes that Paul is not interpreting the Christian Supper by the heathen meals, but the latter by the former. Only it is not the eating of sacrificial food (which Paul permits) but direct participation in idolatry that will separate the Christian from Christ, and no more than the Israelites of old will he escape; his sacraments will preserve him from the moral consequences of idolatry, and from rejection and retribution, no more than did
theirs. Paul sums up the situation in unambiguous terms: **You** 21
cannot drink the cup of the Lord (*the cup of blessing*, verse 16, which means participation in the benefits of Christ's blood-shedding), **and the cup of demons; you cannot partake of the table** (here and in the next clause the word *table*, τράπεζα, rests upon Isa. lxv. 11; but see also Philo, *De Specialibus*

Legibus i. 221, quoted above p. 235, and invitations, preserved in papyri, to eat at the *table*, κλίνη, of such-and-such a god) **of the Lord** (where to eat of the one loaf unites the participant with Christ and his people in the one body), **and of the table** (the use of this word, as of *cup*, with both *the Lord* and *demons* cannot be used to prove identity of meaning in the rites in question) **of demons.** For the notion that eating at the table of demons could lead to demon-possession see Schoeps, *Theologie und Geschichte des Judenchristentums* (1949), p. 192. There is a very full note on ancient cult-meals in Lietzmann, and Moffatt illustrates and explains the attractions such festivals must have continued to have for many Christians. But only a clean break with idolatry is possible for the Christian; Paul takes the word *Lord* (cf. xii. 3) seriously. The parallel between vi. 18 and x. 14 is not fortuitous. Fornication and idolatry are both impossible for a Christian because of his exclusive relationship with Christ.

22 Paul adds a warning. **Or are we to provoke** (taking παραζηλοῦμεν as subjunctive, with M. ii. 196; cf. Gal. iv. 17) **the Lord? Are we stronger than he?** That is, Do we suppose that we (even though we regard ourselves as 'the strong'—cf. viii. 7, 10) can play fast and loose with our loyalty to him (as some in Corinth were disposed to do), and get away with it? The language is based on Israel's provocation of God, but here *the Lord* probably means Jesus Christ. Compare Gal. vi. 7: God is not mocked.

23. x. 23–xi. 1. NATURE, EXTENT, AND LIMITATIONS OF CHRISTIAN FREEDOM

(23) 'All things are permitted'; but not all things are expedient. 'All things are permitted'; but not all things build up. (24) Let no one seek his own ends, but let each one seek the other man's. (25) Eat everything sold in the market, and make no inquiries based on conscientious scruples; (26) for 'the earth is the Lord's, and so is everything it contains'. (27) If any unbeliever invites you, and you wish to go, eat everything set in front of you, and make no inquiries based on conscientious scruples. (28)

But if anyone says to you, 'This is sacrificial food', do not eat it—on account of the man who pointed it out, and for conscience' sake. (29) When I say 'conscience', I mean not one's own, but that of the other man. For to what end is my freedom to be exposed to the judgement of another's conscience? (30) So long as I partake of my food with thanksgiving, why get myself blamed for that over which I give thanks?

(31) Whether then you eat or drink, or whatever you do, do all things to the glory of God. (32) Be men who lay no stumbling-block before Jews, or Greeks, or the church of God, (33) just as I myself seek to please all men in all ways, not seeking what is profitable to myself, but what is profitable to the majority, that they may be saved. (1) Be imitators of me—as I am of Christ.

The question of food sacrificed to idols has now been under discussion, more or less directly, for three chapters (since viii. 1). It is time to sum up in terms of practical advice and precept (see already viii. 9, 13; x. 14, 21). This Paul proceeds to do, repeating a quotation from a Corinthian source that he has
already used in another connection. **'All things are per-** 23
mitted'; but not all things are expedient. So, almost word for word, in vi. 12; see the notes. There Paul developed the argument on individualist lines. A man who acts on the principle that he is free to do anything he likes is in danger of losing his freedom through becoming enslaved to the practices for which he feels himself to be free. Here Paul develops his argument in a corporate direction. **'All things are permitted'; but not all things build up,**—that is, build up the community. There is a negative form of this point in Rom. xiv. 20, where the 'work of God', which a self-willed Christian may destroy for the sake of food (which he rightly thinks to be permitted), is the community. It is not a Christian duty to seek out things that a man may be permitted to do; it is a Christian duty to build up the church. 'The freedom of the Christian is the freedom to play his part in the upbuilding of the community' (Barth, *C.D.* III. ii. 305 f.). This he will do not by thinking of his own rights and
privileges, but rather by considering others. **Let no one seek** 24

his own ends (literally, *that which is his own*; cf. xiii. 5), **but let each one** (*each one* is not expressed in the best texts of the Greek, but may be taken out of *no one*; this is a good classical usage—see B.D. §479) **seek the other man's.** This somewhat colloquial expression is not merely close verbally to the Greek (literally, *that which is the other's*) but is also more accurate that 'his neighbour's', since *neighbour*, like the Latin *proximus*, suggests the 'man who is near to me', which easily passes over into the 'man who is like me', the 'man who is my friend', whereas, as the rest of the paragraph shows, we are rather to think here of the 'man who is unlike me', the 'man with whom I instinctively disagree'. This is the man—for example, the man who disagrees with me about food sacrificed to idols—whose interests I must consider rather than my own.

25 **Eat everything sold in the market** (primarily, perhaps, but not exclusively, the meat-market), **and make no inquiries based on conscientious scruples.** For details here and throughout the paragraph see 'Things sacrificed to Idols'. Not all the food sold in the market had been offered to an idol, but undoubtedly some of it had; Paul is therefore saying: You do not need to find out which food has been offered and which has not, for you may freely eat food that has been offered. So far as the essential point of principle is concerned he is at one with the strong Christians (cf. Rom. xv. 1); neither food nor abstention from it will commend us to God. He makes a clean break with Judaism, where conscience demanded of the devout Jew the most searching inquiry before he might eat. Paul had in fact ceased to be a practising Jew (see the notes on ix. 20 f.).

26 Paul supports his point by quoting Ps. xxiv. 1; **'The earth is the Lord's, and so is everything it contains'.** 'God the Creator is stronger than demons' (Harris). It has been said that this verse was used by Jews as, or in, a grace said at meals; this is not so, but the verse was used as an argument that grace ought to be said, and this use of it would probably be known to Paul. See verse 30. Paul assumes that the Christian, like the Jew, will recognize with an expression of gratitude that everything he eats is a gift from God. On the Jewish use of this Psalm, especially in *Tosephta Berakoth* iv. 1, see E. Lohse, in *Z.N.T.W.* xlvii (1956), 277-80.

In verses 25 f. Paul is thinking of the Christian as he brings in his own supplies of food for use in his own home; he now considers the case of a Christian invited to eat away from home.
If any unbeliever invites you (it is implied that social con- 27
tacts between believers and unbelievers continue; cf. v. 10; whatever 2 Cor. vi. 14–vii. 1 means it cannot be intended to justify, or demand, the creation of a Christian ghetto), **and you wish to go** (it is wrong to see here the implication that Paul would prefer the invited Christian not to accept; the language is normal; cf. Xenophon, *Memorabilia* I. iii. 6, εἰ . . . κληθεὶς ἐθελήσειεν . . . ἐλθεῖν), **eat everything set in front of you** (almost exactly the same words are used at Luke x. 8, where they probably reflect the practice of the Gentile mission—missionaries must assume that everything offered them for Jesus' sake (Rengstorf, ad loc.) is clean), **and make no inquiries based on conscientious scruples** (cf. verse 25). In these circumstances, as in the market, it could not be assumed that all the food, or even any of it, would necessarily have been offered to an idol, but the possibility was always present that some of it might have been so offered. Paul's advice implies therefore that a Christian may eat such food without either doing or suffering harm. There is however a difference between taking part in a meal with others and the individualist activity of shopping for a meal at home. At a meal, one's table-companions also must be considered. **But if anyone says to you, 'This is sacrificial food', 28
do not eat it. The word Paul has used up to this point for 'food sacrificed to idols' (εἰδωλόθυτον, which the majority of MSS. wrongly substitute here) is that which Jews and Christians used, and contains the pejorative force of the word *idol*; those who did not wish to express this pejorative sense because they themselves approved and took part in the worship of idols used a different word (ἱερόθυτον; see on viii. 1), which Paul here puts on the lips of either the non-Christian host, or a fellow-guest, possibly also not a Christian. We must say more about this informant later. In the circumstances described, the Christian should not eat. Why? **On account of the man who pointed it out, and for conscience' sake.** In Greek *the man who pointed it out* and *conscience* are more closely co-ordinated than in the English, being governed by the same preposition; the next

sentences will show (against Wendland, who distinguishes the heathen *who pointed it out* from the weak Christian, whose *conscience* is involved) how close the co-ordination is: it is the *conscience* of the man, and it is *his* conscience that you must
29 consider. **When I say 'conscience', I mean not one's own** (ἑαυτοῦ; this might stand for σεαυτοῦ, *your own*, but the more generalized meaning is better—M. ii. 181), **but that of the other man** (cf. verse 24; the man who gave warning). Who is this man? He might be the host (defined in verse 27 as an unbeliever), who, perhaps out of kindly consideration, perhaps with a measure of *Schadenfreude* (hosts have been known to entertain it), informs his Christian guest of the nature of what he is eating, or is about to eat. He might be a fellow-guest, either a non-Christian, or a weak Christian. It is not easy to see how a non-Christian's conscience could enter into the matter, and it is therefore best to suppose that we have to do with a second Christian guest, whose weak conscience, though it permitted him to attend the meal, has led him to make inquiries (cf. verses 25, 27) of his host or in the kitchen, and who, using the most courteous word available, now passes on the fruit of his researches to his stronger Christian brother. The meal is evidently a private one; if it were a cult banquet there would be no need to inquire, or to pass on self-evident information; nor would a weak Christian be present. For the general position, compare viii. 7-13; the strong Christian must be governed by his weak brother's conscience (cf. Rom. xiv. 13-16, 20-3; xv. 1).

At the end of this verse a large number of MSS. add, 'For the earth is the Lord's, and so is everything it contains'. The words are borrowed from verse 26, but here they must be given a somewhat different application. It is not because articles of food are evil in themselves (for they are all part of God's good creation) that you must abstain, but with an eye to the welfare of your fellow-man.

The next sentence is notoriously difficult. **For to what end is my freedom** (to eat whatever I think good) **to be exposed to the judgement of another's** (literally, *another*, but this is scarcely English) **conscience?** It is not easy to see how this question is to be connected with the flow of thought in the paragraph, but, though a marginal gloss has been suspected, it is better not to run away from the problem. (1) It is attractive to suppose that in these words we hear an interjection made by a strong Christian who objects to being limited by the conscience of others. This is all very well, he says, but why should my freedom be thus hedged in? There are two reasons for rejecting this view: the sentence should be introduced by *but*, not *for*; Paul never answers the supposed complaint. (2) Paul gives here a further reason for self-control on the part of the strong Christian Why should I, by exercising my freedom to eat what I like, cause it to be evil spoken of by others, scrupulously conscientious? Compare Rom. xiv. 16. This position is most strongly put by Heim, who argues that the situation contemplated here is different from that of chapter viii, where a strong Christian simply abstains from taking advantage of his rights in order not to lead his weaker brother to do what is against his conscience. Here a new point is made. 'Abstain from eating on the ground that, by eating, you bring yourselves into the unpleasant situation of being criticized, at a heathen's table, by a Christian table-companion, and for conscientious reasons at that, and that in this way slander will be uttered.' Verse 31 follows on this, with the sense, Let your eating and drinking be conducted in such a way as to bring glory (not dishonour) to God. This exegesis is very complicated, and there is no good reason for denying affinity between the situation described in chapter viii and that of chapter x. (3) The best view is that Paul is simply reinforcing the point that he has just made. Verse 29 is to be explained thus; 'Not because one's own conscience requires abstention, but for the sake of the other man's, the weak man's conscience, in order that he may not be caused to act against his conscience. If I were to suppose that I must abstain on account of my own conscience, then I should have submitted myself to the judgement of another, and given up my freedom; in the abstract I remain quite free to eat what I can enjoy with thanksgiving (that is, with a good conscience); but neither do I give up my freedom if I abstain out of regard for the conscience of another' (Bultmann, *Theology*, pp. 215 f. (E.T., 217 f.); the whole context should be consulted for Paul's use of *conscience*). It is to be noted that, as in Rom. xiv, xv, Paul places himself unambiguously among the strong and free; he is firmly of the opinion that (apart from considerations of love to fellow-Christians) the Christian is always free to eat any food whatever. His conscience, though there may be occasions when he does not take advantage of the liberty it allows him, remains always his own, and free, and is not called in question by the judgements of others. Compare iv. 3 f. This means, among other things, that Paul has ceased to practise Judaism, except occasionally, and by way of concession.

30 The sense of verse 30 has already been given. **So long as I partake of my food with thanksgiving, why get myself blamed for that over which I give thanks?** Paul is still justifying abstention by the strong. It matters least of all what I eat (for a Christian ought not to be a slave to his appetite or his tastes); it matters far more that I should avoid strife, and give no occasion for evil speaking within the church; it matters most of all that I should act with a good conscience, and this is shown (as far as food is concerned) by the fact that I say grace over my meal.

It is time to leave the subject of eating and drinking (which nevertheless played a very large part in early Christian controversy, and made it possible, as here, for important questions
31 of principle to be hammered out). Paul generalizes. **Whether you eat or drink, or whatever else** (on the ellipse of *ἄλλο* in Greek see B.D. §480) **you do, do all things to the glory of God.** This verse puts positively what has hitherto been put negatively. I do not act to the glory of God if I give to an idol some of the honour due to God alone; nor if I cause scandal or ill-feeling in the church, or cause a fellow-Christian to fall from his faith. These statements apply the obligation of giving glory to God in the field of eating and drinking; Paul does not here offer comparable statements applying the same principle in other fields, and it is not for a commentary to do what Paul does not attempt. Paul does however make it clear that such applications ought to be made.

32 **Be men who lay no stumbling-block** (which might make it difficult for them to believe, or make them fall from their faith) **before Jews, or Greeks** (that is, non-Jews), **or the church of God** (that is, the assembly, probably the local assembly, of God's people). Paul not infrequently links to-

gether Jew and Greek (e.g. Rom. i. 16); it is seldom that he adds Christians as a third group. Presumably he is still thinking of food laws, and of the principle he enunciated for himself in ix. 19, 23. His aim is not to enjoy, or for that matter to renounce, freedom in respect of food and drink, but to win all men for the Gospel; and this should equally be the aim of his readers. Thus they must not wantonly outrage Jewish scruples. It would be a good deal harder to find Gentile scruples that could be flouted (except among particular groups, such as the Pythagoreans, who observed strict dietary laws); Paul adds *Gentiles* probably because they form his usual pair with *Jews*, possibly because excessive scrupulosity might evoke pagan ridicule (Héring). Weak Christians were certainly liable to take offence; we have already seen that their consciences should be protected. On *the church of God* see pp. 31 f.

In this kind of behaviour the Corinthians have an example: **as I myself seek to please** (the present tense is to be taken as conative; Paul could hardly claim that he succeeded in his attempt!) **all men in all ways** (cf. ix. 22), **not seeking what is profitable to myself** (cf. verse 24; xiii. 5), **but what is profitable to the majority** (or perhaps, taking *οἱ πολλοί* in the sense of 'the many' in the Qumran MSS., *the community*), **that they may be saved** (again cf. ix. 22). Elsewhere (Gal. i. 10; cf. 1 Thess. ii. 4; and especially 1 Cor. vii. 32 ff., with the notes) Paul speaks of pleasing men as an evil thing; but there is no contradiction. Pleasing men is evil when it is done with a view to currying favour with them, or so as to avoid persecution; it is good when it is done so as to lead them to the faith. It is not simply that the value of behaviour is affected by its motive. Paul knows that the Christian message is necessarily and intrinsically offensive (e.g. i. 23); it is the more important that Christianity should offend for the right and not for the wrong reason, because it is a placarding of Christ crucified, and not because Christians are inconsiderate of the scruples and convictions of their fellows.

The parallels with ix. 22 have already implied that Paul believed that the Corinthians might profit from his example; the
point is now made explicit: **Be imitators of me—as I am of** 1
Christ. This verse is much more closely connected with what

precedes than with what follows; our chapter division is unfortunate. Paul several times expresses the thought that he was not merely a teacher and preacher to his churches, but one whose conduct should be imitated (cf. Phil. iii. 17; 1 Thess. i. 6; 2 Thess. iii. 7, 9); part of his apostolic role was to manifest with special clarity the pattern of the Christian life (e.g. iv. 9-13). This pattern was based upon the life of Christ himself; Paul's only claim to be worthy of imitation lies in the fact that he himself imitates Christ. Paul does elsewhere urge his readers to imitate Christ directly (e.g. Rom. xv. 2 f.); there is no hierarchy of mediated imitation here. But Paul is wise enough to know that his own imitation of Christ was, if imperfect, a good deal more accessible than the historic life of Jesus.

(c) THE CHRISTIAN ASSEMBLY

24. xi. 2-16. MEN AND WOMEN

(2) Now I praise you that you are always remembering me, and hold fast the traditions as I handed them on to you. (3) But I wish you to know that Christ is the head of every man, the man is the head of the woman, and God is the head of Christ. (4) Every man who prays or prophesies with a veil hanging down from his head disgraces his head; (5) but every woman praying or prophesying with unveiled head disgraces her head, for it is one and the same thing as if she had been shaved. (6) For if a woman is not veiled, let her cut her hair short too; but if it is a disgraceful thing for a woman to cut her hair or to shave, then let her be veiled. (7) For a man ought not to veil his head, since he is the image and glory of God, but the woman is the glory of man. (8) For man did not come from woman, but woman from man; (9) for man was not created for the sake of woman, but woman for the sake of man. (10) For this reason a woman ought to have authority on her head, on account of the angels. (11) Only in the Lord neither is the woman anything

apart from the man nor the man apart from the woman; (12) for as the woman was taken out of the man, so also man comes through the woman; and all things come from God. (13) Decide among yourselves: is it fitting for a woman to pray to God unveiled? (14) Does not nature itself teach you that if a man has long hair it is a dishonour to him, (15) but that if a woman has long hair it is a glory to her? For her long hair has been given her as a covering.

(16) But if anyone means to be contentious—we have no such custom, nor have the churches of God.

We have seen reason (vii. 1, etc.) to think that in this epistle Paul refers from time to time to a letter sent to him from Corinth. In this letter the Corinthians asked questions, but also did not hesitate to express the conviction that things were going well with their church. Paul could not always agree with them, but here he is able to preface critical observations with praise;
contrast xi. 17. **Now I praise you** (many MSS. add 'brothers') 2
that you are always (or *in all things*) **remembering me, and hold fast the traditions as I handed them on to you.** The language was probably formulated in Corinth, but Paul uses it himself (xi. 23; xv. 1, 3; see also Rom. vi. 17; 2 Thess. ii. 15; iii. 6). *The traditions* (as the other references show) were the central truths of the Christian faith, handed on at this stage (before the emergence of Christian literature) orally from evangelist and teacher to convert. The context suggests that training in Christian conduct was included. Later (xv. 2) Paul will throw some doubt on whether the Corinthians did indeed *hold fast* the teaching he had given them; here he accepts at its face value their claim to do so. It is not clear what leads him to the subject discussed after this *captatio benevolentiae*; possibly the Corinthian letter contained an inquiry whether it was still necessary to observe conventional distinctions (see Introduction, p. 6; Hurd, pp. 182-6) in a community in which there were no longer male and female (Gal. iii. 28), and women as well as men were manifestly moved by the Spirit to pray and prophesy (verse 5). Alternatively, Paul may have been acting on information received from Chloe's people (i. 11), from Stephanas,

Fortunatus, and Achaicus (xvi. 17), or in some other way. The question raised is that of the relation between men and women, especially in public worship. Related themes are treated in chapters vi and vii.

3 I am glad, then, that you think so kindly of me, **but** I should prefer to see behaviour in the church ordered in accordance with Christian principle. **I wish you to know that Christ is the head of every man** (subject and predicate could be reversed in this clause, but in the two following clauses *head*, being anarthrous, is predicate, and these carry the present clause with them)**, the man** (or possibly *the husband*) **is the head of the woman** (or possibly *the wife*)**, and God is the head of Christ.** In this verse (which is to be contrasted with 4, 7, 10 below) the word *head* (κεφαλή) is evidently used in a transferred sense. In the Old Testament *head* (*rosh*, sometimes but by no means always translated into Greek as κεφαλή) may refer to the ruler of a community (e.g. Judges x. 18); this use, however, though it was adopted in Greek-speaking Judaism, was not a native meaning of the Greek word (for details see H. Schlier, in *T.W.N.T.* iii. 674 f.). In Greek usage the word, when metaphorical, may apply to the outstanding and determining part of a whole, but also to origin (e.g., in the plural, to the source of a river, as in Herodotus iv. 91). In this sense it is used theologically, as in an Orphic fragment (21a): Zeus is the head, Zeus the middle, and from Zeus all things are completed (Ζεὺς κεφαλή, Ζεὺς μέσσα, Διὸς δ᾽ ἐ̃κ πάντα τελεῖται; that some MSS. have ἀρχή instead of κεφαλή adds to its significance; see also S. Bedale in *J.T.S.* v (new series), 211-15). That this is the sense of the word here is strongly suggested by verses 8 f. Paul does not say that man is the lord (κύριος) of the woman; he says that he is the origin of her being. In this he is directly dependent on Gen. ii. 18-23, where it is stated (a) that woman was created in order to provide a helper suited to him, and (b) that she was created by the removal of a rib from Adam's body. It is true that Paul might have reached a different conclusion if he had started from Gen. i. 27, where from the beginning creation seems to have been of male and female alike (perhaps—as some ancient Jewish interpreters thought—of an androgynous being). Paul is indeed partly influenced by this verse when in verse 7, after writing that man

is the image and glory of God, he says that woman is the glory of man—not his image, for she too shares the image of God, and is not (as some commentators have thought) more remote from God than is man.

So far we have concentrated on one clause. *Man is the head of woman* in the sense that he is the origin, and thus the explanation of her being. That *God is the head of Christ* can be understood in a similar way. The Father is *fons divinitatis*; the Son is what he is in relation to the Father. There can be no doubt that Paul taught a form (we may call it an innocent form) of subordinationism; see further iii. 23; xv. 28, with the notes. The Son would no longer be the kind of Son we know him to be if he ceased to be obedient to and dependent on the Father.

It is harder to explain the clause that states that *Christ is the head of every man*—of every man, not simply of the Christian; for it is scarcely legitimate (with Robertson-Plummer) to take *every* to mean simply 'whether married or unmarried'. The reference is probably to Christ as the agent of creation (cf. viii. 6: *through him*); possibly however the thought goes further: as the existence of Christ is given in the existence of God, and as the existence of woman is given in the existence of man, so the existence of man is given in the existence of Christ, who is the ground of humanity (cf. Col. i. 16, In him all things were created). Thus a chain of originating and subordinating relationships is set up: God, Christ, man, woman. From this proposition practical consequences are deduced.

Every man who prays (that is, in public and aloud, as any 4
Christian might do in the assembly) **or prophesies** (for the gift of prophecy see xii. 10, et al.) **with a veil** (throughout this paragraph *veil*—always a paraphrase, since the Greek word κάλυμμα does not occur—is to be understood as a head-covering concealing the hair and upper part of the body, not as a covering for the face—so Schlatter, who shows that the reference is to the practice of the devout and modest Jewess; see *Ketuboth* vii. 6: What transgresses Jewish custom? If she goes out with her head uncovered . . .) **hanging down from his head** (κατὰ κεφαλῆς; so Robertson, pp. 606 f., M. iii. 268; it is worth while to retain this somewhat pedantic rendering because, as we have seen, κεφαλή is sometimes used metaphorically; Héring takes κατά to mean

not 'coming down from', but 'coming down upon'—thus 'with a head-covering') **disgraces his head.** For Jewish customs, see further S.B. iii. 423-6. The word *head* at its first occurrence undoubtedly refers to the man's physical head; what of the second occurrence? Some take it to mean physical head again: man's unveiled head is the mark of his freedom, the image and glory of God (verse 7), and it would be disgraceful if it were concealed. Others take this verse to be a consequence of the preceding verse (which otherwise would have no purpose—cf. Weiss's suggestion that it is a gloss), and argue that the second use of *head* must refer not to the man's physical head, but to Christ, the head of every man. Moreover, in the ancient world a cap, not a bare head, was the sign of freedom; and the Jewish custom is for men to be covered at worship, though it is not certain that this prevailed in the first century. Allo suggests that both interpretations, the literal and the metaphorical, may be right. He refers to 2 Cor. iii. 18. The Christian, with his unveiled head, reflects the glory of Christ. If (like Moses) he were to wear a veil and conceal his head he would rob his own head of its chief function of reflecting the glory of Christ, and he would at the same time rob Christ of the glass in which his glory should be reflected. This interpretation seems probable but is by no means certain; and, since my note already owes much to Allo, I shall borrow for myself his last sentence too: '*Si quelqu'un donne une meilleure interprétation, je m'y rangerai*'.

So much for men. They must be bare-headed when they
5 take part in public worship. **But every woman praying or prophesying with unveiled head disgraces her head, for it is one and the same thing as if she had been shaved** (literally, *she is one and the same thing with her that has been shaved*; cf. B.D. §131). The verse is meaningless unless women were from time to time moved, in the Christian assembly in Corinth, to pray and prophesy aloud and in public (not simply in family prayers and other small groups—Bachmann). If moreover Paul had thought it wrong for them to do this he would certainly not have wasted time in discussing what, in these circumstances, they should do with their heads; he would simply have forbidden the practice. This observation will create a

problem when we reach xiv. 33-6 (cf. also 1 Tim. ii. 11 f.), but this problem will be considered then (see pp. 331 ff.). In the present chapter Paul assumes that women will offer public prayer, and utter the kind of public speech known as prophecy, and simply regulates the way in which they shall do this.

A woman must not speak in the assembly with unveiled head (it is not a necessary implication of Paul's words that provided she does not speak she need not be veiled). She is thus sharply and visibly differentiated from man; the oneness of male and female in Christ (Gal. iii. 28) does not obliterate the distinction given in creation. Man disgraces his head by wearing a veil, woman disgraces hers by not wearing one. What is meant here by *her head*? Some think that her husband is intended (he is disgraced by her shameless behaviour), but the subsequent reference to shaving suggests that her physical head is meant. Tacitus, *Germania* 19 (the husband of an adulterous wife cuts off her hair, strips her naked, and drives her from the house) is a parallel more likely to occur to a modern commentator than to a Corinthian; Aristophanes, *Thesmophoriazusae* 838 (the mother of unworthy children should have her hair shorn), or something like it, might be more familiar. Compare Lucian, *De Syria Dea* 6. A Jewish woman was always veiled in public: Jeremias, *Jerusalem zur Zeit Jesu* (1958), II B 232. Kümmel argues that Paul is not here combating a movement for the emancipation of women, but seeking to introduce into Greece an oriental custom; see also S.B. iii. 427-34. This makes it the more necessary to ask the question whether Paul is here simply dependent on custom, so that 'in communities where it is no longer a disgrace for a woman to be "shorn", the argument has lost its point' (Hooker, *N.T.S.* x. 410—see below, p. 253). This is probably not so; Paul thinks that *nature* (see verse 14) expects a woman to be covered, so that for her to be uncovered is not only an offence against custom but also an unnatural act. Whether his understanding of *nature* is legitimate is a question that will call for discussion below. Veiling, cutting the hair, shaving, all belong together. 'If you throw off the veil imposed by the law, throw off that imposed by nature too' (Chrysostom). **For if a woman** 6
is not veiled, let her cut her hair short too; but if it is a disgraceful thing for a woman to cut her hair or to shave

(reading ξυρᾶσθαι, aorist infinitive middle of ξυρῶ; B.D. §317; M. iii. 57), **then let her be veiled.** No new thought is introduced here, but the repetition reinforces the view that Paul is thinking of a natural rather than a merely conventional propriety.

He now takes up again the more definitely theological point.
7 **For a man ought not to** (literally, *is not under obligation to*, but the parallel in verse 10 shows that Paul thinks it not merely unnecessary but wrong for a man to be veiled) **veil his head, since he is the image and glory of God.** Paul means, presumably, that to veil his head would be to obscure God's image and diminish his glory; these therefore in some sense reside in the head. According to Gen. i. 26 man (both male and female being included in this term) was created in the image of God; that is, in contrast with the rest of creation, resembling him. This thought, however, Paul does not develop. It does not appear in verse 7c, where it would be inappropriate (Adam begot a *son* in his image), and in this context Paul values the term image only as leading to the term glory. The sense in which Adam was God's glory has already been brought out (p. 250); he was the direct product of God's own creative activity, made by God himself to serve his purpose. Man exists (ὑπάρχων) to give glory to God (Rom. i. 21; see the notes), and in fact does give glory to God by being what he truly is, God's obedient and believing creature. This, however, he truly is only in Christ (in whom alone the race is restored from its fallen state), and worship is meaningless unless it manifests his being in Christ. Thus God's glory is revealed. **But the woman is the glory of man.** Paul now follows not Gen. i. 26, but Gen. ii. 18-23, as the next two verses show. (It is a flaw in Barth's argument in *C.D.* III. i. 191-206 that he does not, on p. 203, recognize this trans-
8 ference). **For man did not come from woman** (since he was in existence before any woman came into being), **but woman from man** (being made out of a rib drawn from Adam's side,
9 Gen. ii. 21); **for** (parallel to the *for* which introduces verse 8) **man was not created for the sake of woman** (since he was created before—in the primitive narrative—God had even thought of making woman), **but woman for the sake of man** (after God had created the animals in a vain search for a helper

suitable for Adam, Gen. ii. 19 f.). Thus as Adam was brought forth directly from God, and was made for his sole service, so the woman was brought forth from man, and was intended from the beginning to be his helper. In the sense therefore in which man is the glory of God, she is the glory of man, deriving her being from man (though not man but God is her creator), and finding her fulfilment in serving him. This is her role in creation; it is not her role in Christ, in whom such distinctions are removed, but Christians remain created beings, and whatever he may have meant by Gal. iii. 28 Paul cannot have meant that the created difference between the sexes had ceased to exist—his discussion (in chapter vii) of marriage problems within the church is sufficient to show this.

After his statement that *woman is the glory of man* we expect Paul to complete the parallelism of verse 7 by adding, It follows that a woman ought to be veiled (as a man ought not). He does not do this. After developing in verses 8 f. the relation between
man and woman in creation he continues, **For this reason a** 10
woman ought to have authority on her head, on account of the angels. *For this reason* (διὰ τοῦτο) is most naturally taken to point backwards: for the reasons just given. These reasons are supplemented by another (unless we take *for this reason* to point forwards, in which case this is the only reason), namely, *on account of the angels*. In this verse two points are notoriously obscure: (a) Why does Paul say that a woman should have on her head (not a veil but) *authority* (ἐξουσία)? (b) Why does he refer to angels? On these two questions, and especially the former, reference should be made to an article by Dr M. D. Hooker (in *N.T.S.* x. 410-16), to which these notes are much indebted.

The angels have often been explained in terms of the narrative of Gen. vi. 1 f., in which the 'sons of God' (angels) assaulted the daughters of men; against such potential attackers women need protection. It is not however clear how the wearing of a veil while they pray or prophesy can serve their purpose. Is this the only time at which lustful angels may prey upon them? It might have been thought that women would be safest when thus engaged. We cannot use the argument that 'nowhere else in the New Testament are angels thought of as evil' (there are e.g. angels of Satan; for Jewish views of angels see S.B. iii.

437-40), but even so there seems inadequate ground for this interpretation. Setting aside such bizarre patristic interpretations as that the angels are bishops (cf. Rev. ii. 1, etc.), the alternative remains that the angels are the guardians of the created order (less probably the guardians of the women). As such they would be particularly offended by variation from the principles set out in verse 3. This view is accepted by Miss Hooker; it finds support in an article in *N.T.S.* iv. 48-58 by J. A. Fitzmyer, who adduces Qumran evidence for the belief that angels were present in the assembly, and liable to be offended by lapses from due order. It should perhaps be varied a little, in that we may think of the angels as watchers of the created order (cf. iv. 9, referred to by Dr Hooker). Some are ready to uphold it, others perhaps ready to pounce on any lapse from the security it affords.

Why does Paul use the word *authority* when we expect veil? Miss Hooker (loc. cit.) has no difficulty in showing that most of the current interpretations of the word are impossible. Kittel's suggestion that it is based on an ambiguity in Aramaic (the root *sh-l-ṭ* gives rise to words meaning *power*, *authority*, and also to one meaning *veil*) presupposes linguistic knowledge that cannot have been common in Corinth, and other suggestions break down in Greek, where Paul's word (ἐξουσία) does not mean *dignity*, *protection*, or 'a sign of authority (the husband's) submitted to'. What seems to be the true explanation must be given in two stages.

(a) A woman must be veiled because whereas in herself she is the glory of man (verse 7) in worship (she is praying or prophesying) God only must be glorified. 'If she were to pray or prophesy with uncovered head, she would not be glorifying God, but reflecting the glory of man, and in God's presence this must inevitably turn to shame. The glory of man must therefore be covered, lest dishonour is brought upon the woman's "head". Although Paul's argument is based upon theological premises, it may perhaps reflect practical expediency; it is likely that it was the men of Corinth, rather than the angels, who were attracted by the women's uncovered locks, and that it was in this way that attention was being diverted from the worship of God' (p. 415).

(b) But why *authority*? 'According to Paul, . . . it is man, and not woman, who is the glory of God, and who will therefore naturally play the active role in worship . . . Yet now woman, too, speaks to God in prayer and declares his word in prophecy; to do this she needs authority and power from God. The head-covering which symbolizes the effacement of man's glory in the presence of God also serves as the sign of the *ἐξουσία* which is given to the woman' (pp. 415 f.). That is, her veil represents the new authority given to the woman under the new dispensation to do things which formerly had not been permitted her.

Not the smallest argument in support of the interpretation that has now been given is that it leads naturally to the next two verses which, accepting the natural, and unaltered, differences between man and woman, emphasize their mutual dependence in the purpose of God, and its final execution in the Christian
dispensation. **Only in the Lord** (not simply, as is shown by 11
what follows, *in the realm of the Christian life*; perhaps, *in the Lord's intention*, in the original creation and in its restoration) **neither is the woman anything apart from the man, nor the man apart from the woman.** One would be inclined here to see a reference to the Jewish belief that the first human creature of Gen. i. 26 f. was bisexual, were it not that the next verse
points plainly to Gen. ii. **For as the woman was taken out of** 12
the man (in creation; see Gen. ii. 21)**, so also man comes through the woman** (in the ordinary process of childbirth). Thus each owes his existence to, and cannot continue without, the other. Together they make a unity in which each member is essential. **And all things come from God.** Men and women alike owe their existence to God and depend on him. God himself is asserted to be the source of human existence, of sexual differentiation, and of the sexual function of procreation. If for particular reasons Paul can advise against marriage, it is not because he thinks that sex is of the devil. Schlatter compares *Genesis Rabbah* viii. 8 (It is not man without woman, nor woman without man, nor the two of them without the *Sh^{e}kinah*); this sentence refers however more explicitly to the procreation of children.

Paul returns, after this parenthesis, to the question of women's dress in worship. Why? Is it likely that, having established his

point on serious theological grounds he should doubt their value, and make a blustering appeal to custom and prejudice? One would think not. It is probable therefore that there is more
13 in Paul's words than some commentators have found. **Decide among yourselves:** perhaps, *in yourselves*, that is, in your own minds and by using your own mental resources. It would be foolish to deduce that the unaided human intellect is capable of finding divine truth. The readers are Christians, and Paul appeals to them to reach a common-sense decision in that capacity; compare v. 4 f., 12; x. 15. **Is it fitting for a woman to pray to God unveiled?** Undoubtedly the sentence expects the answer no. The Corinthians should be able to reach this
14 conclusion themselves, without instruction from Paul. **Does not nature itself teach you that if a man has long hair it is**
15 **a dishonour to him, but that if a woman has long hair it is a glory to her?** Paul uses the word *nature* (*φύσις*) at Rom. i. 26; ii. 14, 27: xi. 21, 24; Gal. ii. 15; iv. 8 (cf. Eph. ii. 3). These passages do not all express identically the same idea, but the notion common to them all is that of correspondence with things as they are found truly to be, without artificial change. The best parallel to the present passage is Rom. i. 26 (cf. the use of *φυσικός* in Rom. i. 26 f.). The idea is not an abstruse theological one; Paul is thinking of the natural world as God made it, rather than (in the Stoic manner) of Nature as a quasi-divine hypostasis. *Nature* (i.e., God) has made men and women different from each other, and has provided a visible indication of the difference between them in the quantity of hair he has assigned to each; that is, in point of fact men have short, women have long hair, and though art can reverse this difference, the reversed distinction is, and is felt to be, artificial. Whether or not this corresponds with scientific observation, it would certainly correspond with Paul's observation, as study of Hellenistic portraiture will confirm. There is a good parallel to the thought in Epictetus I. xvi. 9-14. 'Let us leave the main works (*ἔργα*) of nature (*φύσις*), and behold her minor works (*πάρεργα*). Is there anything less useful than the hair on the chin? What then? Has not nature used this also in the most fitting way possible? Has she not by means of it distinguished the male and the female? Has not the nature of each one of us immediately cried out from

afar, I am a man; on this understanding approach me, speak to me, seek nothing else; here are the signs? Again, in regard to women, as she has mingled something gentler in the voice so she has taken away the hair (of the chin) . . . For this reason we ought to keep the signs that God has given, we ought not to throw them away, nor to confound, so far as we can, the distinctions of the sexes.' That it is, correspondingly, *un*natural for a woman to shave (like the most manly, ἀνδρώδεις, of athletes) is outspokenly illustrated by Lucian, *Dialogi Meretricii* v. 3. If this dialogue is a pointer to the context of thought implied (and it does seem probable that horror of homosexualism is behind a good deal of Paul's argument in this paragraph) it is certainly not *fitting* for a woman to cut off her hair. Her long hair is *a glory to her. Glory* is here used in a sense different from but related to that of verse 7. Human beings must give glory to God by being (e.g. in their unconcealed and unperverted sexual differentiation) what God intended them to be; at the same time, obediently to be what God intended them to be is the highest glory that human beings can achieve. To wear her hair long, in a womanly fashion, is an outward sign that a woman is fulfilling her role in creation. A further ground is given for this: **For her long hair has been given her** to serve **as** (ἀντί, literally, *in place of*) **a covering.** Paul (essentially a Jew) did not believe that women only should be covered; a man also must hide his nakedness. But woman has been given in her hair a primitive form of covering which man lacks. In this she has the advantage of him, and she must follow the hint her naturally long hair supplies.

Paul, probably feeling that he has disputed long enough
about trifles, breaks off the argument. **But if anyone means to** 16
be (the construction is not classical; this use of δοκεῖ is affected by, though not the same as, the correct use of δοκεῖ μοι) **contentious** (about this matter)**—we have no such custom, nor have the churches of God.** Paul cannot prevent divergence of opinion, or even contention. Indeed, he has invited the former by his *Decide among yourselves* (verse 13), and an appeal to *nature* which is really an appeal to nature as understood in the Hellenistic age. Contentiousness (cf. Luke xxii. 24, where the noun corresponding to Paul's adjective is used; neither appears

elsewhere in the New Testament; a cynical observer could regard contentiousness as characteristic of philosophers—Lucian, *Icaromenippus* 29) is not a Christian virtue, however, and anyone who wishes to argue against Paul's view on this matter should remember that he is putting himself in a minority of one. This should make him think twice. If *we* means Paul (as it probably does), the sense is: I have never permitted the custom of unveiled praying or prophesying by women, and no church has introduced it. Alternatively, *we* may mean Paul and the church at Ephesus (where the letter was written; Introduction, p. 5), or the Corinthian church (up to now); in this case *the churches of God* must mean the *other* churches. On the church see further pp. 31 f. The plural is used here as at Rom. xvi. 4, 16; 1 Cor. (iv. 17); vii. 17; xiv. 33, (34); xvi. 1, 19; 2 Cor. viii. 1, 18, 19, 23, 24; xi. 28; xii. 13; Gal. i. 2, 22; 1 Thess. ii. 14; 2 Thess. i. 4. This is Paul's most common way of referring to the totality of God's people, though occasionally he uses the singular in this sense (xii. 28; xv. 9). It emphasizes the fact that the universal church is made up of a number of local churches, differing from one another in detail, though not in regard to the custom under discussion. They are the churches *of God* (see the note on i. 2), and therefore stand under his authority.

By *custom* Paul must mean praying and prophesying by unveiled women; he cannot mean contentiousness (Bachmann). Would he 'think it necessary to say that Apostles have no habit of contentiousness?' (Robertson-Plummer).

25. xi. 17-34. THE SUPPER

(17) In giving you this charge I have no praise[1] for you; for when you assemble it is not to make things better but to make them worse. (18) For, in the first place, I hear that, when you come together in assembly, there are

[1] The text translated, παραγγέλλων οὐκ ἐπαινῶ, is read by ℵ G and the majority of MSS.; A C* and the Latin and Syriac have παραγγέλλω οὐκ ἐπαινῶν; B has παραγγέλλων οὐκ ἐπαινῶν; D* and a minuscule have παραγγέλλω οὐκ ἐπαινῶ. See the commentary.

divisions among you; and in part I believe it, (19) for there must be factions among you, in order that the genuine among you may stand out. (20) So then, when you assemble together, it is not to eat a supper in honour of the Lord; (21) for in eating each one gets ahead with his own supper, and one goes hungry and another gets drunk. (22) What! have you not houses for eating and drinking? or do you despise the church of God, and do you want to put to shame the poor? What am I to say to you? Am I to praise you?[1] In this matter I do not praise you.

(23) For I received from the Lord, that which I also handed on to you, that the Lord Jesus, in the night in which he was betrayed, took a loaf, (24) and when he had given thanks broke it, and said, This is my body, which is for you; do this as my memorial. (25) In the same way he also took the cup, after they had had supper, saying, This cup is the new covenant in my blood; do this, as often as you drink, as my memorial. (26) For as often as you eat this loaf, and drink the cup, you proclaim the Lord's death, until he comes.

(27) It follows that whoever eats the Lord's loaf or drinks the Lord's cup unworthily, shall be guilty of the body and blood of the Lord. (28) Let a man test himself; that is how he should eat of the loaf and drink of the cup. (29) For he who eats and drinks,[2] eats and drinks judgement to himself, if he does not distinguish the body.[3] (30) This is why many among you are sickly and ill, and a number are sleeping. (31) But if we examined ourselves, we should not be judged; (32) but when we are judged by the Lord we are disciplined, that we may not be condemned with the world.

(33) So, my brothers, when you assemble for a meal, wait for one another. (34) If anyone is hungry, let him eat at home, that the end of your assembly may not be judgement. The other matters I will put right when I come.

[1] ἐπαινέσω; ἐπαινῶ (P^{46} B and others) is probably due to adaptation to the next occurrence of the verb (Zuntz, p. 92).

[2] The Western Text adds ἀναξίως, *unworthily*.

[3] The Western Text, followed by the majority of MSS., has *the Lord's body*, τὸ σῶμα τοῦ κυρίου.

Still speaking of disorder in the Christian assembly, Paul goes on to deal with a new point, more serious perhaps than man-imitating women, which he must be allowed to introduce in
17 his own words. **In giving you this charge** (Paul's *τοῦτο* should refer to what precedes; a reference to what follows would more naturally be given by *τάδε*; if the whole charge—chapters vii-xiv—were intended no pronoun would have been used) **I have no praise for you; for when you assemble it is not to make things better but to make them worse.** The MSS. show much variation in the forms in which the verbs *to give a charge* (*παραγγέλλειν*) and *to have praise for* (*ἐπαινεῖν*) are given; see note 1 on p. 258. In the translation, those MSS. are followed which give the first as a participle, the second as an indicative; this seems best because the next clause (*for when you assemble* . . . gives the reason why Paul does not praise his readers. Some prefer to follow MSS. which make the first verb indicative and the second a participle, thus: I give this charge, because I do not praise . . . (causal use of a participial clause). But this makes *this* (*τοῦτο*) refer to what follows; it is better taken as referring to what precedes. Others (B.D. §430) follow a very small number of MSS. in making both verbs finite: I give this charge . . . I do not praise . . . This reading, with its asyndeton, is probably an accidental error. Paul means: I have given you a charge in respect of one matter in the church's assembly for worship. I cannot deal with this subject with any pleasure, because you are worthy not of praise but of blame. So far short of the mark do your assemblies come that instead of building up the community they damage it; you are not better but worse
18 off for having met. Here is a particular example. **For, in the first place** (no *secondly* follows, but Paul in verse 34 refers to *other matters*, and goes on, in chapters xii and xiv, to deal with further regrettable features in the Corinthian assembly, and his *πρῶτον μέν*, without answering *δέ*, is at least excusable; see B.D. §447), **I hear that** (it is necessary to bring these words forward in English in order to make the right connection of thought), **when you come together in assembly** (or *in church*, *ἐν ἐκκλησίᾳ*; see below), **there are divisions among you.** It is natural to recall the *divisions* of i. 10 ff., but it must not be assumed (as e.g. by Lietzmann and Schlatter) that the divisions

referred to here are identical with those (G. Bornkamm, *Gesammelte Aufsätze* ii (1959), p. 141). The divisions that make themselves manifest at the Supper are, in part at least, the result of class distinction between rich and poor, though it is not impossible that a meal may also have provided Jewish Christians, if they insisted on *kosher* food, with an occasion for separating themselves from their Gentile brothers. It appears that, notwithstanding the divisions, the whole company of believers still came together in one *assembly*. This translates a Greek word (ἐκκλησία) usually rendered *church* (as e.g. at i. 2). In non-biblical Greek, however, it denotes the citizen body of a town assembled for deliberative or executive purposes, and in the Greek Old Testament it translates a Hebrew word (*qahal*) which often refers to the people of God assembled. It corresponds with these facts that in a number of passages, especially in 1 Cor. xiv, the word means not simply the people of God, but the people of God assembled. This seems to be the sense here.

Thus the Corinthian assembly (ἐκκλησία) is marked by division. The unity of x. 17 is not yet achieved; indeed it is denied at the Supper itself. This is not treated as a reason for giving up the Supper, which, in Paul's view, does not wait upon the realization of perfect unity, but is rather a means towards this realization.

So far hearsay: *I hear* . . . It does not seem probable that the Corinthians, proud as they were of their own achievements (e.g. i. 4 ff.; v. 2), told Paul of the divisions at the Supper in their letter to him (vii. 1, etc.). He heard the news probably either from Chloe's people (i. 11), or from Stephanas, Fortunatus, and Achaicus (xvi. 17). **And in part I believe it:** *in part*, because he is unwilling to credit so scandalous a story, yet *I believe* because the informants are credible people; also because division is in
itself readily believable: **for there must be factions** (Paul uses 19
a fresh word, αἱρέσεις, without any significant change of meaning—if there were such a change the connection of thought would break down) **among you, in order that the genuine among you may stand out** (or, *in order that the genuine may stand out among you*). That is, unless there are factions, the genuine will not be distinguishable from the rest. *The genuine*

(δόκιμοι) suggests in the first instance those whom God approves (for the opposite, cf. ix. 27, ἀδόκιμος); but Rom. xvi. 10 (the word is also found at Rom. xiv. 18; 2 Cor. x. 18; xiii. 7) shows that the word can be used in a moral sense: Apelles was not the only man 'acceptable to God'; he was an outstanding Christian. So here: *the genuine* are what they are in the last resort because of God's choice and approval, but they are also marked out as true Christians by their behaviour. Paul does not mean: . . . that those who are Christians by God's election may stand out from those who are not; but: . . . that those who behave in a truly Christian manner may stand out from those who do not. Yet it is also true (as Kümmel points out against Lietzmann) that Paul is not in this sentence simply resigned or ironic; the verse 'describes a divine, eschatological necessity (cf. xv. 25, 53; 2 Cor. v. 10 . . .): the appearance of divisions contributes to the making of a clear decision at the judgement (cf. iii. 13)'. A similar prediction of division was ascribed to Jesus; see J. Jeremias, *Unknown Sayings of Jesus* (1964), pp. 76 f.

Division may be inevitable, but it is not edifying, or to the
20 credit of the church in which it takes place. **So then, when you assemble together** (the English is pleonastic, in imitation of the Greek; ἐπὶ τὸ αὐτό means much the same as ἐν ἐκκλησίᾳ in verse 18), **it is not to eat a supper in honour of the Lord.** The last five words represent a Greek adjective (κυριακόν), qualifying *supper* and meaning 'pertaining to the Lord' (κύριος). 'The Lord's Supper' is familiar, but the possessive case fails to make clear the relation of the Supper to the Lord. 'In memory of the Lord', 'under the authority of the Lord', 'in the presence of the Lord', might all be used to help out the rendering chosen here; in fact, the sense in which the Supper is 'the Lord's' can only be brought out through the ensuing paragraph as a whole; the contrast in the next verse suggests for the present the translation given. The Supper (as conducted at Corinth) brings
21 no honour to the Lord (as it should do), **for in eating each one gets ahead with** (προλαμβάνει, takes it before others have theirs; contrast verse 33) **his own supper, and one goes hungry and another gets drunk** (μεθύει can hardly mean less than this). It is clearly implied that the occasion included an ordinary meal, as well as symbolic acts and significant words.

It is wrong that one should go hungry and another be drunk; if the Supper were rightly conducted, none would be hungry, none drunk, but all moderately supplied with food and drink. A further implication (see especially verse 22) is that the members of the church were expected to share their resources, the rich, presumably, to bring more than they needed and to make provision for the poor. In fact, the rich were bringing but eating and drinking the extra supplies themselves. This was not to eat the *Lord's* supper, but their *own*. Small wonder that Paul is
indignant. **What! have you not houses for eating and** 22
drinking? On the surface this seems to imply that ordinary, non-cultic eating and drinking should be done at home, contradicting the inference drawn above that the Corinthian supper included an ordinary meal. But Paul's point is that, if the rich wish to eat and drink on their own, enjoying better food than their poorer brothers, they should do this at home; if they cannot wait for others (verse 33), if they must indulge to excess, they can at least keep the church's common meal free from practices that can only bring discredit upon it. Their behaviour shows contempt of the community as a whole. **Do you despise the church** (or perhaps we should again render *assembly*, as at verse 18; see the note) **of God, and do you want to put to shame** (the verb καταισχύνετε is in the present tense, and should be understood as conative) **the poor** (literally, *those who do not have*, τοὺς μὴ ἔχοντας; possibly, *those who do not have houses*)? The poor man, who can bring little or no supper with him, will naturally, though wrongly, feel ashamed when he sees the food and drink brought and eaten by his fellow-Christian. The rich man's actions are not controlled by love (see Rom. xiv. 15; also Jas. ii. 1 f., and *Taanith* iv. 8, . . . that none should be abashed which had them not [white raiments]); they therefore amount to contempt not only of the poor, but also of God, who has called into his church not many wise, not many mighty, not many nobly born (i. 26). God has accepted the poor man, as he has accepted the man who is weak in faith and conscience (viii. 9-13; x. 29 f.; Rom. xiv. 1, 3 f., 10, 13; xv. 1, 7); the stronger (whether in human resources or in faith) must accept him too. It is by failure here that the Corinthians profane the sacramental aspect of the Supper—not by liturgical error, or by

under-valuing it, but by prefixing to it an unbrotherly act (Bornkamm, op. cit., p. 145). This view will be reinforced if, with H. Kosmala (*Novum Testamentum* iv. 81-94) we see in *as my memorial* (verses 24 f.) a special emphasis on discipleship and imitation of Jesus.

What is happening in Corinth is so flagrant a denial of Christian principle and practice that even an apostle is at a loss. **What am I to say to you? Am I to praise** (reading ἐπαινέσω, and taking it as aorist subjunctive; see note 1 on p. 259) **you?** Compare verses 2 and 17; it seems that the Corinthians were seeking praise from the apostle, and therefore representing their church in the best possible light. **In this matter I do not praise you.** It would be equally possible to punctuate, *Am I to praise you in this matter? I do not praise you.* But the punctuation chosen is better. There were some matters in which Paul could give at least qualified praise; not in this one.

Paul is not at a loss for long. He deals with the situation (so far as it is to be dealt with by letter; see verse 34) by recalling the words and acts of Jesus at the Last Supper—recalling, for he had already communicated this material to the Corinthians. It should not be simply assumed (though this is often done) that the words that follow (in verses 23 ff.) were already in liturgical use at the celebration of the Lord's Supper. Paul gives no indication that he is using words that the Corinthians would recognize in this sense, nor does he make the point that the Corinthians' behaviour was inconsistent with words that they themselves used in the course of their meal. The Lord's death was proclaimed (verse 26), and this may have included an account of the Last Supper (as this is contained in the passion narratives in the gospels), but this is not the same as a liturgical formula. Paul here asserts, without claiming that the assertion should already be familiar, that the words and acts of Jesus at the Last Supper should be taken as controlling the supper eaten
23 by the church in his own day. This is the point of the **for** (γάρ)
with which the next verse begins.

I received from the Lord, that which I also handed on to you. The language is the language of tradition in the technical sense, and corresponds to that which had been established in

Judaism. *Received* (παρέλαβον) corresponds to the Hebrew *qibbel*, and *handed on* (παρέδωκα) to *masar*; compare xv. 1, 3. It should however be remembered that both words were used in this sense in ancient Greek long before this was in any way influenced by Jewish usage; it is therefore wrong without further evidence to read a full rabbinic content into them. Schlatter notes for example the use of both words with a military password in Josephus, *Antiquities* xix. 31. It is certain that accounts of what Jesus had said and done were passed from one to another in the primitive church; it is from such accounts that the gospels grew. To say this is in itself to pass no judgement, whether favourable or unfavourable, on the historical value of the gospels (or of such passages as the present one), for traditions are sometimes accurately, sometimes inaccurately and tendentiously, preserved, and there is little evidence that the elaborated techniques of Jewish tradition were applied to the very different material, handed down in very different circles, by Christians. In what sense did Paul receive this tradition *from* (ἀπό) *the Lord*? Discussion has usually turned upon two possibilities. (a) The Lord himself was the origin of the tradition in the sense that he was the first link in a chain reaching from him to Paul. Eyewitnesses reported to others what the Lord had said and done, these repeated it to others again, and so in due course the tradition reached Paul, who thus had it *from the Lord* not immediately but by unbroken transmission. (b) The Lord communicated immediately to Paul the truth in question, in the Damascus road experience, or in some similar visionary way. Paul received it from the Lord directly, without any kind of mediation. It is against (b) that Paul uses the language of tradition; it is against (a) that he stresses elsewhere (Gal. i. 12: *οὐδὲ . . . παρέλαβον*) his independence of human teaching. The preposition used has been much discussed; it does not seem to be decisive (M. i. 237, 246), but some think it must denote the originator of the tradition, and not the person from whom Paul immediately received it. A possible compromise solution is that Paul received the factual tradition by human means, but received the interpretation of it directly from the Lord; better, perhaps (see O. Cullman, *The Early Church* (1956), pp. 55-99; also Bornkamm, op. cit., p. 148; F. Hahn, *Christologische Hoheitstitel* (1964), p. 93), we may see the authority of the Lord operating with, and through, the human tradition (which now is enshrined in Scripture).

Paul, then, had previously learnt, and previously taught the Corinthians, **that the Lord Jesus, in the night in which he was betrayed** (or, better perhaps, *was handed over*—that is, by God, to death; cf. Rom. iv. 25; viii. 32; but the word may have been used differently in the tradition, for whose wording Paul
24 was not responsible)**, took a loaf, and when he had given thanks, broke it.** The *night* referred to is presumably that before the crucifixion, when all the evangelists relate that Jesus took supper with his disciples. John relates no special acts and words of Jesus in relation to loaf and cup (but see John vi. 51-8); Matthew, Mark, and Luke contain a narrative similar to Paul's, but differing from it in details, most of which will be noted below. The supper must be understood as having taken place in the immediate context of the crucifixion. What Jesus is here related to have done would have been done at any meal (but with special solemnity at a Passover meal) by the head of any Jewish household. The blessing (cf. x. 16), or thanksgiving, over bread was, 'Blessed art thou, O Lord our God, King eternal, who bringest forth bread from the earth.' It need not be said that neither Paul nor any of the evangelists thought that he was narrating merely commonplace acts; but the acts derive their significance from the context, and the words that follow. Jesus **said, This is my body, which is for you** (we might say, *is given*; but, though many MSS, add *broken*, the Greek has no verb; it is an awkward addition, made smoother in Luke xxii. 19)**; do this as my memorial.** The words are ascribed to Jesus himself, present in the body (at the Last Supper), and physically distinct from the loaf of which he spoke. The word *body* is to be noted (even if it be held, with Jeremias (*The Eucharistic Words of Jesus* (1964), pp. 198-201), that what Jesus historically said was, *My flesh*; it may be noted here, once for all, that this Commentary cannot deal with the historical question concerning what actually happened at the Last Supper, but only with the use Paul makes of the incident), and should probably be understood in the light of the reference, in *Pesahim* x. 4, to the 'body of the Passover (lamb)'. This (Jesus says of the loaf) is *my* body.

Already (v. 7) we have seen that Paul regarded Jesus as the new Christian Passover; he seems to make the same point here. The Passover to the Jews was the sacrifice and festival of deliverance. 'He brought us out from slavery to liberty, from sorrow to joy, from mourning to holiday, from darkness to great light, from servitude to redemption' (*Passover Haggadah*). Christ, the crucified (cf. i. 23), by his death, has effected a like deliverance (cf. Rom. iii. 25, and the note), and this is represented in the Supper. It is in this sense that the body of Jesus is *for you*. It is worth while to note that there is no reference to the theme of x. 17; Paul could see more than one line of interpretation in the Supper.

In 1 Corinthians (and at Luke xxii. 19b, but not in Matthew and Mark), the words continue with a command, *Do this* (that is, say a thanksgiving, and break and distribute the loaf) *as my memorial*. Standing as they do in a Greek text these words naturally suggest the memorial feasts that were a not uncommon feature of Greek and Roman life. Many examples are given by Weiss and Jeremias, one of the most striking being from the testament of Epicurus (Diogenes Laertius x. 16-22), who made provision for an annual celebration 'in memory (εἰς τὴν μνήμην) of us (i.e., me) and Metrodorus'. The earlier tradition (see Jeremias, op. cit. p. 82) did not contain this clause, and it is probable that its formulation owes much to Hellenistic custom, though it is true that the pagan memorial meals seem to have been held less frequently than the Christian. Differences, however, are not surprising; Epicurus, for example, was not believed, as Jesus was, to have risen from the dead. In this respect there is a nearer parallel in Lucian's account (*de Syria Dea* 6) of the feasts in 'memory of the passion' (μνήμη τοῦ πάθεος; cf. Justin, *Trypho* 41) of Adonis. Pagan memorial feasts, however, may not have contributed the whole content of the clause, or provide a sufficient interpretation of it. The Passover, as we have seen, was itself a memorial rite (see Exod. xiii. 9), but it recalled not a person so much as a divine act. The Christian Supper also recalled an act of deliverance, but it was more closely connected with a more significant person, and the memorial was naturally his memorial. He had given himself on behalf of his people, who shared in the benefits of his passion as they shared in eating a loaf in a meal held in his memory. See also the reference to Dr Kosmala on p. 264 above.

25 **In the same way** (that is, taking, saying a thanksgiving, and handing to his disciples) **he also took** (*he took* is not in the Greek, but is a necessary supplement) **the cup, after they had had supper** (cf. x. 16; *the cup of blessing* was drunk after the meal had been eaten; Bornkamm, op. cit., p. 154, sees here an indication that according to the Pauline tradition the whole meal intervenes between loaf and cup, and, in this, a decisive argument for dating the Pauline account earlier than Mark's), **saying, This cup is the new covenant in my blood.** Paul's wording here differs markedly from that in the gospels:

> Matt. xxvi. 27 f.: Drink of it, all of you; for this is my covenant blood which is poured out for many, for the forgiveness of sins.
>
> Mark xiv. 24: This is my covenant blood which is poured out on behalf of many.
>
> Luke xxii. 20: This cup is the new covenant in my blood, which is poured out on your behalf.

It is often argued that the Pauline form is secondary, for it avoids the direct identification of the wine contained in the cup with blood, and the implied thought, particularly revolting to a Jew, of drinking blood. This argument is probably sound, but it is not impossible that it should be reversed. Jesus was himself a Jew, and might therefore have avoided (or, to be more cautious, the Palestinian tradition might have avoided) the identification of wine with blood; this identification might have been made, and the original form of the saying modified, at a later stage, when the Gospel had moved into a Gentile environment, and the parallelism of *This is my body* forced the companion saying into the form, *This is my blood.*

There is little difference in meaning between *This is my covenant blood*, and *This cup is the new covenant in my blood.* Each form of the saying presupposes that the shedding of the blood of Christ inaugurated a new covenant between God and man (it is better to connect *in my blood* with *covenant* than with *cup*). In the background stand two Old Testament passages: Exod. xxiv. 8 and Jer. xxxi. 31-4 (on the significance of the latter in New Testament theology see C. H. Dodd, *According to the Scriptures* (1952), p. 45). When the covenant of Sinai was made, Moses sprinkled the people with the blood of sacrificial victims, using the words, 'Behold the blood of the covenant which the Lord has made with you'; and Jeremiah, after the failure of the old covenant, foretells the establishment of a new covenant, including the forgiveness of sins and personal knowledge of and communion with God. It is implied that the new covenant has now been inaugurated, and inaugurated, as the old covenant was, by means of sacrifice. The new sacrifice is not (like that of Exod. xxiv. 5) of oxen, but of Jesus. The shedding of his blood is the founding of the new covenant in which men's sins are forgiven (cf. xv. 3) and knowledge of God is conveyed. The Paschal framework of the Last Supper and of the crucifixion (cf. v. 7) provides, however, a new context into which the idea of the covenant sacrifice is inserted; in particular it provides a new means by which the sacrificial blood may be applied to those who are to benefit from it. The cup of blessing, drunk by all the participants in the meal, becomes (not, in Paul, actually the covenant blood, but) the means by which the covenant is entered. To drink the cup is to enter into the covenant, the covenant established *in* (that is, *by means of*, or possibly *at the cost of*) Christ's blood. In this way the drinking of the cup connects with what is said in x. 17 about the eating of the loaf which constitutes the one body in which believers are joined: those who enter into covenant with the Lord naturally enter at the same time into covenant with one another, and a covenant community is thereby established.

The parallelism with verse 24 is completed by a further clause: **Do this** (see the note on verse 24; neither there nor here does *do*—*ποιεῖν*—have in itself any necessary sacrificial content; it means, Take a cup, say the blessing over it, and distribute it), **as often as you drink, as my memorial.** *Drink* has no expressed object. It is possible to understand as object the *cup* just referred to, but possibly better to understand wine. The additional clause (which has no parallel in verse 24) has a limiting effect. Christians must *do this* not every time they have a meal, but whenever they drink wine. Bread was always available; in ordinary households (cf. i. 26) wine was not. It would be more likely to be present at gatherings of the church than on ordinary domestic occasions, but might not always be drunk at such gatherings. When it was not available, the broken bread would adequately represent the Lord's death and the benefits derived from it (this may be why Paul—contrast Mark—added *which is for you*); the cup of wine, and the blood it represented, would make the meaning of the covenant sacrifice clearer.

It is probable that the material received by Paul from the tradition (verse 23) ends at verse 25; he may have added to it the words *which is for you* (see above). He now adds a further sentence underlining the connection between the Supper and the death of Christ, and indicating the sense he gave to the words,
26 *Do this as my memorial.* **For** (*γάρ*, giving the ground of something; it is hard to see what the new sentence explains if not the memorial character of the Supper) **as often as** (*ὁσάκις*, as in verse 25; it is not a Pauline word, but Paul could easily have taken it up here if he had just quoted it from the tradition) **you eat this loaf, and drink the cup** (that is, as often as you *do this*; verses 24 ff.), **you proclaim the Lord's death, until he comes.** *Proclaim* (*καταγγέλλετε*) has been taken (e.g. by Weiss) to mean, 'You represent symbolically, by means of the broken loaf and the outpoured wine', as by a visible word (*visibile verbum*, used by Augustine of baptism, *In Joannis Evangelium Tract.* lxxx. 3); it seems certain however (see J. Schniewind, in *T.W.N.T.* i. 68-71) that it must mean *proclaim*, announce by word of mouth. That is, when Christians held a common meal they recalled aloud the event on which their existence was based. This recalling (which closely resembles the narration of the exodus from Egypt in the Jewish Passover) must have had some narrative content, and the fact helps to explain the relative continuity and fixed form of the Passion Narrative in the gospels. The story had very often been repeated before it was written down.

The repetition of the story of the Lord's death is to continue *until he comes* (back from heaven, it is implied). There may be more here than a time limit. The Greek expression used (*ἄχρι οὗ* with the aorist subjunctive, and without *ἄν*) '*always* introduces the prospect of the attainment of the eschatological goal: Rom. xi. 25; 1 Cor. xv. 25; Luke xxi. 24' (Jeremias, op. cit.

p. 118). Dr Jeremias connects this with his interpretation of the word *memorial* (ἀνάμνησις), which he takes to have a Godward reference—the intention is that God shall *remember* his Messiah by bringing about the *parusia*. This interpretation may possibly be valid for an earlier stage of the tradition, though not, it seems, for Paul; nevertheless Dr Jeremias's conclusion at this stage may well be right. The Greek expression (ἄχρι οὗ ἔλθῃ) 'obviously plays upon the maranatha of the liturgy, with which the church prays for the eschatological coming of the Lord. That is, the meal is' a memorial (ἀνάμνησις) 'of the Kyrios—not because it reminds the church of the past event of the passion, but because it proclaims the beginning of the time of salvation and prays for the breaking in of complete fulfilment' (p. 118). Compare *Didache* x. 5; but see the discussion of *maranatha* at xvi. 22.

For the coming of the Lord compare xv. 23. There is little doubt that Paul when he wrote 1 Corinthians expected that he would live to see this event. The church as it met round the supper table would form a living link between the beginning and the end of the interim between the two comings of the Lord. It is striking that Paul makes no reference here to the resurrection. The reason may be that for him the resurrection was rather the exaltation of Jesus than a return to ordinary life with his old associates. It is true that he appeared to them (xv. 5-8), but the sequence of appearances lasted a short time, and was evidently exceptional. The Supper was not to Paul (whatever it may have been to other groups of Christians) a perpetuation of fellowship meals between Jesus and his disciples. He refrains from identifying the wine with the blood of Jesus (verse 25; cf. Mark xiv. 24), and though he quotes the words about the loaf, *This is my body*, he means, as we have seen, This is the (or a) means by which the benefits of my broken body may be received. Later eucharistic liturgies speedily incorporated the theme of resurrection (e.g. the *Church Order* of Hippolytus, iv. 11: *memores igitur mortis et resurrectionis*) but this is not Paul's emphasis; and in this Paul seems to have been in agreement with the original understanding of the Supper. The historic meal in the night in which Jesus was betrayed was an anticipation, held in the shadow of the cross, of the glorious banquet of the kingdom of God; the resurrection did not essentially alter the situation, though it confirmed the hope and faith of the disciples participating in the meal. They still ate in the circumstances of 'shame' and looked forward to a 'glory' they had not yet experienced (for the language see the Passover regulations of *Pesahim* x. 4; in telling the story, the head of the household 'begins with the shame and ends with the glory'). See further Introduction, p. 26.

The Christian Supper was thus founded on the sacrificial death of Jesus, an act of divine deliverance by which sins were forgiven and a new covenant set up between God and men, who, being reconciled to God, were now united among themselves. It was to be accompanied by a recital of the act of atonement, in which God's love was commended to sinful men (cf. Rom. v. 8). How then should it be observed in practice? Certainly not as it was being observed in Corinth; and Paul accordingly proceeds to stern warning and rebuke. E. Käsemann (*Essays on New Testament Themes* (1964), p. 126) notes the accumulation of juridical and legal terms here, and says 'The Corinthians have to be reminded of this particular content of the Supper because in their enthusiasm they fondly imagine that they have been withdrawn from the jurisdiction of this justice and the tribunal which administers it. The self-manifestation of Christ calls men to obedience and this means that, at the same time, it calls them to account before the final Judge who is already today acting within his community as he will act towards the world on the Last Day—he bestows salvation by setting men within his lordship and, if they spurn this lordship, they then experience this
7 act of rejection as a self-incurred sentence of death.' **It follows that** (ὥστε, expressing result) **whoever eats the Lord's loaf or drinks the Lord's cup** (*the Lord's*, τοῦ κυρίου, stands only once in the Greek, but applies to both loaf and cup) **unworthily, shall be guilty of the body and the blood of the Lord** (that is, of an offence against the body and blood of the Lord: the somewhat unusual use of the Greek word, ἔνοχος, may reflect the construction of the rabbinic *ḥayyab*). What Paul means by *unworthily* is explained by verses 21 f.; he is thinking of the moral failings of factiousness and greed which marked the Corinthian assembly. One who so eats takes not the Lord's Supper, but his own (verse 21). In what sense is he guilty of the

Lord's body and blood? Paul does not think of these as physically or substantially present, for he does not identify the wine with the Lord's blood, and, as we have seen, the identification of the bread with the body means that the bread is a means of partaking of the benefits of Christ's work. That *body* is not to be interpreted here as equivalent to *church* is shown by the addition of *blood*. It seems necessary to interpret verse 27 in the light of verse 26. The eating and drinking are accompanied, and interpreted, by the proclamation of the Lord's death, in virtue of which his body and his blood are understood to be *for us*. But to eat and drink *unworthily* (in the sense indicated above) is to contradict both the purpose of Christ's self-offering, and the spirit in which it was made, and thus to place oneself among those who were responsible for the crucifixion, and not among those who by faith receive the fruit of it. Compare viii. 12.

What then must a would-be participant in the Supper do?
Let a man test (δοκιμαζέτω) **himself; that is how he should** 28
(literally, *and so let him*) **eat of the loaf and drink of the cup.** *Test* looks back to *the genuine* of verse 19. Compare also 2 Cor. xiii. 5 f. The decision is God's but man may ask himself what decision he is likely to earn. Paul does not require that a man be morally faultless before he takes part in the meal; he does require that he should be applying moral scrutiny to his life and
behaviour. **For** (γάρ, introducing the reason, or a further state- 29
ment of the reason already given in verse 27, why a man should test himself) **he who eats and drinks** (many MSS. add *unworthily*; see note 2 on p. 259; also K. W. Clark in *Studia Paulina*, pp. 60 f.), **eats and drinks judgement to himself** (cf. *Acts of Thomas* 29: This eucharist shall be unto you for compassion and mercy, and not for judgement and retribution), **if he does not distinguish the** (many MSS. add *Lord's*; see note 3 on p. 259; also Clark, loc. cit.) **body.** The added words represent one possible interpretation of the original text; they are textually secondary, but the interpretation they offer is not for that reason necessarily wrong. They have the effect of identifying unworthy eating and drinking with not distinguishing the Lord's body. It will however be wise to approach this difficult verse by noting a number of parallels with other clauses in the context.

The verse as a whole deals with one who *eats and drinks*—a participant in the Lord's Supper. Such a man *eats and drinks judgement* (κρίμα) *to himself*; that is, he exposes himself to judgement, not simply in the sense that all men must appear before God for judgement (Rom. xiv. 10; 2 Cor. v. 10), but in a special sense. This clearly recalls verse 27, where *guilty* (ἔνοχος) is a forensic word. It was noted above that 'judgement' words are common in this passage. We have already had *guilty* and *judgement* (this recurs in verse 34); *distinguish* (διακρίνειν) occurs in verses 29, 31, *judge* (κρίνειν) in verses 31, 32, and *condemn* (κατακρίνειν) in verse 32; compare also *test* in verse 28. To bring out the verbal relationships in English seems impossible, but they are a significant feature of Paul's Greek. The persons in question thus incur judgement, expose their own guilt, when they come together to the Lord's Supper. They do so, because they fail to *distinguish the body*. It is impossible to find a consistent rendering of the word *distinguish* (διακρίνειν) because Paul does not use it consistently. At iv. 7 it means to mark one out as different from others; at vi. 5, to decide between two disputing brethren, to determine which is right and which wrong; at xiv. 29, to give critical attention to what the prophets say. Rom. iv. 20; xiv. 23, the only other Pauline uses, are not relevant because the verb is used as a deponent. In the immediate context the verb is used reflexively: verse 31, *if we examined ourselves*; compare also verse 28, *Let a man test himself*. It has been suggested (but for a fuller account of this view of Ehrhardt's see below) that in the present verse *body* is used as a sort of reflexive pronoun. This is certainly possible in Hebrew (*gupho*), and there are at least partial parallels in Paul, in vi. 18, 20; vii. 4; ix. 27; xiii. 3; Rom. vi. 12; xii. 1; 2 Cor. iv. 10; Gal. vi. 17; Phil. i. 20. If this were the meaning, however, Paul would probably have written not *the body* but *his body* (τὸ σῶμα αὑτοῦ). Alternative explanations are: (a) he fails to distinguish the eucharistic from common food; (b) he fails to distinguish the Lord's body in the bread which he eats; (c) he fails to perceive and to give due weight to the church, assembled at the Supper as the body of Christ ('without a proper sense of the body', Moffatt). None of these is entirely satisfactory. (a) introduces a distinction that does not appear in the context, and, as Dr Bornkamm (op. cit., pp. 142 f.) points out, it appears from x. 1-13 that the Corinthians made too much rather than too little of their sacraments; (b) would demand *the body of the Lord*, instead of simply *the body*; (c) also would require a genitive with *body*, and strains the meaning of the verb (διακρίνειν). An original interpretation was suggested by A. A. T. Ehrhardt (*The Framework of the New Testament Stories* (1964), pp. 256-74; there is much of value in this, as in all Ehrhardt's essays, even though this point is unconvincing), who took *judgement* in this passage to be a desirable (not, as is usually supposed, an undesirable) thing. He who eats and drinks places himself under judgement, unless he separates or withdraws his body (himself) from the process. It is a mark of this judgement that cases of sickness and death take place (verse 30). These are something to rejoice in. If we did withdraw ourselves (verse 31), we should not be judged; and the consequence of this would be that instead of enduring temporal punishment only we should be condemned with the world. This suggestion involves too many improbabilities, and though the verse remains problematical and uncertain, it is best, in view of the parallelism between verses 27 and 29 to go back to (b) above, and to interpret *the body* (29) in the light of *the body and blood of the Lord* (27), which is now taken up again in shorthand form. It may be (Bornkamm, op. cit., p. 169) that the Corinthians took the word *body* in a sacramental, Paul in a 'fellowship' sense.

Paul sees the *judgement* worked out in concrete expressions.
This is why many among you are sickly and ill, and a 30
number are sleeping the sleep of death. The words are not metaphorical; compare v. 5. The Lord preserves the sanctity of his own table by his own means. Perhaps the gravity of the punishment was felt most in the thought of death before the *parusia*; compare 1 Thess. iv. 13. The means by which the physical punishment worked is probably suggested by x. 20 f. Those who abused the Lord's table were exposing themselves to the power of demons, who were taken to be the cause of physical disease. This verse is first an explanation of events known to be taking place in Corinth, and secondly a threat directed against those who continued to misuse the Supper. Only in a derived sense is it (as Ehrhardt suggests) comfort for the sufferers and the bereaved: better thus to suffer physical

31 punishment now than to be condemned hereafter. **But** (not *for*, as some MSS. read, giving the wrong connection) **if we examined** (διακρίνειν again, but, unless we follow Ehrhardt, it is impossible to use the same translation as in verse 29) **ourselves, we should not be judged:** that is, we should escape the judgements (illness, and so forth) described in verse 30.
32 **But** the judgements are not wholly to be deplored, because **when we are judged** (κρίνειν) **by the Lord we are disciplined** (by means of the punishments he inflicts)**, that we may not be condemned** (κατακρίνειν) **with the world,** that is, the mass of men who are not Christians. Again compare v. 5. The goal of punishment is not destructive, but remedial and educative (παιδευόμεθα). Those whom the Lord loves he disciplines (Heb. xii. 5 ff.), giving them opportunity and incentive to repent and amend their ways. If Paul seems here casually to consign *the world* as a whole to perdition it must be remembered (a) that for him, as often in the New Testament, *the world* signifies not so much the vast mass of mankind who have never heard the Gospel, as the beings, human and demonic, who oppose it (cf. i. 20 f.; ii. 12); and (b) that he was prepared to take any steps 'in order to save some' (ix. 22)—and that this was not pious sentiment but a task to which he devoted all his energies, an object for which he was prepared to endure any suffering.

33 After his exhortations Paul comes to practical advice. **So, my brothers** (cf. i. 1; sometimes with Paul the means by which a hard blow was softened)**, when you assemble for a meal** (literally, *to eat*; there is little to tell us what proportion of church meetings was held for this purpose; see the notes on xiv. 23, 26)**, wait for one another.** Paul does not say, Wait for so-and-so, or for such-and-such an official, to preside over your gathering, though this might seem to have been the easiest way of reducing the chaotic Corinthian assembly to order (cf. xiv. 33). Apparently there was no such person (though there were leading and responsible members of the Corinthian church: xvi. 15 f.). It is implied that a proper distribution of food should first be made, and that all should then eat together (contrast
34 verse 21). **If anyone is hungry, let him eat at home.** This, like verse 22 (see the note), might at first seem to contradict the observation that the Lord's Supper was still at Corinth an

ordinary meal to which acts of symbolical significance were attached, rather than a purely symbolical meal; and it has been suggested (e.g. by Schlatter) that this instruction represents a beginning of the separation of the eucharist (or symbolical meal) from the *agape* (or fellowship meal). This however is not so. Paul simply means that those who are so hungry that they cannot wait for their brothers should satisfy their hunger before they leave home, in order that decency and order may prevail in the assembly. This is **that the end of your assembly may not be judgement.** See verse 29. It here appears clearly that (notwithstanding its uses—verse 32) *judgement* is not in itself and absolutely a good thing. It is well to avoid it, though God can use it for Christians' good.

There were other faults in the Corinthian supper, but they were presumably not so serious as those that have now been dealt with. They can wait till Paul's arrival in Corinth (iv. 19; xvi. 5-9). **The other matters I will put right when I come.** 'Whenever I shall have arrived' (M. i. 167) is correct but pedantic as a translation. The paradox of personal humility, and authority derived from the word of God, is especially characteristic of the Corinthian letters.

(d) SPIRITUAL GIFTS

26. xii. 1-3. THE FUNDAMENTAL TEST: (a) JESUS IS LORD

(1) About spiritual gifts, brothers, I have no wish that you should remain in ignorance. (2) You know that, when you were Gentiles, how you would be led astray and carried away to the dumb idols. (3) So I make it plain to you that no one speaking in God's Spirit says, Jesus is anathema; and no one can say, Jesus is Lord, except in the Holy Spirit.

We noted that at xi. 2 Paul turned to questions connected with the assembly of the Corinthian Christians for worship. He has not done with that theme, and has much more to say about it in chapter xiv; but, having dealt with the Supper, he moves on at this point to a distinct theme, perhaps raised by the Corinthians in their letter (see vii. 1, and cf. the opening of this chapter), possibly suggested by information otherwise received (cf. i. 11; xvi. 17). The assembly formed an excellent opportunity for members of the church to display the spiritual gifts of which they were evidently proud (i. 5-8; iv. 8). The new theme is thus related to that of xi. 17-34, for spiritual, like material, resources should be employed within the brotherhood of the body of Christ, which is paralysed by egocentric exploitation of wealth. Paul raises the new subject of discussion in a familiar way (cf. vii. 1; viii. 1; xvi. 1).

1 **About spiritual gifts** (πνευματικῶν; the adjective may be neuter—spiritual gifts, cf. ix. 11; xiv. 1; xv. 46; or masculine—spiritual persons, cf. ii. 15; iii. 1; xiv. 37; it seems impossible to find objective ground for a decision between the two possibilities, and little difference in sense is involved—spiritual persons are those who have spiritual gifts), **brothers** (cf. i. 1), **I have no wish that you should remain in ignorance** (a Pauline
2 phrase; cf. x. 1). **You know** (it is characteristic of Paul to appeal to—sometimes perhaps to flatter a little—his readers' own knowledge; cf. e.g. viii. 1, 4) **that, when you were Gentiles** (it is evident that many, though not all, of the Corinthian Christians had been non-Jews; cf. Acts xviii. 5, 6, 8), **how** (ὡς, pleonastic after the preceding *that*, ὅτι; Paul, it seems, started the noun clause a second time; there can be no doubt that this difficult text is original) **you would be** (accepting the iterative sense of ἄν[1]—M. i. 167; Robertson, p. 974; alternatively one could take ἀνήγεσθε as one word, or ὡσάν as one word with ἀπαγόμενοι, 'carried away, as it were') **led astray and carried away to the dumb idols.** The main point of this verse is contained in the word *carried away* (ἀπάγεσθαι), which is reinforced by the simple form (ἄγεσθαι), here rendered *led astray*. It suggests moments of ecstasy experienced in heathen religion, when a human being is (or is believed to be) possessed by a supernatural; for example, in Lucian's *Dialogi Mortuorum* xix. 1, Paris, speaking of the power of love, says, A sort of god (δαίμων)

[1] See the additional note on p. 399.

carries us away (ἄγει) wherever he wills, and it is impossible to resist him (further evidence is given in Betz p. 40, note 10; for Paul's use of ἄγειν cf. Rom. viii. 14; Gal. v. 18). Paul himself in this verse appears to think of demons as ravishing those who take part in heathen worship; compare x. 20. The idols themselves are lifeless—*dumb*, unable to give an answer to prayers addressed to them. The thought is in the Old Testament (e.g. 1 Kings xviii. 26-9; Ps. cxv. 4-8; Isa. xlvi. 7), and was retained in Judaism. Possibly Paul means to contrast the silence of the idols with the noisy (demon-inspired) outcry of their worshippers.

Paul's readers are *Gentiles* no longer; but neither are they Jews. He does not describe them as a 'new' or 'third race' (e.g. *Diognetus* 1), but the thought is not far away.

Paul now proceeds to answer the question implied by verse 1.
So (that is, in view of the *you know* of verse 2) **I make it plain** 3
to you (γνωρίζω, as at xv. 1; 2 Cor. viii. 1) **that no one speaking in God's Spirit** (neither Paul nor his readers doubted that there were other spirits capable of inspiring ecstatic speech) **says, Jesus is anathema; and no one can say, Jesus is Lord, except in** (that is, under the influence of) **the Holy Spirit.** Paul assumes the existence of a community in which the phenomena of inspiration were present, and indeed common. He neither denies the right of such phenomena to exist within the church, nor affirms that in themselves they are a proof of the presence and activity of the Spirit of God. That is, Christian 'enthusiasm' is neither attacked nor defended, but presupposed and analysed. The analysis is to continue through chapters xii, xiii, xiv, but the decisive touchstone is mentioned at once. Not the manner but the content of ecstatic speech determines its authenticity. *Anathema* here must mean *accursed* (cf. Rom. ix. 3), a sense derived mainly from its use in the LXX to describe objects devoted to the 'ban' (*ḥerem*; there is however some Hellenistic evidence for this meaning—for details see J. Behm in *T.W.N.T.* i. 356 f.). It is not easy to conceive the circumstances in which one might cry out, Jesus is anathema, and be in danger of supposing that he was inspired by the Holy Spirit. Several suggestions have been made; the most important are the following. (a) Christians brought for trial before the courts

should make the confession 'Jesus is Lord' (see below). They might however in weakness be persuaded to say, 'Jesus is anathema' (cf. Pliny, *Epistles* x. 96: Those who denied that they were or had been Christians, when . . . they invoked the gods . . . and cursed (*male dicerent*) Christ, none of which things, it is said, genuine Christians can be compelled to do, I considered it right to release), and might subsequently attempt to justify themselves by claiming that their words (which enabled them to continue in freedom, and to be secret Christians) were inspired by the Spirit. This is a neat explanation, but there is nothing in the context to suggest it, and it presupposes the circumstances of a later time. (b) The court in question might be that of the synagogue; or the reference might be to the rejection of Jesus by the synagogue, claimed to be the result of the leading of the Spirit. This suggestion is supported by the Jewish background of the use of *anathema* in the sense of curse (this is emphasized especially by Schlatter, who refers to Deut. vii. 26; *Nedarim* v. 4; also Acts xviii. 6), but it does not do justice to the fact that Paul is dealing with the testing of (supposedly) inspired speech. (c) It may be that Paul simply made up *Jesus is anathema* as a counterpart to *Jesus is Lord*: these were two possible extremes, and only one of them could point to genuine inspiration. This view may be partly right, but it is doubtful whether Paul would present to the Corinthians a purely hypothetical and artificial possibility. (d) The ecstatic heathen worship which Paul recalls in verse 2 might provide the setting in which the words *Jesus is anathema* could be understood. Against this however is the fact that Paul is not here concerned to say (though he certainly believed) that the heathen rejection of Jesus (so far as it was by this time explicit) was mistaken; he was providing tests by which what purported to be *Christian* inspiration taking place within a *Christian* gathering could be judged. (e) Allo is probably right with the suggestion that Paul is referring to the cries of Christian ecstatics who were resisting the trance or ecstasy they felt coming upon them, 'in the manner of the Sibyl who foamed as she resisted the inspiration that was taking possession of her, or of Cassandra, who curses Apollo in Aeschylus's *Agamemnon*'.

A similar but more developed situation appears in 1 John iv.

1-3, where the simple anathema is displaced by the docetic denial of the human life of the Son of God in the flesh. For the process of discrimination compare xiv. 29; 1 Thess. v. 21.

The true Christian watchword is, *Jesus is Lord*. Compare Rom. x. 9, and the commentary; also the note on xvi. 22. It is true not because it is the right or orthodox formula but because it expresses the proper relation with Jesus: the speaker accepts his authority, and proclaims himself the servant of him whom he confesses as Lord (*κύριος*). It is this relation (and not Christology) with which Paul is concerned here: inspiration as a religious phenomenon is in itself indifferent, and gains significance only in the context of Christian obedience.

It is doubtless true that sincerely to confess Jesus as Lord is a sign of the Spirit's work, whether the marks of inspiration are present or not, but this is not Paul's intended meaning here. He is dealing with the phenomena of inspired, ecstatic speech, and indicating how such speech should be judged. For this reason the question of the sincerity of the man who says Jesus is Lord is not raised here; it is not the man who speaks, but the Spirit (Weiss). Paul follows the lead of the Old Testament (Deut. xviii. 21 f.; and especially xiii. 2-6) in claiming that content, not manner, is the criterion. Having laid down this fundamental proposition, in its Christian form, he is free to go ahead with the general discussion of spiritual gifts and persons.

27. xii. 4-31. DIVERSITY OF GIFTS IN ONE BODY

(4) There are distributions of gifts, but the same Spirit; (5) there are distributions of services, and the same Lord; (6) and there are distributions of operations, but the same God who operates all things in all men. (7) To each one is given his own manifestation of the Spirit, with a view to mutual profit. (8) For to one there is given, through the Spirit, a word of wisdom; to another, in accordance with the same Spirit, a word of knowledge; (9) to another faith, in the same Spirit; to another gifts of

healing, in the one[1] Spirit; (10) to another the working of miracles,[2] to another prophecy, to another the power to distinguish between spirits, to another various kinds of tongues, to another the interpretation of tongues. (11) All these things the same one Spirit puts into operation, distributing individually to each one as he wills.

(12) For as the body is one, and has many members, and all the members of the body, many though they are, are one body, so also is Christ. (13) For in one Spirit we were all baptized so as to become one body, whether we were Jews or Greeks, slaves or free men, and we were all given one Spirit as drink. (14) For a body does not consist of one member, but many. (15) If the foot should say, Because I am not a hand I do not belong to the body; saying this will not mean that it does not belong to the body. (16) And if the ear should say, Because I am not an eye I do not belong to the body; saying this will not mean that it does not belong to the body. (17) If the whole body were eye, where would hearing be? If the whole body were hearing, where would smelling be? (18) But in fact God has put the members, each several one of them, in the body, as he saw fit. (19) If the whole were one member, where would the body be? (20) But in fact there are many members, and one body. (21) The eye cannot say to the hand, I have no need of you; or the head to the feet, I have no need of you. (22) But, much rather, the bodily members that are accounted weaker are necessary, (23) and those we consider to be the relatively less honourable parts of the body we clothe with special honour, and our unseemly members have the greater seemliness, (24) while our seemly parts have no need of this. But God has put the body together and given special honour to the

[1] Many MSS. (including ℵ D) have *same* (αὐτῷ). This is due to assimilation to the preceding clause, but P[46] may possibly be right in having no adjective at all.

[2] P[46] D it (vg) and others have the singular, δυνάμεως, which would refer simply to the effect of one supernatural power; the plural, which gives a more conventional sense, could be a (mistaken) correction. So Zuntz, p. 100; but the authorities in question differ among themselves (though all have δυνάμεως), and are not entirely convincing.

member that lacked it, (25) in order that there may be no division[1] in the body, but that all the members may have the same care for one another. (26) If, on the one hand, one member suffers, all the members suffer with it; if, on the other, a member is glorified, all the members rejoice with it. (27) Now you are Christ's body, and, individually, members.

(28) Further, there are some whom God has set in the Church, first apostles, second prophets, third teachers; then miracles, then gifts of healing, gifts of support, gifts of direction, various kinds of tongues. (29) Are all apostles? Are all prophets? Are all teachers? Are all able to work miracles? (30) Do all have gifts of healing? Do all speak with tongues? Do all interpret? (31) But strive for the greater gifts; and I am going on to show you a yet better way.[2]

The radical criterion of spiritual phenomena can be laid bare in a few words: it is the work of the Spirit of God to bear witness to the lordship of Jesus Christ. He alone can do this; that which does not do this does not spring from him. Inspiration that is not from God is thus already excluded by xii. 3; but inspiration that does come from God is so diverse that its variety can give rise to a further set of problems. Which are the most important spiritual gifts? Can a man who does not have them be counted a Christian at all? Is it not to be expected that a true Christian will manifest them all? To questions such as these Paul applies himself in chapters xii, xiii, and xiv, turning aside (as his main theme justifies him in doing, or even requires him to do) to consider the being of the church in which the gifts are at work.

There are distributions (διαιρέσεις; not *varieties*, though 4
this is implied; Paul thinks of the gifts as given, not in the abstract) **of gifts** (χαρίσματα; see i. 7), **but the same Spirit.** The main point of the whole section is already made. Gifts are shared out among Christians; all do not receive the same gift, but all the gifts come from the Spirit, so that there is no room

[1] Many MSS. (including ℵ D*) have the plural, σχίσματα, *divisions*; this is due to assimilation to i. 10.

[2] For ἔτι, P[46] D* have εἴ τι. See the commentary.

for rivalry, discontent, or a feeling of superiority. Paul con-
5 tinues in this vein. **There are distributions of services**
(*διακονίαι*, but the word here has nothing to do with 'ministry'
in the technical sense; *gifts* are not occasions for boasting but
opportunities of service, to the community and through the
community to the Lord), **and the same Lord,** to whom ultimately all the services are rendered, since Christians are his
6 slaves (see iv. 1; also Rom. i. 1, with the note). Further, **there
are distributions of operations** (that is, of ways in which the
divine power is applied), **but the same God who operates all
things in all men** (or *in all things*, *πᾶσιν*—so Héring; but since
Paul is speaking of spiritual operations which are effected in
and through human beings it is better to take the word to be
masculine than neuter).

Paul's point in this opening paragraph is clear. Christians differ from each other, not only in natural make-up but in the spiritual gifts distributed to each. Uniformity of experience and service is not to be expected; unity lies ultimately in the Spirit who gives, the Lord who is served, the God who is at work—the Trinitarian formula is the more impressive because it seems to be artless and unconscious. Paul found it natural to think and write in these terms. With a possible reference to
Ps. lxviii. 19 (quoted at Eph. iv. 8), he sums up the argument so
7 far: **To each one is given his own manifestation** (literally,
a manifestation, but the point is that each member of the
church has one appropriate to himself) **of the Spirit, with a
view to mutual profit,** that is, the profit of the church as a
whole (cf. xiv. 12). Each member of the church has a gift; none
is excluded. No member has his gift for his own private use; all
are intended for the common good.

8 The variety of gifts is now illustrated. **For to one there is
given, through the Spirit** (that is, as a supernatural endow-
ment), **a word of wisdom; to another, in accordance with
the same Spirit** (Paul varies the wording, but the new phrase
is intended to mean precisely the same as *through the Spirit*;
attempts to distinguish the phrases are not convincing; cf. *in* in
verse 9), **a word of knowledge.** When the church is assembled
(cf. xiv. 26) the Spirit bestows on some of its members the gift
of instructive discourse. It is the discourse, not the wisdom or

knowledge behind it, that is the spiritual gift, for it is this that is of direct service to the church (Schlatter). It is not clear how (or indeed whether) *a word of wisdom* and *a word of knowledge* are to be distinguished. Some have noted the essentially practical character of wisdom in the Old Testament, and the fact that knowledge (γνῶσις) may be speculative. *A word of wisdom* would then represent a practical discourse, consisting mainly of ethical instruction and exhortation, and *a word of knowledge* an exposition of Christian truth. But in this epistle *knowledge* is connected with practical matters (e.g. viii. 10 f.), and some kinds at least of wisdom (see pp. 67 f..) can be speculative enough. Probably Paul is varying his speech, as he does with *gifts*, *services*, and *operations* in verses 4 ff. Similar variations occur as the sentence continues. **To another** (ἑτέρῳ, a 9
different word from that in the last clause; Paul differentiates the two at Gal. i. 6 f., but here, for the sake of variety, he uses them as synonyms, as at 2 Cor. xi. 4; Homer could do the same —*Iliad* xiii. 730 ff., cited by Robertson-Plummer) **faith, in** (that is, *in the power of*) **the same Spirit; to another** (here, and in the following clauses, Paul reverts to ἄλλῳ, without changing his meaning) **gifts of healing, in the one Spirit** (again the wording changes slightly, but the meaning does not); **to** 10
another the working (ἐνεργήματα, translated *operations* in verse 6) **of miracles** (see note 2 on p. 282), **to another prophecy, to another the power to distinguish** (διακρίνειν, for this word see the note on xi. 29) **between spirits, to another various kinds of tongues, to another the interpretation of tongues.** No doubt all these spiritual gifts were familiar to Corinthian Christians in the first century. Some are imperfectly clear to the modern reader. *Faith* cannot be that faith by which alone the Christian life is begun and maintained, for this could not be spoken of as a gift enjoyed by some Christians but not others. Compare xiii. 2; this verse suggests that the faith in question is to be connected with the miracles referred to in the next few lines. Some but not all Christians had that extraordinary faith that was able to claim from God extraordinary manifestations of power in the natural world, for example, *gifts of healing*. Paul himself is related to have healed the sick (e.g. Acts xiv. 8 ff.), and there is no doubt that miraculous cures

were believed to take place in the church in the apostolic age. *Miracles* will cover a wider range of abnormal activity; how wide a range we have no means of knowing, though presumably the nature miracles in the gospels give us a pointer. For *prophecy* see especially chapter xiv. It was uttered in ordinary though probably excited, perhaps ecstatic, speech. It was not for this reason true; hence the necessity for a further gift, which enabled the possessor *to distinguish between spirits*. Here *spirits* signifies the Holy Spirit and other possible sources of ecstatic phenomena. It was necessary (and it required another gift) to know whether the inspired speaker (who is probably to be distinguished from those who uttered a word of wisdom or of knowledge) was actuated by the Spirit of God, or by some demonic agency (cf. xii. 3). For *various kinds of tongues* see xiii. 1 and chapter xiv. Here unintelligible speech is in mind, and not only discrimination but also *interpretation* is needed; this too is a spiritual gift. Paul places gifts related to tongues at the end of his list (cf. verse 28); it is probable that the Corinthians rated them much higher.

Paul's aim at the moment is not however to establish a rating or hierarchy of gifts, but rather to insist that all gifts whatsoever, important or unimportant, showy or obscure, come from the
11 same source. **All these things** (just listed) **the same one Spirit** (literally, *one and the same Spirit*) **puts into operation** (ἐνεργεῖ, cf. verse 6 above, where it is used of God; the word suggests that the Spirit is the source of boundless and manifold energy and power—a thoroughly biblical thought), **distributing** (cf. verses 4 ff.) **individually** (ἰδίᾳ; see e.g. M. iii. 18; it would be possible to write the word ἴδια, and translate *his own gifts*) **to each one** (it is again implied that each Christian receives some gift) **as he wills.** Thus it is not for Christians to dictate to the Spirit what gifts they (or others) should have, though they should strive for the greater (and perhaps less spontaneous) gifts (verse 31). The Spirit chooses what gift shall be given to each Christian, so that none has occasion for boasting, or for a sense of inferiority. As his work, the gifts are a sign of the free grace of God by which the church exists, and of the place the church occupies at the dawn of the new age. They naturally lead Paul to think of the church itself.

The various members of the church have different gifts and exercise different functions; to express this fact Paul uses an analogy frequently employed in the ancient world, and compares the church to a body. Livy (ii. 32) ascribes the use of the metaphor to Menenius Agrippa (*c.* 494 B.C.), who turned it to good effect in persuading the mutinous Roman *plebs* that their interests were the same as those of the patricians (another part of the same body), and that they should therefore not withdraw their services. It is important that Stoics (e.g. Seneca, *Epistles* xcv. 52: All this that you see, in which things divine and things human are included, is one (*unum est*); we are members of a great body (*membra corporis magni*); Epictetus II. x. 3 f.: You are a citizen of the world and a part (μέρος) of it . . . [one should act] as the hand or the foot would do if they had reason and understood the natural order . . .) compared the universe as a whole to a body, and that Gnostics (see e.g. *Corpus Hermeticum* ii. 2 f.: Is then this world so great that no body is greater? Agreed. And compact?—for it is full of many other large bodies, or rather, of all the bodies there are. So it is. Well then, the world is a body? It is. And one that moves? Yes, indeed; cf. iv. 1; vii. 3; xi. 19) took up the same theme. The cosmos was a body, informed by mind (νοῦς) or reason (λόγος), and all men, being members of this body, achieved their proper being and function by acting in the one body in accordance with the one mind. Paul begins like a Stoic moralist; for the parallel (and also for
the differences) see Sevenster, *Seneca*, pp. 170-3. **For as the** 12
body is one, and has many members, and all the members of the body, many though they are, are one body, . . . If he continued in this vein he would add: So also is the church, and you ought therefore to recognize the value of one another's gifts, use your own for the common good, and live in harmony. This he does indeed go on to say; but verse 12 concludes: . . . **so also is Christ.** Paul takes two steps in one. It would not have been wrong to conclude: so also is the church. But the church (as is stated specifically in verse 27) is the body of Christ, so that Christ himself may be said to be a body made up of many members, diverse from each other but working together in harmony. This does not amount to a simple identification of Christ with the body of believers. Such an identification

would be unthinkable for Paul, who has just (xii. 3) stated, as the principle by which the work of the Holy Spirit may be distinguished, the confession, Jesus is Lord; he is Lord over the church, and in this sense eternally distinct from it. Yet men are in the body of Christians only as they are in Christ (Rom. xii. 5), and though it is scarcely true to suggest, as Calvin does, that Christ would be 'mutilated in some way, were he to be separated from his members', it is in relation to them that Paul says *so also is Christ*. Christ however remains always the prototype of the relationship. For the church as the body of Christ see further the notes on the remainder of the paragraph, and on Rom. xii. 4 f., and especially the article (σῶμα) by E. Schweizer in *T.W.N.T.* vii. 1024-91.

The next verse has already been drawn upon in the above
13 discussion. It opens with a **for** (γάρ) which explains (by the process of incorporation) how it can be said that Christ is a body. He is so because **in one Spirit we were all baptized so as to become** (εἰς, not local, but describing the result of the process—so Weiss) **one body,** his body. Baptism signifies (see especially Rom. vi. 3 ff.) dying and rising with Christ; by this means the Christian, not in himself but in Christ, experiences the eschatological events of suffering and vindication which were anticipated in the events of Good Friday and Easter. In Christ, he is a new creature, belonging to the new age, though this fact is one that becomes factually apparent only partially, and through the sanctifying work of the Spirit. If, however, the Christian, has, in baptism, put on Christ, so have other Christians too (Gal. iii. 27); if the Spirit is now at work creating the image of Christ in and upon him, the same Spirit is at work in and for other Christians too. Hence there comes into being the body which belongs to Christ (verse 27), which is in Christ (Rom. xii. 5), since all Christians who have put on Christ are one person in him (Gal. iii. 28). Not by nature, as the Stoics taught, nor by a mystic *gnosis*, but by grace, men are incorporated into the cosmic unity. By nature, on the contrary, they are essentially diverse from and alien to one another: **Jews** and **Greeks, slaves** and **free.** Compare Gal. iii. 28; Col. iii. 11. It seems evident from these passages that, though the thought of a unity analogous with that of the cosmos, and based perhaps on the

thought of Adam as the universal ancestor of mankind (W. D. Davies, p. 57), is not absent from Paul's mind (it will find fuller development in Colossians), his main intention is practical; the various national and social groups, and the dissident religious cliques at Corinth (i. 11 f.), have all entered into the unity of the body of Christ, which they ought to express, and not deny, by means of their various gifts. The exuberance of spiritual phenomena must be (not suppressed—Paul never suggests this, though it might have been the easy way out of a problem) harnessed to this end.

There is no reason to think that *we were baptized* refers to anything other than baptism in water (together with all that this outward rite signified). The death and resurrection of Christ are certainly implied and stand behind the rite, but Paul is thinking of the act in which each Christian individually participated, and it is the more striking that he sees this most individualistic act, in which a man makes up, and expresses, his own mind to be a Christian, as the foundation of unity in the one Spirit and the one body, choosing this rather than the corporate act of the church in its common meal. The relation of this meal to the unity of the Christian society has already been expressed (especially in x. 17), and some (e.g. Calvin, Schlatter, Wendland) see it also in the next clause: **we were all given one Spirit as drink.** This is however unlikely. The new verb (ἐποτίσθημεν) is in the same aorist tense as *we were baptized* and probably refers not to a repeated act (as the Supper would be) but to a single occasion. It was used of the watering of plants at iii. 6, but there is no reason to suppose that Paul still has this metaphor in mind. The new figure is a necessary supplement to the statement that we were baptized (that is, immersed) in the Spirit; the Spirit not only surrounds us, but is within us. It would be wrong to press Paul in regard to all the details of the analogy, yet its effect is to give a somewhat impersonal view of the Spirit (which was thought of in earlier times, and also by the Stoics, in quasi-physical terms). Contrast verse 11.

The primary point is now established. Christians, who are members of Christ, constitute one body, Christ's body. This is one metaphorical way of describing the church, but among Paul's metaphors (planting, building, and so forth) it holds an

important place, and Paul proceeds to develop it. The first thing
he notes about a body (in relation to the Corinthian situation) is
its diversity. Christians should not expect to have identical
gifts (this proposition is implied by the *for* with which the next
14 clause begins), **for a body** (not specifically Christ's body, but
any body: generic use of the article in Greek) **does not consist
of** (literally, *is not*) **one member, but many.** The point is
made explicitly (cf. Plato, *Protagoras* 330A: Each one of them
has its own proper function, like the parts of the face; an eye is
15 not like the ears, nor is its function the same . . .). **If the foot
should say, Because I am not a hand I do not belong to
the body; saying this will not mean that it does not
belong to the body** (literally, *it does not for this reason*, παρὰ
16 τοῦτο, *not belong to the body*). **And if the ear should say,
Because I am not an eye I do not belong to the body;
saying this** (παρὰ τοῦτο again) **will not mean that it does not
belong to the body.** That is, if a Christian who has the gift of
healing should say, Because I do not have the gift of tongues I
am no member of the church, he deludes himself, and his complaint has no validity. He is as much a Christian as the man who
speaks with tongues. The variety which exists is highly desirable,
17 indeed necessary. **If the whole body were eye, where would
hearing be? If the whole were hearing** (ἀκοή, possibly *ear*),
where would smelling be? That is, if all Christians pro-
phesied, what would become of other proper Christian activities, such as the working of miracles? But, as every one knows,
18 it is not so. **God has put the members, each several one of
19 them, in the body, as he saw fit. If the whole were one
member** (cf. verse 17), **where would the body be?** It would
20 simply not exist as a body. **But in fact there are many
members, and one body.** This is true of the human body,
with which all Paul's readers are familiar; it is true also of the
Christian body: God wills its variety.

21 Paul now turns to a somewhat different point. **The eye cannot say to the hand, I have no need of you; or the head to
the feet, I have no need of you.** In truth, each member needs
all the rest. That is, the Christian who has the gift of tongues
cannot boast his independence of his brother who has the gift
of prophecy; each needs the other. Boasting (which Paul is never

slow to condemn; cf. i. 29 ff.) is quite the wrong attitude. **Much** 22
rather, the bodily members that are accounted weaker
(delicate organs, such as the eye; invisible organs, such as the
heart) **are necessary, and those we consider to be the** 23
relatively less honourable parts of the body (whose functions we normally conceal) **we clothe with** (the verb περιτίθεμεν suggests this; cf. the shame felt by Adam and Eve, and their primitive clothing—Gen. iii. 7, 10, 21) **special** (more abundant) **honour, and our unseemly members** (cf. Phil. iii. 19, interpreted by Gal. vi. 13) **have** (receive from us in clothing)
the greater seemliness, while our seemly parts have no 24
need of this. So the weaker (cf. viii. 7-13; ix. 22; x. 28 f.; Rom. xiv. 1; xv. 1) and humbler (i. 26; xi. 22) members of the church should not be despised but treated with special honour; this is how God has treated undeserving mankind as a whole. **God has put the body together** (συνεκέρασεν; Robertson-Plummer quote the use of this word by Alcibiades, in Thucydides vi. 18, with reference to the united action of the city) **and given special** (as in verse 23) **honour to the member that lacked it** (it appears that Paul has now left the metaphor and is speaking directly of the church, though what he says is superficially not unlike the Stoic doctrine of the συμπάθεια of the cosmos), **in order that there may be no division** (σχίσμα; cf. i. 10, 25
and see note 1 on p. 283) **in the body, but** (Paul now moves on to a positive point for which there can be no real physical analogy) **that all the members may have the same care for one another.** We have already met examples of what Paul means: thus the Christian who is strong in faith and conscience must, in regard to food sacrificed to idols, consider not only his own freedom and taste but also the scruples of his weaker
brothers (viii. 7-13; x. 28 f.). Paul develops the theme: **If, on the** 26
one hand, one member (of the body) **suffers, all the members suffer with it.** To some extent this is true physically; local injuries affect the well-being of the whole body (cf. Plato, *Republic* v. 462 CD: . . . as when a finger is hurt, the whole bodily unity (κοινωνία) suffers with it . . . and so we say that the man has a pain in his finger). **If, on the other, a member is glorified, all the members rejoice with it.** Here the physiological metaphor fails (a clear indication that in the

description of the church as *the body* we are dealing with metaphor, no more); members of the body are not glorified and do not rejoice. It must be remembered that Paul is speaking to the Corinthian situation in regard to spiritual gifts. If one member of the church appears to be deficient in such gifts, this is no occasion for the rest of the church to despise him. He is not the only sufferer; the whole church suffers through the deficiency. If another member has more than the usual share of inspiration, neither should he boast nor the rest be envious and resentful. All should rejoice together in the gift God has bestowed on the one for the benefit of all (verse 7), has indeed bestowed on the whole group, through the one.

The argument is rounded off with the comprehensive state-
27 ment **Now you are Christ's body, and, individually** (this seems to be the meaning of *ἐκ μέρους*), **members.** Paul's main intention is still strictly practical. The members of a human body are various, and inter-related; they are diverse, but form a unity. This (as we have seen) had been said about other societies; it was certainly true about the Christian society, whose members differed in the gifts given to them and were, because the differences arose out of the action of a divine person, the more various and the more interdependent. But the very fact that they were, individually and collectively, constituted by spiritual gifts shows that they were not simply the body of Christians (which would have been a natural expression to use) but the *body of Christ*, since it was only in Christ that the spiritual gifts existed, and since the spiritual gifts were bestowed in order to make it possible for the human community to do the work of Christ. The genitive (Χριστοῦ) is not of identity but of possession and authority; not, the body which is Christ, of which Christ consists, but, the body that belongs to Christ, and over which he rules (as Head, as later epistles will say: Col. i. 18; ii. 19; Eph. i. 22; iv. 15; v. 23; cf. 1 Cor. xi. 3), separate from the body even though continuous with it. Since the resurrection (in some anticipated sense, perhaps, before it) Christ has been the new humanity living in the new age. His members have their place in this eschatological entity, and, as members of it, must live accordingly. What this kind of living means will be made especially clear in chapter xiii, but the paragraph that closes

here has given particular examples. Paul now returns to the unified diversity of spiritual gifts and operations (cf. verses 4-11) describing concretely (though sometimes obscurely) the different services performed in the church. In Eph. iv. 11 there is a similar list, more developed in form.

Further (καί, developing the thought of the church as an 28
organic structure), **there are some** (οὓς μέν, which expects an answering οὓς δέ, *others*, but the construction breaks off, because instead of saying 'some . . . others' Paul chooses to give a numbered list) **whom God has set in the church** (ἐν τῇ ἐκκλησίᾳ; whether the local or the universal church is intended is a matter of dispute—Paul uses the word in both senses (see pp. 31 f.), and its meaning probably changes as this verse proceeds: apostles in the universal church, prophets in the assembly of the local church), **first apostles . . .** *Apostle* (ἀπόστολος) is a verbal noun derived from a verb (ἀποστέλλειν) which Paul uses only three times, but always significantly: in Rom. x. 15; 1 Cor. i. 17 of the sending of men to preach, and in 2 Cor. xii. 17 of Paul's own sending of men as his deputies. A synonymous verb (πέμπειν) is used rather more frequently but on the whole with less relevance to the interpretation of *apostle* (Rom. viii. 3, of God's sending his Son; 2 Thess. ii. 11, of God's sending a deceiving influence; 1 Cor. iv. 17; xvi. 3; 2 Cor. ix. 3; Phil. ii. 19, 23, 25, 28; Col. iv. 8; 1 Thess. iii. 2, 5, of the sending of human messengers). An apostle is, in Paul's understanding, one called by Christ and sent by him to preach the Gospel. He himself was such an apostle, commissioned by Christ; some might dispute the fact, but his own converts at least, such as the Corinthians, should have no doubt of it (Rom. i. 1; xi. 13; 1 Cor. i. 1; ix. 1, 2; xv. 9; 2 Cor. i. 1; xii. 12; Gal. i. 1; Col. i. 1; 1 Thess. ii. 7). There were however other apostles too. Phil. ii. 25 is perhaps to be taken in a different sense; the word may mean only that Epaphroditus was an envoy of the Philippian Christians, charged with conveying their gift to Paul. This in itself has nothing to do with an appearance of and a charge from Christ, and with preaching the Gospel, though it is perhaps not quite impossible that Epaphroditus was an apostle (in the larger sense) whom the Philippians entrusted with a task they were not able themselves to fulfil. 2 Cor. viii. 23 is certainly about church

delegates. Other missionary apostles undoubtedly existed: 1 Cor. xv. 7 (see the note); 2 Cor. xi. 5; xii. 11 (where Paul seems to speak ironically, but not to deny the apostleship of those he speaks of; see the note); Gal. i. 17, 19. We should probably include here Rom. xvi. 7 (see the note). It will be seen that Paul nowhere identifies these apostles with the Twelve, whom indeed he mentions only once, and that probably in a quotation (xv. 5; see the note). For him the apostles constituted a limited but not clearly defined body; if sight of the risen Jesus was an indispensable qualification (cf. ix. 1) Paul was the last to be appointed (xv. 8). The present verse shows clearly enough their pre-eminent position in the church. Their work did not simply bear witness to the deeds of God in the last days; it was itself part of the eschatological events, and in the Gospel they preached the righteousness of God was manifested (Rom. i. 17). Paul at least understood his work to be that of a pioneer (Rom. xv. 18-21; 2 Cor. x. 12-16); he was a founder of churches (iii. 6, 10; ix. 1), but he also cared for and built up the churches he founded, though this was a task in which others joined. In this work he had authority (ix. 4, 5, 6, 12, 18), but it was authority for building up and not for casting down (2 Cor. x. 8; xiii. 10), and he did not claim to be a lord over his converts' faith (2 Cor. i. 24), though not all his colleagues seem to have shared his views in this respect. Yet he writes not of himself only but of apostles in general when he declares that their office brings them into disrepute and scorn (iv. 9-13; 2 Cor. vi. 4-10). Paul's apostolic situation was complicated by the fact that his relations with his apostolic colleagues were not always easy, and that there were in addition false apostles who though they claimed to be apostles of Christ were in truth angels of Satan (2 Cor. xi. 13). For these complications, and the relation of Paul's understanding of apostleship to others which appear in the New Testament, see Introduction pp. 21 f., and the commentary on 2 Corinthians. The *apostles* referred to here are eschatological (see A. Fridrichsen, *The Apostle and his Message* (1947); also 'The Apostles in and after the New Testament', in *Svensk Exegetisk Årsbok* xxi (1956), pp. 30-49) evangelists, who preach the good news, and manifest the death and resurrection of Jesus in their own lives and in the establishing of converts in churches.

Apostles are not the only servants of Christ, or indeed the only preachers of the Gospel. Perhaps their only really distinctive feature in the present list is that they were itinerant. There were also, **second prophets, third teachers.** *Prophets* take the second place in the Ephesian list also. Paul refers elsewhere (Rom. i. 2; iii. 21; xi. 3; 1 Thess. ii. 15) to Old Testament prophets; only in 1 Corinthians does he use the word of Christian prophets, though these are implied by Rom. xii. 6; 1 Thess. v. 20. We must suppose that they were men who exercised the gift of prophecy described at length in chapter xiv. The prophets of that chapter are local, not travelling, Christians, inspired to address the word of God to the church, and, at least on occasion, to non-Christians also, who might be converted by their speech (xiv. 24). *Teachers* take a lower place in the Ephesian list. Presumably they were mature Christians who instructed others in the meaning and moral implications of the Christian faith; compare Gal. vi. 6; possibly (as some think) they expounded the Christian meaning of the Old Testament.

This threefold ministry of the word is, according to Paul, the primary Christian ministry. By it the church is founded, and built up. Other activities, such as baptism (i. 17) can occupy only a secondary place. The significance of the first three groups is underlined by a twofold break in the sentence. The numerical sequence is pursued no further (possibly because, though Paul can place all the remaining gifts on a lower level than apostleship, prophecy, and teaching, he does not feel that he must, or wishes to, distinguish narrowly between the lower gifts), and, instead of persons, gifts are now mentioned (the reverse change takes place in Rom. xii. 6 ff., showing that Paul was concerned rather with gifts and functions than with persons and their status). The further gifts are as follows: **miracles** (cf. verse 10), **then gifts of healing** (cf. verse 9), **gifts of support** (ἀντιλήμψεις: the rendering must be to some extent a guess, but the word is used, notably in papyri referring to the Ptolemies, of defence or succour given by a higher authority), **gifts of direction** (κυβερνήσεις: properly *steering*, of a ship, but used metaphorically), **various kinds of tongues** (cf. verse 10). *Support* may foreshadow the work of deacons (διάκονοι), whose main task in the early church was that of ministering the church's aid to the needy, and *direction* that of bishops (ἐπίσκοποι), the name sometimes given to those who presided over the church's affairs (cf. Rom. xii. 8). These were local ministries (cf. Phil. i. 1), in contrast with the peripatetic ministry of apostles, and secondary to the ministry of the word exercised by prophets and teachers. Gifts of a self-assertive kind, *direction* and *tongues*, which appear to have suited the Corinthian taste, are placed at the end of the list.

There is nothing to suggest that more than one gift or function could not be exercised by one person; but Paul checks the idea, perhaps gaining currency at Corinth, that all—or perhaps all of a group who thought themselves superior
29 Christians—might enjoy every gift. **Are all apostles?** Perhaps some in Corinth thought the answer should be Yes (see Barth, *C.D.* III. ii. 309; and cf. iv. 8); but it must be No, for the apostles confront the church with a word which it did not originate (cf. xiv. 36), a word by which it is both created and judged. **Are all prophets?** This is not for man but for the Spirit to decide and show (*as he wills*, xii. 11). **Are all teachers?** iii. 1 suggests that they were not. **Are all able to work miracles?** (literally, *Are*
30 *all miracles?*—Paul's sentence breaks down). **Do all have gifts of healing? Do all speak with tongues? Do all interpret** (that is, interpret the tongues with which others speak)? It was evident that the answer was No.

The lesson the Corinthians had to learn was that the church was a whole, a body. No one member of it could exercise all the necessary functions. Each depended on the ministries of the rest, and there was in this no ground for discontent, no ground for a feeling of superiority. Yet it was proper to give the advice,
31 **Strive for** (be ambitious to acquire) **the greater gifts**—proper because the Corinthians evidently valued too highly what Paul regarded as one of the lowest of gifts, that of speaking with tongues. Thus the Corinthians might seek—by prayer and self-preparation—the gift of prophecy, or of teaching. These gifts would enable them to make a maximum contribution to the life of the church. Even so, however, the last word has not been said. **I am going on to show** (bringing out the force of the present tense, δείκνυμι) **you a yet better way.** This seems to be the meaning of an awkward sentence. The phrase (ἔτι καθ'

ὑπερβολήν), here taken adjectivally, is sometimes taken adverbially with *show*: Beyond all this, beyond all that I have so far said, I show you a way. The prepositional phrase in question, as Schlatter points out, goes with the verb in 2 Cor. i. 8; iv. 17. The problem is accentuated by puzzling textual variation; see note 2 on p. 283. What appears to be a Western reading has some support from P^{46}, and is preferred by B.D. §272, followed (apparently) by M. iii. 221: If there is anything beyond, I show you the way. But we cannot be certain exactly how to read the evidence of the papyrus ('It is tantalizing that these very lines are damaged in the papyrus: the last but one on the page had some letters, now lost, which may have contained the solution of this ancient puzzle'—Zuntz, p. 90), and it would be unwise to commit oneself to the Western text.

It may be that the awkwardness of the sentence is due to the fact that the connection between chapter xii and chapter xiii is somewhat artificial. It suggests the view (see further pp. 299, 314 f.) that chapter xiii, though written by Paul, was not written by him freshly for the present occasion, but was inserted because he saw its relevance to the argument, and to the Corinthian situation. Chapter xiii makes good sense as a unit complete in itself, and when it is done Paul returns to the matter-of-fact discussion of spiritual gifts, with special reference to speaking with tongues and prophecy, and xiv. 1 (*Strive for spiritual gifts*) takes up the wording (ζηλοῦτε) of xii. 31a. As we shall see, chapter xiii is admirably suited to the context, because love provides the scale by which other gifts may be tested and measured, and also is the means by which the unity of the body is maintained. At Gal. v. 22 it is mentioned first among the products of the Spirit; here it seems to be distinguished from spiritual gifts in general (see especially xiv. 1), and all Christians are expected to have it. But for this reason the chapter was (and is) suited to other contexts as well as the Corinthian, and was probably inserted into 1 Corinthians as a ready-made piece.

28. xiii. 1-13. THE FUNDAMENTAL TEST: (b) LOVE

(1) If I speak with the tongues of men and of angels, but have no love, I am like clanging bronze or a shrill cymbal. (2) And if I have the gift of prophecy, and know all mysteries and all knowledge, and if I have complete faith, so as to remove mountains, but have no love, I am nothing. (3) And if I use all my property for feeding others, and if I hand over my body to be burned,[1] but have no love, that does me no good. (4) Love is long-suffering, love is kind; love is not envious, does not brag, is not puffed up, (5) does not behave in an unseemly way;[2] it does not seek its own ends,[3] is not touchy, does not put evil down to anyone's account; (6) it does not rejoice at unrighteousness, but joins in rejoicing at the truth; (7) it supports all things, believes all things, hopes all things, endures all things.

(8) Love never fails. But prophecies—they shall be done away with; tongues—they shall cease; knowledge—it shall be done away with. (9) For we know in part, and we prophesy in part, (10) but when totality comes, that which is partial shall be done away with. (11) When I was a child, I used to speak as a child, I used to think as a child, I used to reckon as a child; but now I have become a man I am done with the things that belong to childhood. (12) For now we look through a glass and see obscurely; then we shall see face to face. Now I know in part, then I shall know even as also I have been known. (13) But now there abide these three: faith, hope, love. But the greatest of them is love.

[1] *καυθήσομαι* or *καυθήσωμαι* is read by C D G, the great majority of Greek MSS., the Latin and Syriac versions, and many fathers; *καυχήσωμαι* is read by P^{46} ℵ A B and some important minuscules. See the commentary.

[2] *ἀσχημονεῖ*; P^{46} has *εὐσχημονεῖ*, 'does not put on a fine (outward) show (of good manners)'. The reading is interesting but may well be due to a slip.

[3] Instead of *τὰ ἑαυτῆς*, P^{46} B have *τὸ μὴ ἑαυτῆς*, 'does not seek that which is not its own'. This is impossibly trite. It describes 'heathen honesty', not Christian love.

The 'Hymn to Love', as it has been called—and indeed it has a rhythmical though not a regular structure—falls into three parts. In verses 1-3 love is contrasted with other religious actions and attitudes ('it is love alone that counts'); in verses 4-7 (with which cf. Col. iii. 12 ff.) love is described, mainly in negative terms (it is 'love alone that triumphs'); in verses 8-13 the theme of contrast returns, and it is brought out that when other things perish love persists into the eternal world (it is 'love alone that endures'—Barth). Many attempts have been made to write out the chapter in the form of verse. This does not seem profitable. The chapter is prose, and its rhythmical patterns are not regular enough to warrant presentation in the form of poetry. This is not to deny its high literary quality; the balance of the sentences and the point and power of the vocabulary are seldom equalled by Paul, or indeed in Greek literature generally. This adds weight to the view that the passage may have been separately composed and polished, and inserted at this point (see p. 297). It must be emphasized that this does not mean that the chapter was not written by Paul, or that it was not intended by him to stand at this place. It 'stands to the whole discussion on Spiritual Gifts in a relation closely similar to that of the digression on self-limitation (chapter ix) to the discussion of' things sacrificed to idols (Robertson-Plummer). In Romans also (xiii. 8 ff.) moral exhortation reaches its climax in a description of love (Schweitzer, *Mysticism*, p. 386).

On the chapter as a whole see, in addition to commentaries, G. Bornkamm, 'Der köstlichere Weg (1. Kor. 13)', in *Das Ende des Gesetzes* (1952), pp. 93-112 (also for literature), and Barth *C.D.* IV. ii. 824-40.

The first contrast is with speaking with tongues (see xii. 10; xiv. 2), a true gift of the Spirit, possessed by Paul (xiv. 18), but not valued as highly by him as it appears to have been by his
readers. **If I speak with the tongues of men and of angels,** 1
but have no love, I am (*γέγονα*; *I have become* would be pedantic) **like clanging bronze, or a shrill cymbal.** The *tongues of men* presumably represent ordinary human speech, and the meaning is 'not only with . . . but also with . . .'. Apparently Paul thought that the unintelligible speech (unintelligible except to inspired interpretation) used by inspired participants in

Christian worship was that in use among angels; this was not normally understood by human beings, if we may follow Rev. xiv. 2 f., and the rabbinic tradition (S.B. ad loc.) that Johanan ben Zakkai, because of his outstanding piety and learning, was able to understand the speech of the angels. Compare also 2 Cor. xii. 4. But to speak in this way is to make no more intelligible communication than inanimate objects, which make a noise when struck. This is the main thought in Paul's mind, but both nouns suggest that he is thinking also of pagan worship. *Bronze* (or copper, χαλκός), used as a substantive, stood both for the metal, and for vessels or implements made of it (especially for armour, so that 'clanging armour' would be a not impossible rendering here); compounds occur in descriptions of the worship of Demeter and of Cybele (see L.S. s.v.). The *cymbal* (κύμβαλον; see K. L. Schmidt in *T.W.N.T.* iii. 1037 f.) though not confined to was widely used in religious practices. The noise may have been intended to call the god's attention or to drive away demons (Betz, p. 65); its probable effect was to excite the worshippers. Metaphorically the word was used to describe an empty philosophizing. Thus Paul asserts that a church speaking with tongues but not practising love is a meaningless phenomenon; more than that, it is mere paganism. Schmidt is perhaps right in suggesting further that Paul's attitude is that of the prophets who condemned Israelite worship (which was not without music: e.g. Ps. cl. 5, Praise him upon the loud cymbals, ἐν κυμβάλοις εὐήχοις . . . ἀλαλαγμοῦ; Josephus, *Antiquities* vii. 306, The cymbals prepared by David were large broad plates of bronze) as no better than pagan, if it was not accompanied by obedience to the will of God.

After tongues, prophecy and knowledge (cf. xii. 8, 28; xiv. 1,
2 et al.): **If I have the gift of prophecy, and know all mysteries and all knowledge . . .**; and faith (xii. 9): **and if I have complete faith, so as to remove mountains** (cf. Mark xi. 23 and parallels), **but have no love, I am nothing.** Prophecy, unlike speaking with tongues, cannot be described as mere noisy sound; it is one of the highest Christian activities. Even so, if the prophet does not love, his Christian achievement is nil. The gift of prophecy is coordinated with that of understanding *mysteries*, the secret truths, made known in the Gospel, of God's

eschatological purposes and acts; see ii. (1), 7; iv. 1; xv. 51; also Rom. xi. 25; xvi. 25; 2 Thess. ii. 7. Occurrences of the word in Ephesians and Colossians represent a somewhat more developed use. To *know all mysteries* is thus to have a perfect understanding of the eschatological situation of the church—though it is possible that Paul is not using the word in his own technical sense but means simply pieces of information not generally known. This might apply also to the word *knowledge* (*γνῶσις*), for this was often knowledge available only to the few, the elect. If it is to be distinguished from *mysteries* it may suggest (see the note on xii. 8) the moral and other implications to be drawn from the data of the Christian revelation, but it is probable that Paul is here piling up words without too nice a regard for the distinctions between them. 'I may know everything there is to know, but if I have no love I am nothing.' Paul describes miracle-working faith (not the faith through which men are justified, which all Christians share; see the note on xii. 9) in the terms used by Jesus in the synoptic gospels. He gives no indication that he is quoting from Jesus, and was probably not doing so. ' "To uproot" or "to tear out mountains" is a proverbial expression, which means "to make what seems impossible possible" ' (S.B. i. 759; for a Hellenistic parallel see Lucian, *Navigium* 45). Paul very seldom refers explicitly to the words of Jesus; see the notes on vii. 10. For the thought see also Matt. vii. 22 f.

In Paul's view, prophecy, knowledge, and miracles stand higher than speaking with tongues, but even so they are not comparable with love. We come nearer to love in the full sense in the next sentence, but still do not quite reach it. **If I use all** 3
my property for feeding others (*ψωμίσω*; literally, I feed with small morsels, as a child, or invalid; it may be that Paul is thinking of the morsels rather than of feeding, and means, 'If, for the purpose of almsgiving, I divide all my property into fragments;' the word is obscure), **and if I hand over my body to be burned, but have no love, that does me no good.** It seems clear that the bestowal of all one's property on others may be motivated by love. Paul does not deny this (any more than he denies that speaking with tongues, prophecy, knowledge, and faith may be accompanied by love); but he affirms the possibility

that charitable acts may proceed from lower motives. Better that they should do so than that the poor should starve; but the givers deserve, and at the judgement will get, no credit (*that does me no good*). Both text and meaning of the next clause are uncertain; see note 1 on p. 298. Both variants, *to be burned* and *in order to glory*, have ancient attestation, and both have received support from modern textual critics. 'In order to glory' might, as an unworthy motive, apply either to giving away one's property, or to handing over oneself (presumably for sale into slavery so that the proceeds might be used for the benefit of others; cf. 1 Clement lv. 2); but 'handing oneself over' is a far from explicit expression (Clement is much clearer), and needs a supplementary clause, such as *to be burned*, in order to make it clear. Lietzmann and Bornkamm rightly point out that *to be burned* is parallel to *so as to remove mountains*, and that the parallelism confirms the text. Moreover, an act performed *in order to glory* is already by definition an act without love, and if this variant were accepted the sentence would scarcely make sense. See the conclusive discussion by Zuntz (pp. 35 ff.); on the other side, but unconvincingly, Clark in *Studia Paulina*, pp. 61 f.

To be burned is the better reading; but what does it mean? No suggestion is free from difficulty. It might refer to martyrdom, but though Christian martyrdoms had taken place when Paul wrote (if Acts is right he had not forgotten that of Stephen, though he does not explicitly mention it in the epistles) we have no evidence for martyrdoms by fire before the Neronian persecution (Tacitus, *Annals* xv. 44). Paul found the imperial courts on the whole friendly, though Christians who were not citizens may have had different treatment. Christians as such would not be liable to the Jewish penalty of burning, which was reserved for him 'that has connexion with a woman and her daughter, and the daughter of a priest that has committed adultery' (*Sanhedrin* ix. 1). It is unlikely that *to be burned* means *to be branded as a slave*, so that the sentence means (as above), If I sell myself into slavery with a view to benefiting others. Slaves were not normally branded. It is more likely than this that Paul may have had in mind the practice of self-immolation. Lucian (*de Morte Peregrini* 21-5, on which see Betz, p. 122) describes the self-burning of the Christian charlatan Peregrinus, and an

Indian was well known to have ended his life in this way in the time of Augustus (Plutarch, *Alexander* 69; Strabo XV. i. 73; Dio Cassius liv. 9). Suicide of this kind Paul would be unlikely to approve, but he might well have thought in terms of self-sacrifice (Bachmann), remembering perhaps Dan. iii. 25 f. (LXX). 'If in some great cause I give myself up to the most painful of deaths, but have no love, even this is no credit to me.' This would provide a powerful climax for the first part of the chapter, in which Paul describes 'man—and indeed the *homo religiosus Christianus*—in the highest possibilities open to him' (Bornkamm) only in order to show his deficiency if he lacks love.

Love is the indispensable addition which alone gives worth to all other Christian gifts. What then is love? It is a contradiction of the natural man (Bornkamm), and Paul finds it easier to answer the questions, What does love do? and what does it not
do? **Love is long-suffering;** that is, a man who has love is 4
long-suffering; he does not lose patience or temper, whatever he may have to put up with from others. Further, **love** (that is again, as throughout the paragraph, the man who is actuated by love) **is kind** (the positive counterpart to *long-suffering*; love does good to those who do harm); **love is not envious** (though Paul uses here the verb—ζηλοῦν—which he uses in xii. 31 in telling the Corinthians to aim at the greater gifts), **does not brag** (the word is used by the Stoic moral philosophers, not elsewhere by Paul, but it is apt in the letter to Corinth), **is not puffed up** (this is Paul's, equally appropriate, word; see iv. 6,
18, 19; v. 2; viii. 1), **does not behave in an unseemly way** 5
(the word, ἀσχημονεῖ, is that used at vii. 36, and discussed in the note there: love never treats anyone unfairly, as a man would do who provoked a girl's passions and refused to marry her; see also note 2 on p. 298); **it does not seek its own ends** (cf. x. 24). See note 3 on p. 298. Love not merely does not seek that which does not belong to it; it is prepared to give up for the sake of others even what it is entitled to. Love **is not touchy** (is not provoked to anger; the word, παροξύνεται, like several others in this chapter, does not occur elsewhere in Paul's writing, but see Acts xv. 39 for a παροξυσμός in which he is said to have taken part), **does not put evil down to anyone's account.** The

verb (λογίζεται) is used again at verse 11 in a different sense, and Zechariah viii. 17; Testament of Zebulun viii. 5 suggest that it might mean here 'plots evil against no one'. This makes good sense. But the word has an important use in some distinctive Pauline passages (notably Rom. iv. 1-12; 2 Cor. v. 19), and there is no reason why this use should not apply here. If it is asked, What then does love do with evil? the final answer must be that it takes evil upon itself, and thus disposes of it.

6 Love **does not rejoice at unrighteousness,** either from the pleasure it takes in being censorious, or in its sense of superiority. Rather it **joins in rejoicing** (here, in contrast with the preceding sentence, we have the compound verb συγχαίρει; this may be only a strengthening of the verb—'rejoices greatly'; or the change may have been made for the sake of rhythm; but these alternatives seem less probable than the translation given) **at** (not *with*; *the truth* does not rejoice) **the truth.** Love does not seek to make itself distinctive by tracking down and pointing out what is wrong; it gladly sinks its own identity to rejoice with others at what is right. 'Righteousness' would have made a better balance than *truth*, but righteousness has special meanings of its own in Paul (see e.g. i. 30; 2 Cor. v. 21; Rom. i. 17; iii. 21, all with the commentary), and may have been avoided for this reason.

7 Love **supports all things** (πάντα στέγει). The verb occurs at ix. 12; 1 Thess. iii. 1, 5, and normally means 'to endure'. It may simply have this meaning here; if, however, it does, it is almost exactly repeated a few lines further on (where in my translation *endures* renders ὑπομένει). This is not impossible; Paul does sometimes repeat himself. But it may be suggested that the meaning here is related to the saying of Simeon the Just (third century B.C.): By three things is the world sustained: by the Law, by the Service (that is, the worship of the Temple), and by the doing of kindnesses (*Aboth* i. 2; one may note here, but not exaggerate, the distinction Barth makes between 'love' and 'acts of love'—*C.D.* IV. ii. 831). Love is the support of the world. This interpretation of the clause accords with the use of Paul's verb in Greek generally (it is related to στέγη, roof). An alternative possibility is to interpret on the lines of 1 Pet. iv. 8: love conceals rather than exposes evil.

Love **believes all things:** not 'always believes the best about people', but 'never loses faith'; **hopes all things:** similarly, 'never ceases to hope'. Héring translates happily, '*plein de foi, plein d'espérance*'. Compare the connection of faith, hope, and love in verse 13. Love **endures all things:** no hardship or rebuff ever makes love cease to be love. Compare verse 8.

Paul returns to his contrast between love and the spiritual gifts he discusses elsewhere, but now it is made in terms of the
enduring quality of love. **Love never fails** (literally, *falls*). It is 8
not easy to distinguish now between love as a human quality (human in that it is practised by men, though never without divine aid), and love as an activity of God (who alone practises love in its fullness). 'Love is not love, that alters where it alteration finds'; in this sense, by definition, *love never fails*. If my relationship with my fellow-man is soured by his rebuffs, then it is not love; genuine love will always persist. This affirmation can in truth be made only about God. He only persists without variation in his love; yet it is his love that is reflected and reproduced in the Spirit's gift of love, which, since it reflects the nature of God as no other gift can do, belongs to a category of its own. Barth quotes Troeltsch: love is 'the power of this world which already as such is the power of the world to come'. Schweitzer (*Mysticism*, p. 305) writes similarly: 'It is the pre-eternal thing which man can possess here and now in its true essence'. **But prophecies—they shall be done away with.** It is the nature of predictive prophecy that it should be fulfilled, and in the moment of fulfilment the prophecy as prophecy ceases to exist. Similarly, though perhaps not so clearly, prophecy that is the inspired declaration of the truth about God and his will vanishes in the presence of God himself. **Tongues—they shall cease.** These are essentially indirect and mysterious communication about God, and when prophecy ends they will *a fortiori* be silenced. **Knowledge—it shall be done away with.** Knowledge (γνῶσις) is secret information about God; when God manifests himself at large no man can boast about his secret stock of knowledge. Prophecies, tongues, and knowledge are all at best partial revelations of the God who is love (1 John iv. 8, 16). As such, they have their place, and it is

9 no unimportant place; yet it is both limited and temporary. **For we know in part, and we prophesy in part** (there is no need
10 now to mention tongues), **but when totality comes, that which is partial shall be done away with.** The adjective (in the neuter gender, and with the article, τὸ τέλειον) rendered *totality* is fairly common in Paul; see ii. 6; xiv. 20. It takes its precise meaning from the context, and here, in contrast with ***in part*** (ἐκ μέρους) it means not perfection (in quality) but *totality*—in particular the whole truth about God. This totality is love; in comparison with it, other things (true and valuable in themselves) may be left behind like the ways and achievements
11 of childhood. **When I was a child, I used to speak as a child, I used to reckon** (ἐλογιζόμην, the verb used in verse 5, where see the note; the thought of calculation, estimation, seems inseparable from it; perhaps Paul is hinting that it was childishness that led the Corinthians to overvalue tongues and to undervalue love; see iii. 1) **as a child; but now I have become a man I am done with the things that belong to childhood.** This reference to childhood is an illustration, suggested by the use of the word *totality*, which, in other contexts (ii. 6) denotes maturity. Paul does not mean that he himself is now mature in the sense that he is able to dispense with prophecy and knowledge, and practise perfect love (Phil. iii. 12). For him (unlike Stoics and other Greek thinkers) *totality* remains an eschatological notion to be realized only at the future point of time determined by God. In this age, in which men love imperfectly, there is room for other instruments of revelation, imperfect though they too may be. Before God we are all, including apostles, little children.

Verse 11, however, is an illustrative parenthesis, and the *for* with which the next verse begins gives the ground of verse 10.
12 **For now we look through a glass** (looking-glasses were made in Corinth) **and see** (the last two words are not in the Greek) **obscurely; then** (at the End, when God finally consummates his purpose; see xv. 24) **we shall see face to face. Now I know in part** (cf. verse 9); **then I shall know** (not the simple word γινώσκειν, but the compound ἐπιγινώσκειν; the change is probably intended to bring out not a different kind of knowing —I shall recognize—but the completeness of future knowledge;

man's present knowledge will be done away not in the interests of ignorance but of fuller understanding) **even as also I have been known** (that is, by God; again the verb is ἐπιγινώσκειν). The general drift of the verse is clear; it brings out the inadequacy of man's present knowledge of God in contrast with (a) God's knowledge of man now, and (b) the knowledge of God that man will have in the future. Then, not now (as in gnostic thought), there will be complete mutuality of knowledge. Such perfect mutuality Paul finds, at least for the present, an adequate account of the eschatological future (cf. xv. 28—God all in all). Several points remain for study.

In *through a glass* the use of the proposition (διά), though discussed at length by some commentators, will cause no difficulty to Englishmen who have read *Alice*; the (virtual) image produced by a plane mirror appears to lie on the further side. The metaphor is sometimes used, especially by Philo, to describe an indirect and partial knowledge of God, but this is not its necessary sense. A mirror image can suggest clear and full knowledge of God; for example, *Abraham* 153, a clear image (ἐναργὲς εἴδωλον) as through a mirror (of something in itself invisible); *On the Decalogue* 105, through it [the number seven] the Maker and Father of all things is most clearly seen, for, as through a mirror, the mind forms a picture of God acting and creating and administering the universe. Compare 2 Cor. iii. 18 (if in this verse κατοπτρίζοντες means 'beholding as in a mirror'). The fact is that the metaphor of the glass must take its sense from the context; always the glass is an instrument of revelation, sometimes the stress lies simply on the revelation, sometimes on its indirectness. The latter use obtains here, but the ambiguity of the metaphor acounts for the addition (for which some odd explanations have been supplied) of a further qualification, *obscurely* (literally, *in a riddle*, ἐν αἰνίγματι). In this Paul is probably dependent not so much on Hellenistic usage as on Num. xii. 8, where God says that he will speak to Moses face to face (cf. verse 12b), not obscurely (*through riddles*, δι' αἰνιγμάτων). But the expression would be fully comprehensible to Corinthians unfamiliar with the Greek Old Testament. The Chorus complains of Cassandra that she speaks in riddles (ἐξ αἰνιγμάτων; Aeschylus, *Agamemnon* 1112); this is because she is inspired by

Apollo, whose custom it is to deliver obscure oracles. Paul means that in the present age all knowledge of God (all *gnosis*) is incomplete and unclear. On the background ('Hellenistic commonplace') see further Knox, *Gentiles*, p. 121, note 4.

Man's knowledge of God is imperfect; Paul remembers this when he uses gnostic language. Thus at Gal. iv. 9 he changes his account of the Galatians' conversion from 'having come to know God' to 'having been known by him'. Even in the Gospel man does not fully know God, and he ought not to deceive himself into thinking that he does; but God knows him, and this is the all-important truth, for when God knows, recognizes, man, he acts on his behalf. Hence Paul can describe the future as bringing to men comparable knowledge of God: *then I shall know even as also I have been known.* The gnostic found a saving relationship with God in the mutual knowledge that existed between the elect, gnostic, man, and God. According to Paul, this is not a possibility. Man's knowledge is not only dependent on God's gracious initiative, it is at best partial. It can therefore (even if the gnostic premises are accepted) mean only partial relationship and salvation. In a sense this must always be true as far as this age is concerned. But only in a sense, for there is another word to say; or rather, another three.

13 **But now** (*now in fact*, over against all the transient qualities and activities mentioned, νυνὶ δέ—contrast ἄρτι in verse 12, which means *at this present time*) **there abide these three: faith, hope, love.** *Abide* (μένει) could be rendered 'remain'; that is, when tongues, prophecy, miracles, and other charismatic gifts have been dismissed as bringing only partial knowledge of God, three are left over, which represent a total, saving relationship between man and God. The verb, however, is usually taken to mean that its subjects last on, enduring not only in this age but also in the age to come, and this meaning seems to be required by the contrast with verse 8; compare 1 Esdras iv. 38. There is no reason why both thoughts should not be present. All three, then, faith, hope, and love abide (against Calvin, and others, who think that in the age to come faith and hope will cease; see below).

Faith is now no longer the miracle-working faith of verse 2, but faith in its full Pauline sense; see *Romans*, Index s.v. It is not the same thing as knowledge, but the grateful and trustful acceptance of God as he is. A man may be weak in faith (e.g. Rom. xiv. 1), but if he has faith at all it is faith in God, faith in the whole true God (as human knowledge can never in this age be knowledge of the whole true God). The whole true God, manifested in Christ, is accessible to faith (as he is not to knowledge); hence faith is distinguished from all other gifts of the Spirit. Faith, the thankful recognition of the gracious God, will be in place as long as God continues to be gracious; that is, faith is an eternal mark of the true relationship between God and man. Whatever is not of faith is sin (Rom. xiv. 23), and it follows that the life of the age to come will rest on faith as completely as does the Christian life now. The contrast between faith and sight (2 Cor. v. 7) is not in mind here.

Hope, 'perseverance in faith' (Calvin), is faith with the main stress lying on its future aspect. It is directed towards what is not yet seen (Rom. viii. 21-5; cf. 2 Cor. iv. 18), and therefore means patient endurance, the endurance that finds the meaning of the present moment not in itself, but in God (see Rom. ii. 7, with the note). If this is so, it may be asked how *hope* can be held to *abide* in the age to come, when the temporal things of 2 Cor. iv. 18 have passed away, and we see no longer in a glass but face to face, and know as we have been known. The answer is not that the life of the age to come, or of heaven, admits of progress and development (we do not know whether this is true or not). It is because hope 'does not refer to the realization of a picture of the future drawn by man, but because it is a trust in God that looks away from itself and from the world, a trust that waits patiently for God's gift, and, when he has given it, is still not in full (*verfügenden*) possession, but in the serene (*getrosten*) confidence that what God has given God will maintain' (Bultmann, *T.W.N.T.* ii. 529). Further, like faith, hope presupposes and expresses a genuine and therefore unalterable truth about God. God is faithful (πιστός); that is, one in whom faith (πίστις) is properly reposed. Similarly, God is our hope; that is, one in whom hope is properly reposed. It is because they are thus rooted in the truth about God that faith and hope express a permanent truth about man. Compare xv. 19. This is why Paul can speak 'of faith, hope and love as things which will not cease, even when that which is perfect is come ... In other words he can conceive no state of perfection in which the unworldly is a mere possession. The openness of Christian existence is never-ending' (R. Bultmann, *Primitive Christianity in its Contemporary Setting* (1956), p. 208).

Finally, *love*. All through the chapter, as we have seen, the word has tended to shift in meaning. At first, we are dealing with the affirmation that it is better that men should love one another than that they should, for example, speak with tongues, or work miracles. As however Paul's description of love proceeds, it becomes apparent not only that the only human model he can have used is Jesus of Nazareth, but that the description is a description of the love of God, who alone loves spontaneously and without motivation (the language is Nygren's). Ideally, men should imitate (iv. 16; xi. 1) this love, and, through the gift of the Spirit, may in part do so, but even when they reproduce it least inadequately they must recognize that their love is derivative. 'We love, because he first loved us' (1 John iv. 19). Love, then, is a manifestation of God himself, proceeding from God himself, a manifestation both clearer and more profound than any that can be derived from prophecy or knowledge. Love never fails (verse 8), but abides even in the age to come, because it is the nature and being of God himself, and because (unlike prophecy and knowledge) it is an essential manifestation in human relations of what God is. It is not a virtue, among others, that men must achieve for themselves. 'Every attempt to understand love as a virtue and a work inverts the Gospel of 1 Cor. xiii into a law' (Bornkamm, op. cit., p. 111). It means, rather, the presence of Christ himself in the church.

Faith, hope, love: nowhere else does Paul quite so clearly combine these three words, but it is evident that his thought tended to bring them together, and to represent them as the central, essential, and indefectible elements in Christianity. See Col. i. 4 f.; 1 Thess. i. 3; v. 8. This makes unconvincing the view that 'the arrangement of the essential gifts into a group of three Paul borrowed from the style of the Hellenistic age' (Knox, *Gentiles*, p. 120; see also Lietzmann's excursus, which contains valuable information, though it is rightly corrected by Kümmel). Even less convincing is the suggestion that Paul derived his trilogy from a Hellenistic tetralogy, faith, *eros*, *gnosis*, and hope, by striking out *gnosis*.

Faith, hope, and love are all of eternal importance; **but the greatest** (Paul uses the comparative, *μείζων*; perhaps because he is putting *love* over against *faith* and *hope* considered as an alternative unit; more probably because the superlative, *μέγιστος*, was uncommon in Hellenistic Greek, occurring once only in the New Testament, at 2 Pet. i. 4—see M. i. 78) **of them is love.** *Love* is a property of God himself. When men put their trust in God they manifest the fact that he is trustworthy, and thus that he is love. As sinners, themselves unloving, there is nothing they can do but trust him, and trust—faith (*πίστις*)—is thus the indispensable condition not only of entering but of continuing in the Christian life. But God does not himself trust (in the sense of placing his whole confidence in and committing himself to some other being); if he did, he would not be God. When men hope in God they acknowledge that he is the Lord of the future, and that as they are dependent upon him now so they will always be. Man's hope bears witness to the eternity of God, and to his sovereignty. But God does not himself hope; he is what he is, and what he will be; though he accommodates himself to us in time he is not determined by the sequence of past, present, and future. If God hoped he would not be God. But if God did not love he would not be God. Love is an activity, the essential activity, of God himself, and when men love either him or their fellow-men they are doing (however imperfectly) what God does. '*Deus non dicitur fides aut spes absolute, amor dicitur*' (Bengel). It is above all in this sense that love is the greatest of gifts, though it is also true that it, beyond any other, such as miracle-working, is able to build up a Christian community in harmony and unity. There is no contradiction here with what Paul says elsewhere about faith. The faith by which alone man lays hold upon the gracious gift of justification expresses itself in love (Gal. v. 6).

29. xiv. 1-40. THE TESTS APPLIED TO TONGUES AND PROPHECY

(1) Pursue love as your aim, but strive for spiritual gifts, and especially that you may prophesy. (2) For he who speaks with a tongue speaks not to men but to God, for no one can understand him as in the Spirit[1] he speaks mysteries. (3) But he who prophesies speaks to men, and gives them edification, exhortation, and comfort. (4) He who speaks with a tongue builds up himself, but he who prophesies builds up the assembled company. (5) I wish you all to speak with tongues, but even more that you should prophesy; for he who prophesies is greater than he who speaks with tongues (unless the latter interprets what he says). (6) But now, brothers, think: if I come to you speaking with tongues, what good shall I do you, unless I speak to you in revelation, or in knowledge, or in prophecy, or in[2] teaching? (7) In the same way, inanimate objects that emit sound, whether flute or lyre, unless they make a distinction between the sounds they produce, how will anyone know what is being played on the flute or lyre? (8) And if the trumpet gives an undistinguishable call, who will arm himself for battle? (9) So is it also with you, when you speak with a tongue, unless you utter intelligible discourse, how will the substance of your speech be known? For you will be speaking into the air. (10) There are I don't know how many kinds of language in the world, and nothing is without its own language; (11) if then I do not know the meaning of the language, I shall be a foreigner to the man who is speaking, and in my eyes[3] the man who is speaking will be a foreigner. (12) So with yourselves, since you are men who strive for spiritual gifts, seek that you may abound in them for the building up of the church.

[1] For *πνεύματι*, G it have *πνεῦμα*.

[2] *ἐν* (before *διδαχῇ*) is omitted by P46 ℵ* D* G.

[3] *ἐν* is omitted by P46 D G 1739, wrongly; either to make this clause parallel with the preceding one, or to avoid the possible interpretation, He that speaks in me (that is, the Spirit) will be a foreigner. Zuntz, p. 104.

(13) So let him who speaks in a tongue pray that he may interpret it. (14) For if I pray in a tongue, my spirit prays, but my mind is inactive. (15) What is to be done then? I will pray[1] with the spirit, but I will pray[1] with the mind too. I will sing praise with the spirit, but I will sing with the mind too. (16) For if you say a blessing in the spirit, how will the man who occupies the place of the simple listener say the Amen to your thanksgiving? For he does not understand what you are saying. (17) You indeed are giving thanks well enough, but the other man is not being built up. (18) I thank God, I speak[2] with tongues more than any of you; (19) but in the assembly I desire to speak five words with my mind, that I may instruct others too, rather than tens of thousands of words in a tongue.

(20) Brothers, do not be children in intelligence; in wickedness be mere infants, but in intelligence be mature. (21) It is written in the Law, I will speak to this people by men of strange tongues and by the lips of strangers,[3] yet even so they will not listen to me, saith the Lord. (22) It follows that tongues serve as a sign not for the believing, but for the unbelieving, prophecy as a sign not for the unbelieving, but for the believing. (23) If then the whole church assembles together, and all its members are speaking with tongues, and unbelieving outsiders come in, will they not say that you are mad? (24) But if all are prophesying when an unbelieving outsider comes in, he is convicted by all, he is judged by all, (25) the secrets of his heart are laid bare, and so he will fall on his face and worship God, declaring that God truly is among you.

(26) What is to be done, then, brothers? When you assemble, each one of you has a hymn, a piece of teaching, a revelation, a tongue, an interpretation. Let all these

[1] In each case the subjunctive (προσεύξωμαι) appears as an alternative to the future indicative.

[2] I translate λαλῶ; the majority of MSS. have λαλῶν, P[46] has λαλεῖν. These are probably 'improvements', and should be rejected.

[3] For ἑτέρων, P[46] D G, the majority of Greek MSS., and the Latin and Syriac, have ἑτέροις. This reading, though ancient, is probably to be rejected as an assimilation to the ending of ἑτερογλώσσοις; Zuntz, p. 174.

be exercised for the building up of the community. (27) If there is speaking with tongues, let it be by two or at most three on each occasion, and one at a time, and let one member interpret. (28) But if there is no one to interpret, let the man who would speak with tongues keep silence in the assembly, and speak to himself and to God. (29) Let either two or three prophets speak, and let the others test what they say. (30) If a revelation is given to another sitting by, let the first keep silence; (31) for you can all prophesy, one by one, that all may learn and all receive exhortation. (32) And the spirits by which prophets speak are under the control of the prophets, (33) for God is not a God of disorder but of peace, as in all the churches of the saints.

(34)[1] Let women observe silence in the assemblies, for they do not have leave to speak, but must be in subjection, as also the Law says. (35) If they wish to learn anything, let them ask their own husbands at home; for it is a disgraceful thing for a woman to speak in assembly. (36) Or was it from you that the word of God went forth? Or are you the only people it has reached?

(37) If anyone thinks himself to be a prophet or spiritual person, let him recognize that what I am writing to you comes from the Lord;[2] (38) if anyone does not recognize this, he is not recognized.[3]

(39) So, my brothers, strive after the gift of prophecy, and do not forbid anyone to speak with tongues; (40) and let all things be done in a decent and orderly manner.[4]

The new chapter, though it begins by recognizing the primacy of love (chapter xiii), links up most naturally with xii. 31, and it is thereby confirmed (see pp. 297, 299) that chapter xiii, though

[1] D G and the Old Latin place verses 34 f. after verse 40. See the commentary.

[2] The translation follows the short text of D* G, and the Old Latin. Many MSS. add either *ἐντολή* or *ἐντολαί*.

[3] Reading *ἀγνοεῖται* with ℵ* A* G. Zuntz, pp. 107 f. prefers *ἀγνοείτω*, supported by P^{46} and B as well as the majority of MSS. But if the commentary is right *ἀγνοεῖται* is not as difficult as he thinks. D* has *ἀγνοεῖτε*, in which *-ε* may be no more than a phonetic error for *-αι* (M. ii. 70).

[4] See note 1.

entirely apposite, was probably written independently of its present context. Love is not mentioned among the gifts listed in xii. 28 because it does not stand on the same footing and belongs to a higher category. It is well to remember that the higher category exists, and forms a standard by which other gifts are judged; love is in fact the most practical consideration in dealing with a situation like that at Corinth; but there are other practical considerations to take into account too.

Pursue (διώκειν; cf. Rom. ix. 30 f.; xii. 13; xiv. 19; it is, as 1
near as may be, synonymous with the next verb, and, as Weiss points out, the awkwardness of this distinction which does not distinguish emphasizes the artificiality of the links between xii, xiii, and xiv) **love as your aim.** This charge applies to all Christians, and is fully consistent with the operation of gifts of all kinds. Assuming it, we can continue: **Strive for** (ζηλοῦν; this verb marks out the connection with xii. 31) **spiritual gifts, and especially that you** (addressed, according to Schlatter, to the *church*, which may be said to *prophesy* if there are prophets in it; but it is more probable that the same second person plural runs throughout the sentence—all should desire to love, to have spiritual gifts, to prophesy) **may prophesy.** We have already noted (p. 286) the Corinthian tendency to exaggerate the importance of the gift of speaking with tongues, and Paul's unwillingness to agree with this valuation. He now makes the point explicitly. *Especially* is not (as the English may suggest) a superlative, but a comparative (μᾶλλον), and, as the following verses show, it is with tongues that Paul is comparing prophecy. Not that speaking with tongues is anything other than a good gift from God; since it is a gift God chooses to give it would be wrong if men were to misprise it. It has its own value. **For he who speaks with a** 2
tongue speaks not to men (who cannot understand what he says) **but to God** (who himself inspires the speech and therefore understands it, even though it is cast in a form unintelligible by ordinary standards; cf. Rom. viii. 26 f.). It is clear that tongues are not directed to men, **for no one can understand** (literally, *hears*) **him as in the Spirit he speaks** (literally, *but in the Spirit*; there is an attractive but not quite convincing Western variant, 'but the Spirit speaks') **mysteries.** For *mysteries* see xiii. 2; xv. 51, and the notes. Here the meaning is simply

'secrets'; the speaker and God are sharing hidden truths which
3 others are not permitted to share. **But he who prophesies** (the word evidently refers much less to prediction than to exhortation and exposition of Christian truth) **speaks to men, and gives them** (the last three words are not in the Greek but are needed in English, which cannot make the following nouns the direct object of *speaks*) **edification** (that is, builds them up in the Christian life and Christian community; cf. iii. 10-17, and many other passages), **exhortation, and comfort.**

It is not to be thought that speaking with tongues does no good, but the good it does is limited by failure of the congrega-
4 tion at large to understand what is said. **He who speaks with a tongue builds up** (the verb cognate with *edification* in verse 3; the verb 'to edify' seems to be one that should be avoided because of its overtones in modern English, though there is no substitute for the noun) **himself** (and thus his speaking is a profitable exercise as far as he himself is concerned), **but he who prophesies builds up the assembled company** (not 'the church', for ἐκκλησίαν does not have the article; literally, *an assembly*, but the sense is *the assembly of which he is one member*; ἐκκλησία in the sense of *assembly* is frequent in this chapter).
5 The inevitable conclusion follows: **I wish you all to speak with tongues** (for speaking with tongues is a good thing, a gift from God by which you may all be individually built up), **but even more that you should prophesy** (since by this means the whole society will be built up). Otherwise put, **he who prophesies is greater than he who speaks with tongues (unless the latter interprets what he says).** He is greater, because he is a better servant (Mark x. 43 f., and parallels). Interpretation, it seems, often accompanied speaking with tongues (see xii. 10); it had the effect of turning tongues into prophecy. The last clause (bracketed in my translation) is expressed in an unusual construction (ἐκτὸς εἰ μὴ διερμηνεύῃ; not unnaturally, there are several variants), but there is no serious doubt of its meaning; on the grammar see B.D. §376.

Here one might expect the discussion to end. Paul has made his point. That he takes it up again probably means that the importance of tongues was being so warmly pressed in Corinth that he felt it necessary to emphasize his opinions as strongly as possible. **But now, brothers, think** (the last word is not in the Greek): **if I come to you** (the use of the first person singular makes the argument more urgent but is not essential to it; cf. *Romans*, p. 152) **speaking with tongues, what good shall I do you, unless I speak to you** (in addition, that is, or perhaps by an interpretation of the tongue) **in revelation, or in knowledge, or in prophecy, or in** (there is evidence—see note 2 on p. 312—for omitting this preposition) **teaching?** Paul sometimes uses the word *revelation* (ἀποκάλυψις) to denote the apocalyptic manifestation at the last day (Rom. ii. 5; viii. 19; 1 Cor. i. 7; 2 Thess. i. 7), but also for supernatural revelations, of the Gospel (Rom. xvi. 25—if this is Paul's), of celestial truths (2 Cor. xii. 1, 7), and of Christian duty (Gal. ii. 2). In the latter sense it is not easy, and perhaps not necessary, to distinguish it from prophecy. For *knowledge* see xii. 8, etc. If the preposition *in* is omitted before *teaching*, the effect is to make prophecy and teaching stand together as a pair, more closely connected with each other than either is with *revelation* and *knowledge*; it may be doubted, however, whether the shorter reading is original, and whether, if it is, it was intended by Paul to make a subtle distinction. For *teaching* (διδαχή) see Rom. vi. 17; xvi. 17, which are not closely parallel, and 1 Cor. xiv. 26; also, for the verb, Rom. xii. 7 (cf. Gal. vi. 6). The elucidation or application of Christian truth is intended. All these activities, which shade too finely into one another for rigid distinctions to be profitable or even accurate, are of advantage to the Christian assembly, but, without them, speaking with tongues is (as far as the assembly is concerned) sheer sound, signifying nothing. 6

The matter is brought out by an illustration. Its general drift is clear. Just as a man may (if he speaks with tongues) utter unintelligible noises which are of no use to those who hear him, or (if he prophesies) address them with rational speech, so a musical instrument may produce an ordered sequence of distinguishable notes (that is, a recognizable tune), or may simply make a noise. What is not clear is the construction of the Greek. This is because the first word in the sentence, here translated *In the same way*, has different meanings according to its accent. The translation assumes one accentuation (ὁμῶς); but it is possible to adopt another (ὅμως), which would require the

rendering, *yet*, *still*, *nevertheless*. Both ways of taking the word are accompanied by difficulty. The former occurs very seldom in Hellenistic Greek, though Paul appears to use it again at Gal. iii. 15, and Hellenistic examples have been adduced by J. Jeremias and R. Keydell, in *Z.N.T.W.* lii. 127 f.; liv. 145 f.; the latter involves disorder (hyperbaton) in the sentence, which we should have to render more or less as follows, 'Inanimate objects, though capable of sound, yet, if they do not distinguish . . ., how shall it be known. . .?'. There is no reason why Paul should not have occasionally used an uncommon word (perhaps he was abbreviating ὁμοίως, which he uses at vii. 3, 4, 22; Rom. i. 27), and we may (with B.D. §450; M. iii. 337 hesitates) choose the rendering given, though without re-
7 garding the matter as certain. **In the same way, inanimate objects that emit sound, whether flute or lyre, unless they make a distinction between the sounds they produce** (not sounding them all at once; cf. the sounds of xiii. 1), **how will anyone know** (literally, *how shall it be known*) **what is being played on the flute or lyre?** This is especially true and im-
8 portant when a particular tune is used to convey a message. **If the trumpet gives an undistinguishable call, who will arm** (Paul's word, παρασκευάζεσθαι, may be more general, but it is used with *arms*, ὅπλα, and the context justifies the rendering here) **himself for battle?** The answer is so evident that Paul
9 does not need to express it. **So is it also with you, when you speak with a tongue, unless you utter** (these two clauses are not really consistent with each other; for the double anticipation of the protasis see K. Beyer, *Semitische Syntax im Neuen Testament* I. i (1962), p. 82) **intelligible** (εὔσημον, here standing as the opposite of *undistinguishable* in verse 8; Alexander the false prophet, in ecstasy, utters φωνὰς ἀσήμους—Lucian, *Alexander* 13) **discourse, how will the substance of your speech be known? For you will be speaking into the air.** Compare ix. 26: a boxer whose blows fall only on the air will not win his fights; a speaker whose words do not enter into men's ears and minds will not convey his meaning. The expression was proverbial; examples are given by Weiss.

Again, Paul seems to have completed his argument but proceeds to drive it home further with another analogy before

turning to the practical application. **There are I don't know** 10
how many (εἰ τύχοι; cf. xv. 37) **kinds of language in the**
world, and nothing (Paul writes only the pronoun, οὐδέν; it is
attractive to think, as Lietzmann suggested, that he meant οὐδὲν
ἔθνος, *no race*) **is without its own language.** The point made
in this verse is simply that there are very many languages, so
many that no man can know them all. **If then I do not know** 11
the meaning of the language (in which I am addressed), **I**
shall be a foreigner (βάρβαρος) **to the man who is speaking,**
and in my eyes (ἐν ἐμοί; see note 3 on p. 312, and M. i. 103 f.;
B.D. §220) **the man who is speaking will be a foreigner.**
The Greeks (and Romans) used the word transliterated *barbarian* to denote anyone whose language, because they could
not understand it, sounded like mere babbling. Ovid (*Tristia*
v. 10 37), banished to Tomi on the Black Sea, declares, *barbarus*
hic ego sum, quia non intellegor ulli. **So with yourselves, since** 12
you are men who strive for (Paul uses the noun, ζηλωταί,
cognate with the verb used in verse 1) **spiritual gifts** (literally,
spirits; Paul normally uses the word, πνεῦμα, in the singular, with
reference to the Spirit of God, but here thinks of various
spiritual agencies producing various spiritual gifts; see verses
14, 15, 16, 32, and cf. 1 John iv. 1), **seek that you may abound**
in them (the last two words are not in the Greek) **for the**
building up of the church (or perhaps *the assembled company*;
cf. the use of the word ἐκκλησία in verse 4, with the note). This
recapitulates the argument of verses 1-5.

So let him who speaks in a tongue pray that he may 13
interpret it. This will have the effect of converting it into prophecy, or teaching; compare verse 5. Paul moves slightly now
to deal with prayer, which may be uttered in a tongue (cf. verse
2, *he speaks to God*), or rationally. **For if I pray in a tongue, my** 14
spirit prays, but my mind is inactive (literally, *unfruitful*,
i.e., it produces nothing, contributes nothing to the process).
It is evident that the *mind* is the rational element in man's being,
prized by many of Paul's contemporaries as the highest and
intrinsically good part of human nature. Paul did not rate
rationality so high; the *mind* is not sinless, but needs to be
renewed (Rom. xii. 2). *My spirit* is not so easy to understand. It
must be taken with the wording of the next verse, where *spirit*
recurs (without the possessive pronoun, though it would be

wrong to lay much stress on this). There are three main possibilities. (a) *My spirit* is part of my psychological make-up, a non-rational part serving as the counterpart of *my mind*. (b) My *spirit* is the spiritual gift entrusted to me, as in verse 12, or rather the particular spiritual agency which induces my inspired speech. (c) *My spirit* is the Holy Spirit as given to *me*. The verse would then correspond with Rom. viii. 26, where the Spirit is said to make intercession for the elect in unutterable speech. (a) is supported by the parallelism, but not by Paul's usage elsewhere. (c) would seem the most probable view if it were not for the pronoun *my*. To describe the Holy Spirit as in any sense *mine* is intolerable, and certainly not Pauline. (b) is the best view, though if stated as baldly as by Calvin (' "My spirit" will mean exactly the same as "the gift conferred on me" ') it is open to the objection that the gift itself cannot be said to pray. Paul's language lacks clarity and precision here because he is compressing into a few words the thoughts (1) that it is the Holy Spirit of God that is at work, inspiring Christian worship and prayer; (2) that the work of the Spirit is crystallized into a specific gift; (3) this gift is given in such personal terms to *me* that I can speak of it as *mine*—in short as *my spirit*, which, being what it is, operates through appropriate psychological channels independently of *my mind*.

The upshot of the matter is that if I pray in a tongue, part, and that a most significant part, of my nature remains out of action. This is not good for me, and it is not good for the com-
15 munity I ought to serve. **What is to be done then? I will pray with the spirit** (the pronoun is now dropped, but it is also dropped with *mind*), **but I will pray with the mind too.** See note 1 on p. 313; possibly *Am I to pray . . .? Let me pray. . . .* Rational prayer is not less spiritual than irrational. **I will sing praise** (ψάλλειν, originally 'to play the harp', then 'to sing to the harp'; here the Old Testament usage, e.g. Ps. vii. 18, is decisive; no different principle from that of prayer is involved) **with the spirit, but I will sing praise with the mind too.** The motive for this is clear; as always Paul is thinking of the benefit of the church as a whole. Just as a Christian is not free to exercise his liberty in regard to idolatrous food without consideration for his brother (viii. 13; x. 29), so he is not free to act

as he pleases in worship, but there too must consider the needs
of others. **For if you say a blessing** (cf. x. 16; a prayer of 16
thanksgiving is most naturally suggested, and this is confirmed
at the end of the verse, but Jewish usage, e.g. the well-known
synagogue prayer known as the Eighteen Blessings, shows that
any kind of prayer may be included) **in the spirit** (that is, in
the spirit *only*, not with the mind), **how will the man who
occupies the place** (that is, *fills the role*; for the expression cf.
Epictetus II. iv. 5, and the talmudic *male' mqom* . . ., quoted by
Bachmann; there is no ground for thinking of a specific location within the assembly, assigned e.g. to catechumens) **of the simple listener** (ἰδιώτης; transliterated into Hebrew and Aramaic, where it retains the sense of one who stands outside a particular activity or office—see especially Schlatter; here now one, now another is forced in to the role of ἰδιώτης as the gift of tongues goes round, but in verses 23 f. the ἰδιώτης is contrasted with *you*, and is therefore not a Christian) **say the Amen to your thanksgiving?** It was Jewish and early Christian custom for the congregation to signify its concurrence with the prayer by responding *Amen*; see Deut. xxvii. 14-26; Ps. cv. 48; 2 Esdras xv. 13; xviii. 6; S.B. iii. 456-61; Rev. v. 14; vii. 12; xix. 4; Justin, *Apology* I. lxv. 3; lxvii. 5. In these circumstances however the response becomes impossible; **for he does not understand what you are saying.** The responsibility of the church as a whole to hear, understand, test, and control is underlined; compare Schweizer 7fk, 23c.

It is not that speaking with tongues is in itself wrong; see
verse 2. **You indeed are giving thanks well enough, but the** 17
other man (a literal rendering of ὁ ἕτερος; for this expression cf. x. 29; Rom. xiii. 8) **is not being built up.** Compare verse 4. Speaking with tongues is a good thing; Paul himself does it, and
is glad to do it. **I thank God, I speak** (reading λαλῶ, in asynde- 18
ton; for the reading see note 2 on p. 313, and B.D. §415 against M. iii. 160) **with tongues more** (probably quantitative rather than qualitative; possibly both) **than any of you.** If this opinion is to be qualified at all it will be in the interests of *the other man.*
But in the assembly (ἐκκλησία; cf. verse 4) **I desire to speak** 19
five (a round number, used as such in Judaism—S.B. iii. 461 f., also G. Kittel, *Rabbinica* (1920)) **words with my mind** (cf. verse

14), **that I may instruct others too** (cf. verse 3), **rather than** (*rather* is not expressed in Greek; the use of ἤ alone may reflect Semitic idiom, but there are classical parallels; see M. ii. 442; iii. 32; B.D. §245) **tens of thousands of words in a tongue** (which I should speak not to men but to God). *Instruct* is a new word (κατηχεῖν), not used at xii. 8, 28 f.; xiv. 3, 6; see Gal. vi. 6. Evidently Paul considered instruction to be a particularly suitable activity for the Christian assembly. It should be noted that Paul does not contrast 'speaking with the mind' with 'speaking with the Spirit' (Bornkamm, *Gesammelte Aufsätze* ii (1959), p. 134), but with 'speaking with a tongue'. Prophecy and tongues are closely allied in that each is a speaking in Spirit, differentiated in that the prophet speaks with the mind also.

20 **Brothers** begins a new paragraph, and softens an outspoken command (cf. e.g. x. 1). It is time the Corinthians learned to adjust their scale of values and to make mature Christian judgements. Compare iii. 1 ff. **Do not be children in intelligence,** hankering after what is merely showy and outwardly impressive. **In wickedness** (cf. v. 8; Rom. i. 29) **be mere infants** (Paul uses here a different word from that of the first clause; possibly only for variation, but a younger child is suggested—παιδία; νηπιάζεσθαι), **but in intelligence be mature** (τέλειοι; for this word cf. ii. 6, 13). It is sufficiently evident from the epistle as a whole (and from 2 Corinthians) that the Corinthians had still a good deal to learn. They were proud of their achievements, but bickered among themselves, and preferred tongues to other gifts. Paul supports his argument by using the Old Testament.

21 **It is written in the Law** (the quotation comes from Isa. xxviii. 11 f., so that *law*, νόμος, is here used not for the Pentateuch alone but for the Old Testament generally; this usage appears elsewhere in the New Testament—Rom. iii. 19; John x. 34; xii. 34; xv. 25—and is rabbinic), **I will speak to this people by men of strange tongues** (ἑτερογλώσσοις) **and by the lips of strangers; yet** (καί is used adversatively) **even so they will not listen to me, saith the Lord.** This quotation is not given in agreement with the LXX; there is some evidence (Origen, *Philocalia* ix. 2) that Paul may have used here a version known also to the later Old Testament translator Aquila. It was probably the word 'men of other tongues' that caught his eye

and suggested the application of the passage to his discussion of 'tongues'. It is this, rather than the historical setting of the prophecy, in which Isaiah threatens his people, who have failed to listen to his words, with the foreign speech of Assyrian invaders, that is in Paul's mind. His point is simply that (according to the Lord himself) when he speaks to men by means of strange tongues they will not listen—that is, they will not hear in obedience and faith. Tongues therefore are (as Paul has said throughout the chapter) ineffective as a means by which persons other than the speaker may be built up. **It follows** from this 22
(i.e. from the fact that God has foretold that the wonder of strange tongues will not be attended to) **that tongues serve as** (not the Semitic predicative use of εἶναι εἰς; see B.D. §145) **a sign not for the believing, but for the unbelieving.** In what sense? Presumably, as a sign of judgement, as in, for example, a nearby passage in Isaiah (xx. 3), the naked and barefooted prophet is a sign of impending doom, of military overthrow and social servitude. When they are not met with faith (cf. Heb. iv. 2) tongues *serve* to harden and thus to condemn the unbeliever (cf. verses 23 f.); this is not their only purpose (as it was not the only purpose of the parables of Jesus, notwithstanding Mark iv. 11 f.), for they also serve to build up the speaker, and, though they do not build up, will at least not offend a Christian assembly that understands what is going on. For this twofold effect of one phenomenon we may compare Paul's use (in Rom. ix. 33) of another verse from Isa. xxviii together wth Isa. viii. 14: of the same Stone it can be said that it is a stone of stumbling and a rock of offence, and that he who believes in it (him) shall not be ashamed. So it is with tongues: the point might perhaps be more clearly put if it were said that they are a sign by which believers are distinguished from unbelievers, since the latter reveal themselves by the reaction described in verse 23.

Paul has now used his Old Testament quotation to bring out his point about speaking with tongues. Throughout the chapter so far, however, he has been concerned to contrast speaking with tongues with prophecy, and having said that *tongues serve as a sign not for the believing, but for the unbelieving*, it is natural for him to add as a balancing clause that **prophecy** serves **as a sign** (*serves as a sign* is not in the Greek but must be understood from the preceding sentence) **not for the unbelieving, but for the believing.** The question is whether the new clause really does balance the former. It is often said that *sign* must now be taken in a new sense: not as a sign of judgement, but as a sign of grace. Prophecy, by inviting and stimulating faith, indicates the gracious presence of God in the community in which it occurs. It is true that Paul's thought continues through the next few verses on these lines, but in the present verse the connection appears to be that prophecy acts upon the Corinthian believers in the same way that tongues act upon 'outsiders'. The Corinthians tend to shut their ears to prophecy because they gain more satisfaction from listening to tongues than from hearing their faults exposed and their duties pointed out in plain rational language. Thus they incur judgement (cf. xi. 34).

Paul's exposition in verses 20 ff. is both more profound and more coherent than some commentators appear to have recognized, but it is certainly obscure; his thought clears up as he turns to the practical demands of the church's evangelistic task.

23 **If then the whole church assembles together** (the English is pleonastic, in imitation of the Greek συνέλθῃ . . . ἐπὶ τὸ αὐτό; Paul uses this verb of the church assembly not only in verses 23, 26, but also in xi, 17, 20, which suggests that the two chapters are dealing with the same gathering—see below, pp. 325 f.), **and all its members** (the last two words are not in the Greek but are naturally to be understood) **are speaking with tongues** (not necessarily all at once, though verse 27 suggests that this sometimes happened, and made confusion worse confounded), **and unbelieving outsiders come in, will they not say that you are mad?** *Unbelieving outsider* renders two Greek nouns, connected by *or*: the first is the word (ἰδιώτης) used in verse 16 and there translated 'simple listener', the second that which we meet in verse 22 (and frequently in Paul and elsewhere). It seems clear that the first is now used in a new sense, since in verse 16 it referred to a member of the church (see the note). Neither in verse 16 nor here can it refer to an 'intermediate' group, half-way between the full Christian and the complete outsider. That it here refers to one who is not a member of the church, or even a catechumen, is shown by verses 21 f., and by his comment, *You are mad*. The two words in fact express (as is

brought out in the translation) one idea; as Lietzmann says, they are respectively the subjective (*unbelieving*) and objective (*outsider*) description of one who is not a Christian. It is significant that the order is reversed in verse 24. These outsiders are important; they are 'the real yardstick for estimating the value of ministries' (Schweizer 22 f, cf. 28c).

It is important to note that such persons could find their way into the Christian assembly at Corinth. Paul does not say that this always happened, but he evidently has no difficulty in conceiving it. It happened in the synagogue, and in pagan religious gatherings too (Apuleius, *Metamorphoses* xi. 15: *Videant irreligiosi; videant, et errorem suum recognoscant* (Let the outsiders see; let them see, and recognize their error—that is, as you take part in the religious procession of Isis; this certainly was followed by a rite that Lucius was not at liberty to divulge)). This raises the question what kind of assembly Paul is describing in chapter xiv. It is often said, with reference to verse 26, that the assembly of chapter xiv is an informal kind of 'service of the word', in which hymns, prayers, and various kinds of sermon have their place, but not the Christian supper. There is no evidence to support this view, apart from the fact that in chapter xiv nothing is said about eating and drinking; this silence is quite inconclusive, since in this chapter Paul is dealing with various forms of Christian speech, and sticks firmly to his point. It is important not to assume for the Pauline churches practices that became usual at a later time, and there is no reason why xi. 17-34 and xiv. 1-40 should not refer to the same gathering; see G. Bornkamm, *Das Ende des Gesetzes* (1952), p. 113, note 2, and the references there; also Allo's excursus on the question, though Allo holds, without giving any reason, that outsiders who had taken part in the fellowship meal were excluded, and the doors shut, before the eucharist properly so-called began. The Corinthian supper (see the commentary on x. 16-22; xi. 17-34, and Introduction, p. 26) was a common meal, in the course of which a loaf was broken and distributed (by whom we do not know), and a cup of wine shared. This was probably the main, perhaps the only, weekly meeting of the church; and in a church so given to speaking with tongues it is hard to think that no such speaking, and no prophesying, accompanied the meal—that is, the material of chapters xi and xiv belongs together. There is no reason, further, to suppose that these meetings always took place indoors. Not every Jewish community had a building to meet in (cf. Acts xvi. 13). Whether out-of-doors or inside, unbelievers might arrive by chance, or be brought as guests by friends who were Christians. The next verse shows good reason why such visits should be encouraged.

The outsider's comment on a gathering speaking with tongues must not be misunderstood. *You are mad* (μαίνεσθε) does not mean, You are suffering from mental disease, but You are possessed; it could suggest something like the Bacchic frenzy of men believed to be overpowered and used by a superhuman force. A modern observer (and some ancients, such as Festus—Acts xxvi. 24) might well suppose the Corinthians to be out of their wits; many of their contemporaries will have seen in the same events a supernatural phenomenon. To accept the supernatural origin of tongues, however, is not in itself to be a Christian; see xii. 1 ff. The great deficiency of the gift of tongues is that it fails to make clear the fundamental proposition, Jesus is Lord. Tongues are thus a quite inadequate evangelistic agency. Compare Acts ii. 13, where the speakers are taken to be drunk.

24 **But if all are prophesying when** (Paul's καί, *and*, gives a
slightly Semitic turn to the construction) **an unbelieving outsider** (see above) **comes in, he is convicted** (ἐλέγχεται; cf.
John xvi. 8, and my note; the word is used by Greek moralists
of the work of the conscience) **by all, he is judged** (ἀνακρίνεται;
cf. iv. 3—the work of the Spirit in prophecy is no purely human
25 judgement) **by all, the secrets of his heart are laid bare.**
The man's conscience is exposed and quickened. There is no need to see here (as e.g. Héring does) a miraculous gift of thought-reading. The moral truth of Christianity, proclaimed in inspired speech, including no doubt the testimony of those who had been fornicators, idolaters, and the like, but had been washed, sanctified, and justified (vi. 9 ff.), the prophetic word of God, which is sharper than any two-edged sword (Heb. iv. 12), are sufficient to convict a sinner. God's word effects its entrance through the conscience, and then creates religious conviction. **So he will fall on his face** (for this attitude of worship cf. e.g. Gen. xvii. 3; Luke v. 12; Rev. vii. 11; xi. 16; it bears witness to a

profound sense of unworthiness, as well as of the immediate presence of God) **and worship God, declaring that God truly is among you** (ἐν ὑμῖν, not *in you*, which might be the impression of enthusiasm produced by speaking with tongues). Moral conviction distinguishes New Testament Christianity from other forms of religious feeling. Dionysus might evoke frenzy (such as speaking with tongues) in his devotees, but it is the God whom Paul knew from the Old Testament, and as the Father of Jesus Christ, who is the judge of all the earth. Paul may have had in mind 1 Kings xviii. 39 (Schlatter), or Dan. ii. 47; Isa. xlv. 14; Zech. viii. 23 (Wendland). No indication is given that such a convicted sinner was to be excluded from any part of the supper-gathering; the opposite is implied. See xvi. 22, with the note; and compare G. Bornkamm, *Das Ende des Gesetzes* (1952), p. 126.

Final instructions on the conduct of a church assembly, in which speaking with tongues and prophecy take place, follow.
What is to be done, then, brothers? The motivation of the 26
discussion is not exclusively practical, since important questions of principle and priority are involved, but the conclusion can and must be given practical form. **When you assemble, each one of you** (the last two words help out the English, and are supplied by many, but not all, Greek MSS.) **has a hymn** (ψαλμόν, but a fresh, perhaps spontaneous, composition, not an Old Testament psalm, is intended; cf. Col. iii. 16; Eph. v. 19), **a piece of teaching** (for this and the next word cf. verse 6), **a revelation, a tongue** (that is, a communication made in an unintelligible tongue), **an interpretation** (of a communication made in a tongue). *Each one* must be taken seriously here, as at xii. 7. Church meetings in Corinth can scarcely have suffered from dullness, and no doubt Paul's exhortation was relevant: **Let all these be exercised for the building up of the community.** The last three words are not in the Greek, but repeatedly (e.g. verse 4) Paul chooses to apply the metaphor of edification to the whole body of Christians rather than to the individual. That many in Corinth exercised their gifts in the interests of self-development and even of self-display can hardly be doubted; this was contrary to the law of love which regulates all Christian behaviour. It is possible (Lietzmann) that Paul's

meaning is, 'Let each one who has a hymn ... exercise it for ...'; but this is not what the Greek says, and there is no
27 difficulty in taking it literally. **If there is speaking with tongues** (a paraphrase; literally, *if anyone speaks with tongues*), **let it be by two or at most three on each occasion** (κατά is used distributively), **and one at a time** (on ἀνὰ μέρος see Moule, p. 67), **and let one member interpret.** Speaking with tongues had value only if interpretation (cf. verse 5) made it possible for the church as a whole to understand what was being said; if more than one spoke at once, or even if a large number spoke consecutively, interpretation would become impossible. Interpretation might also fail through lack of a Christian with
28 the appropriate gift. **If there is no one to interpret, let the man who would speak with tongues** (no subject is expressed in Greek; one is required in order to avoid ambiguity) **keep silence in the assembly** (ἐν ἐκκλησίᾳ; see verse 4, and cf. verse 33; he will waste the assembly's time, and repel any outsider who may be present; what he does at home, privately, is another matter). Let him **speak** only **to himself and to God.** Compare verse 2. The two datives (ἑαυτῷ, τῷ θεῷ) ought perhaps to be translated differently: *to* God, but *for* himself, for his own advantage. Paul does not suggest that prayer in a tongue is self-addressed delusion. It is genuine prayer, addressed to God, though only the speaker can participate in it.

29 Rules for prophets follow. **Let either two or three prophets speak** (that is, in any meeting of the church; here, and with those who speak with tongues, the limitation is imposed by time), **and let the others test** (διακρίνειν; cf. xi. 29, 31, and the notes) **what they say.** *The others* may mean 'the other prophets, who do not on this occasion prophesy', or 'the other members of the church'. The latter is more probable; Paul gives us no ground for thinking that only prophets were capable of testing prophetic messages, and the whole church appears to be involved in passages such as 1 Thess. v. 21; compare also 1 John iv. 1; *Didache* xi. 2-7. Indeed, the long section on spiritual gifts, which began in chapter xii, proceeds on the assumption that all spiritual manifestations must be tested, and the test provided in xii. 3 is one that can be applied by any Christian, whether himself a prophet or not.

We are reminded by the next verse that it is supernaturally inspired speech (and not prepared sermons) that is in question.
If a revelation is given (the verb, ἀποκαλυφθῇ, cognate with 30
the noun, ἀποκάλυψις, *revelation*, used above at verse 6) **to another sitting by, let the first** (i.e., the one who has first begun to prophesy) **keep silence** (cf. verse 34). It is clear that the spirit now wishes to communicate a fresh truth through a different speaker; his is the only authority capable of determining and revising the proceedings of a church gathering; see Schweizer, 7m, 24l (against Knox, *Gentiles*, p. 121). It is implied (and will shortly be stated) that prophets, though inspired, are
able to control their speech. **For you can all prophesy, one** 31
by one, that all may learn, and all receive exhortation. It seems natural that *all* should be taken in the same sense at each occurrence; all members of the church, therefore, may, on occasion, prophesy. This means that the *prophets* of xii. 28 may (notwithstanding xii. 29) turn out to be a group co-extensive with the church itself (cf. Num. xi. 29; Acts ii. 16 ff.). Paul does not however assert that all Christians necessarily will take part in the activity technically described as prophesying, only that all may do so. It is not any human decision that makes a man a prophet, or prevents him from being a prophet. The decision lies wholly within the freedom of the Holy Spirit, and prophecy is a function rather than an office.

Having emphasized that every member of the church may at the will of the Spirit act as a prophet Paul returns to the necessary practical caution. **The spirits by which prophets speak** 32
(literally, *prophets' spirits*; for this use of *spirit* in the plural cf. verse 12 above) **are under the control of the prophets** (so that a prophet cannot plead, as some in Corinth may have done, that he must continue speaking because the Spirit compels him to do so; if there is reason for him to be silent he can be silent),
for God is not a God of disorder but of peace. God himself 33
is not characterized by, and is therefore not the cause of, disorder. If disorder appears in the Corinthian assembly it has been caused by some agent other than God. Conversely, peace in the society is a mark of the presence and work of God. This is true (ideally) not only in Corinth, but universally—**as in all the churches** (or assemblies) **of the saints** (cf. i. 1). This

thought is taken up in verse 36, with perhaps the suggestion that there are Christian assemblies elsewhere from whose example the Corinthians might learn a lesson; they are not to think of themselves as the beginning or the end of the Gospel, nor are they the whole people of God. It may be that verse 36 should follow immediately upon verse 33; see below.

Verse 33b, however, is sometimes taken closely with verse 34 which introduces a reference to a special example of disorder in the Corinthian assembly. It is against this that *in the churches* and *in the assemblies* (both translating ἐν ταῖς ἐκκλησίαις) follow very awkwardly, and verse 34 is best taken as a new beginning. This observation is important, because verses 34, 35 are placed by the Western Text (see note 1 on p. 314) after verse 40, and, taking them as a unit, it is possible to argue either that this is their rightful place, or that they were not an original part of the epistle, but a marginal note, based on 1 Tim. ii. 11 f. and inserted by copyists at different points. It is a strong argument in favour of the latter view that there appears to be a contradiction between verses 34 f. and what is said about the role of women in worship in xi. 5. On the other hand, it may be argued that verses 34 f. appear to interrupt the discussion of prophecy in the assembly, and might for this reason have been moved from their original place by copyists wishing to produce a smoother text. The textual problem turns to some extent upon exegesis, and we must therefore consider the meaning of verses 34 f., and return to the question of their authenticity and position.

34 **Let women observe silence in the assemblies** (of the church), **for they do not have leave to speak, but must be in subjection** (reading the imperative, ὑποτασσέσθωσαν; it changes the construction—see B.D. §479—but not the sense, on which see Barth *C.D.* III. iv. 172-6, if the infinitive of the Western Text is read), **as also the Law says. Paul does not** say to which part of the Old Testament (*the Law* can mean so much; see verse 21) he refers; presumably Gen. iii. 16. For the relation between man and woman see the discussion in xi. 3-15, and the commentary. The present passage seems more wooden, less flexible, and to take less account of the renewal of the created order in Christ; this may be because we have here the work of a Deutero-Pauline writer (such as the author of 1

Timothy), or because Paul is here refraining from discussion and stating a practical conclusion without giving reasons and qualifications. The command that women should be silent does not mean that they should take no interest in what happens in the assembly, of which they are members. They will contribute
nothing, but **if they wish to learn anything, let them ask** 35
their own husbands at home. The verse contemplates married women, whose husbands are Christians. *A fortiori*, unmarried women and the wives of unbelievers will not speak in the assembly; if they wish to learn they must presumably persuade married friends to put questions to their husbands. Nothing is said of any minister or teacher who may or should be consulted about the content, interpretation, or application of Christian truth. As at xi. 13 f., Paul appeals (not only to the Old Testament but also) to the common feeling of mankind. **It is a disgraceful thing for a woman to speak in assembly** (ἐν ἐκκλησίᾳ; perhaps here the sense would be given by 'in public'). The reader will recall Aristophanes's *Ecclesiazusae*, in which the women of Athens take over the city's *ecclesia* (assembly). This is comedy to Aristophanes, but the sort of comedy that must certainly have confirmed Paul in his view, if he ever saw it played. Kümmel aptly quotes Plutarch, *Conjugal Precepts* 31, Not only the arm but the voice of a modest woman ought to be kept from the public, and she should feel shame at being heard, as at being stripped. The next paragraph, 32, contains an equally apt sentence: She should speak either to, or through, her husband. 'In gatherings for worship the ancient synagogue did not on principle forbid women to speak in public, but did so in practice' (S.B. iii. 467).

Is it possible to reconcile these verses with xi. 5, where Paul, assuming that women will pray and prophesy, orders them to be veiled when doing so? It cannot be said that in xi. 5 he only grudgingly permits them to speak, or refers to a practice of which he disapproves; there is nothing to suggest either this, or that the speaking referred to in xi. 5 takes place in a private house-gathering, and not in the church assembly. Only special pleading (Schlatter is very unconvincing here) can deny that chapter xi concedes the right of women (suitably clothed) to pray and prophesy in a public meeting of the church. Nor is it very convincing to argue that *to speak* (in verse 34, λαλεῖν) does not refer to such praying and prophesying, but to uninspired speech, especially the asking of questions that might seem to pass judgement (verse 29) on what had been said. It is true that the verb does in Classical Greek bear the meaning 'to chatter', and it would be understandable that Paul should wish to stem an outburst of feminine loquacity; but in the New Testament, and in Paul, the verb normally does not have this meaning, and is used throughout chapter xiv (verses 2, 3, 4, 5, 6, 9, 11, 13, 18, 19, 21, 23, 27, 28, 29, 39) in the sense of inspired speech. It is not impossible that Paul should now use it in a new sense (promptly reverting to the old in verse 39), but it is unlikely. It must be remembered that according to Acts xxi. 9, women prophets were not unknown in the church. Only two possibilities are worthy of serious consideration.

(a) Paul did not write verses 34 f. They were added later as a marginal note (there is little to be said for the view that they were Paul's own marginal addition), at a time when good order was thought more important than the freedom of the Spirit. There is much to be said for this view, especially since the language of these verses can be explained as based upon 1 Tim. ii. 11 f., but the textual evidence is not quite strong enough to make it compelling. The Western editors may have moved the verses because they seemed out of place. If any significant MS. omitted the verses altogether it would probably be right to follow it.

(b) Paul had been informed of feminist pressure (possibly of feminine chatter) which was contributing seriously to the disorder of the Christian assembly in Corinth, and took energetic measures to stamp it out. He cannot have disapproved on principle of contributions made by women to Christian worship and discussion or he would not have allowed xi. 5 to stand in his epistle, but in the interests of peace and good order he could command the women to be silent, precisely as he could give orders for a male prophet to be silent if his continued speech was likely to prove unedifying (verse 30). Sevenster (*Seneca*, p. 198) may be right in saying that 'Paul is probably alluding in the first place to a passion for discussion which could give rise to heated argument between a wife and husband'.

(a) is supported by the fact that verse 36 links up well with verse 33. (b) may find some support in that it seems to refer to a specifically Corinthian practice or argument, such as could suggest the reply of verse 36. On the whole, (a) may be preferred though the matter is not certain. Calvin, though he does not refer explicitly to the problem of contradiction with xi. 5, may be given the last word. 'The discerning reader should come to the decision, that the things which Paul is dealing with here, are indifferent, neither good nor bad; and that they are forbidden only because they work against seemliness and edification.'

The Corinthians will be well advised to have an eye to general Christian practice; they do not have a monopoly of the Gospel, or of its interpretation. **Was it from you that the word of God** 36
went forth? The next clause shows that this question does not carry the implication that Jerusalem, the ultimate origin of the Christian mission, alone had the right to decree church practices. **Or are you the only people it has reached?** There are now many Christian churches, and, though Paul does not exclude the possibility that all but one may have fallen into error (he certainly believed that the Jerusalem apostles could err: Gal. ii. 11), it would certainly be temerarious on the part of the Corinthians to suppose that they were right and the rest of the Christian world wrong.

This thought, and the fear that he would encounter opposition in Corinth, lead naturally to the closing verses of the chapter, which are in fact a conclusion of the whole argument, and not simply a resumption of the earlier discussion of prophecy. **If anyone thinks himself to be a prophet or spiritual person** (cf. xii. 1; here the reference is undoubtedly to *person* not *gift*) **. . .** No doubt there were (as this verse implies) some who wrongly supposed this; perhaps this was what had happened with the women, some of whom may have confused a natural desire to talk with the operation of the Holy Spirit. It will be a mark of true spiritual inspiration that one should **recognize that what I am writing to you comes from the Lord** (see note 2 on p. 314; many MSS. have '. . . is the Lord's command', or 'commands'; it is much more likely that the short text was made more explicit by the addition of *command(s)* than *vice versa*). Compare vii. 25, 40. Paul does not mean that

he is quoting the teaching of Jesus, but that 'he too has the
38 mind of Christ', and has 'authority for building you up'. **If anyone does not recognize this, he is not recognized.** See note 3 on p. 314. Paul means that he does not recognize the man in question as inspired in his opinion, not that he does not recognize him as a Christian. There is nothing here to suggest excommunication, nor is it necessary to suppose (with e.g. Lietzmann) that the man *is not recognized*, known, by God. Compare however 1 John iv. 6 (Allo).

39 Paul now sums up for the last time. **So, my brothers, strive after** (ζηλοῦν; cf. verse 1) **the gift of prophecy, and do not forbid** (possibly conative: Make no attempt to prevent . . .; M. i. 125; but probably the prohibition is general) **anyone to speak with tongues.** This acceptance of tongues, and preference for and cultivation of prophecy, is in accord with the argument of the chapter as a whole. Compare 1 Thess. v. 19 ff.

40 **Let all things be done in a decent and orderly manner**—by following the advice of verses 26-33 (35). For *decent* compare vii. 35; xii. 23 f.; Rom. xiii. 13; 1 Thess. iv. 12. The group of words is characteristically Pauline. *Orderly* suggests (but is not exhausted in) the idea of members of the church doing things one at a time, not all at once. The motive of Paul's advice goes back to verse 33a.

(e) THE RESURRECTION

30. xv. 1-11. THE COMMON GOSPEL

(1) I draw your attention, brothers, to the Gospel which I preached to you, which you also received, by which also you stand, (2) through which also you are saved; I ask you to note with what form of words I preached the Gospel to you—supposing that you hold it fast,[1] unless indeed you believed to no purpose. (3) For, first of all, I handed on to you that which I too received, namely that

[1] For εἰ κατέχετε D G have ὀφείλετε κατέχειν, *you ought to hold it fast.* This is an 'improvement'. B.D. §478 regard εἰ (omitted by P^{46}) as another, but the text as translated, though difficult, is not impossible and should be preferred. There is a very important note in Zuntz, pp. 254 f.

Christ died for our sins according to the Scriptures, (4) and that he was buried, and that according to the Scriptures he was raised on the third day, (5) and that he appeared to Cephas, then to the Twelve;[1] (6) then he appeared to more than 500 brothers at once, of whom the majority remain to this day, though some have fallen asleep; (7) then he appeared to James, then to all the apostles. (8) Last of all, as to one hurried into the world before his time, he appeared to me too. (9) For I am the least of the apostles, not worthy to be called an apostle, since I persecuted the church of God. (10) But by God's grace I am what I am; and the grace which he bestowed upon me did not prove vain, for I laboured more abundantly than all of them—though it was not I, but the grace of God with me.[2] (11) Whether then it was I or they, so we preach, and so you believed.

Most of the sections of the epistle have begun with a clear reference to the reasons that had led Paul to write them—news, for example, received from Chloe's household (i. 11), or questions asked in a Corinthian letter (vii. 1, etc.). No such reference is made in the present paragraph, and it is not till xv. 12 that we learn that there were some in Corinth (of whom Paul had heard, possibly through Stephanas, Fortunatus, and Achaicus—xvi. 17) who held the view that there was no resurrection of the dead. Throughout chapter xv Paul deals with this erroneous opinion, its presuppositions and its consequences. In doing so he finds it necessary to begin some way back; hence the present paragraph, which is intended to call to mind that the resurrection of Christ played an essential part in Paul's preaching, and indeed in all Christian preaching. Paul plunges directly into the theme.

I draw your attention (γνωρίζω, at xii. 3 translated *make* 1
plain; essentially it means 'I cause to know' but naturally it derives its precise meaning from the context, which here is somewhat embarrassed—Paul is reminding the Corinthians of what they ought never to have forgotten; cf. Gal. i. 11), **brothers**

[1] The Western Text pedantically corrects to *Eleven*. There is no need to treat the whole clause as a gloss (Weiss).

[2] For σὺν ἐμοί, P^{46} with many other MSS. has ἡ σὺν ἐμοί. This is textually secondary but gives the right interpretation.

(cf. i. 1), **to the Gospel** (see i. 17) **which I preached to you, which you also** (*καί*, here and in the next two clauses, introduces the succeeding steps which should follow the preaching of the Gospel) **received** (see verse 3), **by which also** (*καί*) **you stand** (the following discussion, like many earlier passages in the epistle, will throw much doubt on the security of the Corinthians' faith, but Paul always believes, and writes, the
2 best of his people; for the thought cf. Rom. v. 2), **through which also** (*καί*) **you are saved.** In view of Paul's common usage of the verb *to save* (*σώζειν*; Rom. v. 9 f.; cf. xiii. 11) we should probably take *you are saved* as a futuristic present. Unless men have believed in vain (a serious possibility; see verse 10), salvation, though still to come, is assured. The opening clauses have, perhaps, flattered the Corinthians a little (every good teacher and pastor knows how to use what may look like flattery but is really encouragement), but they have also opened the way for a summary of the Gospel.

First, however, possible ill-effects of the *captatio benevolentiae* must be guarded against by an outspoken warning; the parenthetical position—in thought as well as in grammar—of the warning is possibly the cause of the grammatical obscurity of the next verse. There are two principal ways (much fuller accounts in e.g. Héring and Allo) in which it can be taken. (a) The opening word is an interrogative pronoun (*τίνι*), and we may place a full stop after *you are saved*, and continue with a direct question: With what form of words (or, With what reasoning—*λόγῳ*) did I preach to you....? (b) Preferably (Robertson, pp. 738, 954; also Kümmel), we may continue the verb (*I draw your attention*) from verse 1, and take the pronoun to introduce an indirect question which is virtually indistinguishable from the relative clauses that precede it (*which I preached, which you received, by which you stand, through which you are saved*). For the purpose of our translation it is convenient to introduce a verb in order to keep the sentence going. **I ask you to note with what form of words I preached the Gospel to you.** *Form of words* seems appropriate, for Paul is about to quote material, apparently in the form in which he had committed it to his converts.

This material, the Gospel itself, ought to be familiar; but

Paul cannot be certain of this, and adds, ... **supposing that you hold it fast** (see note 1 on p. 334), **unless indeed** (ἐκτὸς εἰ μή; the same construction as at xiv. 5) **you believed to no purpose.** The exact meaning of *to no purpose* (εἰκῇ) is not clear; probably Origen is right in his definition, 'Those who believe for a time, and in time of trial turn away, believe *to no purpose* (εἰκῇ)'. On this view, 'to hold fast' (cf. xi. 2) and 'to believe to no purpose' are opposites, and the same thing is said twice, positively and negatively. There is no reason why this should not be so, and no reason to complain that Paul's conditional sentence is illogical (on the ground that he could point out the wording of his Gospel whether the Corinthians held fast to it or not). He is simply giving utterance to his uncertainty whether he can depend on the Corinthians or not, before coming to the substance of his Gospel.

For, first of all (this English phrase is intended to retain 3
the ambiguity of the Greek ἐν πρώτοις, which may indicate priority either in time or in importance—naturally the two may well coincide), **I handed on to you that which I too received.** Paul is not the originator of tradition, but a link in the chain (Schweizer, note 306). For the language compare xi. 23. Here Paul does not say that he received the message in question *from the Lord*, but the omission is probably not important. In chapter xi he was emphasizing the authoritative origin of what he had handed on to the Corinthians; here the content rather than the origin of his teaching bears the stress. It is not possible on the basis of this passage to draw a nice distinction between the apostle's preaching in which he set forth the Gospel publicly, and his private teaching of converts and catechumens. The content of his public proclamation was Christ crucified (ii. 2), and the next few verses show that what he handed on was the same. That is, though the use of language proper to traditionary processes is important, and shows Paul's concern for the preservation of true Christian doctrine, it must not be pressed too far; Paul was a Christian rabbi, handing on a body of established truth within the circle of his pupils, but at the same time he was an evangelistic preacher; he preached what he taught, and he taught what he preached.

The content of the Gospel is summed up in three short

clauses. Paul's teaching was **that Christ died for our sins**
4 **according to the Scriptures, and that he was buried, and that according to the Scriptures he was raised on the third day.** The three clauses are linked in simple parataxis by the word *and* (*καί*). This recalls the Semitic style of the gospels, but ought not too readily to be described as a Semitism; the short independent propositions, not subordinated to one another, reflect the nature of proclamation.

The first proposition explicitly relates the death of Christ to sin, but gives no precise indication what the relation is. *Christ died for* (*ὑπέρ*) *our sins.* The preposition normally means 'on behalf of' (and is thus usually used with persons, e.g. Rom. v. 8), but this meaning is clearly impossible here; indeed it means nothing different from the preposition (*περί*) used in the similar statement at Gal. i. 4 (cf. Rom. viii. 3). Both mean 'concerning', 'with reference to', 'in order to deal with'. The distinction between the prepositions was wearing thin in Hellenistic times (see M. i. 105), though it had not quite disappeared: the word Paul uses here may convey a hint of a double meaning—Christ died on our behalf, that is, to deal with our sins. How the death of Christ dealt with our sins is a question not discussed here. The primitive proclamation was, it seems, content to affirm that it was so; Paul elsewhere devotes his theological powers to explaining the affirmation; here he does not do so, partly because his main intention was simply to indicate the content and wording of the preaching, and partly because it was the resurrection not the death of Christ that occupied his attention.

Some theological exposition however is given in the words *according to the Scriptures.* Christ's death happened in fulfilment of Scripture. This means that it was not fortuitous, but willed and determined by God, and that it formed part of the winding up of his eternal purpose, that is, that it was one of those eschatoogical events that stand on the frontier between the present ag e and the age to come, in which the divine purpose reaches its completion. It is perhaps reasonable to add that a death that happened *according to the Scriptures* further invites interpretation in Old Testament categories—for example, of sacrifice, of punishment and atonement, of the remnant, and of the sufferings endured by the people of God on their way into the good time to come. So much may be said in general terms, but it is necessary also to ask the question, What Scriptures were they that Paul (and his apostolic colleagues) believed to have been fulfilled in the death of Christ? It has often been answered that the chief passage in mind is the prophecy of the Suffering Servant of the Lord in Isa. lii. 13–liii. 12; this however should not be too easily assumed. In favour of the identification see O. Cullmann, *Christologie des Neuen Testaments* (1957), pp. 75 f., 79 (E.T., 76, 79); against, M. D. Hooker, *Jesus and the Servant* (1959), pp. 117-20; F. Hahn, *Christologische Hoheitstitel* (1964), pp. 56 f., 197-213. The connection with *our sins* is not decisive, since this phrase may be a Pauline addition to the primitive formula (Hooker, op. cit., p. 119); in any case, Paul is capable of discussing the relation between the death of Christ and sin without allusion to Isa. liii, and in fact very seldom makes any reference to this passage. It may well be that the general allusion to the Scriptures was made before specific passages were alleged in support of it. Christian conviction saw in the death of Christ a divine act that must have been foretold because it was a manifestation of the eternal will of God; out of this conviction arose the search of the Old Testament which in due course produced an armoury of testimonies. Compare Héring, who notes that allusions to Ps. cxviii. 22 and Deut. xxi. 22 do not seem probable. Schlatter adds as possible allusions (which are nevertheless not probable) Ps. cxliii. 2 (Rom. iii. 20; Gal. ii. 16), Ps. lxix. 10 (Rom. xv. 3), the reference to Passover in 1 Cor. v. 7, and that to the means of atonement in Rom. iii. 25.

It is surprising to find specific reference to the fact *that he was buried*. Probably 'the burial was included in the *kerygma*, not because it had any specific significance in itself, or fulfilled the Scriptures, but because it was the necessary stage between death and resurrection, and moreover confirmed the reality of both' (Hooker, op. cit. p. 120). If he was buried he must have been really dead; if he was buried, the resurrection must have been the reanimation of a corpse. Paul does not go on to narrate the discovery, reported in the gospels, of the empty tomb. This may mean (since 1 Cor. xv. represents a tradition earlier than any of the gospels) that the story of the empty tomb is a late construction, based on the conviction, itself grounded in the appearances, that Jesus was alive. On the other hand, it may be urged that this inference, if made, was valid: if he was buried, and was subsequently seen alive outside his grave, the grave must have been empty, and may well have been seen to be empty.

The third clause is expressed with a different tense of the verb: *and that . . . he was raised* (ἐγήγερται, perfect). In contrast with *died* (ἀπέθανεν), and *was buried* (ἐτάφη), both of which are aorist tenses, the new clause suggests both that the raising happened, and that it remains in force. Christ died, but he is not dead; he was buried, but he is not in the grave; he was raised, and he is alive now (cf. M. ii. 137, 141; B.D. §342; Robertson, p. 896). The order of words in the Greek suggests, though it does not require, that *according to the Scriptures* should be taken with *on the third day*. It is not impossible however to connect the Scripture reference with *he was raised* (so B. M. Metzger, *J.T.S.* (new series) viii. 118-23, comparing 1 Macc. vii. 16 f.), and the translation is intended to leave open both possibilities. It is not easy to produce Old Testament documentation for *the third day*. Hos. vi. 2 is not very convincing; Jonah ii. 1 f. is used in Matt. xii. 40, but no other New Testament writer shows a similar interest in Jonah and the whale; 2 Kings xx. 5; Lev. xxiii. 11 are not more helpful (B. Lindars, *New Testament Apologetic* (1961), p. 60). The story of the resurrection of Jesus has no exact parallel or explicit forecast in the Old Testament, but early Christian writers found some passages (e.g. Ps. xvi. 10; Isa. liv. 7) relevant. It is probably best here too to suppose that the resurrection experience and faith came first; then the conviction that the resurrection must have been foretold; then the documentation.

The outline of Christian preaching which Paul evidently regards as normative and essential consists of factual statements about the end of Jesus' life (not at all about the course of his ministry): he died, he was buried, he was raised. These historical statements (for so even the third may be understood—see below) receive two kinds of interpretation: (a) the whole process constituted a fulfilment of part of the eternal purpose of God, already disclosed in Scripture, and (b) the death of Jesus was intended to deal with sin, which (it is clearly implied) is the predicament from which man needs to be delivered.

The resurrection has been referred to as a historical event. This is true only to a limited extent. Paul states it in the passive voice—*he was raised*—and the passive implies an active: God raised him from the dead (verse 15; vi. 14; and elsewhere in Paul). This is an affirmation about God which historical evidence as such cannot demonstrate (or, for that matter, disprove). Yet it is not unrelated to history, for the affirmation began to be made at a particular point in time, which can be dated by historical means, and it was motivated by occurrences which can be described in historical terms. These occurrences Paul goes on to list in outline, in a brief account of appearances of the risen Jesus to various witnesses. It is evident that these appearances, vitally important as they were in the origins of primitive Christianity, cannot prove more than that, after the crucifixion, certain persons believed that they had seen Jesus again; they cannot prove the Christian doctrine of the resurrection, since this involves a statement about the action of God incapable alike of observation and demonstration. If Paul used them as such a proof, he was for the moment losing his grip on his own subject-matter and line of argument (Bultmann, *Theology*, pp. 290, 300 (E.T., 295, 305)); in fact however he includes them as part of the primitive Christian testimony which he begins to quote at verse 3b, and because he is able to continue them (with a reference to the appearance to himself) in such a way as to underline heavily the main point of the paragraph—that the resurrection of Jesus formed an essential part of every known kind of Christian preaching.

The list of appearances is given in simple, paratactic style.
He appeared to Cephas, who was not unknown at Corinth; 5
see i. 12; ix. 5. The gospels do not recount but give some support to a special appearance to Peter: Luke xxiv. 34; compare Mark xvi. 7. This appearance (in addition to his natural gifts) may account for the prominence of Peter in the early chapters of Acts; it may possibly have been the occasion of some such words as Matt. xvi. 18. After this, he appeared **to the Twelve.** This is the only place where Paul refers to *the Twelve*—a fairly clear indication that he is here quoting a formula he did not himself make up, and that the notion of a group of twelve special disciples is pre-Pauline, and therefore very early. The

Twelve appear to have played some part in the story of Jesus, and to have served as witnesses who could prove the continuity between Jesus of Nazareth and the risen Lord, but not to have been significant figures in the church, at least after the earliest period. The gospels contain accounts of appearances to the Twelve (or more precisely the Eleven, Judas Iscariot being removed from the original number—see note 1 on p. 335): Matt. xxviii. 16 f.; Luke xxiv. 33-51 (but here others are present with the Eleven); John xx. 19-23 (here Thomas is absent, but others may be present), 26-9 (Thomas is included); compare Acts i. 3.

At this point the primitive tradition appears to cease (so J. Jeremias, *The Eucharistic Words of Jesus* (1964), pp. 101 ff.; according to Héring it ceases at verse 4; others think it continues to verse 7).

6 The appearance **to more than 500 brothers at once, of whom the majority remain to this day** (twenty years or so later)**, though some have fallen asleep** (for death as sleep cf. vii. 39; xi. 30; xv. 18, 20, 51; 1 Thess. iv. 13, 14, 15; see Barth *C.D.* III. ii. 638 f.; O. Glombitza, in *Novum Testamentum* ii. 285 f., strangely thinks Paul's meaning to be that some of the 500 have continued their apostolic task but others have given it up) has no parallel in the gospels; on some occasions, noted above, others are said to have been with the Eleven when Jesus appeared to them, but it is never suggested that as many as 500 persons were involved. It has been suggested that this event should be identified with that described in Acts ii as the gift of the Holy Spirit to about 120 disciples (see Acts i. 15), who were quickly joined by thousands of converts (Acts ii. 41). This is possible; the early tradition (including Paul—and John) knows nothing of a corporate bestowal of the Holy Spirit distinct from appearances of the risen Jesus, and it may be that Acts ii is a Lucan rewriting of what originally was a resurrection appearance. Though possible, this is beyond proof, and it may be better to recognize that the Pauline list and the gospel narratives of resurrection appearances cannot be harmonized into a neat chronological sequence; it is hardly to be expected that they should. Another question that cannot be precisely answered is whether all these 500 became apostles (cf. ix. 1). Some at least may have done so, if we accept the wider Pauline view of

apostleship rather than the narrower one of the author of Acts. Indeed, if the latter did evolve the Pentecost story out of a resurrection appearance he may have been influenced not only by his interest in the Holy Spirit but also by the desire to keep apostolic qualifications (cf. Acts i. 21 f.) within relatively narrow limits.

No appearance **to James** (presumably the Lord's brother) is 7
narrated in the canonical gospels; see however the Gospel according to the Hebrews (fragment 21, in M. R. James, *Apocryphal New Testament* (1924), pp. 3 f.; Jerome, *de Viris Illustribus* 2). Whether Paul considered James an apostle is not clear; see Gal. i. 19. Nor is it clear who are meant by **all the apostles,** though the reference to them has the effect of underlining Paul's disparaging reference to himself in the next verse. The order of the words in Greek (*τοῖς ἀποστόλοις πᾶσιν*) lays stress on the noun (B.D. §275; M. iii. 200); this may have the effect of excluding James from their number, but this conclusion is uncertain. Some (e.g. Heim, following Holl) think that the reference is to the Twelve with James. This is not probable. Paul is now adding (see above) to the primitive list, and it is unlikely that he would simply reduplicate the earlier reference to the Twelve, and unlikely also, by the same reasoning, that he means 'the Twelve with James'. It seems reasonable to suppose that he here uses *apostles* in his customary sense (see xii. 28, and the note), with reference to a group of missionaries, wider than the Twelve but not unlimited in scope—more limited perhaps than the group of 500 mentioned in verse 6.

All the apostles evidently means 'all except me'; Paul was in no doubt about his own apostleship, though he knew that it was disputed. The disputes probably arose in the first instance out of doctrinal differences, but his adversaries, it seems, supported their case against him by pointing out that there was already an established group of apostles while Paul was still a persecutor. It is pointless to ask whether the initial series of appearances had been closed by the Ascension, and to inquire how Paul can have seen Jesus after Jesus had ascended into heaven. This may be a problem in Acts, but it is not so for Paul, who knows nothing of such an ascension as is described in Acts i. 9 ff.

The last of the witnesses of the risen Christ was Paul himself.

8 It is true that **last of all** could be taken to mean 'least in importance', and this would agree with verse 9; but at the end of a list, punctuated by *then* ... *then* ... *then*, the other possible meaning of the word must be accepted. This point granted, the chronology must have some bearing on the difficult words that follow (see J. Munck, in *New Testament Essays: Studies in Memory of T. W. Manson* (1959), pp. 180-93; T. Boman, in *Studia Theologica* xviii. 46-50). **As to one hurried into the world before his time** (τῷ ἐκτρώματι: the suggestion that we should read τῳ ἐκτρώματι, *a kind of untimely birth*, would be more convincing if the form τῳ occurred elsewhere in the New Testament), **he appeared to me too.** It is true that Paul's word describes not a process (untimely birth) but the result of the process (for which in English the same words would serve), yet the result is the result of the process, and as such the time element is not unimportant. At first, the word seems inappropriate; as Christian and apostle Paul came into being not early, but later than others. It could however be said that in comparison with other apostles who had accompanied Jesus during his ministry he had been born without the due period of gestation. The last of the apostles was nevertheless born before his time—he had to be if he was to be an apostle at all. It must be admitted however that the word was an odd one to choose for this purpose, and it is probable that Paul took it up from the lips of his adversaries. It suggested the characteristics of an unformed, undeveloped, repulsive, and possibly lifeless foetus. The word may even have been used not only of Paul's supposed deficiencies as a Christian and apostle, but also with reference to his bodily characteristics. 2 Cor. x. 10 shows that his adversaries were not above mocking his physical appearance. As an apostle (if an apostle at all) Paul could be dismissed as a freak. In this epistle ix. 1 f. is enough to show that Paul's apostolic status had been called in question; there is much more of this dispute in 2 Corinthians, especially in chapters x-xiii. In his epistle to the *Romans* ix. 2, Ignatius probably alludes to this passage, without however giving to the word (ἔκτρωμα) any precise meaning.

The appearance of Christ (ix. 1), and the call, had made Paul an apostle, and from this conviction he could never withdraw;
9 but he made no attempt to hide the truth about his past. **For I**

am the least of the apostles (cf. Eph. iii. 8; also 1 Tim. i. 15), **not worthy** (more fully, *who am not worthy*, but in modern English this sounds stilted) **to be called an apostle, since I persecuted the church of God.** In this statement worthiness is reckoned from the standpoint of Christ himself, not from that of Paul's critics. As far as they are concerned he is ready to insist that he is in no way inferior to the superlative apostles (2 Cor. xi. 5; xii. 11). But it is Christ's judgement that matters (cf. iv. 3 f.), and it is his creative love—grace (verse 10)—that has made Paul an apostle. For Paul's work as a persecutor see Acts viii. 1, 3; ix. 1, 2; xxii. 4, 5; xxvi. 9 ff.; Gal. i. 13; for the *church of God* see i. 2; also xii. 28. It is unlikely that the church of Jerusalem is meant, probable therefore that *church* is used in the sense of the whole company of Christian believers.

Paul's career as a persecutor serves to bring out more clearly what is true of all Christians—his dependence on the goodness
of God. **By God's grace I am what I am**—that is, a Christian 10
and an apostle. Compare John xv. 16. All Christians live under grace (Rom. vi. 14); further (for Paul uses the word in more senses than one, though all the senses are related) they are all given grace in such a way that the gift issues in qualification for particular services (Rom. xii. 6). Already in 1 Corinthians Paul has referred to the grace given him for his own task as an apostle (iii. 10). In the second epistle (vi. 1) he begs his readers not to receive God's grace in vain; he himself had not done so. **The grace which he bestowed upon me did not prove vain.** Presumably there was a real possibility that this might have happened; compare verse 2—the Corinthians might have believed *to no purpose*.

That Paul was, by God's grace, truly a Christian and truly an apostle was demonstrated by his apostolic activity. **I laboured more abundantly than all of them**—all the other apostles. Paul gives more details in 2 Cor. xi. 23-7, though these verses emphasize his greater troubles and sufferings, whereas here he is thinking rather of his greater achievements, probably in terms of the fact that whereas his colleagues might be content to work in churches that others had founded he made it his aim always to break new ground and to take the Gospel to those who had not heard it (Rom. xv. 20; 2 Cor. x. 12-16). But this is not something for him to boast of; the activity is not his, but God's—**it was not I, but the grace of God with me.** See note 2 on p. 335. Paul means, if he did not write, *the grace of God* which was *with me*; this is the subject of the verb (to be understood) *laboured.*

The discussion of detail has led Paul from his main point, which was that the resurrection of Christ is an inalienable element in all Christian preaching. He comes back to this, and
11 quickly sums up the paragraph. **Whether then it was I or they** (presumably, other apostles, as referred to in the list of resurrection appearances, and possibly, whether or not by their own choice, ranged in some sense as rivals to Paul), **so we preach, and so you believed.** We all announce that Christ died, was buried, and was raised. There is no Christianity without this affirmation. And, Paul adds, you accepted it. If you are Christians at all you are committed to the belief that Jesus Christ was raised from the dead. You must now be prepared to draw the consequences of this confession of faith.

31. xv. 12-22. IMPLICATIONS OF THE GOSPEL

(12) Now if this proclamation of Christ asserts that he was raised, how can some among you say that there is no resurrection of the dead? (13) If there is no resurrection of the dead, then Christ was not raised; (14) and if Christ was not raised, then our proclamation goes for nothing, and so too does your faith. (15) Moreover, we prove to be bearers of false testimony about God, for we have testified of God that he raised up Christ—whereas, if, as they say, the dead are not raised, he did not raise him up. (16) For, if the dead are not raised, then Christ was not raised. (17) But if Christ was not raised, your faith is vain, you are still in your sins; (18) yes, and those who have fallen asleep in Christ have perished. (19) If in this life we have hoped in Christ—that and nothing more—then we are the most pitiable of all men.

(20) But now in fact Christ has been raised from the dead as the firstfruits of those who are asleep. (21) For since by man came death, by man also came the resur-

rection of the dead; (22) for as in Adam all die, so also in Christ shall all be brought to life.

The main point that Paul needs as the foundation of his argument is now established. The Christian preaching does not in itself contain any proposition about the immortality or resurrection of Christians. In this it differed from some contemporary 'Gospels', which consisted mainly in the offer of immortality to the hearer. In the Christian Gospel all this is left as implication, but the implication is secure, because the preaching is based upon the death and resurrection of Jesus. From this
Paul proceeds. **Now if this** common **proclamation of Christ,** 12
shared by Paul and all other preachers, **asserts that he was raised** (here and in the following verses the perfect tense of xv. 4 is repeated, but it is unnecessary to bring it out in translation, because Paul's thought is now concentrated on the main fact of the once-for-all act in which God raised Jesus up), **how can some among you say that there is no resurrection of the dead?** Compare verses 16, 29, 32. If the chapter is read over quickly one gains the impression that Paul's opponents were materialists, who denied any kind of life after death whatever. It may however not have been so simple; could sceptics of this sort have been Christians (*among you*) at all? According to Schweitzer (*Mysticism*, p. 93), Paul's opponents believed that only those who survived till the *parusia* would enter the kingdom of God; those who died before this would be lost. Alternatively, it may be that what was denied was the idea of resurrection, while some kind of immortality or survival was affirmed; this is suggested by Lietzmann, who quotes Justin, *Dialogue with Trypho* 80: [There are false Christians, not to be credited as Christians,] who say that there is no resurrection of the dead, but that at death their souls are received up into heaven. Some think that this was the situation, and that Paul misunderstood it, wrongly supposing that to deny resurrection was to deny all forms of future life. But again, it was not so simple (see Kümmel, in criticism of Lietzmann). Jews, Paul among them, had immortality in their tradition as well as resurrection. We shall probably be right in recalling iv. 8. One aspect of Corinthian error appears to have been the belief that eschatological conditions

have already been fulfilled; compare 2 Tim. ii. 18—according to Hymenaeus and Philetus the resurrection had already happened. So, in a sense, did Paul himself believe, for in his view also Christians had been raised with Christ (Rom. vi. 5-8; 2 Cor. v. 15; Gal. ii. 19 f.; Col. iii. 1-4); the resurrection of Christ was not simply a test case which proved that resurrection was a possibility, but the actual source of supernatural life; yet in Paul's view this had not happened in such a way as to leave nothing over for a resurrection in the future. In fact, as we continue through the present chapter we shall see that Paul is maintaining, against his adversaries, not only the notion of resurrection, but also that the resurrection is something expected to happen in the future. The idea of a resurrection that has already happened is genuinely Christian, but it is one that Christians of a gnostic type were able to adopt and press in a one-sided way. Paul affirms both resurrection, and its futurity.

13 The next stage of the argument follows easily. **If there is no**
resurrection of the dead, then (to bring out the force of οὐδέ,
14 *neither*) **Christ was not raised; and if Christ was not raised,**
then our proclamation goes for nothing (since Christ's
resurrection is an essential part of it)**, and so too does your**
faith (since you professed to receive what was proclaimed).
More literally, proclamation and faith alike are declared to be
empty (κενόν, κενή); take out the resurrection, and there is
nothing left. 'No one can give himself to a dead man; no one
can expect anything, or receive anything, from a dead man'
15 (Schlatter). See also verse 17. **Moreover, we prove to be**
bearers of false testimony about God, for we have testi-
fied of God that he raised up Christ—whereas, if, as they
say (a classical use of ἄρα; B.D. §454)**, the dead are not raised,**
he did not raise him up. If there is no resurrection, the
Christian proclamation is a lie placed where it is likely to do
most damage, in a statement about God. The next clause is
scarcely necessary, but Paul does not intend to allow his oppo-
16 nents to escape his logic. **For, if the dead are not raised, then**
(οὐδέ, once more) **Christ was not raised.**

Paul's next step is to point out that more is involved here than
simple historical statement, in which a historian might well make
17 an honest mistake. **If Christ was not raised, your faith is**

vain (not the word of verse 14, but ματαία—unable to secure forgiveness, or a future life), **you are still in your sins; yes,** 18
and (ἄρα καί) **those who have fallen asleep in Christ have perished.** In other words, Christianity is completely destroyed: you might as well never have believed at all. It follows, since justification is by faith, that you are still related to God in terms of sin—not merely that you still commit sin, but that the sin you commit determines God's judgement of you. Paul will argue later in the chapter (xv. 56) that the sting of death is sin; here he notes that, since with a vain faith in a dead Christ you continue in your sins, death retains its victory (cf. Rom. vi. 23; also iv. 25; v. 10; vi. 10 f.). Indeed, as Lietzmann notes, *those who have fallen asleep in Christ* is already an impossible expression, since if Christ was not raised from the dead there is no one in Christ; if being in Christ is a real possibility, those who have fallen asleep (cf. xv. 6) in him will be no more finally dead than he is. At first sight Paul appears to make the Christian faith completely dependent on historical research into the fact of the resurrection; it is in fact not dependent on the historical method to this extent, for the resurrection of Christ is itself, as we have seen, an event which is accessible only to faith. To say this is to run the risk of entering into a circular argument, in which it is asserted that faith is grounded in faith, and thus justifies its own existence. Faith, as Paul knew it, is more vulnerable than this: it would be destroyed by the discovery of the dead body of Jesus, but it cannot be created simply by the discovery of an empty tomb.

The next sentence is difficult both to translate and to interpret.
If in this life we have hoped in Christ—that and nothing 19
more—then we are the most pitiable of all men. (a) *We have hoped* is not expressed in the usual Greek perfect tense (ἠλπίκαμεν), but by means of a participle and part of the verb *to be* (ἠλπικότες ἐσμέν). So-called analytic tenses of this kind are not uncommon in Greek, but the doubt often exists whether a genuine tense is being formed, or whether the verb is a simple copula and the participle expresses a substantive; so here some would render 'we are men who have hoped', 'we are hopers'. (b) At the end of the protasis stands the word *only* (μόνον), and it is not certain to what element in the sentence it should be

applied. 'In this life only' (Moule, p. 170, but with hesitation; cf. 2 Baruch xxi. 13: If there were this life only, which belongs to all men, nothing could be more bitter than this)? Or 'We have only hoped' (M. iii. 228)? In the translation I have made it apply to the whole clause (so Bachmann, Harris); its position at the end seems to justify this, and if it is done the question raised under (a) becomes less urgent. If Christian life means simply hoping in Christ during the present life, it is indeed but a poor shadow of itself, and Christians have lost both their present enjoyment of eternal life, and the future to which they look. But Paul says more than this: not merely that they are pitiable, but that they are the most pitiable of all men. It may be that this is rhetorical exaggeration, intended vividly to depict the wretched state of those who are suddenly reduced to the same level as that of their fellow-mortals and fellow-sinners. Such rhetoric would not be un-Pauline, or unmeaning. It is more probable however that Paul means exactly what he says. If Christ was not raised, Christians would be bearing about in their body the dying of Jesus (2 Cor. iv. 10), without any prospect that his life also might be manifested in them. They would not merely be pursuing a figment of their imagination, but embracing death. Much better, as Paul is to say later (xv. 32), eat and drink, and use the present life to the full (vii. 31).

All this, however, is unreal speculation, of value only in that it reminds the reader of what life without Christ would be. Paul—and his Corinthian readers—know that the truth is
20 different. **But now in fact** (another great *but*, νυνὶ δέ, in the Pauline manner; cf. Rom. iii. 21) **Christ has been raised from the dead.** So all Christian preachers affirm; there is no Christian faith without this affirmation. Further, he has been raised not in isolation but **as the firstfruits of those who are asleep,** in death (cf. verse 18). For *firstfruits* compare Rom. viii. 23; xi. 16. The word is used in a different sense at 1 Cor. xvi. 15—see the note; for the sense compare Col. i. 18 (Christ is the beginning—ἀρχή, whereas *firstfruits* is ἀπαρχή—, the firstborn from the dead); also Rom. viii. 29. As the passages in Romans clearly show, Paul (in dependence on the Old Testament) takes the word to mean the first instalment of the crop which foreshadows and pledges the ultimate offering of the whole. Because Christ has been

raised from the dead, the resurrection of the rest of mankind (or at least of those who are in Christ; see below) is assured. The general sense is clear; it is less certain that there is a specific allusion to the offering of the first sheaf of harvest (LXX, ἀπαρχή) on the day after the Sabbath after the feast of Passover (Lev. xxiii. 10 f.)—that is, on the day on which (according to the gospels) Jesus rose from the dead. This view however is possible, and finds some support in the fact that, according to Philo, this occasion was described as 'firstfruits' (ἀπαρχή). In *De Specialibus Legibus* ii. 162 f. Philo goes on to explain the use of the name: 'The Jewish nation is to the whole inhabited world what the priest is to the State.' Paul may have been familiar with some such interpretation of the rite and of the word (he need not have read Philo), and the more readily have applied the word to the relation between Christ and the rest of mankind, which he is about to state in the next two verses. This however cannot be positively affirmed, and it is even less certain that Paul used this imagery (and that of v. 7) because he was writing at about Passover time (for the date of the epistle see Introduction, p. 7).

The next two verses are of great importance, and set out, in double parallelism, Paul's understanding of Christ and of his relation to mankind at large.

Since by man came death, 21
by man came also the resurrection of the dead;
for as in Adam all die, 22
so also in Christ shall all be brought to life.

The two verses may be taken together, since the latter serves to make the former more precise, though the former is also important as interpreting the latter: it is in Adam *as man* that all die; it is in Christ *as man* that all are brought to life. In these two figures (see *Adam*) the story of mankind as a whole is not only summed up but also activated, or set in motion. The theme is taken up again and handled in more detail later in the chapter (verses 45-9; see the notes). Death entered the world through Adam (whom Paul treats as a historical character), because Adam in transgressing the divine commandment brought upon himself the sentence of death threatened in Gen. ii. 17. Adam's historic sin marked the historic entry of death as a phenomenon

—his own death. This does not explain why all men should die *in Adam*. Rom. v. 12 suggests (though it may be taken differently—see the Commentary) that others died because they too sinned, as Adam had sinned and died. The rest of Rom. v, however, shows that Paul has in mind more than this. Such is the solidarity of the human race that the sin of its first father constituted the mass of mankind as sinners (Rom. v. 19), not in that it made them, independently of their own will, morally bad men, but in that it introduced them into a society which was as a whole alienated from God. The present passage is less explicit, but can be—and in the absence of evidence to the contrary should be—understood on similar lines. *By man* and *in Adam* (Adam is a Hebrew word that means *man*), that is, as members of the human race which has departed from its original vocation in God's intention, all men inherit death as their destiny. This restatement (though Paul would not have been interested in the fact) involves no assumption about the historicity of Adam.

The parallel statement about Christ and the resurrection, though similar, differs in important particulars. Its parallel form suggests at first that Paul means that, as from the time of Adam all men die, so now the lot of all men is resurrection. But this can hardly be said to fit the context, in which, as in Paul's thought generally, resurrection seems to be the privilege of those who through faith are in Christ. Though the wording has been affected by the parallel clause, his meaning appears to be that all who are in Christ shall be brought to life; compare 1 Thess. iv. 16: The dead in Christ shall rise. This is not a denial that all men may ultimately come to be in Christ; indeed, this may be implied. Christ's act of grace and righteousness, which more than counterbalances Adam's transgression, is described in Rom. v, and presupposed here; in virtue of it, God's purpose that man should have dominion over the universe is restored, though beyond death. The pattern of death-resurrection becomes the framework of human life; perhaps a more meaningful pattern than the untried innocence and bliss of Adam before the fall—Augustine's *felix culpa*. It must however be remembered that in this epistle, as well as elsewhere, Paul speaks of those who perish: i. 18; iii. 17; v. 13; vi. 9 ff.; ix. 27; compare x. 12; xi. 30. See further *Romans*, pp. 225-8; *Adam*, pp. 113-19.

At this point a second difference appears. Sin and death, traced back by Paul to Adam, are a description of humanity as it empirically is. For this reason the historicity of Adam is unimportant. It is impossible to draw the parallel conclusion that the historicity of Christ is equally unimportant. The significance of Christ is that of impingement upon a historical sequence of sin and death. Sin and death (to change the metaphor) are in possession of the field, and if they are to be driven from it this must be by the arrival of new forces which turn the scale of the battle, that is, by a new event. As Paul knew, this event had happened very recently, and its character as historical event raised no doubt or problem in his mind. This observation is not intended as a defence of the gospel narratives as historical documents; they are entirely open to question and must stand their own ground. But so far as the 'Second Adam' or 'Heavenly man' figure is mythological (see pp. 373-8), the myth has been historicized by Paul, and that not only because he was aware of Jesus as a historical person, but because a historical person was needed by the theological argument.

The exposition based on the figures of Adam and Christ does not return explicitly till xv. 45-9 (see however verses 25, 27, with the notes). Paul now turns aside to take up the theme of resurrection in apocalyptic terms, as he was bound to do if, as was argued above, it was necessary for him to establish resurrection as a future event. An apocalyptic passage (not irrelevant, though formally it may appear to be a digression) follows from verse 23 to verse 28, and is resumed in verses 50-7; Paul may well have divided an existing apocalypse in two and edited it, working it in with other practical and dogmatic themes. The join at this place is satisfactory, though it is easy to see the change of theme. Verses 21 f. state a principle; verse 23 begins to work it out in chronological sequence.

32. XV. 23-28. CHRISTIAN APOCALYPSE (a)

(23) Each one, however, will be brought to life in his own rank: Christ himself as the firstfruits, then, at his coming, those who belong to Christ. (24) Then comes the End,

when he hands over the kingdom to him who is God and Father, when he shall have brought to nought every Ruler and every Authority and Power. (25) For Christ must continue to reign in his kingdom until he shall have set all his enemies under his feet. (26) Death is the last enemy to be brought to nought.

(27) Now when it says that all things shall have been placed in subjection, it is plain that this is with the exception of him who subjected all things to him. (28) But when all things shall have been subjected to him, then the Son himself also shall be subjected to him who subjected all things to him, that God may be all in all.

The new section is very closely connected with the preceding one; indeed, the first clause has no verb of its own, but must be supplied with one from verse 22. *In Christ all shall be brought*
23 *to life*; **each one, however, will be brought to life** (the last five words are not in the Greek) **in his own rank.** I have made a break between verse 22 and verse 23 because it appears that at this point Paul embarks upon a new range of material. In verses 12-22 he argued first on general logical principles, and then on the basis of his Adamic Christology (this description makes it look more systematic than it is), to the idea of resurrection; this cannot be denied without denying Christ's resurrection, and his relation to Adam and the human race. The Adamic argument will recur from verse 45, but there intervenes first the present apocalyptic paragraph (which is taken up again in verse 50), and then two more, containing different arguments. The new paragraph is entitled to consideration on its own.

As far as Christians are concerned (though not for Christ) resurrection is a future concept (see above, pp. 347 f.). *Rank* (τάγμα) is a word which in classical Greek is used almost (though not quite) exclusively in a military sense, and denotes a body of troops, which can be disposed according to the decision of the commanding officer. In later Greek (including the LXX) its use widened, so that it could be applied to any sort of group, military or civilian, and could mean place, or position, or even ordinance (see Allo; and note 1 Clement xxxvii. 3; xli. 1, showing two senses in one author). I have used the word *rank*, because it conveys something of the ambiguity the Greek word suggests, and is less precise than group, division, or detachment would be. The difficulty commonly felt in the rendering which is in accord with Greek usage as a whole is that 'each one in his own group' seems to imply more than is stated in the following words: **Christ himself as the firstfruits, then, at his coming, those who belong to Christ.** These seem to speak of one individual person, and one group. At a pinch this might suffice: Christians must not suppose that the resurrection has already happened; Christ has indeed been raised (for *firstfruits* see xv. 20), and they will be raised, but not at the same time. The difficulty would be set aside if we could accept the rendering of verse 24 which is rejected in the notes on that verse. We should then have a list of three groups, raised up at different times: Christ alone, already raised on the third day after his crucifixion; Christians, who will be raised at the time of the *parusia* of Christ; and thirdly, those who are not Christians, raised at a later point. But in fact we cannot find the third group in verse 24; the verse does not mean this. The solution of the problem is to be found in xv. 50-3, helped out by 1 Thess. iv. 15 ff. Paul distinguishes between those who have died before the *parusia* and those who are still alive when it happens. It is true that he does not make this distinction in verses 23-8, but it is made in what appears to be a later part of the same apocalypse, and may be assumed here. We know at least that the distinction was one entertained by Paul. If this is accepted the difficulty disappears. Christ has already been raised, a foretaste and pledge of the resurrection still to come; there will be brought to life those who belong to Christ, who will be separated into those who have already died, who must be in the simplest sense *brought to life*, and those whose mortality must be clothed with immortality (xv. 53; 2 Cor. v. 3 f.). *Those who belong to Christ* (cf. iii. 23; Gal. iii. 29; v. 24) are presumably Christians, but in view of the fact that Paul cannot have hoped to evangelize the whole world before the time at which he thought the *parusia* likely to happen (see pp. 380 ff.) we should perhaps understand 'the elect'.

On the view adopted here nothing is said about the future life of those who are not Christians, and with this silence we must be content. The evidence of the other epistles is not conclusive.

This question leads however to the interpretation of the next
24 verse. **Then comes the End** (τὸ τέλος), **when he hands over the kingdom to him who is God and Father.** Allusion has been made above to a way of interpreting this verse that finds in it a reference to a third group of persons who participate in the resurrection. For this purpose the Greek word here translated *End* must be taken to mean, *rest*, *remainder*: first Christ, then Christians, then (after an interval in which Christians reign with Christ) the rest of mankind. It cannot be said that attempts (notably Lietzmann's) to demonstrate this meaning have succeeded (see Kümmel, Allo, Héring, and others). Even if the meaning stood out clearly in the two or three passages in which it is supposed to occur (and it does not), these would be worth little against the very many passages where the meaning is simply *end*. The meaning *end* is secure, and it is better to read the word as a noun than to take it adverbially: *then*, *finally*. . . . 'The general Resurrection, and the immediately following judgement upon all men and the defeated Angels, are not mentioned in the series of events enumerated by Paul in 1 Cor. xv. 23-8. All this falls for him under the general concept of "the End" (τέλος, 1 Cor. xv. 24), and is taken for granted as well known' (Schweitzer, *Mysticism*, pp. 67 f.). This may include too much, but it is on the right lines.

Uncertainties nevertheless remain. The *parusia* of Christ has just been mentioned in verse 23; *then comes the End*—immediately, or simply as the next significant event? On the latter view it would be possible to find room here (between the *parusia* and the end of all things) for the millennial kingdom which some Christian apocalypses predict (see Rev. xx. 6). Such a *Zwischenreich* is found here by, for example, Schweitzer and Lietzmann, but it seems unthinkable that Paul, if he believed in such a kingdom, should pass it over without a word, and *then* (εἶτα) may well mean *thereupon*. See a full discussion in W. D. Davies, pp. 291-8. The *parusia* of Christ, accompanied by the resurrection of Christians, ushers in the end, at which the main event is the handing over of the kingdom by Christ to God—the *God* and *Father* presumably of Christ himself; there is a strong vein of subordinationism in this passage (see especially verse 28). This is the moment of the establishing of the kingdom of God. The apocalyptic scheme of thought takes God as the rightful king of the universe. In some way (never specified by Paul), however, authority has come into the hands of evil powers, whom God has to dispossess in order to reassert his own sovereignty. In the passage before us Christ appears to reign during the period in which this dispossessing takes place, one enemy after another (cf. verse 26) being overpowered. When the kingdom has been fully re-established, the Son hands it over to the Father, and the kingdom of Christ gives place to the kingdom of God. There is, as has been said, nothing to suggest that this developing reign of Christ falls between the *parusia* and the End; it culminates in the *parusia*. This is supported in the following verses, in which it is said that Christ reigns until all his enemies are defeated, and that the last enemy to be overcome is death; the defeat of death however is naturally taken as belonging to the time of the resurrection of Christ's people (verse 23). For Paul, God is an ultimate term, Christ a penultimate. Creation is from God, through Christ; redemption is through Christ, to God (viii. 6). This does not necessarily imply difference of status, but it does imply difference of role and operation *ad extra*. Col. i. 13 (if this is genuine) is the only other Pauline reference to the kingdom of Christ.

The next words have already been drawn into the commentary. The transference of the kingdom from Christ to God takes place **when** the former (there can be no doubt here of the subject of the verb; καταργήσῃ must have the same subject as παραδιδοῖ) **shall have brought to nought** (for the word cf. ii. 6) **every Ruler and every Authority and Power.** The Greek tense changes (παραδιδοῖ; καταργήσῃ), and it is not pedantic to make a change in the English. The one clause defines what happens at the End, the other when the End will happen. *Ruler* translates what is properly an abstract noun (ἀρχή; cf. Rom. viii. 38); the meaning is probably the same as that of the related noun (ἄρχων) at ii. 6, 8 (this is reinforced by the statement in the earlier chapter that the Rulers are being *brought to nought*. *Authority* (ἐξουσία) is used as at Col. ii. 10, 15; *Power* (δύναμις) as at Rom. viii. 38. It is idle to attempt to distinguish between these nouns; they represent the evil powers (not good, angelic powers, who simply lose their function in the age to

come: Barth *C.D.* III. iii. 501 f., 511) under whose control the world has come. At the time Paul writes, in the midst of the Christian mission, they continue to exist, and as enemies, but
25 their days are numbered and their defeat is certain, **for Christ** (in Greek *he*, but there is no doubt what subject is intended) **must continue to reign in his kingdom** (bringing out the present infinitive *βασιλεύειν*) **until he** (it is not so clear here what subject should be supplied; see below) **shall have set** (the tense is that of *shall have brought to nought* in verse 24) **all his enemies under his feet.**

The last sentence is a loose quotation of Ps. cx. 1:

> The Lord said to my Lord, Sit at my right hand,
> Until I set thy enemies as the footstool of thy feet.

Paul takes the Psalm to refer to the Messiah (cf. Mark xii. 35 ff.; Acts ii. 34 f.; on the use of the Psalm see F. Hahn, *Christologische Hoheitstitel* (1964), pp. 126-32), and to be a prediction of his ultimate victory. The use of the quotation suggests that the subject of *shall have set* (*θῇ*) in verse 25 is God; the same will be true in verse 28. Christ's reign means his session at the right hand of God, during which one enemy after another is sub-
26 dued. **Death is the last enemy to be brought to nought.** Paul uses the present tense (though the defeat of death lies in the future) because he looks at the process as a whole. A more literal rendering would be, Death (this, having the article in Greek, will be the subject) is brought to nought as the last enemy (these words, having no article, are predicative). Compare 2 Tim. i. 10, but the sense is different there, since 'brought to nought' is in a past tense. Paul uses the word to mean not so much 'to annihilate' as 'to rob of efficacy'; it is accordingly arguable that even after this point death continues to exist, no longer as an effective enemy (to God) but as an instrument in his hand, which could be used, for example, against those whom God saw fit to punish.

The quotation of Ps. cx. 1 leads Paul (by the exegetical device *g^e^zerah shawah*; see *Romans*, p. 89) to a similarly worded passage in Ps. viii. 7 (see C. H. Dodd, *According to the Scriptures* (1952), pp. 32 f., 120, 122):

> Thou didst subject (*ὑπέταξας*) all things under his feet.

A different verb is used (in Greek; in Hebrew it is the same), but verbal parallelism between the two Psalms is close. The new passage however is not directly messianic, but deals with man, or the son of man (Ps. viii. 5). It is this Man to whom all creation is subjected. Messiah and Man can thus be used to interpret each other. This connection must be remembered as we proceed with Paul's own words.

Now when it says. . . . This translation takes the un- 27
expressed subject of the verb (εἴπῃ) to be Scripture, and also gives to the construction (ὅταν with the aorist subjunctive) a different rendering from that which has been given in verse 24. The alternative is, When he shall have said. . . . In this rendering, 'He' might be either God (declaring that all things have now been subjected to Christ, or to himself) or Christ (declaring that all things have now been subjected to God, or to himself—so Bachmann). We need not however attempt to decide between these alternative possibilities, because the continuation of the sentence shows that, for the moment, Paul is not continuing the narrative but explaining Scripture, and, in particular, excluding an apparently possible but false interpretation of his text. Scripture then asserts **that all things shall have been placed in subjection.** It is not stated here to whom all things are being subjected, and we might think either of Christ (to whom in the first place submission is made) or of God (to whom Christ hands over dominion, when he has established it). That the former alternative is correct is shown by the sequence of the next clauses. In verse 28, *him who subjected all things to him* must refer to God's subjection of all things to Christ; this determines the meaning of the same words in 27b; and this in turn determines the meaning of 27a. Thus Paul sees the fulfilment of Ps. viii in the representative man, Jesus Christ. To him, not now but in an assured future, all creation will be subjected. All creation, but nothing more: when Scripture speaks of the subjection of all things to the representative man (for this theme see further below, verses 45-9, and the notes), **it is plain that this is with the exception of him** (that is, God) **who subjected all things to him** (that is, Christ). One would have thought it perhaps unnecessary to refer explicitly to this exception. Paul does so partly in order to prepare for the next verse—so far from

its being true that God is subjected to Christ, Christ is subjected to God; partly also perhaps because of a Corinthian belief (of which we have no other evidence) that at his exaltation Christ became the one supreme God. Whether or not this was believed in Corinth, it was not true. Obedience was and would through eternity continue to be part of the divine virtue of the Son.

28 **When all things shall have been subjected** (again, ὅταν with the aorist subjunctive) **to him** (that is, to the Son), **then the Son himself also shall be subjected** (M. i. 163 takes the voice as neutral—'shall be subject'—but it may be best to align it with the other passives, though evidently without the implication of a third, active, party who subjects the Son to the Father; the Son subjects himself, willingly) **to him** (God) **who subjected all things to him** (Christ), **that God may be all in all.** The Son has been entrusted with a mission on behalf of his Father, whose sovereignty has been challenged, and at least to some extent usurped by rebellious powers. It is for him to reclaim this sovereignty by overcoming the powers, overthrowing his enemies, and recovering the submission of creation as a whole. This mission he will in due course execute, death being the last adversary to hold out, and when it is completed he will hand the government of the universe back to his Father. This mythological account of salvation is evidently closely parallel to the developed gnostic scheme; it is not closely related to the primitive Christian scheme of preaching, which Paul quotes in xv. 3-5, and it is probable that Paul, though developing it himself, took it over in part from a source in which it already existed in outline.

It is the last act in the myth that shows that Paul has radically Christianized it. Elsewhere (Phil. ii. 6 ff.) he will show that the story originates in the humility and readiness to serve shown by the Son (or representative Man); this quality is retained to the end, when the Son voluntarily takes second place (cf. verse 24; the two verses refer to the same thing). There is an element of subordinationism here (cf. *Adam*, p. 102), which is inevitably bound up with Christ's representative fulfilment of Ps. viii. According to this Psalm, man exercises his appointed lordship over the rest of creation in his being 'a little lower than God'. This is in harmony with the creation narrative (Gen. i. 28). It is when man strives to rise above his appointed place and put himself on God's level that he falls below it and loses his dominion (Gen. ii. 17; iii. 17 ff.; Rom. i. 21 ff.; v. 12-21). In the obedient service of the representative man Jesus Christ, man's dominion is being restored, but its security lies only in the unvarying submission of Jesus the Son to his Father. See further the notes on xv. 45-9; and compare O. Cullmann, *Christologie des Neuen Testaments* (1957), p. 300 (E.T., 293 f.): 'Here is the key to all New Testament Christology. To speak of the Son has meaning only in reference to God's revelatory action, not in reference to God's being. But precisely for this reason, Father and Son are in this action really one. As of the Logos, so also of the Son of God we can now say: He is God, in so far as God reveals himself in the saving event (*Heilsgeschehen*).'

The end is *that God may be all in all*. This is to be understood in terms of Rom. xi. 36; 1 Cor. xv. 54-7; 'soteriologically, not metaphysically' (Bachmann; cf. Knox, *Gentiles*, p. 128). It is not the absorption of Christ and mankind, with consequent loss of distinct being, into God; but rather the unchallenged reign of God alone, in his pure goodness.

Here the chapter might end. But Paul (cf. xiv. 5) has more arguments to expend on those Corinthians who are foolish to deny the resurrection.

33. xv.29-34. *AD HOMINEM* ARGUMENTS FOR AND ABOUT RESURRECTION

(29) If there is no resurrection, what will those people do who are baptized on behalf of the dead? If the dead are never raised, why are they baptized on their behalf? (30) Why do we too go in danger every hour? (31) By the boasting that I have of you in Christ Jesus our Lord, brothers, I die daily. (32) If it was on purely human terms I fought with wild beasts at Ephesus, what good does that do me? If the dead are not raised, 'Let us eat and drink, for tomorrow we die'.

(33) Don't be misled. 'Bad company ruins good ways.'

(34) Wake up properly to a sober life, and stop sinning; for what some people have is ignorance of God. I say this to shame you.

In verse 28 Paul concluded the first stage of his argument that resurrection is a necessary part of the Christian faith, and that it is to be understood in eschatological terms. It is part of the total intention of God for mankind. It is true that it raises problems; these come under explicit consideration in verse 35, and the discussion of them leads, after an important Christological digression in verses 45 ff., to a further apocalyptic statement of the Christian hope (verses 50-57). Before turning to these further points however Paul sees additional means of demonstrating that Christian existence can be fully understood only in terms of the future. He argues on the basis of Christian institutions, Christian suffering, and Christian ethics.

He first invites his readers to consider a practice no doubt
29 as familiar to them as it is puzzling to us. **If there is no resurrection** (ἐπεί, 'since otherwise'; cf. v. 10; vii. 14), **what will those people do who are baptized on behalf of the dead? If the dead are never** (ὅλως) **raised, why** (τί καί, emphatic; B.D. §442; What conceivable reason can they give?) **are they baptized on their behalf?** *What will they do?* may be taken in two senses: (a) What will they achieve by the course they adopt? (b) What will they do next, when it is discovered that the dead on whose behalf they have acted are dead and done with, since there is no future resurrection? (a) and (b) are not mutually exclusive, and the point may perhaps be paraphrased, Will not these people look fools when it turns out that there is no resurrection, and that they have wasted their labour? *Baptized*, without further explanation, can hardly have any other than its normal Pauline meaning. It is true that for Paul baptism is baptism into death (Rom. vi. 3), but this does not justify Schlatter in the view that here 'those who are baptized' are Christians (especially apostles) who have died in order to act as witnesses to the dead. The primary reference is to Christian baptism: certain people (οἱ βαπτιζόμενοι suggests a particular group, not all Christians) undergo the rite of Christian baptism —in what appear to be very strange circumstances. They are

baptized *on behalf of the dead.* The second part of the verse follows clearly enough. If the dead are dead and now beyond recall, there is no point in taking this or any other action on their behalf. But what was the practice of baptism for the dead, and did Paul approve of it? An account of the history of the interpretation of this passage is given by M. Rissi, *Die Taufe für die Toten* (1962).

It is very unlikely that with the adjective *dead* (νεκρός) a noun such as *works* (cf. Heb. vi. 1) should be supplied. Throughout this chapter (and in Paul usually) 'the dead' are dead men. It is equally unlikely that *on behalf of* (ὑπέρ) is to be taken in a local sense, and that the reference is to baptism carried out *over* the dead, that is, over their graves. The most common view is that Paul is referring to some kind of vicarious baptism, in which a Christian received baptism on behalf of someone, perhaps a friend or relative, who had died without being baptized. There is evidence for some such rite among various heretics (among other quotations Lietzmann cites Chrysostom, on this passage: When a catechumen among them [the Marcionites] dies, they hide a living man under the dead man's bed, approach the dead man, speak with him, and ask if he wishes to receive baptism; then when he makes no answer the man who is hidden underneath says instead of him that he wishes to be baptized, and so they baptize him instead of the departed), and there were precedents in Greek religious practices, though not close precedents (see Schweitzer, *Mysticism*, pp. 283 f.). Stauffer lays great stress on 2 Macc. xii. 40-5. Apart however from 1 Corinthians there is no evidence that a rite of this kind arose as early as the 50's of the first century. This does not make it impossible; many strange things happened in Corinth. But would Paul have approved of it? It is true that in this verse he neither approves nor disapproves, and it may be held that he is simply using an *argumentum ad hominem*: if the Corinthians have this practice they destroy their own case against the resurrection. This is the view held by some, and it is possible; but it is more likely that Paul would not have mentioned a practice he thought to be in error without condemning it. Of those who accept this position some draw the conclusion that vicarious baptism cannot be in Paul's mind, others that, if he did not practise the custom himself, he at least saw no harm in it, since he too held an *ex opere operato* view of baptism that bordered on the magical. A recent view (M. Raeder, 'Vikariatstaufe in 1 Cor. xv. 29?', in *Z.N.T.W.* xlvi. 258 ff.) is that *on behalf of the dead* is a phrase implying purpose. *The dead* are departed Christians; those who are baptized are converts who accept Christianity in order that, at the resurrection, they may be united with their loved ones. This is not altogether impossible, but this use of the preposition is rare, and it is not easy to see why Paul should express himself in this way. The context provides no positive evidence in support of Schweitzer's view (*Mysticism*, pp. 283-6) that the aim of this baptism was that the dead might rise at the beginning rather than at the end of the messianic kingdom; see p. 356. Nor is there much to be said for Bachmann's interpretation: What will the baptized do for the dead (that is, themselves—in the future)?

The idea of vicarious baptism (which is that most naturally suggested by the words used) is usually supposed to be bound up with what some would call a high sacramental, others a magical, view of baptism. Immersion in water is supposed to operate so effectively that it matters little (it seems) what body is immersed. The immersion of a living body can secure benefits to a dead man (at any rate, a dead catechumen). This however was not Paul's view. He did not himself give close attention to baptism (i. 14-17), and though it is probable that most of the members of his churches were baptized it is quite possible that some of the Corinthian Christians had not been baptized, and by no means impossible (even if we do not, with Rissi, think of an epidemic or an accident) that a number of them may have died in this condition. There was no question of making these persons Christians; they were Christians, even though unbaptized. But baptism was a powerful proclamation of death and resurrection, and in this setting it is not impossible to conceive of a rite—practised, it may be, only once—which Paul, though he evidently took no steps to establish it as normal Christian usage, need not actively have disapproved. And what would be the sense of it, if the dead are not raised?

And what would be the sense of running the risks to which an
30 apostle was exposed? **Why do we too** (the καί is attached to ἡμεῖς, *we*, not to the sentence as a whole) **go in danger every**

hour? Whatever exactly the baptism referred to in verse 29 may have been, it was, as was said above, a proclamation of death and resurrection. Paul was concerned with other modes of the same proclamation, and in the process incurred innumerable hardships summed up at a time not long after the writing of 1 Corinthians in 2 Cor. xi. 23 ff. Death itself is hardly too strong
a term to describe them. **By the boasting that I have of you in** 31
Christ Jesus our Lord, brothers (cf. i. 1; but there there is strong evidence for the omission of the word)**, I die daily.** The strong asseveration (introduced by the particle *νή*, usually followed by the name of a god or goddess, and in the whole of the Greek Bible used only at Gen. xlii. 15 f. in addition to this verse) is called for not so much by the violence of the language (Paul uses similar expressions elsewhere without similar support: e.g. iv. 9-13) as by Paul's desire that the Corinthians should understand what the lot of an apostle truly is, and should see it in its proper context. Paul's boasting in the Corinthians is in their conversion, in the fact that they have been won to Christ out of the heathen world. This is worth many deaths. It is not human boasting in human achievement, but boasting in the Lord (cf. i. 31), of what the Lord has done. Paul not infrequently speaks of his converts in this way; compare for example Phil. iv. 1.

A particular example of the endurance of suffering and danger in the light of the resurrection hope follows. The circumstances were no doubt well known in Ephesus, and not unfamiliar in Corinth; to us they are completely obscure, and nothing but the
discovery of new evidence can illuminate them. **If it was on** 32
purely human terms I fought with wild beasts at Ephesus, what good does that do me? The grammar, like the historical background, is uncertain. *On purely human terms* represents a phrase (*κατὰ ἄνθρωπον*) used by Paul at iii. 3 (in accordance with human standards); ix. 8 (with ... human authority); Rom. iii. 5 (... these human arguments); Gal. i. 11; iii. 15. It may draw attention to a human turn of speech or experience, used in order to illustrate theological truth, but more often draws attention to a human standard of judgement, which Paul repudiates. It seems to have the latter sense here, and is brought forward to the beginning of the protasis for emphasis. The conditional sentence

(lacking ἄν in the apodosis) seems to be of the simple kind with an open condition in past time: If I did this, then that follows. It is, however, not unknown for this kind of apodosis (without ἄν) to occur with an unfulfilled condition in the protasis, which would give: If I had fought (as I did not), what would....? In fact Paul's meaning falls somewhere between these alternatives for the protasis consists of two parts, one of which was fulfilled (Paul did fight with beasts), the other not (he did not do so on purely human terms).

We still have to inquire what he meant by *fighting with wild beasts*. It is difficult to think that the word (θηριομαχεῖν) was meant literally. Notwithstanding the apocryphal acts of the martyrs, even apostles seldom emerged alive from exposure to wild beasts; moreover, if Paul had been sentenced to this punishment he would have lost his Roman citizenship, which, according to Acts xxii. 25, etc., he still had after this time. The list in 2 Cor. xi. 23 ff., though detailed and explicit, makes no mention of beasts, and it seems likely that Luke, if he had heard of so dramatic an event, would have made use of it in Acts. The word could be used metaphorically, and was so used by Ignatius (possibly in imitation of Paul; he admired the apostle, and had read 1 Corinthians) at *Romans* v. 1: From Syria to Rome, by land and sea, I am fighting with wild beasts (θηριομαχῶ) . . . being bound to ten leopards, by which I mean a detachment of soldiers. It is probable that Paul uses the word in some such way; it is to be noted that metaphorical use does not remove the reality and gravity of the danger and hardship endured. Compare iv. 9. It may be that the occasion was that of the riot in Acts xix. 23-40; this must remain quite uncertain, but if the occasion did not involve danger of death it loses relevance in the context (Weiss). Compare Rom. xvi. 4.

Whatever the occasion, if Paul had endured his hardships with no more than human resources and grounds of hope, what good would that have done? Only the Christian hope makes sense of, and offers reward for, such experience.

It has been argued that in this verse the words *in Ephesus* cannot have been written in the city itself; this does not seem cogent.

Paul continues: Take away the Christian hope, and not merely will a man lose the motive for endurance; his moral standards will collapse. **If the dead are not raised, 'Let us eat and drink, for tomorrow we die'.** The quotation is taken, word for word, from Isa. xxii. 13, though the context in Isaiah is different. More appropriate quotations can in fact be found in non-biblical settings, both literary and non-literary. For example, Deissmann (*Light from the Ancient East* (1910), p. 296) quotes a gravestone of the imperial period from Cos, in which the dead Chrysogonus addresses the passer-by: Drink, for you see the end. If death is the end, there is little left to do but pluck the pleasures of the passing moment. Not all who deny the resurrection draw this conclusion from their premiss; Paul suggests that it would be reasonable to do so. Perhaps some at Corinth did.

Such moral carelessness, whatever may inspire it, and however attractive it may seem, is not for Christians. **Don't be** 33
misled (as at vi. 9). **'Bad company ruins good ways** (or, possibly, *characters*).**'** This quotation is not from the Old Testament, but from Menander's lost comedy *Thais*. It is the only quotation from a non-biblical source in the genuine Pauline literature; compare Acts xvii. 28 (quoting Aratus) and Titus i. 12 (quoting Epimenides). It is unnecessary to suppose that Paul had read or seen the play; the quotation, like others from Menander, had become proverbial (and if Paul had recognized the verse he would have elided, and written χρήσθ' ὁμιλίαι, not χρηστὰ ὁμιλίαι; though it seems that in this period elision was more often spoken than written; see M. i. 45; ii. 61, 63; Robertson, p. 207; B.D. §17). The Christian behaviour of the Corinthians will be ruined if they mix much with those who, not sharing the resurrection hope, live as they please. Earlier (v. 10) Paul had made clear to the Corinthians that he did not expect them to come out of the world, and he was prepared for them to continue to join in dinner parties with their heathen friends (x. 27); but deliberately to cultivate bad company and take pleasure in it was another matter. Perhaps, moreover, as Héring suggests, the bad company was inside the church.

The rest of the epistle suggests that the Corinthians were by no means free from fault in this respect, and this is confirmed by the sharp reminder that follows. **Wake up properly** 34
(δικαίως; not *righteously*; for this sense see Kümmel) **to a sober**

life, and stop sinning. Paul's first imperative (ἐκνήψατε) calls for a number of English words. The verb means to sleep off a bout of drunkenness, but the aorist tense suggests the completion of the process in recovered sobriety. The second imperative (with the negative μή) is in the present tense, and implies the ending of a course of action already in progress. Paul is aware of dangerous tendencies at work in his church. And he knows the cause of them. We have already seen reason to conclude that some kind of primitive gnosticism existed in the Corinthian church (cf. i. 5; viii. 1; xiii. 2, 8; also 'Christianity at Corinth'); at least, if the term gnosticism seems too definite, there were Corinthian Christians who claimed to have knowledge, by which they were able to regulate their conduct, for example in regard to food sacrificed to idols (viii. 1-13). So far as their knowledge leads them to the moral indifferentism of verse 32, they are mistaken. **What some people** (Paul does not intend to use names—there is no point in causing unnecessary embarrassment or disturbance) **have is** not knowledge (*gnosis*) but **ignorance** (*agnosia*) **of God.** Compare Mark xii. 24. This verse provides strong evidence for the existence of a Corinthian group claiming to have a special knowledge of God, and suggests that Paul believed that this *gnosis* would eventually have, if it had not already produced, regrettable moral consequences. This sort of speculation is not for Christians. **I say this to shame you.** The contrast with iv. 14 shows how strongly Paul feels about this; but compare vi. 5.

34. xv. 35-49. THE OLD MANHOOD AND THE NEW

(35) But some one will say, How are the dead raised? With what kind of body do they come? (36) Fool! What you yourself sow is only brought to life if it dies. (37) And as to the seed you sow, you do not sow that body that is to be, but a bare grain, of wheat, it may be, or of some other cereal. (38) It is God who gives it a body, and he does so as he himself has chosen, and to each seed he gives its own body. (39) Not every kind of flesh is the same flesh,

but there is one kind for men, another for beasts, another for birds, and another for fish. (40) Also there are heavenly bodies, and earthly bodies; but the glory of the heavenly bodies is one thing, and the glory of the earthly bodies is another. (41) There is one glory of the sun, another of the moon, and another of the stars; yes, and star differs from star in glory. (42) So it is also with the resurrection of the dead. The sowing takes place in corruption, the raising up in incorruption; (43) the sowing takes place in dishonour, the raising up in glory; the sowing takes place in weakness, the raising up in power. (44) A natural body is sown, a spiritual body is raised up.

If there is a natural body there is a spiritual body too. (45) And so it stands written: The first man Adam became a living soul. The last Adam became a life-giving Spirit. (46) Only it is not the spiritual body that came first, but the natural; then the spiritual. (47) The first man came out of the ground, made of dust; the second man comes from heaven.[1] (48) Corresponding to the one man made of dust are the men who are made of dust; and corresponding to the heavenly Man are the heavenly men. (49) And as we have borne the image of the man made of dust, we shall bear[2] also the image of the heavenly Man.

The preceding paragraph was a digression, though closely related to the main point. It began with *ad hominem* arguments in support of Paul's doctrine of resurrection, and turned to moral exhortation in the light of the moral disorder that may be expected to arise if the doctrine is abandoned. But the doctrine itself has not yet been fully expounded or adequately grounded, and the new paragraph turns to these points. The questions of verse 35 are (in view of the uncomplimentary epithet in verse 36) to be taken as objecting questions, seeking to apply a *reductio ad absurdum* to Paul's position, but Paul uses them as the jumping-off ground for the next stage of his exposition.

[1] The text translated is almost certainly correct; many MSS. add that the second man is *lord* (κύριος); P⁴⁶ that he is *spiritual* (πνευματικός).

[2] φορέσομεν. The majority of MSS. have φορέσωμεν, *let us bear*, pronounced identically (M. ii. 74), so that only exegesis can determine the original sense and reading. See the commentary.

35 **But some one** (not one may suppose, an imaginary figure; see xv. 12) **will say** (for the formula cf. Rom. ix. 19; xi. 19; the lively style is that of the diatribe), **How are the dead raised?** For the discussion of this question between the schools of Hillel and Shammai see S.B. iii. 473 f. **With what kind of body do they come?** It would be possible to paraphrase the latter question, With what kind of body are they provided? But Paul is probably thinking of a real *coming*—out of graves, with Christ. It may be that Paul and the objector (cf. vi. 13; the same persons may be involved—Heim) are at cross-purposes, and that Paul to some extent misunderstands his opponent. The latter thinks that Paul teaches a rising up of physical bodies; to raise the question of bodies will therefore discredit the doctrine. But this is not Paul's meaning, and he is not at all disturbed by the question. There is an analogous discussion in Apocalypse of Baruch l, li. Paul's reply reminds the questioner that nature is
36 full of change and variety. **Fool!** For the epithet compare Ps. xiii. 1. **What you yourself sow is only brought to life if it dies.** The same point is made (with more specific reference to Christ himself) in John xii. 24; the same process underlies some synoptic material (e.g. Mark iv. 30 ff.). Paul is not here using the figure to bring out the necessity of death; rather, the
37 fact of transformation through death and revivification. **And as to the seed you sow** (literally, *what you sow*, ὃ σπείρεις, an accusative of apposition), **you do not sow the body that is to be** (that is, the matured crop), **but a bare grain, of wheat, it may be, or of some other cereal** (perhaps, *of some other plant*; literally, *or of one of the others*). There is no need to particularize in the illustration; sowing, germination, and growth are the same whatever seed one thinks of. Man sows the
38 seed; he does not produce the plant. **It is God who gives it** (the sown seed) **a body** (that is, in the analogy, a plant-body), **and he does so** (these four words are not in the Greek) **as he himself has chosen** (his choice not being determined by man's act of sowing), **and to each seed he gives** (*he gives* is not in the Greek; *pertains* would be another possible supplement) **its own body.** In this verse Paul moves from one analogy to another. His first point is that death, though not an end, means change; his second is that *body* does not always and necessarily

mean the same thing—there are many kinds of body, and God himself appoints and chooses them for various purposes. Paul's statement recalls, though it is not identical with, that of Rabbi Meir (*Sanhedrin* 90b), who answered the question, When the dead rise, will they rise naked or in their clothes? thus: From a grain of wheat one can draw a conclusion *a minori ad maius* (*qal waḥomer*). If the grain of wheat, which is put in the earth naked, grows up in who knows how many garments, how much more does that apply to the righteous, who are buried in their clothes! See further W. D. Davies, pp. 305 ff.

Paul now proceeds to develop his second point, though in doing so he for the moment changes his word from *body* (σῶμα) to *flesh* (σάρξ)—an unfortunate change in view of the special theological connotation *flesh* has in some of his writing (see *Romans*, pp. 155-62), but not here. God has provided variety
in nature; thus **not every kind of flesh is the same flesh,** 39
but there is one kind for men, another for beasts, another for birds, and another for fish. This is pure physiology (correct or not, it was familiar in Judaism—S.B. iii. 475 f.), and enters theology only as analogy. Paul returns to the word *body*, this time with a distinction between heavenly and earthly bodies.
There are heavenly bodies, and earthly bodies. The latter 40
have just been mentioned: men, beasts, birds, fish. The former are stars, thought of as living beings equipped with bodies emitting light (possibly, in Paul's view, made of some light-substance). Hence **the glory of the heavenly bodies is one thing, and the glory of the earthly bodies is another.** The word *glory* is expressed only once in this sentence, but the grammar requires that it be understood twice, notwithstanding the objection (made, e.g. by Lietzmann) that earthly bodies have no glory. So far, however, as earthly bodies have *glory* they do not manifest it, as the heavenly bodies do, in light. But even among the heavenly bodies distinctions (it is the existence of
distinctions that is Paul's main point) have to be made. **There** 41
is one glory of the sun, another of the moon, and another of the stars. Paul means that they do not shine with equal brightness. **Yes, and** (γάρ, which cannot here mean *for*) **star differs from star in glory** (brightness).

Thus throughout the natural order variety reigns. The

resurrection of the *body* must be understood in the light of this fact; now that it has been established, Paul is in a position to pro-
42 ceed. **So it is also with the resurrection of the dead.** Resurrection means transformation. This is set out in a series of couplets in antithetical parallelism (see B.D. §490); there is no reason for seeking a poetical origin for them, since they are a perfectly natural prose expression of parallel but antithetical facts. **The sowing takes place** (it is best to take the verbs, *σπείρεται*, *ἐγείρεται*, in verses 42 f. as impersonal passives; so Allo) **in corruption, the raising up is in incorruption.** Paul does not mean only that the body placed in the grave is in a process of physical decomposition, though this is part of the truth and the clearest expression of it. *Corruption* is an evil power, by which the world is dominated in the old age (Rom. viii. 21). It affects not only human life, but the whole of creation. Its dominion will be ended in the age to come, at the beginning of which the resurrection takes place. Thus Paul's point is not simply that we shall have a new body, no longer subject to change and decay, but that the new body will be appropriate to the new age in which God, having reasserted his sovereignty, is *all in all* (xv. 28). The next two couplets come nearer to describing the change
43 in the body itself. **The sowing takes place in dishonour** (*ἀτιμία*; Paul seems to use this word as the term contrasting with *δόξα*, which has no direct negative)**, the raising up in glory; the sowing takes place in weakness, the raising up in power** (*δύναμις*, often an eschatological term—e.g. Mark ix. 1).
44 Paul's next step is plainly to contrast two kinds of body. **A natural body is sown, a spiritual body is raised up.** Exactly what Paul means by *natural* (*ψυχικόν*) and *spiritual* (*πνευματικόν*) bodies must be worked out in the next paragraph. See also W. D. Davies, pp. 182 ff. Neither English adjective is a very happy rendering of Paul's Greek. *Natural* translates an adjective based on the Greek noun *soul*, or *life* (*ψυχή*); it describes the body, animated by soul, with which a man is clothed and equipped during his life in this age (cf. Bultmann, *Theology*, p. 201 (E.T., 204). *Spiritual* does not describe a higher aspect of man's life; the noun spirit (*πνεῦμα*) on which it is based refers to the Spirit of God, and the *spiritual body* is the new body, animated by the Spirit of God, with which the same man will be clothed and

equipped in the age to come, which he reaches (supposing him to die before the *parusia*) by way of resurrection. Compare 2 Cor. v. 1. The same historically continuous (Kümmel; see also M. E. Dahl, *The Resurrection of the Body* (1962)) *ego* makes use successively of two different kinds of body. That there should be two kinds of body should surprise no one who has followed the argument of verses 38-41; but Paul goes on to support the point with more than *a priori* and naturalistic considerations. Compare Phil. iii. 21.

If there is a natural body there is a spiritual body too. On this proposition the validity of Paul's argument (which accepts the point that a simple reanimation of corpses is unthinkable) depends. He gives here his answer to the question of verse 35, and answers it substantially in the terms in which it was asked. The sceptical inquirer wished to know with what sort of body the dead were to be provided, implying that the restitution of the earthly body was an absurdity which he could not accept. Paul answers that the dead will be provided with a different kind of body, but he is still thinking, not of some kind of universal risen body of Christ, but of the bodies with which the individual dead will appear. Their resurrection is completely dependent on Christ's, but even so they retain their individuality (Whiteley, pp. 192 f.). It is however necessary to begin the argument from Christ, and to view Christ in the right context it is necessary to go back to the creation of man. On the next
verses see W. D. Davies, pp. 43-57. **So it stands written:** 45
The first man Adam became a living soul. This quotation from Gen. ii. 7 is expanded by the addition of two words, the adjective *first* (added in view of the fact that Paul intends to speak of a last Adam), and the proper name *Adam* (added because Paul needs another name to balance Christ, whom in any case he intends to describe as the last Adam). *Soul* (ψυχή) is the noun from which the adjective *natural* (ψυχικόν) is derived (see above, in the note on verse 44), and it is this connection Paul has in mind in introducing the quotation. Adam, the progenitor of the race, had a *natural body*. Such bodies are the common stuff of humanity as we know it. But—and herein lies the force of Paul's argument—to speak of *the first man Adam* necessarily calls to mind the fact that there stands beside him

another comparable figure. Paul does not need to establish his existence, for it was accepted in Judaism, and perhaps beyond. There is little consistency in the various speculations known to have existed about a Primal Man, Archetypal Man, Heavenly Man (and they are too diverse to be summarized in a commentary of this size); this is not surprising. Some sort of consistency could only be achieved when the speculations could be focused upon and interpreted by a historical figure. It may however be asserted that to many of his Jewish contemporaries (though possibly not to so high a proportion of his Corinthian readers) reference to the Adam of Gen. i-iii would suggest another Adam. Hence Paul can add as a natural extension of his quotation, **The last Adam became a life-giving Spirit.** For him, the conception of a New Man is given concreteness by the resurrection, after which, in terms of the Spirit, Jesus became the Son of God in power (Rom. i. 4). The resurrection means the Spirit, and Spirit is (for Paul, as in biblical thought generally) not merely alive but creatively life-giving (cf. John vi. 63). Between Adam and Christ there is analogy (as the very term *last Adam* shows), but it is the sort of analogy that issues in the contrasts as well as the parallels of Rom. v. 15-19 (on which see the Commentary). To the Christological implications of this we shall return; the immediate point is the demonstration of two kinds of body, and as *living soul* points to the *natural body*, so *life-giving Spirit* points to the *spiritual body*. There is no reference here to a *fall* of Adam (Bultmann, *Theology*, p. 173 (E.T., 174)).

The connection just stated must be borne in mind as we proceed to the next verse, where the adjectives *natural* and *spiritual* are used without substantives but in the neuter gender. It is necessary to supply with them not *man* (ἄνθρωπος, masculine),
46 but *body* (σῶμα, neuter). **Only it is not the spiritual body that came first, but the natural; then the spiritual.** Paul's eye is still on the main run of the argument. The doctrine of resurrection is tolerable because there are two kinds of body, a spiritual as well as a natural. The fact of a first man, and a last Adam, proves this to be so. But the sequence is important. This is best explained if we can suppose (cf. O. Cullmann, *Christologie des Neuen Testaments* (1957), pp. 171 ff. (E.T., 167 ff.)) that Paul

was familiar with some such exegesis as that of Philo, who saw (*Legum Allegoriae* i. 31: There are two kinds of men; the one is a heavenly man, the other an earthly;—and elsewhere) in the two accounts of the creation of man in Gen. i. 27; ii. 7 a reference to two men, (a) a heavenly, archetypal man, a Platonic idea of man, and (b) the historic Adam, created out of dust. This dual picture of man Philo was able to build into his philosophical reinterpretation of Judaism. There is no direct evidence that Paul had read Philo, but neither is there reason to think that only Philo entertained this explanation of Gen. i and ii. It seems that Paul knew it, but denied that the relation between the two men, and the two kinds of body they represented, was rightly described by it. The heavenly Man with his spiritual body was not a Platonic pattern of humanity, but an eschatological figure (verse 47). For the rest of mankind too the spiritual body, made in the image of the heavenly Man, belongs to the eschatological future (verse 49), and depends not on the essential nature of things but on a free and gracious act of God. For further contrasts between Paul and Philo see Bachmann, p. 467.

Paul returns to the two men, Adam and Christ, because they not only exemplify the two kinds of body that are important to his argument but also enable him to set forth the act of redemption in virtue of which alone it is possible for men to receive spiritual bodies and share in the life of the age to come.
The first man came out of the ground, made of dust. This 47
is a simple paraphrase of Gen. ii. 7, using some of the language of the LXX. **The second man comes from heaven.** No verb is expressed in either clause. Some part of the verb 'to come' seems to be called for, and the past tense is required in the first clause. In the second it might be better to use the future: The second man will come. But this thought is included in the present *comes*, which also suggests more strongly the thought of origin as well as that of motion. What man may be said to come from heaven? Paul is presumably dependent on the vision of the one like a son of man who according to Dan. vii. 13 was coming on the clouds of heaven. Whatever the original meaning of this vision may have been there were at least some in Paul's day who took it to refer to a heavenly

Man who lived, or was to appear, in heaven. Thus 1 Enoch xlvi. 1 ff.:

> And there [in heaven] I saw One who had a head of days, and his head was white like wool, and with him was another being whose countenance had the appearance of a man, and his face was full of graciousness, like one of the holy angels. And I asked the angel who went with me and showed me all the hidden things, concerning that Son of man, who he was, and whence he was, and why he went with the Head of Days. And he answered and said unto me: This is the Son of man who hath righteousness.

See also 4 Ezra xiii. 1 ff.:

> And it came to pass after seven days that I dreamed a dream by night: and I beheld, and lo! there arose a violent wind from the sea, and stirred all its waves. And I beheld, and lo! the wind caused to come up out of the heart of the seas as it were the form of a man. And I beheld, and lo! this Man flew with the clouds of heaven.

We need not here inquire whether Judaism had already equated this human figure with the Messiah; Paul certainly identified him with Jesus, who was the Messiah. (For variant readings here see note 1 on p. 369). It is not part of Paul's argument here to say that the heavenly Man has already come in the form of earthly man, though his treatment of the cross makes unmistakably clear his estimate of the importance of the life, and especially of the death, of Jesus. He is here pressing forward to the future coming of Jesus as the Man who is the Lord, having recovered the dominion originally assigned to man (Gen. i. 28; Ps. viii. 6) by the humble obedience which was appointed as man's destiny. For this coming see xv. 23; 1 Thess. iv. 16; 2 Thess. i. 7. This is the moment of resurrection, and of completed redemption (Rom. viii. 23).

It is only incidentally here that Paul discusses Christology. He never loses sight of his main theme, which is the vindication of the doctrine of the resurrection. Neither of the two men whom he has mentioned was simply a private individual. Each was an *Adam*, a representative man; what each was, others

became. **Corresponding to the one man** (the Greek does not 48
contain the word *one*, but it helps to point the contrast) **made of dust** (the first Adam; cf. Gen. ii. 7) **are the men who are** simply **made of dust; and corresponding to the heavenly Man** (that is, the man who comes from heaven, verse 47; not 'the divine man'—Betz, p. 102) **are the heavenly men.** The thought of this verse is less complex than may at first appear. It should be remembered that throughout this paragraph Paul's main theme is *bodies*. These are of more kinds than one; there are natural and spiritual bodies. All Adam's descendants, being made of dust as he was, have natural bodies, made of dust and animated by *soul* (ψυχή). But the existence of another Adam with a spiritual body carries with it the existence of a race of men with spiritual bodies. These are received (in the case of Christ as well as in that of the rest of humanity) at the resurrection, only for Christ this has already happened, whereas for men it still lies in the future. This verse is not about morals, and does not declare that Christians will be morally like Christ (though doubtless they ought to be); it says that at the resurrection they will exchange natural bodies for spiritual bodies (cf. Phil. iii. 21), and become a race of heavenly men. For the parallelism of verses 48 f. compare verses 42 ff.

The same point is made once more in the next verse. **And** 49
as we have borne (the past tense does not point to a conversion experience—we still bear) **the image of the man made of dust, we shall bear** (see note 2 on p. 369; copyists who wrote *let us bear* supposed—as Calvin put it—that Paul was giving exhortation, and not *pura doctrina*) **also the image of the heavenly Man.** Paul is not speaking here of the image of God (cf. xi. 7). For the image of the first Adam see Gen. v. 3: Adam lived 230 years and begot (a son) in his likeness (ἰδέα) and in his image (εἰκών). Seth was like his father and belonged to the same order of beings. From this time human beings have continued to have the same kind of body, made in the image of Adam's. We continue to have this kind of body, living on in a state of corruption, up to the time of the resurrection. But then, in the future, *we shall bear* a different image, that of the heavenly Man whose body is spiritual. Paul's thought here must have its roots in Gen. i. 26 f., though he earlier rejected the (Philonic) notion of

a primal archetypal man, made in the image of God. He is probably affected by the notion that Wisdom existed in the image of God (Wisdom vii. 26). But the thought is essentially that of Rom. viii. 29; Phil. iii. 21.

35. xv. 50-58. CHRISTIAN APOCALYPSE (b)

(50) What I say, brothers, is this: Living men cannot inherit God's kingdom, nor does the corruption of death inherit incorruption. (51) Behold, I tell you a mystery. We shall not all fall asleep, but we shall all be changed,[1] (52) in a moment, in the twinkling[2] of an eye, at the last trumpet. For the trumpet shall sound, and the dead shall be raised in a state of incorruption, and we shall be changed. (53) For this corruptible body must put on incorruption, and this mortal body must put on immortality. (54) But when this corruptible body has put on incorruption, and this mortal body has put on immortality, then shall the written word be fulfilled, Death has been swallowed up in victory. (55) Where, O Death, is your victory? Where, O Death is your sting? (56) The sting of death is in fact sin, and the power of sin is the law; (57) but thanks be to God who gives us the victory through our Lord Jesus Christ.

(58) In consequence of this, my dear brothers, be steadfast, immovable, abounding always in the Lord's work, since you know that your labour is not vain in the Lord.

It is now time for Paul to draw the argument of the long chapter to a close. He is defending the thesis that there will be a resurrection of the body. This proposition cannot be reduced to absurdity by the argument that the resuscitation of an immense number of corpses is unthinkable; resurrection is accom-

[1] There are many variations in this verse. The most important are set out in the commentary. See also Clark in *Studia Paulina*, pp. 63 f.

[2] ῥιπῇ; P⁴⁶ D G 1739 lat have ῥοπῇ, in all probability wrongly. See Zuntz, pp. 37 ff.

panied by transformation—*a natural body is sown, but a spiritual body is raised up* (xv. 44). The absurdity indeed lies the other way; religion and morality alike (xv. 14, 32 f.) make no sense if there is no resurrection. That which ultimately makes future resurrection credible is the fact of the resurrection of Christ, and this not only by way of logical precedent (xv. 12) or example, but because Christ as the heavenly Man is the author and head of a new humanity as the first Adam was the author and head of the old humanity. But the establishment and manifestation of this (cf. Rom. viii. 19) lie in the future: whatever has already happened to Christians by faith and in baptism is not the final resurrection and transformation of the body.

What I say, brothers (see i. 1), **is this.** So Paul begins to 50
sum up at vii. 29. **Living men** (literally, *flesh and blood*) **cannot inherit God's kingdom, nor does the corruption of death** (*of death* is not in the Greek; see below) **inherit incorruption.** The meaning of this verse has been established in detail by J. Jeremias (*N.T.S.* ii. 151-9). The Semitic word-pair 'flesh and blood' is 'only applied to living persons; the words flesh as well as blood exclude an application of the word-pair to the dead' (p. 152). In the parallel line, *corruption* is used, as an abstract noun instead of a concrete, for 'corpses in decomposition'. Dr Jeremias sums up: 'The two lines of verse 50 are contrasting men of flesh and blood on the one hand, and corpses in decomposition on the other. In other words, the first line refers to those who are alive at the parousia, the second line to those who died before the parousia. The parallelism is thus not synonymous, but synthetic and the meaning of verse 50 is: neither the living nor the dead can take part in the Kingdom of God—as they are' (p. 152).

This is clearly in accordance with what has been said hitherto about the two different kinds of body—a different kind is needed for the resurrection life—and it also accords with the distinction between those who do and those who do not survive to see the *parusia* which persists through the following verses. Its main importance however is negative. It is not Paul's intention to teach a direct incompatibility between *flesh* and the kingdom of God, only that living and dead alike must experience transformation and be provided with a new spiritual body.

At this point Paul moves into specifically apocalyptic language, describing what is to happen at the End (cf. xv. 23-8). The
51 apocalyptic material is introduced with great solemnity: **Behold, I tell you a mystery.** Paul does not often use *Behold* (*ἰδού*), and, apart from the quotation of Rom. ix. 33 (Isa. xxviii. 16), does so to add emphasis to his words (2 Cor. v. 17; vi. 2, 9; vii. 11; xii. 14; Gal. i. 20). For *mystery* compare Rom. xi. 25, where also it means a secret truth (revealed to and through Paul) about what is to happen at the End. Elsewhere in 1 Corinthians it is used rather differently (xiii. 2; xiv. 2), though at ii. 1 (*si v.l.*), 7; iv. 1 its meaning is related to that of the present verse, since the mystery of the Gospel is an eschatological truth. There is a difference, however, since here the mystery is a secret not essential to the understanding of the Gospel. The events of the last days can safely be left in the hands of God. We are no better off (except that we may be humbled—Rom. xi. 25) if we know what is to happen.

We shall not all fall asleep, but we shall all be changed. According to Robertson, p. 753 the first clause (*πάντες οὐ κοιμηθησόμεθα*) means, 'None shall sleep'. Other grammarians, however (Moule, p. 168; B.D. §433; M. iii. 287), and most commentators, are agreed that in the context the words cannot mean this, but must be taken in the sense 'Not all (of us) shall sleep' (as if the Greek were *οὐ πάντες κοιμηθησόμεθα*; Schlatter compares 2 Cor. vii. 3 to illustrate Paul's habit of attaching the negative to the verb, even when it negates some other part of the sentence). Sleep is an event that will not happen to all; change, however, will. Sleep is Paul's synonym for death (cf. xv. 6), and he means that not all Christians (this is the point of the first person plural) will die, since some will still be alive at the coming of Christ. These, as the following verses will show in more detail, will experience direct change, whereas the dead (as the earlier argument has shown) will rise with a different kind of body, and thus will also undergo a comparable change. It is right to note, before leaving this verse, that it has been transmitted in several different forms. The main alternatives are (a) We shall not all sleep but we shall not all be changed (P^{46}). This looks like a careless repetition of the negative; (b) We shall all sleep but we shall not all be changed (א A C G 33).

Those responsible for this reading failed to grasp Paul's belief that the *parusia* would happen in his own generation; (c) We shall all rise, but we shall not all be changed (D* lat Marcion). This reading imports a new idea of which Paul is not thinking in this paragraph—the fate of the wicked. We may with some confidence accept the text translated here, and from the variants draw at least the comfort of reflecting that we are not the first to find Paul's thought difficult. It follows from verse 50 that some change is necessary both for the dead and the surviving if they are to inherit the kingdom of God.

The change, when the moment comes, will happen instantane-
ously, **in a moment** (*ἄτομον*, used popularly for an indivisible 52
unit of time; but see Aristotle, *Physics* VI. ii. 13), **in the twinkling of an eye** (see note 2 on p. 378; the familiar *twinkling*, though more naturally a rendering of *ῥιπή*, could stand not inadequately for *ῥοπή*; cf. Wisdom xviii. 12, and see Moule, p. 186), **at the last trumpet.** 1 Thess. iv. 16, in a similar context, speaks of God's trumpet. Compare also Matt. xxiv. 31; Rev. i. 10; iv. 1; viii. 2, 6, 13; ix. 14; but it would be wrong to take the *last trumpet* here to means the last of a series (such as the seven in Revelation); it means the trumpet-call that accompanies the End. The notion is Jewish; see Joel ii. 1; Zeph. i. 16; 4 Ezra vi. 23; and other passages noted by G. Friedrich in *T.W.N.T.* vii. 84. Paul has fully adopted this description of the End (conceivably quoting a Jewish apocalypse). **For the trumpet shall sound** (the verb is used impersonally; Paul gives no indication who is to blow the trumpet, though one may reasonably—in the light of other apocalypses—take this to be the work of an angel or archangel), **and the dead shall be raised in a state of incorruption** (whereas at death they are in a state of corruption: xv. 42, 50), **and we shall be changed.** As in verse 50, Paul distinguishes between those who, when the *parusia* happens, are already dead, and those who survive. The distinction is repeated in verse 51, and Paul hints at what he now, it appears, states explicitly: he expects that at the *parusia* he himself will not be among the dead (of whom he speaks in the third person), but among the living (of whom he speaks in the first person). He expected the *parusia* within his own lifetime. Whether he changed this belief is a disputed question, which cannot be

discussed here because it would involve consideration of the whole Pauline corpus. See further the notes on 2 Cor. v. 1-5. It seems probable that if the perspective changes it is because Paul found death nearer rather than because he thought the *parusia* further off. More important than the question of development in Paul's thought, the problem raises acutely the problem of early Christian eschatology. This too cannot be discussed here; it was already perceived and dealt with in the New Testament period, notably by John.

The change that is expected to affect the dead is clear, and has already been stated in xv. 42. The old *natural body* is in process of corruption; it will be replaced by the new *spiritual body*, which is not corruptible. But those who are alive are still clothed with their *natural body*, and a similar change must affect them also.

53 **This corruptible body** (the word *body* is not expressed in Greek, but the adjective is neuter, which would agree with σῶμα; it would be possible to translate more generally, 'this which is corruptible') **must put on** (as clothing; the metaphor is developed in 2 Cor. v) **incorruption** (this point has been sufficiently discussed above)**, and this mortal body** (or, 'this which is mortal') **must put on immortality.** *Mortal* presumably points to human nature which, though not dead, is subject to death, and thus to those who are alive at the *parusia.* They must be changed so as to be no longer subject to the power of death. This change marks the overthrow of death, now at last defeated (xv. 26) since there is no one over whom it exercises authority (unless possibly those who are not in Christ), and the
54 consummation of the new humanity. **But when this corruptible body has put on incorruption, and this mortal body has put on immortality, then shall the written word be fulfilled, Death has been swallowed up in victory** (cf. xv. 26). The reference is to Isa. xxv. 8, but it seems to be a free rendering of the Hebrew (He will swallow up death for ever—*laneṣaḥ*), and not a borrowing from the LXX, which takes the passage differently. The same freedom applies in the next two
55 lines: **Where, O Death is your victory? Where, O Death, is your sting?** Here the reference is to Hos. xiii. 14, where the Hebrew is, O Death, where are your plagues? O Sheol, where is

your destruction? The point in the Hebrew appears to be that Death and Sheol are bidden to bring forth their terrors and apply them in punishment of the guilty people, but there is some evidence that some other Jewish interpreters took the rhetorical questions in the same comforting sense as Paul. See E. E. Ellis, *Paul's Use of the Old Testament* (1957), p. 138; C. H. Dodd, *According to the Scriptures* (1952), p. 76. This is true of the LXX translators, who render, Death, where is your judgement (δίκη)? Hades, where is your sting? This would account for Paul's allusion; he is not however here grounding an argument upon Scripture, but writing freely, in scriptural language, of the ultimate victory over death. Placing himself, as it were, at the time of the End, he mocks death as already defeated, and no longer able to exercise its old sting. He drops the reference to Hades, possibly because the name suggested a heathen god.

Paul is not carried away by rhetoric and enthusiasm. Death is the last enemy that will be overthrown (xv. 26), and the moment for its defeat has not yet come. Death still prevails, and it still has a sting, a sting which has behind it a force which is the more
potent because it is an agent of God himself. **The sting of** 56
death is in fact sin, and the power of sin is the law. The connection between death and sin, which Paul found in Gen. ii. 17, is frequently brought out in his writings (e.g. Rom. v. 12 f.; vi. 23—see the commentary). Considered genetically, the relationship means that sin is the cause of death; here it is considered empirically. Taking death as a given fact, sin is what embitters it, not only psychologically, in that it breeds remorse, but also theologically in that it makes clear that death is not merely a natural phenomenon, but a punishment, an evil that need not exist, and would not exist if man were not in rebellion against his Creator. Once embarked upon the theme, Paul, though he does not develop it, cannot refrain from mentioning the third factor in the complex in which sin and death are two members. Equally related to each of the other two is *law*. For this relationship see Rom. v. 13; vii. 7-25, and the commentary. Law makes sin observable, in transgression, and also multiplies it. Law is the occasion of sin, the jumping-off ground from which sin operates. It is implied by Rom. vi. 14 f. that sin is inevitable where men are 'under law'—not because the law

itself is evil (on the contrary, it is holy, righteous, good, and spiritual—Rom. vii. 12 ff.), but because, since it expresses God's claim in preceptual form, man, who is sold as a slave under the authority of sin (Rom. vii. 14), is provoked either to disobey it or to use it for his own self-centred purposes. It may well be, as Kümmel suggests, that Paul is here using a rabbinic maxim, 'The law is the power of God'. This (as Kümmel notes) is an argument in favour of the originality of this verse, which Weiss (for example) thinks to be most probably an interpolated exegetical note that has crept in between verses 55 and 57. This view (cf. Moffatt: 'a prose comment which could not have occurred to [Paul] in the passionate rush of triumphal conviction') however quite misunderstands the passage, to the climax of which verse 56 notably contributes. It is 'no dry dogmatic gloss'—Bachmann. The earlier verses look into the apocalyptic future, and rejoice in the ultimate defeat of death. Verse 56 soberly considers its present sting and power, and verse 57 exults, not in unfounded optimism but in the victory
57 already won, not only over death but over sin. **But** (for this great
but cf. xv. 20 and the references there) **thanks be to God** (cf. Rom. vii. 24) **who gives us the victory through our Lord Jesus Christ** (cf. Rom. viii. 39). The victory of Jesus Christ was a victory over sin in that he died to sin, a death which men are summoned to share (Rom. vi. 10 f.), so that *the sting of death* is now, in Christ, drawn; and it was a victory over death, in that Christ himself was raised from the dead, and raised as the firstfruits—the pledge that all who are in him will also be raised (xv. 20, 23). The victory is not fully won, for mankind as a whole, until the End (xv. 26), but it is so certain that Paul can speak of it in the present tense: *who gives us the victory* (cf. Rom. viii. 37).

It calls for no great effort of the imagination to hear Paul's vehement preaching in the climax of this paragraph, but he is not the kind of preacher to finish his discourse with a purple patch that evaporates in pure rhetoric. His apocalypse, and the enthusiasm with which he expounds it, are directed to a practical
58 goal. **In consequence of this** (ὥστε), **my dear brothers, be**
steadfast, immovable (the Corinthians had shown themselves to be very easily moved from Christian behaviour and Christian

conviction, for example, in regard to the resurrection), **abounding always in the Lord's work.** Compare iii. 13 ff.; ix. 1; xvi. 10. In all these passages what is meant is the Christian labour of calling the church into being and building it up. This is especially the task of apostles, but also that of their helpers, such as Timothy, and indeed of every Christian, since all are members of the body. The toil would be lost if there were no resurrection, and the workers might then as profitably devote themselves to pleasure (xv. 32), but there is no fear of this, and the Corinthians may more and more (cf. 1 Thess. iv. 1) give themselves to Christian work **since you know that your labour is not vain** (literally, *empty*, κενός; cf. xv. 10) **in the Lord.** *In the Lord* applies both to the *labour* (it is Christian work Paul is speaking of) and to its not being *vain*. Since it is done *in the Lord* it can no more perish than he. Compare iii. 14.

(f) THE COLLECTION

36. xvi. 1-4. INSTRUCTIONS AND PLANS FOR THE COLLECTION

(1) About the collection for the saints, do you also do as I instructed the churches of Galatia. (2) On the first day of each week let each one of you set aside for himself and save up whatever profit he makes, that collections may not be taking place when I come. (3) When I arrive, any whom you approve I will send, authorized by letter, to carry away your generosity to Jerusalem; (4) and if it seems right that I should go too, they shall travel with me.

At vii. 1 it was pointed out that there are several passages in the epistle where it appears that Paul was referring to specific questions or inquiries made by the Corinthians in their letter to him. We are now almost at the end of these passages. It is probable that the Corinthians had heard, perhaps from the Galatians, of the collection Paul was organizing, and had asked what part they were to play in it. **About** (vii. 1; viii. 1; xii. 1) **the** 1

collection (the word λογεία was for a long time thought to be peculiar to biblical Greek; subsequently it appeared in the papyri, mostly in connection with taxation) **for the saints** (for the use of this word for the Jerusalem church cf. Rom. xv. 26; elsewhere, e.g. 1 Cor. i. 2, it is used for Christians generally). At Jerusalem Paul had undertaken to remember the poor (Gal. ii. 10). His activities in this direction are mentioned at Acts xi. 30; xxiv. 17; Rom. xv. 25-8; 2 Cor. viii, ix. His collection has been compared with the Didrachma tax paid into the Temple at Jerusalem by all Jews (J. Jeremias, *Jerusalem zur Zeit Jesu* (1958), I 86; cf. II A 48; II B 118), but Kittel has shown (*T.W.N.T.* iv. 286) that the thought of taxation is misleading; Paul emphasizes the freedom of the voluntary action taken by his Gentile converts in serving the mother church. The only claim of the Jerusalem church was a moral one (Rom. xv. 27), and Paul was in some doubt about the way in which the gift was likely to be received (Rom. xv. 31). He made the collection because he had been asked to do so, because, no doubt, he felt a genuine compassion for the needy, and probably because he hoped that it would cement together the two divisions of the church, which already were showing signs of at least uneasy partnership.

Paul tells the Corinthians what they must do about the collection, at first allusively, in terms we cannot interpret. **Do you also do as I instructed** (for the word, διέταξα, cf. vii. 17) **the churches of Galatia.** We have no record of instructions given to *the churches of Galatia*; presumably the Corinthians had heard of these instructions, and they can be reconstructed from the following verses. They are not given in the Epistle to the Galatians contained in our New Testament; they may have been given orally during the journey described in Acts xviii. 23, or possibly in a special letter. What Paul meant by the term *Galatia* is a notorious Pauline problem which cannot be discussed here. Some see a reference to the churches of the so-called first missionary journey of Acts xiii, xiv—Antioch, Iconium, Derbe, Lystra; more probably we should think of a region in north central Asia Minor, in the vicinity of Pessinus, Gordium, Germa, and Dorylaeum.

2 What is to be done is as follows. **On the first day** (in Greek

the cardinal number, *μίαν*, is used instead of the ordinal; this may be a reflection of the Semitic usage with which Paul would be familiar; cf. Acts xx. 7, and see B.D. §247) **of each week** (that is, on Sunday; it is not mentioned here as a day when Christians meet for worship, but cf. Rev. i. 10) **let each one of you set aside for himself** (not, contribute to a church collection—contrast Justin, *Apology* i. 67; Paul may have wished to avoid the possibility of accusations with regard to misappropriation, and perhaps to avoid misappropriation itself) **and save up whatever profit he makes** (taking the verb as present subjunctive, *εὐοδῶται*—so M. i. 54; ii. 191, 200; at Rom. i. 10 it is used more generally, but its meaning here must be financial), **that collections may not be taking place when I come.** Paul evidently hoped that when he reached Corinth each member would have a prepared sum ready to pay into a central fund. The collection was a good thing, but not one that should engross time and trouble that could be better employed. It was, in the end, to take a long time and much effort to complete the collection in Corinth; see 2 Cor. viii, ix.

After collection, transmission would be seen to. **When I** 3
arrive (see below, verses 5-9), **any whom you approve** (Paul does not intend to pick his own team—again, no doubt, with the motive of avoiding slander; cf. 2 Cor. ii. 16 ff.) **I will send, authorized by letter** (commendatory letters were well known form in antiquity), **to carry away your generosity** (*χάρις*, also used for the grace of God; cf. 2 Cor. viii. 1, 4, 6, 7, 9, etc.) **to Jerusalem.** The reference to letters (*δι' ἐπιστολῶν*) could be taken with the Corinthians' action: 'those whom you approve by letters I will send...'. But this makes less good sense.

Paul's own plans are uncertain. **If it seems right** (so Allo; 4
alternatively, but less probably, *if the amount is worthy*) **that I should go too, they shall travel with me.** When he wrote Rom. xv. 25 Paul was expecting to travel to Jerusalem; and Acts xx. 3—xxi. 17 describes a journey from Greece to Jerusalem, in which Paul is accompanied by a number of colleagues. Acts xx. 4 does not mention a Corinthian, but the success of the Corinthian collection seems to be affirmed by Rom. xv. 26.

For the collection, see further 2 Cor. viii, ix, with the commentary.

D. CONCLUSION

37. xvi. 5-12. WIDER SETTING OF PAUL'S PLANS

(5) I shall come to you when I pass through Macedonia; for my intention is to pass through Macedonia, (6) but with you I will perhaps stay, or even winter, that you may send me on my way wherever I am travelling. (7) For I do not wish to see you now in passing, because[1] I hope to stay with you for some time, if the Lord permit. (8) But I shall stay in Ephesus until Pentecost, (9) for a great and effective door is open to me, and there are many who resist.

(10) If Timothy comes, see that his stay with you is free from fear, for he does the Lord's work as I do myself; (11) so let no one despise him. Send him on his way in peace, that he may come to me, for I am awaiting him with the brothers.

(12) About Brother Apollos:[2] I begged him earnestly to go to you with the brothers, but it simply was not God's will that he should do so now; but he will come when he has the opportunity.

The plan for the collection (xvi. 1-4) culminates in Paul's forthcoming visit to Corinth, when the money will be put together and transmitted to Jerusalem. This leads Paul to a fuller account of his plans for his own future, and thus to the winding up of the epistle. He has told his readers to be ready against his coming to Corinth. When will this be?

5 **I shall come to you when I pass through Macedonia.** At

[1] The point is missed by many MSS. which have δέ, *but*, instead of γάρ.

[2] ℵ* D* G the Old Latin and some Vulgate MSS. add δηλῶ ὑμῖν ὅτι, *I tell you that*. This may be a secondary attempt to improve the sentence; if however Paul was at all embarrassed by the non-appearance of Apollos in Corinth (see the commentary) it would have been characteristic of him to write in this vehement way: As to Apollos, *I tell you* it isn't my fault he hasn't come; I asked him. . . .

the time of writing Paul is in Ephesus (verse 8); thence he
will probably move northward by land and sail from Troas or
thereabouts, or, less probably, will sail direct from Ephesus, to
Macedonia; perhaps to Thessalonica or Beroea. From there he
will move west and south through Macedonia to Athens or to
Corinth. The journey is already planned. **For my intention is
to pass** (literally, *I pass*, διέρχομαι; the present tense cannot
mean, in view of verse 8, that Paul is now on the way, and must
therefore signify firm intention) **through Macedonia** (presumably on a preaching tour; for this use of διέρχεσθαι see e.g.
Acts xx. 25), **but with you I will perhaps stay** (a contrast with 6
the transit through Macedonia), **or even winter, that you
may send me on my way wherever I am travelling.**
Apparently Paul had made no firm plans for his work after the
visit to Corinth; compare xvi. 4—he might or he might not go
to Jerusalem. While at Corinth he determined to go to Jerusalem (Rom. xv. 25). It was a Christian duty to further fellow-
Christians on their travels; cf. verse 11; Rom. xv. 24; 3 John 6.
Paul is evidently anxious that his delayed arrival in Corinth
shall not be misunderstood, and underlines his motive. **For I do** 7
not wish to see you now (ἄρτι; there is a long discussion in
Allo, but the next words clarify the sense sufficiently) **in passing** (an early visit would be a brief one—the alternative to Paul's
present plan would be to pass through Corinth on the way to
Macedonia), **because I hope to stay with you for some time,
if the Lord permit** (cf. Jas. iv. 15). The Corinthians displayed
some aptitude for misunderstanding Paul's motives and plans;
compare 2 Cor. i. 15 ff.

An early move from Ephesus (where Paul is evidently writing)
is impossible. **I shall stay** (or, *I am staying*; ἐπιμενῶ or ἐπιμένω) 8
in Ephesus until Pentecost (the great feast that fell seven
weeks after Passover; see v. 7; xv. 20), **for a great and effec-** 9
tive (ἐνεργής; a strange adjective to apply to a door, but
justified by the metaphor) **door is open to me, and there are
many who resist.** That is, there is a great opportunity for
evangelism, and at the same time there are many (possibly non-
Christians, possibly Jewish Christians) who oppose Paul's work.
Both facts constituted reasons why Paul should stay. It will thus
be some little while before he reaches Corinth, though he will

certainly come. With this compare iv. 19: *I will come quickly.* Some (e.g. Héring) think the difference between the two passages to be so sharp that they cannot belong to the same letter. It must however be remembered that Paul must have spent some time in writing 1 Corinthians, and that there is considerable difference in mood between chapter iv and chapter xvi. In xvi Paul is soberly describing his plans and giving a timetable of his movements; in iv he is rebuking those who think that they can dispense with the apostle and run his church for him. 'Anyone would think I was never going to set foot in Corinth again; but look out! I'll be there sooner than you think.'

So much for Paul's movements. Before they see him the
10 Corinthians may expect a visit from Timothy. **If Timothy comes, see that his stay with you is free from fear.** The opening word, *if*, suggests doubt whether Timothy will reach Corinth. In this there is a contrast with iv. 17, according to which Timothy has already been sent (unless the aorist ἔπεμψα is epistolary; but even if it is, it means no less than that Timothy is setting out with the letter—he does not appear in the greeting of i. 1; contrast 2 Cor. i. 1). It may be that, as with Paul's own movements, chapter iv slightly overstates the matter, so as to give the Corinthians a warning. One can only guess where the uncertainty (in addition to the perils that beset all Christian travellers—cf. 2 Cor. xi. 23 ff.) lay. According to Acts xix. 22 (referring to approximately the period under consideration here) Paul sent Timothy and Erastus into Macedonia. It is possible (one cannot say more) that the same journey is in question. It may be that Erastus is not mentioned in 1 Corinthians because he was a Corinthian (Rom. xvi. 23); he was not visiting Corinth but simply returning home. It may be that Timothy had been sent to Macedonia with the option of going on to Corinth if he saw fit, or if time permitted, or if he received further instructions (which could easily fail to reach him). The translation of the next words is uncertain. The use of the aorist tense (in the clause γένηται πρὸς ὑμᾶς) suggests Timothy's arrival rather than his *stay*, but this does not make good sense. Indeed, we do not in any case know what circumstances might have made Timothy afraid. Paul may have already encountered those aspects of Corinthian behaviour, alluded to in the second

epistle, (2 Cor. x. 10; xi. 6, 7, 29; xii. 11, 16, 21; etc.), which suggest that the Corinthian church could, when it chose, make itself a very unpleasant and threatening society, and have wished to shield his assistant. Evidently there was some reason, or fancied reason, that might have led the Corinthians to *despise* Timothy (verse 11). It may be that the cause of fear lay within Timothy himself, rather than in his environment, though it would then be hard to answer the question why Paul had chosen a coward as his confidential agent. We are bound simply to admit our ignorance.

Paul defends Timothy because **he does the Lord's work as I do myself.** That is, he engages in the same task of evangelism and of building up the churches, and conducts it in the same
manner as Paul. **So let no one despise him.** Compare 1 Tim. 11
iv. 12, where a different verb is used, and youth supplied as a possible ground for despising.

The Corinthians must not ill-use Timothy but **send him on his way in peace** (cf. verse 6; assistance to travelling brothers was evidently an important manifestation of Christian love—without it, one may suppose, it would have been very difficult to carry on the Pauline mission), **that he may come to me** (after Acts xix. 22 Timothy reappears at xx. 4), **for I am awaiting him with the brothers** (it is not clear whether the brothers were waiting with Paul—if so, they may have been Stephanas, Fortunatus, and Achaicus—or travelling with Timothy). For a tentative attempt to reconstruct the events alluded to here see the Introduction, p. 5.

Another notable travelling evangelist of the Pauline group
must be mentioned. **About** (for the construction cf. vii. 1; this 12
may mean that the Corinthians in their letter had inquired about *Apollos*, perhaps asking for a visit, perhaps asking why he had not visited them—had Paul interfered with this?) **Brother Apollos** (see i. 12, and the note): **I begged him earnestly to go to you with the brothers** (perhaps Timothy, if he was accompanied by Christian brothers—verse 11; but we can only guess), **but** (the Greek is *καί*, *and*, but here it must be used in an adversative sense) **it simply** (*πάντως*; cf. ix. 10) **was not God's will** (in Greek, *the will*, and therefore possibly 'his (Apollos's) will'; so e.g. Robertson-Plummer; but see G. Schrenk in

T.W.N.T. iii. 59) **that he should do so** (reducing the number of occurrences of the Greek verb ἔρχεσθαι) **now; but he will come when he has the opportunity.** It is a reasonable guess that Paul and Apollos had decided that the interests of Christian unity in Corinth would be better served by Apollos's absence than his presence; but we do not know. Nor do we know whether Apollos ever visited Corinth again. He is not mentioned in 2 Corinthians. See further Introduction, pp. 8-11, and H. W. Montefiore as there referred to.

38. xvi. 13-24. LAST WORDS TO THE CHURCH, AND GREETINGS

(13) Watch, stand firm in faith, play the man, be strong. (14) Let all you do be done in love.

(15) I make this request to you, brothers. You know that the household of Stephanas is the firstfruits of Achaea, and that they have taken upon themselves the service of the saints; (16) do you for your part subordinate yourselves to such men, and to every one who joins in the work and labours as a Christian.

(17) I am rejoicing in the presence of Stephanas, Fortunatus, and Achaicus, because they have supplied what you could not do for me; (18) for they refreshed my spirit, and in doing so yours also. So recognize such men as these.

(19) The churches of Asia greet you. Aquila and Prisca,[1] along with the church that meets in their house, send you hearty greetings in the Lord. (20) All the brothers greet you. Greet one another with a holy kiss.

(21) The greeting in my—Paul's—hand.

(22) If any one does not love the Lord, let him be anathema. Marana tha. (23) The grace of the Lord Jesus be with you. (24) My love to you all in Christ Jesus.

[1] The Western Text (D G* and Latin versions) adds, *With whom also I am lodging*. This was probably based on Rom. xvi. 4; as Weiss notes, the addition, though textually secondary, may be in substance correct.

In addition to greetings there remain only a few miscellaneous charges, uttered by Paul as he glances back over the Corinthian situation as a whole.

Watch, stand firm in faith (or, *in* the *faith*), **play the man, be strong.** *To watch* (γρηγορεῖν) is often used in the New Testament (e.g. Mark xiii. 37; Rev. iii. 3) not of purely general, moral, vigilance, but in the sense of looking out for eschatological events, expected to happen shortly. It has already appeared that Paul expects the last events to happen soon (xv. 52; cf. vii. 29). Christians must conduct their lives with reference to these events; this attitude alone guarantees a proper seriousness of outlook and purpose (cf. Mark xiii. 35 f.). This is in fact the way to *stand firm*; compare *immovable* in xv. 58. Faith is an attitude to God that means at once confident trust, and obedience; Paul desires both trust and obedience to be unvarying. It makes little difference if (having regard to the fact that the article is used—τῇ πίστει) we translate *Stand fast in* the *faith*; 'the faith' would then mean the Christian religion, the religion which (on the human side) is marked by trust and obedience. *Play the man* (ἀνδρίζεσθε) inculcates a virtue recognized in antiquity; for the word-group see, in addition to the commentaries, Betz, p. 208. 13

Let all you do be done in love. For this chief Christian 14
virtue see especially chapter xiii.

So far in generalization—though generalization, no doubt, that was apt and particular enough at Corinth. Paul now becomes precise and personal. **I make this request to you,** 15
brothers (see i. 1, and the note). **You know that** (straightening the order of the words in Greek, which is varied by hyperbaton) **the household of Stephanas is the firstfruits of Achaea** (that is, the first converts in Achaea, though this fits ill with Acts xvii. 34—perhaps Paul was thinking of Corinth only; cf. Rom. xvi. 5), **and that they have taken upon themselves the service of the saints** (cf. i. 2). The last clause runs literally, *They have appointed themselves for service for the saints* (εἰς διακονίαν τοῖς ἁγίοις ἔταξαν ἑαυτούς). The meaning is given by a closely parallel sentence in Plato, *Republic* ii. 371 C, There are those who, seeing this [a need], appoint themselves to this service (ἑαυτοὺς ἐπὶ τὴν διακονίαν τάττουσι ταύτην). Stephanas and

his family, similarly, becoming aware of a need, undertook service to the saints (cf. 2 Cor. viii. 17). They were not appointed by Paul; they were not appointed by the church; in a spirit not of self-assertion but of service and humility they appointed themselves. In other words, they were appointed directly by God, who pointed out to them the opportunity of service and (we may suppose) equipped them to fulfil it. It is now for the church to recognize this ministry, as Paul does. It is in this recognition of willingness to serve, and of spiritual equipment, that the origins of the Christian ministry lie (see T. W. Manson, *The Church's Ministry* (1948), especially p. 55; and 'The Ministry in the New Testament', in *The Doctrine of the Church* (1964), edited by Dow Kirkpatrick, pp. 39-63). *The saints* here are not those of xvi. 1, since Stephanas has already begun his ministry to them, whereas the collection for the Jerusalem saints is only at this point being set in motion. It may be noted here also that, since *the household of Stephanas have taken upon themselves the service of the saints* they must be adults. This does not prove that Stephanas's household and other households said in other parts of the New Testament to have been baptized (i. 16) cannot have included infants, but we are at least not encouraged to think so. There is, on the other hand, no reason why the *household* should not have included women.

Where natural leaders such as Stephanas arise (cf. xii. 28; Rom. xii. 8; 1 Thess. v. 12 f.) they should be recognized, and
16 the recognition should take practical form: **do you for your part** (imperatival ἵνα; see p. 176) **subordinate yourselves to such men.** From the epistle as a whole it does not appear that the Corinthians would find this easy; the more necessary therefore to remind them that discipline rather than free self-expression is a characteristic of Christian life, and especially of life in the Christian community. No one, not Paul himself (2 Cor. i. 24), is to lord it over another's faith; but all are to serve one another in love (Gal. v. 13).

Stephanas and his household are not the only members of the church whose lead must be valued, respected, and followed. The Corinthians must show a similar spirit of subordination to **every one who joins in the work** (with Paul? or with Stephanas? the preposition in συνεργοῦντι does not make this clear) **and labours as a Christian** (the last three words are not expressed in Greek, but Paul's use of the verb κοπιᾶν elsewhere —e.g. xv. 10—shows how it is to be taken). It is right to remember that in the Corinthian church, which has received a good deal of criticism from Paul—and perhaps with less justice from the commentator—there must have been a number of such persons. One from the neighbouring church of Cenchreae was later to travel abroad—Phoebe (Rom. xvi. 1).

Some have travelled already: the amount of travelling presupposed by the Pauline mission was considerable. **I am re-** 17
joicing in the presence (the word παρουσία could mean 'arrival', but here the arrival is evidently in the past, and the rejoicing in the present, so that the translation in the text is demanded) **of Stephanas** (presumably the man referred to in verse 15), **Fortunatus, and Achaicus** (these two are not mentioned elsewhere in the New Testament), **because they have supplied what you could not do for me** (τὸ ὑμέτερον ὑστέρημα;
possibly, *they have made up my want of you*); **for they refreshed** 18
my spirit (by their Christian fellowship, and by the services they rendered; the news they brought from Corinth cannot have been wholly pleasing), **and in doing so** (the last three words are implied, but are not expressed in the Greek) **yours also**—since the Corinthians will surely be glad to know that their envoys and their service have brought relief to the apostle. **So recognize such men as these.** Compare verses 15 f. They are true servants of Christ in the church.

Concluding greetings follow. **The churches of Asia greet** 19
you. Paul was writing in Ephesus (xvi. 8), but evidently had contacts in various parts of the province of Asia (cf. Acts xix. 10, 26). **Aquila and Prisca** (see Rom. xvi. 3, with the note), **along with the church that meets in their house, send you hearty greetings in the Lord**—i.e., send Christian greetings to their fellow-Christians. Aquila and Prisca are now, it seems, in Ephesus. According to Rom. xvi. 3 they were, when Paul wrote Romans from Corinth, in Rome, unless we take the view that Rom. xvi was originally directed not to Rome but Ephesus (see *Romans*, pp. 12 f., 281 f.). There is no insuperable difficulty in supposing that they had moved. According to Acts xviii. 2 Paul met Aquila and Prisca in Corinth because, as Jews, they

had been expelled from Rome. They might well have reason to return as soon as Claudius's edict was relaxed (at his death in A.D. 54, if not earlier), retaining establishments in the East. Their movements suggest that they were not without money; this would account for their having a house in which a church could meet. Unless we are to think that the whole Christian community in Ephesus was small enough to meet in one house, we must suppose that there were several churches in the city.

20 **All the brothers** (i. 1) **greet you.** These may be the part of the Ephesian church that did not meet in the house of Aquila and Prisca. These need not be covered by *the churches of Asia*, since it would be quite natural to exclude Ephesus from this general category, and reserve it for special treatment. Alternatively, *the brothers* may be Corinthian Christians who had travelled to Ephesus. **Greet one another with a holy kiss.** See Rom. xvi. 16, and the note. Paul's letters must have been communicated to the church members by being read aloud at a meeting of the church. Paul asks them to give one another the salutation he would have given them all had he been present. It is possible that the kiss was already a cult act; see below the notes on verses 22 f.

21 **The greeting in my—Paul's—hand.** For this kind of authentication of a letter compare e.g. Gal. vi. 11. It seems that Paul habitually dictated his letters (see Rom. xvi. 22), but had the habit (attested also in papyrus letters) of adding a concluding paragraph in his own hand. Some of the material in this concluding paragraph is puzzling to us, who are not in a position to pick up all the overtones it suggested.

22 **If anyone does not love the Lord, let him be anathema** (under a curse which separates him from God; see xii. 3; Rom. ix. 3, with the notes). The sentiment is understandable, but it is not immediately clear why Paul should have expressed it here. It seems probable that he is quoting a current Christian formula; he uses not his customary word for *love* (ἀγαπᾶν) but one that occurs here only in his writings (φιλεῖν). Its effect is not unlike that of the 'Jesus is Lord' of xii. 3; the ultimate test of Christian discipleship is personal loyalty to the Lord Jesus. As C. Spicq puts it (*Novum Testamentum* i. 200-4—an article that should be

consulted for its own sake, and also for the wealth of literature on this passage to which it refers): Paul's verb means 'the adoration and religious consecration of the believer to his God'. The formulation of this may not be Paul's own, but the thought fits his purpose. The party-spirit and moral laxity of the Corinthian church would be remedied by devotion to Jesus.

Exegesis of this passage may perhaps be made more precise. The context (see below) is often said to be liturgical. If this is so, it should be noted that there is nothing in the limitation *If anyone does not love the Lord* that could exclude 'unbelieving outsiders', who, through prophecy, have been led to the confession *God truly is among you*, and prevent them, even though unbaptized, from continuing in the Christian fellowship of the Supper. See the notes on xiv. 25, and G. Bornkamm *Das Ende des Gesetzes* (1952), p. 126. Schlatter writes similarly: Paul 'refuses his adversaries communion (*Gemeinschaft*), not because they originate in a different area of the church, not because of their doctrinal opinions, . . . not because of their opposition to his apostolate . . . Paul breaks off communion (*Gemeinschaft*) only if "anyone does not love the Lord".'

Marana tha is Aramaic, transliterated by Paul into his Greek letter, and accordingly here transliterated into the English translation. The words mean, 'Our Lord, come'; but it would be possible (in view of the fact that the early MSS. were written without separation of words) to take them as *Maran atha*, which would mean, 'Our Lord has come'. There is no doubt that both forms make sense; Paul believed both that the Lord had come, and that he would come. The prayer for his coming seems however to make better sense in the context; Paul has, as it were, thinned his readership down to those who 'love the Lord's appearing' (cf. 2 Tim. iv. 8), and having done so express their common desire to welcome him. Compare Rev. xxii. 20, where the same prayer is expressed in Greek (Amen, come, Lord Jesus) also *Didache* x. 6, in a context at once eucharistic and eschatological (Let grace come, and let this world pass away. Hosanna to the God of David. If anyone is holy, let him come; if anyone is not, let him repent. Marana tha. Amen). There is little to be said for the suggestions that *Maranatha* means 'Our Lord is the sign (*'oth*)', or 'Our Lord is the *aleph* and the *tau*' (the first and last letters of the Hebrew alphabet—the *alpha* and the *omega*).

The parallels and connections quoted have led to the popular opinion that in the closing verses of his epistle Paul is using words that belong to the liturgical setting in which, it is supposed, the epistle was first read. It took the place of the sermon; when it was done, the members of the congregation exchanged the kiss, those who were not Christians were excluded (see above), and the words *Marana tha* introduced the Lord's Supper with a prayer that sought the Lord's presence at the meal, and his return in final apocalyptic glory. (O. Cullmann, *Christologie des Neuen Testaments* (1957), pp. 214-18 (E.T., 211 ff.), emphasizes this double aspect of the coming and presence of Christ in the eucharist and at the Last Day; see also F. Hahn, *Christologische Hoheitstitel* (1964), pp. 100-10). That this view (see e.g. J. A. T. Robinson, *J.T.S.* new series iv. 38-41) is less strongly supported by the evidence than is often thought has been shown by C. F. D. Moule (*N.T.S.* vi. 307-10), who himself thinks that *Marana tha* was intended 'to reinforce or sanction the curse or ban'—that is, the *anathema.* It is not impossible to combine this view with that indicated above. The prayer of thanksgiving in the *Didache* (see x. 5) seeks the coming of the Lord that he may gather together the church, and bring it into the kingdom; this gathering together will naturally involve the exclusion of those who do not belong to God's people. So here: the Lord's coming, for which the elect long as their salvation, would confirm the ban on those who do not *love the Lord.*

23 Paul usually concludes his letters with a 'grace', such as **The grace of the Lord Jesus be with you.** Compare Rom. xvi. 20. In Paul's usage, *grace* is most characteristically action and gift (see *Romans*, p. 76, et al.), and in these words Paul prays for a continuation and deepening of what has already been done and given in Corinth (see i. 4). After the familiar formula follows the human (but no less Christian) greeting to the troublesome but
24 always loved (cf. 2 Cor. xi. 11; xii. 15) church: **My love to you** (literally, *My love is with you*, but this does not seem to mean anything essentially different from the familiar English used in

the translation) **all in Christ Jesus.** The last three words may apply to *love* (it is not merely human but Christian love), or to *you all* (all you Christians); probably they were intended to cover the whole sentence. It would not be wrong to say that, in sense, not construction, they cover the whole epistle.

ADDITIONAL NOTE ON XII. 2.

Professor C. F. D. Moule writes to me that he finds difficulty in the placing of ἄν iterative before the verb, yet divorced from a (relative) ὡς. His own suggestion is that " the original was a very clumsy sentence, from which one word fell out by a very early haplography: οἴδατε ὅτι ὅτε ἔθνη ἦτε (=' you know that when you were pagans '), ἦτε . . . ὡς ἂν ἤγεσθε ἀπαγόμενοι (='you were led away (periphrastic), however you happened to be led ')". It seems to me that both Professor Moule and I are forced to do some violence to an exceedingly awkward piece of Greek, he by conjecturing a primitive corruption, I by adopting an order of words which I acknowledge to be un-Greek. The reader may well prefer his violence to mine.

INDEX OF NAMES AND SUBJECTS

Aalen, S., 235, 237
Aboth (Mishnah), 304
Achaea, 393
Achaicus, 4, 13, 23, 42, 248, 261, 335, 391, 394
Acts of Paul and Thecla, 177
Acts of Thomas, 273
Adam, 19, 213, 248, 252 f., 289, 291, 351-4, 373-7, 379
Adonis, 267
Aeschylus, 280, 307
Age, 53, 66, 69 ff., 73, 93 f., 96, 227, 233, 286, 308 f.
Akiba, 121
Alcibiades, 291
Alexander (false prophet), 318
Allo, E. B., 72, 76, 92, 125, 138, 185, 203, 206, 235, 250, 280, 325, 334, 336, 354, 356, 372, 387, 389
Amen, 321
Anacolouthon, 208
Anathema, 279 f., 396, 398
Androgyne, 248, 255
Andronicus, 203
Angels, 253 f.
Anthropology, 19
Anxiety, 179
Apocalypse, 362, 380
Apollo, 2, 280, 308
Apollonius of Tyana, 131
Apollos (and Apollos-party), 3, 5, 8-11, 23 f., 43, 45 f., 51, 81-7, 95, 99 f., 104-8, 388, 391 f.
Apostle, Apostleship, etc., 3, 12 f., 16, 21 f., 24, 30 ff., 44, 49, 59, 84, 88, 95 f., 98-101, 105, 109 ff., 113 f., 116, 124, 133, 168, 190, 196, 200-4, 206 ff., 230, 246, 293 f., 296, 339, 342-6, 364 f., 385
Apostolic Decree, 7 f., 197
Apotheosis, 28
Aquila, 4 f., 43, 322, 395 f.
Aratus, 367
Areopagus, 63
Aristophanes, 251, 331
Aristotle, 381
Arndt, W. F., ix
Ascension, 343
Asceticism, 144, 155, 157, 163, 178 f., 181 f., 184, 186
Assembly, 25, 250 f., 260 f., 316, 319, 324 f., 328-32
Asyndeton, 175
Augustine, 108, 270, 352
Authority, 31, 41, 47, 96, 133, 168, 188, 195, 200, 202, 204, 206 f., 210, 253 ff., 277, 334, 357

Bachmann, P., 40, 49, 63, 79, 115, 138, 141, 158, 185, 206, 250, 258, 303, 321, 350, 359, 361, 364, 375, 384
Baptism, 6 f., 21, 25, 47 ff., 51, 80, 141 ff., 165 f., 217, 220 f., 224, 234, 270, 288 f., 295, 362-5, 379, 397
Barnabas, 202, 204
Barth, K., v, 26, 40, 139, 147, 158, 170, 205, 239, 252, 296, 299, 304 f., 330, 342, 358
Bassus, 131
Bauer, W., 31, 137
Bedale, S., 248
Berakoth (Mishnah), 156
Berakoth (Tosephta), 240
Betz, H. D., 112, 155, 202, 216, 300, 302, 377, 393
Beyer, K., 61, 205, 318
Bikkurim (Mishnah), 220
Billerbeck, P., 101, 112, 115, 121, 132, 135, 154, 161, 183, 206, 223, 225 f., 228, 231, 250 f., 253, 300 f., 321, 331, 370 f.
Binding of Isaac, 130
Bishop, 296
Black, M., 174, 176, 184
Blass, F., 62, 65, 81, 85, 88, 101, 115, 122, 132, 138 f., 156, 175, 185, 191, 206, 209, 211, 213, 215,

221, 236, 240, 244, 250, 252, 260, 297, 316, 318 f., 321 f., 330, 334, 340, 343, 348, 367, 372, 380, 387
Blood, 231 ff., 268 f., 271 ff., 275
Body, 20, 23, 147-51, 181, 218, 232-5, 266, 268 f., 271-5, 287-290, 292, 296, 370-4, 377 ff., 382
Boman, T., 344
Bonnet, M., 177
Bornkamm, G., 53, 261, 264 f., 268, 274 f., 299, 302 f., 310, 322, 325, 327, 397
Brother (sister), 31, 41, 131, 138, 164, 166, 196 f., 202, 220, 322, 335, 384, 391, 393, 396
Brothers of the Lord, 203, 343
Bultmann, R., 69, 72, 111, 125, 142, 155, 171, 177, 188, 191, 193, 233, 243, 309 f., 341, 372, 374
Burial, 339 f.
Burrows, M., 135
Bythos, 74

Caiaphas, 72
Call, calling, 30, 32 f., 49, 55 ff., 59, 168 ff.
Calvin, J., 78, 97, 102, 108, 126 f., 141, 150, 154 f., 165, 205, 223, 225, 288 f., 308 f., 320, 333, 377
Cassandra, 280, 307
Cato, 110
Celibacy, 154 f., 158 f., 162, 174, 176, 182
Celsus, 57
Cenchreae, 1, 395
Cephalus, 102
Cephas (and Cephas-party), 9 ff., 23 f., 43-6, 51, 82, 87 ff., 91, 95, 99, 104, 106, 203 f., 341
Chadwick, H., v, 20, 184
Chiasmus, 156
Chloe, 4, 12 ff., 23, 42, 134, 247, 261, 335
Christ-group, 44 f., 82, 95, 106, 148
Christology, 17 ff., 60, 354
Chrysostom, 78, 251, 363
Church, 23-6, 31 ff., 40-3, 46, 56, 58, 87 f., 91, 95 f., 117, 124, 131 ff., 151, 163, 168, 201, 216, 233, 244 f., 257 f., 261, 263, 270, 273 f., 286 ff., 290, 292 f., 295 f., 319, 324, 329 f., 345, 394 f.
Cicero, 96, 121
Circumcision, 168 ff.
Clark, K. W., 63, 236, 273, 302, 378
Claudius, 396
Clement of Rome, 6, 11, 44, 104, 302, 354
Clementine Literature, 236
Collection, 7, 23, 385-8
Commendatory letters, 387
Communion, 21, 231 f., 235
Conscience, 102, 194 ff., 215, 235, 241-4
Conversion, 143
Corinth, 1 ff.
Corinthians, First Epistle to the:
authenticity, 11 f.
date, 5, 22
integrity, 12-17, 116
Corpus Hermeticum, 63, 69, 80, 287
Corruption, 372, 379, 381 f.
Cosmos, 287, 291
Covenant, 232, 268 f.
Creation, 193, 249, 251-7, 357, 360
Crispus, 4, 47 f.
Cross (crucifixion, etc.), 49, 51, 55 f., 59 ff., 63 ff., 68 f., 71 f., 77, 81, 87, 110, 114, 116, 130, 245, 266, 269, 337 f.
Cullmann, O., 71, 193, 228, 265, 339, 361, 374, 398
Cup of blessing, 231 f., 237, 268
Cybele, 300
Cynic, 54, 93, 100, 182, 200

Dahl, M. E., 20, 373
Daphnis and Chloe, 42
Daube, D., 121, 151, 156, 161 f., 166, 205, 211
Davies, W. D., 73, 75, 193, 214, 289, 356, 371 ff.
Day, 39, 88, 101, 103, 125, 133, 136
Day of Atonement, 126, 128
Deacons, 295
Death, 213, 232, 270, 289, 339, 357 f., 360, 362, 365, 367, 370, 372, 376, 380-4

INDEX OF NAMES AND SUBJECTS

Debrunner, A., *see* Blass, F.
Deissmann, A., 126, 367
Demeter, 42, 99, 300
Demons, 191 f., 194, 225, 232, 236 ff., 240, 357
Depravity, 108
Diatribe, 93, 200, 370
Didache, 233 f., 271, 328, 397 f.
Didrachma, 386
Dio Cassius, 303
Diogenes (Cynic), 223
Diogenes Laertius, 96, 267
Diognetus, Epistle to, 279
Dionysus, 327
Discipline, 132, 134, 163, 175, 217 f., 220, 394
Dishonour, 372
Divorce, 162, 164, 166
Dodd, C. H., 136, 209, 213, 269, 358, 383
Driver, S. R., 205
Dualism, 53, 155

Ecstasy, 278, 280 f., 286
Ehrhardt, A. A. T., 274 ff.
Eighteen Blessings, 321
Election, 191
Elision, 367
Ellis, E. E., 383
End, 109, 227, 272, 306, 356 f., 380 f., 383 f., 398
Enthusiasm, 109, 120, 279
Epaphroditus, 293
Ephesus, 5, 8, 13, 16, 23, 42, 123, 130, 258, 365 f., 389, 395 f.
Epictetus, 54, 80, 90, 99 f., 103, 112, 132, 151, 167, 177, 182, 200, 256, 287, 321
Epicurus, 267
Epimenedes, 367
Epistolary aorist, 116, 130 f., 390
Erastus, 5, 13, 16, 57, 390
Eschatology, 382, 393
Essenes, 31
Euripides, 99
Excommunication, 126, 132 f., 334
Exodus, 220

Faith, 36, 66, 84 f., 190, 214, 224, 227 f., 234, 285, 300, 308, 310 f., 348 f., 352, 379, 393 f.
Fellowship, 39 f., 231 ff., 235
Findlay, G. G., v
First day, 386
Firstfruits, 350, 355, 384, 393
Fitzmyer, J. A., 254
Flesh, 20, 57, 59, 79-82, 149, 176, 206, 233, 235, 266, 371, 379
Ford, J. M., 184
Fornication, 13, 120 ff., 130, 147 f., 150 ff., 155 f., 158, 224 f., 228, 238
Fortunatus, 4, 13, 23, 42, 248, 261, 335, 391, 395
Freedom, 16, 19, 97, 122, 145 f., 177, 188, 197, 200, 210, 218 ff., 239, 242 f., 245, 250, 320
Fridrichsen, A., 294
Friedrich, G., 381
Funk, R. W., ix

Gaius (Christian), 47 f.
Gaius (Roman lawyer), 121
Galatia, 386
Gallio, 5, 31, 135
Gamaliel, 127
Games, 217
Genesis Rabbah, 255
Georgi, D., 23
Gezerah shawah, 358
Gifts, 24, 36, 38, 41, 69, 81, 108, 158, 278, 283 f., 286 f., 290, 295 f., 299, 311, 315, 319 f., 327
Gingrich, F. W., ix
Glombitza, O., 342
Glory, 249 f., 252-7, 371 f.
Glorying (boasting), 59, 61, 209, 213, 290, 365
Glover, T. R., 64
Gnostics, gnosticism (see also Knowledge), 21, 37, 54 ff., 60, 69 ff., 73 f., 79, 82, 109, 120, 144 ff., 188-91, 194 f., 200, 202, 224, 228, 230 f., 287 f., 307 f., 348, 360, 368
Gospel, 16, 19 f., 26, 31, 38, 46, 48 f., 51 f., 58 f., 64, 69, 71, 74, 82, 207-10, 216, 245, 337
Grace, 34 ff., 38, 66, 86, 92, 108, 179, 212, 214, 286, 288, 345 f., 398
Grosheide, F. W., v

Groups (in the church at Corinth), 3 f., 11, 14, 24, 43, 46 f., 51 397
Guph, 274

Hades, 383
Hahn, F., 265, 339, 358, 398
Ḥakam, 138
Halakah, 208
Ḥameṣ, 127
Harris, W. B., 81, 130, 138, 240, 350
Ḥayyab, 272
Head, 248-53
Heim, K., 58, 136, 185, 215, 221, 231, 243, 343, 370
Ḥerem, 279
Héring, J., 12, 14, 38, 67, 72, 91, 120, 130, 139, 155, 171, 194, 196, 221 f., 245, 249, 284, 305, 326, 336, 339, 342, 356, 367, 390
Herodotus, 42, 248
Hillel, 162, 370
Hippolytus, 80, 271
Holiness (saint, etc.), 32 ff., 59 ff., 92, 135, 141 f., 164 f., 180 f., 386, 393 f.
Holl, K., 343
Homer, 1, 191, 285
Homosexualism, 257
Hooker, M. D., 107, 251, 253 f., 339
Hope, 36, 308-11
Horace, 42, 109
Household, 48, 99, 393 f.
Howard, W. F., 99, 322
Hurd, J. C., 4, 6 f., 22, 145, 154, 247
Hymn, 104, 327 f.
Hyperbaton, 393

Idolatry, 7, 13, 150, 188, 191 f., 194, 196, 220, 224 ff., 228-31, 234, 236 ff., 279
Ignatius, 11, 113, 344, 366
Image, 214, 248 f., 252, 377 f.
Imitation, 245 f.
Immorality, 3, 7, 25
Immortality, 347, 382
Imperatival ἵνα, 122, 157, 176, 394
Incorruption, 372, 379, 381 f.
Infant baptism, 48
Inspiration, 279, 281, 283, 332
Interpretation, 285 f., 316, 327 f.
Isis, 325

James, 44, 203, 343
James, M. R., 343
Jeremias, J., 69, 154, 163, 167, 171, 174, 187, 197, 207, 251, 262, 266 f., 270 f., 318, 342, 379, 386
Jerome, 343
Jews (Judaism, etc.), 2, 20, 69, 101, 126, 154 ff., 162, 179, 193, 211, 215, 240, 244 f., 248, 261, 326, 347, 374 f., 386, 395
Jocz, J., 215
Johanan ben Zakkai, 300
Johnson, S. E., 122
Jones, H. S., x
Joseph, 203
Josephus, 31, 115, 197, 265, 300
Judaizers, 20, 89, 91, 169, 179, 389
Judas Iscariot, 203
Judgement, 274 f., 277, 302, 326
Junias, 203
Justification, 39, 59 f., 102, 141 ff., 145, 179, 311, 349
Justin, 267, 321, 347, 387

Käsemann, E., 233, 272
Ketuboth (Mishnah), 249
Keydell, R., 318
Kingdom, 118, 140, 356 ff., 379, 381
Kirkpatrick, D., 25, 394
Kiss, 396, 398
Kittel, G., 254, 321, 386
Knowledge, 18, 25, 36 f., 54, 189 ff., 194, 196 f., 224, 284 f., 300 f., 305, 308, 317, 368
Knox, W. L., 72, 74, 80, 140, 220, 308, 310, 329, 361
Kopher, 113
Kosher food, 91, 261
Kosmala, H., 264
Kümmel, W. G., 48, 51, 77, 165, 182, 184, 221, 232, 236 f., 251, 262, 310, 331, 336, 347, 356, 367, 373, 384

Lamb, 128 f.
Latinism, 101, 122
Law, 106, 145 f., 169, 193, 211-14, 245, 322, 330, 383 f.

Leaney, A. R. C., 232
Leaven, 142, 234
Legalism, 19, 91 f., 145, 213, 215
Levirate marriage, 184 ff.
Libertinism, 144 f., 148
Libertus, 171
Liddell, H. G., 31, 35, 120, 136, 225, 300
Lietzmann, H., 48, 79, 112, 130, 150, 157, 184, 191, 195, 221 ff., 238, 260, 262, 302, 310, 319, 325, 327, 334, 347, 349, 356, 363, 371
Lightfoot, J. B., 33, 38, 49, 53, 63 f., 72, 81, 97, 100, 109, 113, 121, 129, 136, 154 f., 166, 172, 186
Lindars, B., 340
Lipsius, R. A., 177
Litigation, 3, 135, 139 f.
Livy, 287
Lohse, E., 240
Looking-glass, 306 f.
Lord, 193
Love, 11, 16, 22, 36 f., 46, 72 f., 81, 145, 189 ff., 200, 207, 213 f., 216, 224 f., 234, 244, 299, 308, 310 f., 314 f., 327, 393 f., 396, 398 f.
Lucian, 112, 207, 251, 257 f., 267, 278, 301f., 318
Luther, M., 10

Macedonia, 389 f.
McKenzie, R., x
Macrobius, 80
Man (representative, etc.), 19, 359 ff., 374-9
Manna, 221 ff.
Manson, T. W., 20, 33, 44 f., 135, 394
Manumission, 152
Maranatha, 271, 397 f.
Marcionites, 363
Marcus Aurelius, 193
Marriage, 3, 7, 13, 144 f., 153-9, 161, 163, 165 ff., 175-8, 180-6
Martyrdom, 302
Mary, 203
Matthias, 203
Mature, 68 f., 71, 76, 79 f.
Mediator, 60
Meeting-place, 33 f.
Mehaimena, 174
Meir, 371
Memorial, 266 f., 269 f.
Menander, 367
Menenius Agrippa, 287
Merrill, E. T., 11
Messiah, 359, 376
Metzger, B. M., 340
Milligan, G., 125
Mind, 78, 319 f., 322
Ministry, 23 ff., 59, 84, 88, 95, 99, 115, 133, 208, 295 f., 331, 394
Mishnah, 80, 184
Mission, 358, 360, 391
Moffatt, J., 41, 64, 107, 222, 238, 274, 384
Monotheism, 191
Montefiore, H. W., 8-11, 392
Mortal, 382
Moses, 21, 220 f.
Moule, C. F. D., 32, 57, 63, 75, 100, 122, 144, 150, 166, 170, 176, 212, 228, 328, 350, 380 f., 398
Moulton, J. H., 51, 65, 119, 125, 136, 138, 156, 164, 170, 185, 238, 242, 265, 277 f., 311, 314, 338, 340, 360, 367, 369, 387
Munck, J., 45, 344
Mystery, 62, 70 f., 99, 300 f., 315, 380
Mystery cults, 69
Myth, 353, 360

Natural, 372 ff., 377, 379, 382
Nature, 193, 251, 256
Nedarim (Mishnah), 280
Nickle, K. F., 23
Niddah, (Mishnah) 184
Noachian Decrees, 121 f.
Norden, E., 64
Nygren, A., 310

Obedience, 224, 360
Oepke, A., 141
'*olam*, 53
Origen, 57, 73, 322, 337
Orlah (Mishnah), 127
Orphic fragment, 248
'*oth*, 398
Ovid, 319

Paraclete, 74
Paradox, 64
Parataxis, 338
Parusia, 38 f., 271, 275, 355 ff., 373, 379, 381 f., 398
Passover, 127-30, 231, 233 f., 266 f., 269 f., 272, 351, 389
Passover Haggadah, 267
Patria potestas, 183
Patronus, 171
Pausanias, 2
Peace, 34 f., 329, 391
Pentecost, 130, 389
Peregrinus, 207, 302
Pesahim (Mishnah), 266, 272
Peter, *see* Cephas
Philo, 43, 80, 205, 216, 222 f., 235, 237, 307, 351, 375, 377
Philostratus, 131
Phoebe, 395
Pillars, 87
Plato, 64, 86, 102, 139, 214, 290 f., 375, 393
Pliny, 280
Plummer, A., *see* Robertson, A.
Plutarch, 1, 191, 223, 303, 331
Pontius Pilate, 72
Power, 65, 357, 360, 384
Prayer, 247, 249 ff., 253-6, 258, 331 f.
Preaching, 18, 37, 48 f., 53 f., 64 ff., 68, 100, 209 f., 218, 335, 340 f., 346 ff., 384
Predestination, 52, 55, 108
Preisendanz, K., 126
Previous letter, 4, 6 ff., 12, 23, 130, 163
Prisc(ill)a, 4 f., 43, 395 f.
Proselyte, 220
Pseudo-Philo, 222
Pythagoreans, 245

Qahal, 261
Qal waḥomer, 371
Qumran, 69, 75, 123, 126, 135, 245, 254

Raeder, M., 364
Ransom, 152
Redeemer, 221
Redemption, 59, 61, 152, 193, 357, 376
Rengstorf, K. H., 241
Resurrection, 3, 6 f., 13, 18 ff., 147 f., 201, 233, 271, 289, 338, 340-3, 346-50, 352, 354-7, 361 ff., 365, 367, 369 f., 372 ff., 376-9, 385
Revelation, 317, 327, 329
Reward, 86, 88 f., 195, 209 f.
Righteousness, 39, 59 ff., 68, 94, 149
Rissi, M., 363 f.
Robertson, A., 55, 115, 133, 249, 258, 285, 291, 299, 391
Robertson, A. T., 65, 78 f., 110, 117, 125, 132, 138, 150, 174, 176, 206, 208, 249, 278, 336, 340, 367, 380
Robinson, J. A. T., 398
Roux, G., 2
Rulers, 70 ff., 74, 357

Sacrament, 216, 223 f., 226 ff., 237
Sacrifice, 21, 128 f., 207, 269
Sacrificial food, 3, 6 f., 12 f., 16, 21, 132, 146, 188, 191 f., 194-7, 200, 202, 215 f., 219 f., 224 f., 236 f., 239 ff., 320, 368
Sallustius, 80
Salvation, 167, 216, 336, 360
Sanhedrin (Mishnah), 121, 126, 302
Sanhedrin (B. Talmud), 115, 371
Satan, 74, 124 ff., 136, 157, 226, 294
Schlatter, A., 39, 52, 56, 65, 79, 82, 99, 101, 106, 115, 120, 145, 148, 155, 180, 183, 186, 192, 196 f., 211, 218, 222, 249, 255, 260, 265, 277, 280, 285, 289, 297, 315, 321, 327, 331, 339, 348, 362, 380, 397
Schlier, H., 248
Schmidt, K. L., 300
Schmithals, W., v
Schniewind, J., 270
Schoeps, H. J., 127, 130, 177, 228, 236, 238
Schrenk, G., 391
Schweitzer, A., 142, 149, 220, 228, 237, 299, 305, 347, 356, 363 f.
Schweizer, E., 38, 125, 186, 288, 321, 325, 329, 337
Scott, R., *see* Liddell, H. G.
Scripture, 10, 106 f., 266, 338 f., 359, 382

Seal, 201
Seed, 370, 372
Semitism, 61, 64, 72, 99, 104, 119, 138, 205, 254, 322 f., 326, 338, 379, 387
Seneca, 96, 102, 110, 152, 217, 229, 287
Sermon on the Mount, 112
Sevenster, J. N., 69, 96, 102, 110, 153, 170, 172, 229, 287, 332
Severe letter, 5, 12
Sex, 3, 19, 25, 134, 144, 147 ff., 153 f., 156 f., 161, 163, 165, 181 f., 224 f., 232, 234, 251 ff., 255 ff.
Shammai, 162, 370
Shekinah, 255
Shema, 156
Sheol, 382 f.
Sibyl, 280
Sign, 54 ff., 323 f., 398
Silas, 4
Simeon the Just, 304
Sin, 149, 213, 338, 383 f.
Slave, slavery, 170 ff.
Son of man, 19, 359, 375 f.
Sorrowful visit, 5, 12
Sosthenes, 13, 31, 33
Soul, 147, 373 f., 377
Speech, 36 f., 63, 65
Spicq, C., 396
Spirit, 9, 38 f., 65 f., 69, 74-8, 80, 90, 118, 123 f., 141, 143, 147, 149, 151 f., 158, 181, 186, 214, 222 f., 237, 281, 283-6, 288 f., 299, 309, 315, 319 f., 322, 326, 329, 333, 342 f., 372 ff., 377, 379, 382
Spiritual marriages, 6, 25, 183
Stauffer, E., 106, 363
Stendahl, K., 122
Stephanas, 3 f., 13, 23 f., 42, 48, 134, 247, 261, 335, 391, 393 ff.
Steward, 100 f.
Stoic, Stoicism, 74, 93, 96, 102, 109 f., 151, 170 ff., 177 f., 191, 256, 287 f., 291, 306
Strabo, 303
Strack, H. L., *see* Billerbeck, P.
Strong, 195 ff., 215, 238, 240, 242 ff.
Subordination, 249, 360 f., 394
Suffering Servant, 339
Sunday, 387
Supper (Lord's S., Last S., Eucharist, etc.), 3, 6 f., 10, 13, 21, 24, 26, 41, 96, 129 f., 132, 220 ff., 224, 231-5, 237, 261-4, 266-77, 289, 325, 327, 397 f.

Taanith (Mishnah), 263
Tacitus, 251, 302
Talmud, 321
Teachers, 24, 295 f., 317, 327
Temple, 9, 90 ff., 151, 196, 386
Tertullian, 80
Testimony, 62 f.
Thackeray, H. St. J., 51
Thrall, M. E., 100, 170, 176
Thucydides, 1, 42, 291
Timothy, 4 f., 13, 16, 116 f., 211, 385, 390 f.
Titius Justus, 4
Titus, 5, 14, 169
Tongues, 6 f., 22, 25, 37, 81, 285 f., 290, 296, 299, 305, 315-19, 322, 324-8, 334
Torah, 20
Tradition, 247, 264 ff., 268, 337
Transformation, 370, 379 ff.
Trinity, 78, 143, 284
Troeltsch, E., 305
Trumpet, 381
Turner, N., 56, 68, 75, 86, 103, 122, 138 f., 155, 176, 182, 185, 202, 211, 213, 221, 230, 234, 249, 252, 286, 297, 318, 321 f., 343, 350, 380
Twelve, 294, 341 ff.

Unnik, W. C. van, 135

Vegetarians, 197
Veil, 6 f., 13, 249-52, 254 f., 331
Vicarious baptism, 363 f.
Vices (lists), 140
Victory, 384
Virgin, 173-6, 180, 182, 184 f.
Virgines subintroductae, 183, 185

Walk, 168
Weak, 194 ff., 215, 242 f.
Weiss, J., 13 f., 33, 37, 42, 67 f., 73, 77, 84, 97, 99, 103, 109 f., 120, 123, 126, 131, 145, 151, 167,

172, 206, 211, 216, 250, 267, 270, 281, 315, 335, 366, 384, 392
Wendland, H. D., 59, 78, 109, 242
Western text, 31, 41, 50, 67, 259, 297, 330, 335, 392
Whiteley, D. E. H., 373
Wickert, U., 34
Widows, 160, 184
Wilckens, U., v, 68
Wild beasts, 23, 365 f.
Win, 210 ff.
Wisdom, 17 f., 25, 37, 43 f., 49, 52-6, 58-63, 66-73, 77, 80 f., 93 f., 96, 109 ff., 114, 120, 131, 138, 193, 220, 222 f., 230, 284 f., 378
Women, 25, 247-58, 260, 330 ff., 394
Word, 223
Works, 52, 66
World, 53, 58, 66, 75, 93 f., 96, 114, 177 f.
Worship, 248, 250, 252, 254 f., 260, 320 f., 330, 332

Xenophon, 241

Yebamoth (B. Talmud), 165
Yoma (Tosephta), 218

Zeno, 96
Zuntz, G., 32, 35, 50, 55, 62, 79, 82 f., 114, 148, 173, 187, 198, 219, 225, 236, 259, 282, 297, 302, 312 ff., 334, 378

INDEX OF GREEK WORDS AND PHRASES DISCUSSED

ἄγαμος, 180 f.
ἄγειν, 278 f.
αἴνιγμα, 307
αἰών, 53
ἀμέριμνος, 178 f.
ἀνακρίνειν, 77, 102
ἄνομος, 212 ff.
ἀντίλημψις, 295
ἀπάγειν, 278
ἀπαρχή, 350 f.
ἀποδεικνύναι, 110
ἀρχιτέκτων, 86
ἀφιέναι, 162, 164

βάρβαρος, 319

γαμίζειν, 185
γνῶσις, 37

διάκονος, 84
διακρίνειν, 138, 274 ff.
δικαίως, 367

εἰκῇ, 337
ἐκκλησία, 32, 260 ff., 316
ἔκτρωμα, 344
ἔννομος, 212 ff.
ἔνοχος, 272
ἐξουσία, 253, 255
ἐπιθανάτιος, 109
ἔτι καθ' ὑπερβολήν, 296
εὐπάρεδρος, 182
ἕως τέλους, 39

ζημιοῦν, 89

θέατρον, 110
θηριομαχεῖν, 366

ἰδιώτης, 321, 324

καταγγέλλειν, 270
καταχρᾶσθαι, 178
κεφαλή, 248 f.
κλῆσις, 169
κοινωνία, 39, 231, 291
κοπιᾶν, 111
κόσμος, 53
κυβέρνησις, 295

λογεία, 386
λογίζεσθαι, 99
λόγος, 65, 118
λοιπόν, 100, 176

μαίνεσθαι, 326
μένειν, 308
μερίζειν, 46
μεριμνᾶν, 178 ff.
μετασχηματίζειν, 105
μυστήριον, 99

οἰκία, 48
οἰκονόμος, 99 f.
οἶκος, 48
ὀλοθρευτής, 226
ὅλως, 120
ὅμως, ὁμῶς, 317

παίζειν, 225
παραδιδόναι, 265
παρακαλεῖν, 112
παραλαμβάνειν, 265
παρθένος, 182, 184
πειθός, 62, 65
πειθώ, 62
περικάθαρμα, 112
περίψημα, 112
πνευματικός, 76 f., 222, 278
ποτίζειν, 80, 289

σαρκικός, 79, 206
σάρκινος, 79
σοφία, 17, 59
στέγειν, 304
συγκρίνειν, 76

τάγμα, 354
τέλειος, 68
τέλος, 356
τόπος, 33
τυπικῶς, 227
τύπος, 227

ὑπέρακμος, 182 ff.
ὑπηρέτης, 99 f.

φύσις, 256

χάρισμα, 38
χωρίζεσθαι, 162

ψυχικός, 77, 327 ff.
ψωμίζειν, 301

ὧδε, 100